BATTLESHIP NEW JERSEY

The *New Jersey* steams toward Pearl Harbor, Hawaii, in May 1986. *National Archives: DN-SC-86-08803*

BATTLESHIP NEW JERSEY

The Complete History

PAUL STILLWELL

NAVAL INSTITUTE PRESS
Annapolis, Maryland

Naval Institute Press
291 Wood Road
Annapolis, MD 21402

© 2025 by Paul Stillwell

All rights reserved. No part of this book may be reproduced or utilized in any form or by any means, electronic or mechanical, including photocopying and recording, or by any information storage and retrieval system, without permission in writing from the publisher.

Library of Congress Cataloging-in-Publication Data
Names: Stillwell, Paul, author
Title: Battleship New Jersey : the complete history / Paul Stillwell.
Description: Revised edition. | Annapolis, Maryland : Naval Institute Press, [2025]
 | Includes bibliographical references and index. |
Identifiers: LCCN 2025007438 (print) | LCCN 2025007439 (ebook) | ISBN 9781682475676 hardcover
 | ISBN 9781682475768 epub
Subjects: LCSH: New Jersey (Battleship : BB-62)—History
Classification: LCC VA65.N5 S75 2025 (print) | LCC VA65.N5 (ebook)
 | DDC 359.3/2520973—dc23/eng/20250509
LC record available at https://lccn.loc.gov/2025007438
LC ebook record available at https://lccn.loc.gov/2025007439

♾ Print editions meet the requirements of ANSI/NISO z39.48-1992 (Permanence of Paper).
Printed in the United States of America.

33 32 31 30 29 28 27 26 25   9 8 7 6 5 4 3 2 1
First printing

To Carl Stillwell

An exemplary father and human being.

I learned so much from him.

CONTENTS

Preface to the First Edition   IX

Preface to the Revised Edition   XI

Acknowledgments   XIII

CHAPTER I   FROM DRAWING BOARD TO WARSHIP: *September 1940–January 1944*   1

CHAPTER II   WORLD WAR II—EVERYTHING EXCEPT A BATTLESHIP: *January 1944–August 1945*   24

CHAPTER III   POSTWAR DOLDRUMS: *August 1945–June 1948*   55

CHAPTER IV   KOREA, MIDSHIPMEN, AND KOREA AGAIN: *September 1950–July 1953*   81

CHAPTER V   THE IN-BETWEEN YEARS—PEACETIME AND LIBERTY PORTS: *July 1953–August 1957*   114

CHAPTER VI   POLITICS AND THE VIETNAM WAR: *August 1967–December 1969*   147

CHAPTER VII   FROM MOTHBALLS TO LEBANON: *July 1981–May 1984*   183

CHAPTER VIII   BATTLESHIP BATTLE GROUP: *May 1984–November 1988*   218

CHAPTER IX   GOING OUT IN STYLE: *November 1988–February 1991*   252

CHAPTER X   NEW ROLE FOR AN OLD SHIP: *February 1991–Present*   274

APPENDIX I   USS *New Jersey* Commanding Officers   283

APPENDIX II   USS *New Jersey* Ship's Data   284

APPENDIX III   Design Development of USS *New Jersey*   285

Bibliography   289

Index   297

PREFACE TO THE FIRST EDITION

To go to sea in the USS *New Jersey* in the 1980s is to have the sense that she has managed to transcend the normal limitations of time. This feeling probably becomes most evident at night as she glides through the dark sea, the water making a swishing sound as it travels from bow to stern and leaves a luminescent wake beneath the starlit sky. With the coming of night, the eyes no longer focus on the details which command attention during daytime. Instead, the imagination conjures thousands of nights past when this majestic giant has also moved beneath these same stars. The darkness obscures the changes which have been wrought in order to make her again a potent weapon, as she was when she first took to the sea two generations ago.

A look back from the *New Jersey*'s forecastle fills one with a certain knowledge of why battleships have inspired awe for so long. In the foreground loom six gun barrels, each longer than many warships are wide. Beyond them is her towering superstructure, climbing toward the night sky. And one can see also the ship's bridge, illuminated by a dim red glow, as it was more than forty years ago when this was Admiral Bull Halsey's flagship at Leyte Gulf, thirty-five years ago when she steamed with the fast carriers off the east coast of Korea, nearly twenty years ago when her thunderous salvos saved the lives of U.S. Marines ashore in Vietnam, and much more recently when she was protecting Marines in Lebanon. Now, more than four decades after the doomsayers called Pearl Harbor the end of the line for battleships, she steams on yet again with the same red glow from the bridge, the same imposing superstructure, and the same guns which have for so long been a source of awe. This ship, designed in 1938, has accommodated the passage of time and, in a sense, triumphed over it through the installation of today's technology.

During the nocturnal walk about the forecastle comes the realization that there is much more to the ship than steel, guns, and missiles. Hundreds of Navy men breathe life and purpose into her inanimate elements. It is they who give her a soul and they who inherit the legacy from thousands of *New Jersey* men who have gone before. Many of them have probably had feelings similar to those expressed by one of Herman Wouk's characters in *The Caine Mutiny* when he came aboard with the idea of seeing Admiral Halsey. "Can't you feel the difference between the *New Jersey* and the *Caine*?" he asks. "This is the Navy here, the real Navy." I had that feeling myself upon reporting to the crew of the *New Jersey* in 1969 after service in a much smaller ship, the LST *Washoe County*, off the coast of Vietnam. Being part of the *New Jersey*'s crew was more than a source of pride; it was a genuine thrill.

Among my most pleasant moments I count a day in June 1969 when we arrived in Alameda, California. The deep blue sky of Northern California was a dramatic backdrop as hundreds of *New Jersey* men in dark blue uniforms lined up around that towering superstructure and listened as a band played a serenade of welcome. A similar feeling came in the spring of 1983, during a brief visit to the ship. The sun was sparkling off the water as the *New Jersey* completed her refueling one morning from a fleet oiler. As I gazed down from that same superstructure, the hoses from the oiler were unhooked, and the *New*

Jersey's general announcing system played the familiar strains of "Victory at Sea."

The men who have served in the *New Jersey* at various times in the more than forty-three years since her first commissioning have tucked away many of their own special memories of time spent on board, and it is just such memories that form this book. Crewmen have been most generous in sharing their recollections through the medium of oral history and through personal letters. This, then, is a collective insiders' view of what it has been like to live and work in a great battleship in war and peace. To be sure, these men are only a fraction of the total, but in many ways their experiences are representative; one man may speak for dozens or hundreds. All the commanding officers still living have been kind enough to grant interviews. This book places special emphasis on these officers, because they, in their time, have borne the final responsibility for the operation of the ship and the welfare of her crew. And it is they, through the force of their styles of leadership, who have stamped a personality on the ship for a given period.

Even so, running such a vast enterprise is far from a one-man operation. A warship exists as an instrument of national will, and it takes hundreds of men to enable her to execute that will and to spend thousands of hours of training and preparation needed to do so. These are real people, with all their strengths and foibles. In walking about the ship, in daytime or at night, the echoes of the past mingle with the sights and sounds of the present. And there is a certain knowledge that the men who have dwelled here have been, since 1943, the very essence of the USS *New Jersey*.

PREFACE TO THE REVISED EDITION

To the thousands of shipmates who went to sea in the USS *New Jersey*, it was personal. We were a part of the ship; ever since then, she has been part of us. We attend reunions, and the years fall away like flakes of chipped paint. We happily share memories. There is an even more tangible manifestation. Below decks on board the ship is a bulkhead, covered with clear plastic, on which we have signed our names and denoted years of service. As visitors tour the imposing structure that is now a museum and memorial in Camden, New Jersey, evidence of our service is still there. This account tells the story of the ship's history through the experiences of those who served in her.

Serving in the crew of the *New Jersey* was the most enjoyable job of my life. It inspired me to write about the ship's history. In 1986 the Naval Institute published the first edition of this book while the ship was operating. As my father sagely observed at the time, "It's like trying to paint a picture of a moving train." Back then the *New Jersey* still had more than four years of active service ahead. Now that the figurative train has stopped moving, this book brings her story up to date. In the meantime, the economics of publication have dictated a shorter volume than the first, one with a somewhat different format. This updated version complements the original rather than replaces it.

The battleship's last years of active service were remarkable, because her modernization enabled her to operate capably with generations of ships born years after she was. Her missile systems restored the offensive role for which she was built in the early 1940s. And she still had those big guns. Alas, she became too expensive to continue serving. Ironically, she was decommissioned at a time, February 1991, when her sisters *Missouri* and *Wisconsin* were firing their weapons as part of Desert Storm, the Persian Gulf War.

Those active years prior to the final decommissioning led to the purgatory of the mothball fleet in Bremerton, Washington. The *New Jersey* was preserved there with the idea that she might again be needed to support U.S. interests. That need did not come, but she still had the mystique and physical structure that inspire awe. She is one of the few U.S. warships built during World War II that still exists.

Once the Navy concluded that the *New Jersey* no longer possessed military value, she was made available for a new mission. She would henceforth serve as a historical artifact and a teaching tool for present generations and those still to come. She would become as well an inspiration for young Americans to see the Navy as a vehicle in which to serve their nation.

She rode at the end of a long towline from Bremerton to Panama, through the hemisphere-splitting canal, and thence to the East Coast. Competition for a permanent berth involved rival interests in north and south New Jersey. The Navy's decision allocated the ship to the southern location in Camden. She is now across the river from the decommissioned Philadelphia Naval Shipyard, where she was built many years earlier. The subsequent transition from an inert collection of steel and other components into a museum was a challenging process. It required the infusion of large amounts of money, dedication, and the combined efforts of many people. They collaborated to create a new incarnation—to be visited each year by thousands of people.

The process was time-consuming because so much had to be done to overcome the results of years of inactivity in the reserve fleet. Such is the appeal of the great ship that hundreds of individuals volunteered to make her physically attractive and structurally sound. She also needed a newly built dock to be ready for tourists. It has been my pleasure in the years since the *New Jersey*'s memorial/museum opening to visit and revisit the ship. I have been back to the wardroom where my shipmates and I ate our meals. I have gone to my old stateroom and to the fourth-deck combat information center that was my watch station and battle station. Of course, I have gone up on the bow and looked back on the forward 16-inch guns and the majestic superstructure beyond them.

On 23 May 2023 a crowd gathered on the *New Jersey*'s fantail to celebrate the eightieth anniversary of her initial entry into commissioned service. Thanks to her enduring appeal, many more anniversaries are still to come. The people who now serve her so well in her museum role do so for the same reason that former crew members have shared their recollections for this volume. For those who operate the ship and inform visitors, as for those who served in her crew, it is also personal.

ACKNOWLEDGMENTS

The help of Ryan Szimanski, historian/curator of the Battleship New Jersey Museum and Memorial in Camden, has been indispensable in the completion of this revised edition. He and Libby Jones, the museum's director of education, ably responded to my frequent requests and provided valuable material. I am grateful to Phil Rowan, Marshall Spevak, and Jack Willard for their leadership of the organization that operates the memorial. The website is battleshipnewjersey.org.

John Roach, a talented artist, has been a friend for many years through our Naval Reserve connection. He created the superb wraparound painting for the dust jacket. Another painting of his appeared on the dust jacket of my book on the USS *Missouri*.

Carol Comegno, who covered the ship for the South Jersey *Courier-Post* and wrote a book about the *New Jersey*, supplied valuable suggestions concerning the text. Thanks for expert proofreading go to Ed Calouro. He has a gift for spotting typos and errors, and he provided valuable substantive inputs as well.

President Bob Dingman and Vice President Leon Tucker were until recently leaders of the USS New Jersey Veterans, Inc. (www.ussnewjersey.org). During the crew's 2023 reunion, the two of them facilitated my interviews with 1980s–'90s crew members as part of completing the history of the ship's final years in commission.

In 1987 I had the good fortune to meet Lieutenant Commander Steve Chesser, who was then the *New Jersey*'s public affairs officer. We have been in touch ever since. He supplied both photos and material for the text. Two other PAOs welcomed me and provided valuable assistance during my visits to the ship: Lieutenant Commander Eric Willenbrock and Lieutenant Commander Max Allen. Vice Admiral Douglas Katz and his wife, Sharon, went out of their way to be helpful. Another former skipper, Rear Admiral Ronald Tucker, also provided useful material for this updated edition.

Howard Serig, who was a shipmate when I made a two-week information-gathering cruise in the *New Jersey* in 1983, supplied dozens of photos from the ship's Vietnam War period of service. Captain Walt Urban, a longtime friend, is a battleship expert who is frequently involved in events on board the museum ship. I am grateful for his enthusiastic support of this updated edition.

For those at the Naval Institute who helped, the list is long. Adam Kane is the capable Naval Institute Press director who facilitated the creation of this updated version of the ship's story. Steve Catalano has been a constant source of both guidance and support in his role as senior acquisition editor. Jessica Sparks, a Navy veteran, has assisted as well. Former press director Rick Russell and his son, Jack, who does marketing for the publisher, have supplied essential encouragement. Janis Jorgensen, Emily Hegranes, and Brendan Reicherter have been most cooperative in providing access to the Naval Institute's photo collection. Susan Corrado, managing editor of the Naval Institute Press, oversaw the production process involved in turning the disparate elements of text and illustrations into a finished product. I much appreciated her help in providing a digital copy of the text for the original edition so

I didn't have to retype all that material. Production editor Brennan Knight provided capable direction. Claire Noble, Sam Cagguila, and Elena Pelton have been involved in the publicity and marketing of the *New Jersey*'s history. Emily Jerman Schuster did the superb copyediting, and Julie Rushing created the book's design.

I feel a considerable sense of gratitude to the dozens upon dozens of former *New Jersey* crewmen whose recollections of their service make the story come alive.

Finally, as always, I much appreciate the patience, support, and love from my wife, Karen, and our sons, Joseph, Robert, and James.

CHAPTER I
FROM DRAWING BOARD TO WARSHIP
September 1940–January 1944

High above the Philadelphia Navy Yard and the Delaware River, the December sky was laced with tracks of American fighter planes, bombers, and blimps. Their presence was part of the celebration of the christening and launching of the future battleship *New Jersey*. The event was on 7 December 1942, the first anniversary of the Japanese attack on Pearl Harbor. At the head of slipways number two, Mrs. Carolyn Edison, wife of New Jersey's governor, smashed a bottle of champagne across the nose of the still-unfinished ship. The giant hull, which towered five stories above the building ways, began to slide and then moved ever more quickly. The governor's wife blew kisses with both hands.

Applause from the crowd of 20,000 mingled with the hooting of the *New Jersey*'s whistle. After it hit the water following a sixty-second journey down the ways, the 887-foot-long hull described a graceful arc and then reached across for an unscheduled bump against the river's New Jersey shore. Within minutes, a gaggle of tugboats towed it back to the shipyard. Speeches followed from Governor Charles Edison and Under Secretary of the Navy James V. Forrestal.

The design process for the ship began in the late 1930s. On 1 July 1939, with the basic design complete, the Navy awarded the construction contract to the Philadelphia yard. Even as hundreds of shipboard compartments took shape on drafting tables, the name for the planned BB-62 was a subject of interest. Already in 1937, New Jersey citizens, public officials, and war veterans had begun petitioning the Navy to name a new battleship for their state. Especially prominent among the latter, as the

The *New Jersey*'s sponsor, Mrs. Carolyn Edison, prepares to smash the traditional bottle of champagne across the bow to christen the ship as part of the launching ceremony on 7 December 1942. Mrs. Edison's husband, Charles, was then governor of New Jersey. As acting Secretary of the Navy in 1939 he had approved the state's name for BB-62.

Naval Historical Center: NH 95218

campaign picked up in 1938, were veterans of the Spanish-American War.

The requests on behalf of the state bore fruit shortly after the contract was awarded. On 7 July 1939, Secretary of the Navy Claude A. Swanson died after a period of failing health. For months Assistant Secretary of the Navy Charles Edison had acted in Swanson's stead. Now he was officially made acting secretary, and in that capacity he approved the name "New Jersey" on 11 July. Son of the famous inventor Thomas Edison, the acting secretary didn't have his father's creative genius, but he was a capable businessman and solid administrator. Since he was a lifelong resident of the state, his decision was not surprising.

By 1940, the world was in considerable turmoil. The German war machine was on the march in Europe, and the Japanese had made inroads in East Asia. In the U.S. political arena President Franklin D. Roosevelt was considering an unprecedented third term. To disarm his political opponents, he cited the peril facing the nation and added Republicans to his cabinet as Secretary of War and Secretary of the Navy. Charles Edison's status had changed from acting secretary to Secretary of the Navy in January 1940. In June he left the new job when Roosevelt asked him to step aside in favor of Frank Knox. To sweeten the departure, Roosevelt offered his support for Edison to become governor of New Jersey. Edison was elected in November, and the president won his third term.

The physical manifestation of the battleship *New Jersey* had begun on 16 September 1940 when Edison welded the first two keel plates together. In the months to come, that keel grew to considerable length, frames were attached, and collections of steel began to take the shape of a ship. Supervising the work were two naval constructors, Lieutenant Commander Francis Forest and Lieutenant Commander Allan L. Dunning. Building a warship of the *New Jersey*'s dimensions required assembling components produced in various parts of the country. Of necessity, they had to come together and go into place in a fairly rigid sequence.

Former Secretary of the Navy Charles Edison begins construction of the *New Jersey* on 16 September 1940 by welding together the first two keel plates. *Courtesy the Charles Edison Fund*

At any given time, the size of the workforce on the ship's construction amounted to perhaps six thousand to eight thousand men and women, including those in various shops. One of them was Sam Kuncevich, a young shipfitter's helper. He remembered 1940–42 as a time when there was a "spirit to get things done, to get ships built." Eventually, work on the *New Jersey* proceeded around the clock in three shifts. For the day shift, the lunchtime period was a special event. Celebrities were frequently on hand to encourage the yard workers and urge people to buy war bonds. Kuncevich remembered a fight song that included the lyrics "We're gonna have to slap the dirty little Jap, and Uncle Sam's the guy who can do it."

The schedule was especially tight for armor plate. Unlike older generations of battleships, the *Iowa* class had internal side belt armor. Thus, the heavy armor was installed while the ship was still on the building ways rather than after launching. The Midvale Steel

FROM DRAWING BOARD TO WARSHIP 3

In this view, looking forward toward the bow on 8 July 1942, bulkheads are in place in the foreground to form compartments. Machinery is evident in the turret two barbette. Farther forward is a stretch of the armored second deck, surrounding the opening for turret one, and beyond that some of the plating is in place for the main deck in the forecastle area. *Courtesy Philadelphia Naval Shipyard*

Company of North Philadelphia supplied the *New Jersey*'s belt armor. It was routinely shipped to the navy yard by railcars. For one critical section of lower side belt armor, however, a special shipment was made with a low-bed trailer truck accompanied by police escort. The plate was still so hot from its final treatment that workers standing on the plate put an asbestos pad on it to keep their shoes from burning.

The ship's propulsion machinery also had to be installed while the ship was still on the ways. This was necessary so that decks above the turbines and boilers could be built and work on the superstructure could proceed. Lieutenant Harry O. Reynolds was in the shipyard's machinery department. He observed that the boiler components were supplied by Babcock & Wilcox and then erected in the shipyard and lowered into the hull by overhead cranes. The boilers themselves went in during the latter part of 1941. The main engines—one for each of the ship's four propellers—also went into the hull in prearranged sequence. Reynolds said, "Number four was the last one to go in, and I was on pins and needles as to whether we were going to get it in time. We had to leave part of the main deck open just forward of number three turret." The engine barely made it.

The biggest event in the sequence was the launching. To facilitate the first trip into the water, the ways had a slight incline. The hull's immense weight had to be transferred from fixed supports—keel blocks, cribbing, and shoring timbers—to sliding ways that would go with the hull into the water. The wooden sliding ways, 17,000 square feet in area, were matched with ground ways. The two sets were separated by nearly 100,000 pounds of grease—hence the term "greasing the ways." Once the weight of the ship was on the sliding ways, the hull was held in place by triggers in cocked position until released by hydraulically controlled pistons.

Frank Bornack, a longtime shipyard employee, pulled a lever that opened a hydraulic valve. That

The impressive scope of the *New Jersey*'s hull is particularly apparent in this photo taken on the day of her launching. The light gray paint above the waterline is a holdover from the Navy's prewar color scheme. *National Archives: 19-LCM-BB62/C-4*

On 7 December 1942, the first anniversary of the Japanese attack on Pearl Harbor, the *New Jersey*'s hull has nearly completed her launching trip into the Delaware River. *National Archives: 80-G-33590*

knocked out the triggers, and the ship took a minute-long trip. Even in that short space of time, she got up to a speed of 28.3 feet per second—nearly twenty miles per hour. It was entirely a combination of gravity and momentum.

During the launch, one person watching was ten-year-old Joseph Forest, son of the yard's hull superintendent. He held his breath, "wondering if the ship would break free and whether or not she would float once in the water." The hull did float, of course, but then a new problem arose. To check the hull's considerable momentum down the ways, clumps of anchor chain were placed on the riverbank on the vessel's starboard side. To these clumps were attached arresting cables to slew the hull around in an arc to bring it nearly parallel to the course of the river. Shortly before the launching day, someone in the shipyard changed the number of slewing cables from three to two to reduce the possibility of having the cables foul each other. It was to prove an embarrassing miscalculation. Because of the extra motion, the buoyant wooden cradle under the ship was slightly damaged when it struck the New Jersey shore, even though the hull itself was untouched.

Tugboats moved the hull to a water-filled dry dock so the roller paths on which the turrets would turn could be machined. It was better to perform this operation with the ship afloat, because now she was in the position she would be in when the turrets were operated. After the approximately two weeks it took for the turret job to be accomplished, the water in the dock was pumped down. The dock was then refilled, and the hull was supposed to float free from the cradle secured to the dock floor.

The ship started back out of the dock in normal fashion, but when the stern was about seventy feet across the sill of the dock, it stuck. Shipyard divers went under the ship and found the problem to be one of the wedge riders knocked out of position during the unexpected grounding. The solution was to wait for the next high tide to put the ship as nearly as possible into the position at the time the stoppage occurred. Then with power from dock capstans, dock cranes, and yard locomotives, the *New Jersey* was pulled back into the dock. The troublesome wedge rider was then freed. On reflooding of the dock, the ship floated clear of the cradle, and the undocking proceeded normally.

The *New Jersey* was then moved to the shipyard's pier four for outfitting—the installation of the 16-inch turrets, fire control tower, bridge structure, and topside equipment. Next was the precarious operation in January when the gun turret frameworks, called weldments, were put atop the barbettes. The barbettes themselves had been installed by overhead cranes when the hull was still on the building ways, and wooden sheds were built over the openings to protect them from the weather. The weldments were constructed in the yard's turret shop, where Lieutenant Jim Terry was officer in charge. He was instructed to build as much of the framework as he could ashore, because construction was easier there than in cramped spaces on board ship. The limiting factor was the huge hammerhead crane on the fitting-out pier. The crane's rated capacity was 350 tons prior to the launching of the *New*

FROM DRAWING BOARD TO WARSHIP

Having been lifted from a barge, the turret two framework is put in place atop the barbette on 2 January 1943. *Courtesy Philadelphia Naval Shipyard*

After the turret weldments were in place, the lower surface for each turret was jacked up from inside the barbette. Armor for the turrets' sides and back was put in place and machined to fit together. Up above, the crane lowered the 16-inch guns into place, to be followed by roofs. Each gun, with its associated breech mechanism, weighed 167 tons. A 16-inch/50-caliber gun means that the length of the barrel, excluding the part in the breechblock, is measured in the number of inches determined by multiplying barrel diameter, 16, by caliber, 50. The result is 800 inches, with the breech mechanism adding 16 more inches for a total of 68 feet.

As the yard work proceeded in early 1943, forty-seven-year-old Captain Carl F. Holden was chosen as the first commanding officer. He served in Washington as communication officer on Admiral Ernest J. King's U.S. Fleet staff and later was director of naval communications. Holden was a serious, capable,

Jersey, so Terry was authorized to make the turret weldments up to 400 tons.

When the weldment for turret one was ready, a barge went into the shop to transfer it to the ship. Lieutenant Terry had been adding the cumulative weights of the various components, and he concluded the weldment was about 400 tons. Thus, it was more than a little unsettling when he measured the draft of the loaded barge and calculated that the crane would be picking up 416 tons. Once the barge was alongside the ship, the crane lifted the turret weldment and gradually lowered it into place. Lieutenant Terry, mindful that he would be blamed if a mishap occurred, decided to "hold my tongue and STAY UNDER THE LOAD AT ALL TIMES WHEN IT WAS IN THE AIR!" If the crane failed and the load dropped, there would be nothing left of Jim Terry to answer questions. As it happened, the procedure went smoothly, as it did subsequently for turrets two and three.

Captain Carl F. Holden commanded the *New Jersey* from commissioning on 23 May 1943 to 26 January 1945. *USS New Jersey Veterans, Inc.*

and ambitious officer. As he later explained to Naval Reserve Ensign King G. Brandt, "When I heard the *New Jersey* was going to be coming down the line, I put my foot out for it." In all likelihood, Holden had King's support in receiving the assignment.

While yard employees were completing the ship, future crew members were also working to get her ready to operate. Warrant Gunner Robert L. Moore obtained empty powder tanks and dummy 16-inch projectiles in order to check stowage conditions in the projectile flats and the magazines. Lieutenant Harry Reynolds was down in the engineering spaces, lighting off the boilers and conducting tests of the steam lines.

As more and more of the enlisted crew members arrived, they moved into receiving barracks on the Philadelphia naval base. They went to the ship daily to become acquainted with their duty stations. They also received instruction in such requirements as standing by with extinguishers to quell any fires that might break out during welding.

Sometimes the future crew members were involved in the completion of the ship. Gunner's Mate Second Class Ellis Mamroth reported to the pre-commissioning detail from a two-gun 12-inch turret in the USS *Arkansas*. Commissioned in 1912, she was the oldest U.S. battleship to serve in World War II. Going from the oldest to the newest was a distinct pleasure for Mamroth, especially when he observed that the *New Jersey*'s turret arrangement was much safer than that in the *Arkansas*. In the older ship, he could stand in the turret booth and see the breeches of both guns at the same time. In the *New Jersey*, each turret was divided into three separate gun rooms, so an explosion or other problem with one gun wouldn't necessarily disrupt the entire turret.

"By far, my happiest time in the Navy was aboard the *New Jersey*," said Mamroth. "It was what you would call a happy ship." He remembered that Captain Holden seemed to have a lot of regard for everybody in the crew. If there was any sort of gripe about food or living conditions, Holden set about immediately to correct it.

For Ensign Bill Coyne, an officer assigned to fire control for the ship's antiaircraft gun battery, much of the pre-commissioning period was spent in "helping to draw up organization plans, battle bills, cataloging equipment, looking for spare parts, and a myriad of other administrative chores associated with getting the ship ready for active duty." He checked over the four Mark 37 directors that would control the 5-inch guns and familiarized himself with the plotting rooms for those guns, secondary forward and secondary aft. Each contained a Mark 1 antiaircraft computer and stable elements through which a gyroscope maintained a true reference plane so that the guns would remain on target even when the ship was rolling or pitching.

In the three-month period before the *New Jersey* went into commission, the enlisted men slated for the crew went through a large-scale program of psychological testing, interviewing, and evaluation. Commander Percival "Pete" McDowell, the prospective executive officer, established it. The purpose

In this view, taken on commissioning day, the 20-mm gun mount has not yet been installed on the bow. Also still to come is the protective shield that demolished an outhouse at the Philadelphia Navy Yard. *National Archives: 80-GK-884*

was to analyze the requirements of the many jobs on board ship. After evaluating hundreds of men, the command assigned them to appropriate duties. In a paper written afterward, McDowell reported that his program "produced almost spectacular results." Other men on board the *New Jersey* viewed the whole thing with a touch of skepticism. Certainly the testing program achieved better results than if the 90 percent of the crew with no seagoing experience were assigned entirely at random.

The commissioning was on Sunday, 23 May 1943, a warm, beautiful, sunny spring day. Crewmen were called by reveille at 6 a.m. in their barracks, sent for breakfast, and then mustered with seabags and hammocks for the march to the ship. In that era sailors carried hammocks and bedding as parts of their baggage. Among those making the march "after we lashed everything in seagoing fashion" was Fireman Second Class Russell Brown. Initially the crew marched in ranks, but things gradually became more ragged and unsteady as the weight of the baggage took effect. Said Brown, "You started out real good, but toward the end you were leaning way over."

Once on board ship, the men stowed their lockers, made up their bunks, and moved in. Even though commissioning was largely a symbolic milestone, it nevertheless marked the time when control passed from shipyard to crew. More work was needed before the *New Jersey* could go to sea and fight, but she was essentially complete. At the appointed time on commissioning day, the twenty-four hundred officers and enlisted men who composed the crew gathered on the fantail in dress whites.

In the meantime, Lieutenant Jim Phelan had the quarterdeck watch as various VIPs arrived. At one point, he dispatched a messenger to tell Captain Holden of an especially important visitor scheduled to arrive. Instead of going to the inside door of the captain's cabin and thus having to state his business to the Marine orderly on duty, the messenger went in through the door from the 01 weather deck. Hearing

During the *New Jersey*'s commissioning ceremony at Philadelphia on 23 May 1943, the officers and enlisted crew donned dress white uniforms and mustered on the fantail. Two of turret three's 16-inch guns frame the view. *Battleship New Jersey Museum and Memorial*

the captain was in the shower, the messenger told Holden that the officer of the deck had said for the captain to get down to the quarterdeck right away. About ten minutes later, a highly irritated Holden arrived at the quarterdeck and started to chew out Phelan, saying, "A commanding officer does not take orders from the officer of the deck." Fortunately for Phelan, an official car pulled up just then, and the OOD was spared the rest of the tongue-lashing. It was some weeks before he got up enough nerve to raise the subject with the captain and learn of the messenger's unfortunate choice of words.

For the ceremony, admirals and other dignitaries were everywhere, some of them shepherded by Lieutenant (junior grade) Julius C. C. Edelstein, a reserve officer. He looked after the VIPs, who were on a platform aft of turret three. Rear Admiral Milo F. Draemel, commandant of the Fourth Naval District and the Philadelphia Navy Yard, read the commissioning authorization and at 12:38 p.m. directed that the *New Jersey* be placed in commission.

Captain Holden then read his orders and assumed command. Lieutenant Edelstein, whose duties included serving as Holden's speechwriter, helped draft the captain's commissioning remarks. Among his words that day were the following: "This is going to be a smart ship. By smart I mean clean, trim, alert, disciplined. That is synonymous with an efficient ship. It is already a powerful ship. It is going to be a fighting ship."

During the period between the commissioning and the second week in July, the crew and the shipyard force prepared the *New Jersey* to go to sea for the first time. Fuel came on board from a barge alongside. The men of the engineering department were gradually getting used to the propulsion plant, and they were also getting used to the chief engineer, Commander Gerald B. Ogle. Ogle knew his business, for he had been assigned to the Bureau of Ships during the design phase. He was later at the shipyard, helping to get the *New Jersey* ready even before she was launched.

Lieutenant John P. Rossie was head of the *New Jersey*'s A gang, in charge of auxiliary equipment. He said that people in the department learned quickly, or Ogle got rid of them. A number of the department's officers were mustangs, former enlisted men. They and the warrant officers served as instructors in drilling new men on equipment. The learning process was complicated by the fact that completion of the ship was still proceeding. As Rossie put it, "trying to live on a ship when they're working night and day is pretty rough, very noisy."

Men in other departments, particularly gunnery, were undergoing intensive training, including some being sent to antiaircraft gunnery schools. Others went to the General Electric plant in Schenectady, New York, to learn more about the turrets' hydraulic controls. Men traveled to York, Pennsylvania, to be trained on the new 40-mm quad antiaircraft mounts that were being manufactured by York Safe and Lock Company. Inside the *New Jersey*'s turrets, men learned to handle a variety of stations, ranging from handling powder and projectiles far below to ramming them into the breech ends of the 16-inch guns.

In this view on the starboard side, looking forward from amidships, the most prominent structure is the *New Jersey*'s forward stack, flanked on each side by a Mark 37 director for the 5-inch guns. In the foreground is a 40-mm antiaircraft mount. *Courtesy Philadelphia Naval Shipyard*

For the many hundreds of crew members who were new to the Navy, the training covered more than just fighting the ship. It also taught them how to adjust to crowded conditions, lack of privacy, strict discipline and customs, standing in line for meals, and that fresh water was not an unlimited commodity. Commander McDowell, the exec, received reports about high water consumption and problems in the use of shipboard heads. As McDowell explained, "When we realized the standards of these boys were the standards of the subway men's room, the railroad and filling stations, the outhouse and third-rate hotels, we took action. We devoted two hours of drill and instruction in the use of our equipment and got stopped-up drainage under control." Daily fresh water expenditure declined from thirty-five gallons per man to fewer than twenty.

For the senior officers who had come from shore duty and the vast majority of the crew who were new to the Navy, the vigorous pace of training was the closest thing they had yet encountered to combat. An exception was Captain Holden, who certainly knew the value of antiaircraft gunnery, because he was the executive officer of the battleship *Pennsylvania* when the Japanese attacked at Pearl Harbor. Some officers, however, took a jaundiced view. Lieutenant Roman V. "Rosy" Mrozinski was one of the *New Jersey*'s turret officers. He had held a similar position in the heavy cruiser *San Francisco*, a ship heavily damaged by Japanese air and surface attacks off Guadalcanal. Mrozinski remembered, "Some of the people came from Washington; they had had desk jobs, and they were ready to go out and fight the war right then and there, . . . and those of us who had been out in the Pacific and had joined the ship thought this was quite a joke; . . . all we wanted to do at Philadelphia was relax and forget about the war."

A group of the junior officers found even the relaxing to be tiring. They rented apartments in the area a bit north of the shipyard. Lieutenant John W. Sullivan, who was Mrozinski's assistant in turret three, explained that there was a real push to get the ship finished. Work proceeded on "Saturdays, Sundays, and everything else. There was a hell of a lot of welding and painting and grinding and so on going on. It was a madhouse, so that's why we had to go ashore if we were going to get any sleep. We all figured . . . that we're going to be gone for a long time, . . . so we tried to live it up instead of sleeping. And, fortunately, youth came to our assistance."

For Seaman Rafael De La Maza of New York City, not long out of boot camp and a brief attempt at radio school, initial duty on board the *New Jersey* meant the beginning of a three-month period of mess cooking. That included peeling potatoes, washing trays, serving food, and swabbing the mess decks. He had no apartment ashore. For sleeping he had to sling his hammock in the mess area when he first reported. Trying to sleep in a hammock suspended four and

The *New Jersey* steams majestically down the Delaware River on the afternoon of 8 July 1943, not long after leaving the navy yard for the first time. The small chain extending from the bullnose leads down to a ring at the forefoot—the bulbous area where the stem meets the keel. From there a chain attaches to an underwater towing bridle for paravanes to cut mine cables in rivers and coastal waters. *U.S. Naval Institute photo archive*

a half feet above the deck was a new experience, and it gave him a jolt one night when he fell onto a hard steel deck. His day began at 4:30 a.m., when he got up to start breakfast preparations, and ended at 7 or 7:30 p.m. when things were washed and put away.

In the beginning De La Maza's duties did not include the fighting for which he had joined the Navy, but he fell in quickly with the Navy's liberty routine. On off days he went to Shibe Park to watch baseball games. At other times the eighteen-year-old De La Maza went with his new shipmates to Market Street bars to drink beer and listen to a jukebox. Though he had not been drinking before entering the Navy, he and other too-young men followed the example of the older sailors, because, he said, "If you didn't do it, you know, you'd be an outcast."

The men of the *New Jersey* were in their dress white uniforms on the afternoon of Thursday, 8 July, to get the ship under way for the first time. Yard pilot John Vitt was standing up on the 08 level conning position, because the 04 level was not high enough for him to see both bow and stern. Captain Holden stood expectantly nearby, for he was now officially responsible, even though the pilot would be issuing orders to the engines, the helmsman, and the tugs far below. At 1:48 p.m. the last line came free from the shore. The great warship's engines moved slowly astern, and the tugs guided her out into the river and got her headed down the channel on her own power. As she moved down the Delaware River, tugs dropped away one at a time.

That night, after hours getting the feel of the water, the *New Jersey* anchored for the first time in Delaware Bay. Within minutes, three Navy small craft began patrolling on a circle of fifteen hundred yards' radius around the ship. These craft, which were equipped with sound gear, would make sure the new ship was not caught unaware by a submarine, no matter how unlikely the event in the confined waters of the bay.

In the days that followed, the *New Jersey* was under way during the daytime and anchored at night. Each morning, yard workmen came out to the ship by boat, and each night they went ashore. It was a time to test equipment throughout the ship, to provide further training, and to compensate the magnetic compass. The captain and officers of the deck learned the handling characteristics of a vessel that was far bigger than any ship in which they had served. They needed to find out the effect of various speeds, how quickly she would turn, and how big a tactical diameter the turning circle produced when the rudder was put over. The ship's planes were catapulted from the fantail to give their pilots practice and to provide training for the crew in launching and recovering them.

As July passed, the pace quickened. The crew exercised at general quarters and other emergency drills. Boats brought large numbers of officers and shipyard workers from the Philadelphia Navy Yard. Others came from the Bureau of Ships and Bureau of Ordnance in Washington. Early on the morning of Thursday, 22 July, a barge brought James V. Forrestal, Under Secretary of the Navy and the man who had made the principal address when the hull was launched on 7 December 1942. On that previous occasion, he had reminded his audience that when the keel was laid, the ship's announced completion date was 1 May 1944. That date was still more than nine months in the future, but here was the *New Jersey*, virtually complete and ready to fire her guns for the first time. The initial shooting was a structural firing to see what effect the 16-inch naval rifles would have on the rest of the ship.

To the ordnance experts from Washington and the navy yard, these tests were routine—another box to be checked off in the overall process of preparing the battleship for war. For others, the initial firings had considerably larger significance. In his station in radio central, Seaman Bob Westcott had a sense of apprehension that was widely shared among the ship's newcomers. As he recalled, "There were all kinds of rumors coming around. The sound from these guns, they say, is going to be terrible—you know, you're just not going to be able to stand it. And the heat is going to burn the skin off your arms, and all this kind of stuff." Within the experience of most of the *New Jersey*'s crew, there was nothing remotely similar to the firing of these guns.

Throughout the ship, a variety of actions occurred simultaneously in building up to the big event. Computers and radars were operated so the guns could be trained on a safe bearing. Powder cans far down in the magazines were opened and bags transferred through passing scuttles and then put on hoists that would take them up to the turrets. Projectiles were unstrapped from their positions around the insides of the circular barbettes and then sent upward. In the gun rooms projectiles were rammed into the gun breeches, to be followed by six bags of powder for each 16-inch round. Gun captains inserted primers into firing locks in the breech mechanisms. The primers would be fired into the red-colored ends of the rear powder bags, for that section of each bag contained a charge of black powder that would set off the grains of smokeless powder in the six silk bags. Mushroom-shaped plugs sealed the aft ends of the gun breeches so that the ensuing chemical reactions would move in only one direction—out the muzzle ends of the barrels.

Ready lights flashed in turret one to signal to the plotting room on the fourth deck that all was in readiness. Captain Holden gave the order, and at 10:54 that morning the right gun belched forth a ball of yellow-orange flame and expelled a projectile skyward from the starboard side. One by one, the various guns scattered all over the topside spaces of the *New Jersey* took up the action. Included were the deep, thundering 16-inchers, the sharper, cracking 5-inch, and the staccato sounds of the 40-mm and 20-mm antiaircraft machine guns. Hands and minds worked together to produce a cacophony of noise and a spewing forth of flames.

Down in the secondary battery plotting room, Ensign Bill Coyne was encased by steel armor above and on both sides. For him, the noise and heat of the firing were muffled, but the whole ship seemed to shudder and lurch from the impact of the blasts far above. As he described the moment of firing, "The ship herself seemed to hold her breath, along with everyone on board." Later, when he returned to his stateroom, he observed the effects of the day's gunnery. Everything that had not been properly stowed was jarred loose and strewn about the deck. He added, "In fact, throughout the ship all hands were learning the hard way that when the main battery fired, everything in the ship had better be properly secured, or one could expect surprising and sometimes depressing consequences."

The firing of the *New Jersey*'s dozens of guns was impressive but not the whole show as far as 22 July was concerned. After the right gun of turret two fired at 12:10 p.m., the battleship's speed began gradually to build, reaching 32.4 knots at 4:40. Ensign Coyne was also impressed by this aspect of the *New Jersey*'s performance. He recalled, "To see and feel that mammoth ship hurtling through the water at more than 30 knots was a unique experience, one that not only inspired pride and confidence in the ship itself, but also tended to impart a feeling of invincibility—a ship that could do this, just couldn't be stopped." Between her guns and her propellers, the mighty *New Jersey* put on a spectacular show for Under Secretary Forrestal.

The remainder of July took the *New Jersey* first to Norfolk for a few days and then into the Chesapeake Bay for more training. At the end of July and beginning of August, the ship was in Annapolis Roads. For the midshipmen of the Naval Academy, who boated out to the ship, it was an awe-inspiring experience. It was particularly so because many of the plebes had never been on board any ship. One of them was Midshipman Robert C Peniston, who only a few weeks earlier had been at home in Kansas. Now, having had most of his hair shorn off and many other indignities inflicted by hazing upperclassmen, a trip out into the bay provided a rare treat on a Saturday afternoon. To Peniston, it was "a day I'll never forget, because here's this mammoth ship, just looming in the mist. And then as you get closer and closer, the size just seemed to defy all imagination."

After her stay in Annapolis, the *New Jersey* drilled still more in the Chesapeake Bay, although several of her training routines were hampered by the shallowness of the water. Probably the two men on board most concerned with keeping the ship from grounding were Captain Holden and the ship's navigator, Lieutenant Commander Clayton R. Dudley. Years later, Dudley wrote, "Proceeding in Chesapeake Bay up to Annapolis and back to Norfolk, frequently in waters which were only about six inches deeper than our keel, you can imagine how, as Navigator, I began to grow gray hair and consulted the tide tables constantly. . . . However, by the time we had completed our shakedown cruise, I believe he was well satisfied with my performance."

On 9 August 1943, after a brief stay in Norfolk, the *New Jersey* left for her shakedown cruise in the Caribbean. As the battleship moved out into the Atlantic, navigator Dudley could concentrate on keeping the ship on her assigned schedule. He wrote that she did so "like a passenger train running on a railroad—arriving at predicted navigational positions almost always at the predicted time." While she steamed southward in ever-warming latitudes, the battleship was escorted by the destroyers *Sproston* and *Charette*, both of which had been commissioned within a few days of the *New Jersey*. Their sonars pinged ahead into the waters through which the *New Jersey* would pass. In the captain's cabin, Carl Holden paid close attention to a chart marked with colored pins to indicate German submarine sightings of differing degrees of reliability. None of the threats materialized.

On Friday, the thirteenth of August, the *New Jersey* arrived at the nearly landlocked Gulf of Paria. It is formed by the coast of Venezuela and the island of Trinidad. The gulf has only two openings, known as the Dragon's Mouths and the Serpent's Mouth. Since both were easily guarded, the gulf presented warships with a safe haven in which to train, free of concern about submarine attack. The first stop was Trinidad, where Captain Holden went ashore to pay his respects to the commandant of the naval operating base, and where the crew had some memorable liberties.

Lieutenant (junior grade) Gene Hayward was the number-two officer in turret one. He explained that the crew was cautioned before going ashore on the dangers of drinking local rum and then standing in the hot sun. Added Hayward, "Well, that's all they had to say—'Don't do it'—and, of course, they did it." The potent drink had a swift effect. One junior officer fell from a dock into oil-covered water. His white service uniform was instantly transformed into black service. While the officer's cap remained floating on the oil, he and a number of petty officers and nonrated men were hauled back to the *New Jersey* by boat. To Hayward, the liberty parties returning to the ship resembled battle casualties.

The longer some men stayed ashore, the worse their condition became. Petty Officer Leonard Jung said that some of the men returning to the ship "were as good as dead. They were just passed out." A couple of men tried weakly to climb up Jacob's ladders suspended from the side of the *New Jersey* and faced two perils: possible drowning and being squashed between the boat and the side of the ship. After the futility of these efforts became apparent, said Jung, clearheaded men on deck rigged up the ship's crane on the stern with cargo nets and began scooping men onto the fantail.

Seaman Bob Westcott fell out of a liberty boat on his way ashore. Another day ashore in Trinidad brought him a happier outcome. Westcott and a friend decided bananas were healthier than rum, and after a considerable search they found a place where bananas were growing. They liberated a heavy stalk of the fruit and proceeded to carry it—one end on the shoulder of each man. They managed to transport their prize back to the ship, eating quite a few bananas along the way. Once in their living compartment, they hung the stalk from the overhead. "And all through the night," recalled Westcott, "you could hear banana peels go plop on the deck. So in the morning, when we got up, all we had was a pile of banana peels, and that stalk was just as clean as anything."

A number of the ship's officers were detached fairly soon after commissioning, because Captain Holden set a high standard of performance. He expected the *New Jersey* to produce topnotch results, and her chances for that would improve if he got rid of those who didn't measure up. Lieutenant Commander Bill Abhau was then the ship's air defense officer, and he remembered that Holden was "absolutely ruthless in weeding out people that he thought were incompetent. He got rid of two officers that I just couldn't abide, and he got rid of a number that probably—he tended to err on the side of getting rid of them rather than keeping them."

Based on the recollections of the officers and men who served under his command in the *New Jersey*, Captain Holden was a man of many parts. As commanding officer, he took seriously his role as the ship's chief morale officer. He was concerned about the welfare of enlisted crew members and took a warm, fatherly interest in them—paternal without being patronizing. He spoke to the crew over the general announcing system to inform them—within the strict limits imposed by military security—what the ship was doing.

To Seaman Westcott, who served with the radio gang and stood communication watches on the bridge, Captain Holden became an officer with whom he became unusually familiar. That was despite Westcott's initial feeling that a battleship captain was "almost like God" or at least a disciple. During night watches, however, when little else was happening, the two began chatting. It was the captain's practice to inspect the crew's appearance every other Saturday. During an inspection later in the year, Holden took hold of a button on Westcott's peacoat, discovered it was loose, and said, "Bob, I think you'd better do something about that button." Two Saturdays later, Holden came by again, checked once more, and said, "I see you took care of your button."

From time to time when the ship was under way, Captain Holden stopped down in the radio compartment. Doubtless, he was interested because of his previous service as director of naval communications, and he was interested in the radiomen as well. He put on a set of headphones and listened to the dots and dashes of Morse code. On occasion, the radiomen managed to get meat from the ship's butcher shop and cook it in a small skillet on a hotplate they stowed in the compartment. Whenever the metal dogs holding shut the hatch into the compartment were seen to be opening, the radiomen quickly slipped the hotplate and skillet into a tool cabinet because cooking outside the galley was not authorized. Sometimes the individual who appeared through the hatch was Holden himself, and the smoke and aroma of the frying meat lingered in the air. "Fellows," Holden said to the radiomen once, "I'd swear you've been cooking something in here if I didn't know that you know that it's against regulations." Once the captain left, after his stint of listening to the code, the men retrieved the illicit meal from its hiding place, reheated it, and consumed the treat.

With his officers, especially the more senior ones, the captain demonstrated a great deal less tolerance. In fact, it almost seemed there was an inverse relationship between a man's rank and how well he got along with Holden. The officer who bore the brunt of it was Commander McDowell, who had frequent disagreements with the skipper. To some of the more senior officers, Holden seemed unpredictable and arbitrary. He was also strict with regard to disciplinary matters. He was the friend of the enlisted men, but not if they got into trouble. The ship's logs for the early months in commission are replete with sentences dispensed at captain's masts and courts-martial. If someone did get into trouble, he was lucky to have it handled at the division or department level rather than reaching the old man.

The *New Jersey*'s skipper prided himself on his navigation; before the war he had been navigator of the battleship *Idaho*. His knowledge of the subject led to an understandable degree of concern in handling the huge *New Jersey*, because there was virtually no precedent or experience in operating such large ships in the U.S. Navy. When the *New Jersey* went to Trinidad during the shakedown period, Captain Holden would not anchor her inside the net provided for protection against submarines; he considered the water too shallow for the ship's draft of more than thirty-five feet.

From the thirteenth until the end of August, a period of intensive drilling molded the crew of the *New Jersey* into a fighting team. The idea was to do things over and over to improve both speed and reliability so that the teamwork actions in loading and firing the guns would become second nature when it was the time to use them against an enemy. We now call it "muscle memory."

Another purpose of the shakedown was to get the bugs out and correct mistakes. Bob Moore, a warrant gunner in 1943, remembered, "From my point of view our *shakedown* was more of a *breakdown* cruise with 10 percent regulars and 90 percent reserve. Knobs were twisted before their duties were explained or one with experience could arrive on the scene." A number of things thus broken had to be fixed when the *New Jersey* returned to a shipyard in the United States. The inevitable equipment failures and malfunctions had a beneficial aspect, said Bill Coyne, "in that they gave the crew valuable experience in trouble shooting and repair which would prove essential in the months to come."

The Gulf of Paria, less than 12° north of the equator, had the advantage of being a safe haven from submarines, but the crew paid in another way because of the heat of August. Perhaps the foremost victim was the *New Jersey*'s rotund chief engineer, Commander Gerald Ogle. Salt was showing up in the condensate produced by one of the condensers, and it was certainly undesirable to feed salty water into the boilers. So Ogle squeezed through a manhole to get to the saltwater side of the condenser and then to conduct a soap test. By rubbing a bar of soap over a number of tubes, he found in one the leak that was causing the problem. During the time of the test, the August heat swelled up his body, and he was unable to get back out through the manhole by which he had entered. John McCormick, who was Ogle's assistant, described the remedy, "We had to break out the fire hose and play cold water on him to shrink him. That, with the application of grease on his body, enabled him to get thru the manhole."

On 21 August, the *New Jersey* went alongside the oiler *Mattole*, a ship built shortly after World War I. It marked the first time the battleship refueled under way since going into commission. The officer of the deck for the operation was Lieutenant Oscar Gray, who had come from the USS *Mississippi*. He remembered that Captain Holden was only too happy to let the experienced Gray take the *New Jersey* alongside the *Mattole* for the maneuver. This new battleship of theirs, which displaced more than 54,000 tons with fuel, ammunition, and stores on board during the shakedown, was the sort of vessel that merited a healthy sense of respect.

Thousands of rounds of ammunition passed through the *New Jersey*'s guns during the shakedown. The antiaircraft batteries fired at balloons and at target sleeves towed by aircraft. Planes from the light carrier *Monterey*, which was also undergoing shakedown, simulated torpedo attacks against the *New Jersey* to give gunners and fire controlmen a feel for what the experience would be like when the planes were launched by an enemy. The main battery fired both day and night battle practice at target rafts, with the 5-inch guns providing illumination at night by firing star shells. The latter are special projectiles that contain flares; they are equipped with parachutes so that the flares can drift slowly downward and keep targets illuminated for some time.

One of the night practices was conducted in an atmosphere of tragedy. About 6 p.m. on 24 August, the gunnery department was preparing for the upcoming drills by holding alignment checks to make sure that turrets and plotting rooms were working together. While this was going on, Gunner's Mate Second Class Irving S. Doremus opened a hatch in the bottom of the gun pit in turret one and climbed up into the gun pit to get a can of oil near the primer station. The gun captain saw him come up, but he had a mental lapse. When the signal came from the plotting room to match signals, he forgot about Doremus and threw a switch that allowed the guns to go under control of the plotting room. Doremus stepped out from the primer station into the gun pit of the center gun just as the remotely controlled 16-inch barrels were elevated. The huge breech mechanism of turret one's center gun came down and crushed him. He died a few hours later. The crew quickly took up a collection for his pregnant widow.

Late in the afternoon of 31 August, after the training had concluded, the *New Jersey* left the Gulf of Paria via the Serpent's Mouth and steamed to Norfolk. While the ship was in nearby Hampton Roads, Rear Admiral Donald B. Beary, commander, Atlantic Fleet Operational Training Command, came on board and gave the *New Jersey* her annual military inspection on 5 and 6 September. Emergency drills were held at anchor on the first day, and the second day was spent in a mock battle problem.

The *New Jersey*'s three OS2U Kingfisher planes, their cockpits protected from the sea by canvas, ride on the fantail on 3 September 1943 during a transit north from Trinidad to Philadelphia. The ship has a noticeable wake because of a full-power run. *National Archives: 80-G-82695*

The *New Jersey* at anchor in September 1943. Just before heading to Philadelphia for post-shakedown shipyard work, the ship still has a catwalk around the front of the conning tower, rather than an actual bridge. *National Archives: 80-G-204838*

The whole inspection was, in effect, an examination that allowed the crew to demonstrate how well it had learned its lessons during the shakedown.

The *New Jersey* concluded her first underway period on Tuesday, 7 September, almost two months to the day since she had first left Philadelphia. Shortly after noon, the ship anchored in the Delaware River to await the high tide that would give her clearance to move alongside a pier. The ship was under way again in midafternoon, and while she was trying to moor at pier four, one of her paravane chains carried away and was fouled. Then the ship got away from the control of some of the ten tugboats alongside. Dudley, the navigator, recalled the circumstances: "The ship was almost as long as the river was wide so when we reached a heading across channel our overhanging bow was above the right bank (on the navy yard side) and our stern was in shallow water near the other bank. The bulk of the ship acted like a dam across the river channel."

River current shoved the stern aground on the shallow mudbank. The intake of mud fouled the main condenser, stopping the main engines and generators and causing the *New Jersey* to lose electrical power and steering control. Emergency diesel generators went on down in the engineering spaces, but they couldn't get cooling water either, so they soon kicked off as well. Lieutenant John Rossie recalled that the engine spaces "were just as black as could be."

If the whole situation was bewildering down below, it had its frightening aspects topside, particularly for one shipyard worker who was in a restroom at the end of pier four. When the stern grounded in the mud, the bow of the *New Jersey* swung around and headed for the restroom. The worker inside saw the bow coming and went tearing out of the place with his trousers at half-mast. He escaped before the structure was smashed by the bow. Finally the ship was pulled under control and moored to the pier, but the whole episode wasn't quite over. During the yard period that followed the *New Jersey*'s arrival at Philadelphia, a sturdy metal shield was built on the ship's bow to protect the crews of two 20-mm gun mounts being installed there. After the shield was completed, someone in the crew painted on the outside of it the silhouette of an old-fashioned outhouse, much as other ships painted silhouettes of enemy ships sunk or planes shot down. The captain heard about it, and the outhouse symbol was quickly painted over.

Because of the brief grounding, it was time to clean out the condensers again. Earlier, while in Norfolk, it had been done, because the scant clearance above the bottom of Chesapeake Bay had caused a good deal of mud and debris to be scooped up. When the condensers were opened and dumped into the bilges, said John McCormick, the crew found such things as a four-foot shark, a snake, and hundreds of condoms. This time, at Philadelphia, the "gunk" from the bottom of the river was so hard that it had to be broken up with pickaxes.

Still another foul-up occurred on 12 September. A too-sensitive warning system indicated a fire in the powder magazines for turret two. A powder explosion at any time would be a catastrophe, but the effect would be even worse in a shipyard where surrounding facilities might be hit. As a result, Commander Edward S. Addison, the damage control officer, ordered the magazines to be flooded. Later inspection revealed that there had been no fire. Although he realized the necessity for flooding the magazines, Lieutenant Gray, the turret officer, was miffed, because his division was forced to "unload every damn stitch of powder in those magazines." Then his men had to clean the magazines, install new insulation, and repaint the interiors.

The *New Jersey* went into dry dock on 20 September as part of the yard period. The time back in Philadelphia was a post-shakedown availability that enabled the shipyard to fix things that had gone wrong during the first underway period. Moreover, the ship received a new bridge and a new secondary battle control station, thanks to an early September message from Admiral Ernest J. King, commander in chief, U.S. Fleet, who had ordered the shipyard period extended for a time in order to make the modifications.

The purpose of the ship's conning tower was to protect the officers who were inside to direct the

This 16 October 1943 photo shows the newly enclosed bridge that was constructed during the ship's post-shakedown yard period in Philadelphia in September and October. She was the only ship of the class to have a rounded 04-level bridge. Atop the conning tower is the newly installed horizontal antenna for the Mark 3 main battery fire control radar. *National Archives: 80-G-207484*

ship's movements. This was useful for battle, but the narrow viewing slits through the armor were clearly insufficient for normal steaming watches. During the shakedown cruise, the *New Jersey*'s officers of the deck stood their watches on an open catwalk around the front of the conning tower. However, such an arrangement was scarcely adequate for extended steaming in all kinds of weather, because the bridge personnel were completely unprotected. Thus, an enclosed bridge was authorized by Admiral King. Some *New Jersey* officers recalled that Captain Holden made a strong case for a new bridge and got King to agree to it. The resulting bridge followed the curvature of the catwalk around the front of the conning tower, so it was still cramped, but at least it had a roof and windows.

Another change had been approved by Lieutenant Commander Philip W. Snyder, a naval engineer who was senior assistant on the battleship and cruiser desk in the Bureau of Ships. After the first sea trials, the *New Jersey*'s navigator had submitted an alteration request to improve the ventilation in his sea cabin, which was located in the forward part of the superstructure. Commander Snyder disapproved the request because he didn't consider it essential. On the next trials, Snyder's accommodation turned out to be the navigator's sea cabin—a deliberately diabolical assignment, because the passageway outside the cabin was freshly painted. After an uncomfortable night or two, Snyder returned to Washington and promptly wrote to the shipyard at Philadelphia to authorize improvement of the sea cabin's ventilation "on the basis of proven service experience."

On 3 October, the *New Jersey* left dry dock and moored again at pier four. In the ensuing days, she was loaded with 97,920 rounds of 20-mm ammunition and 107,488 rounds of 40-mm. On the twelfth she conducted dock trials of her engineering plant and then got under way the following day. She went to the Chesapeake Bay to test-fire her guns, conduct vibration tests on the engineering plant, and run a battle problem with her crew at general quarters.

At Hampton Roads on 17 October, Rear Admiral Beary came aboard to conduct yet another battle problem and military inspection. This was the final exam. On 18 October, Captain Holden was able to send a satisfying message to Admiral Royal E. Ingersoll, commander in chief, Atlantic Fleet. The message said simply, "Originator reports for duty." The time of training and testing had achieved a satisfactory result; the USS *New Jersey* was at last part of the operating fleet. The crew was able to celebrate with a five-day period of liberty and recreation at Norfolk.

The battleship's first operational assignment was in Casco Bay, off the coast of Maine. There was still training to be done, but now the *New Jersey* was deemed ready to meet the enemy. The battleships *South Dakota* and *Alabama* had operated with the British Home Fleet earlier in the year. They and five destroyers constituted Task Force 22. They served as an immediately available backstop in case German heavy ships such as the battleship *Tirpitz* broke out into the Atlantic and caused the sort of havoc that her sister *Bismarck* had done during her dramatic but ill-fated voyage in May 1941. Admiral King subsequently decided to release the *South Dakota* and *Alabama* for Pacific duty but to keep the *Iowa* and *New Jersey* in the Atlantic for the time being.

While the *New Jersey* was on her shakedown, the *Iowa* had operated in Casco Bay and off Newfoundland, even farther north. She was not providing the kind of direct support that the *Alabama* and *South Dakota* had, but she was an immediately available backstop in case German heavy ships broke out into the Atlantic. In early September 1943, the *Tirpitz* and battle cruiser *Scharnhorst* left Norway briefly to bombard the island of Spitsbergen. After her return to Norway, the *Tirpitz* was damaged later that month by British X-craft midget submarines. As a result, the German threat had eased even before the *New Jersey* came on the scene. This released the *Iowa* to transport President Roosevelt and the Joint Chiefs of Staff to North Africa for a conference of Allied leaders at Cairo, Egypt.

The *New Jersey* arrived off Maine on 24 October 1943, and Rear Admiral Walter S. Anderson, president of the Navy's Board of Inspection and Survey (InSurv) came on board to observe standardization trials over a measured mile course off Rockland, Maine. The highest speed achieved was thirty knots. The shallowness of the water—combined with the ship's deep draft—prevented the *New Jersey* from demonstrating her full capabilities. Assistant engineer officer McCormick recalled that the water was only eighty-nine fathoms deep, with the result that "we could do only about 29 knots without serious vibrations. I soon found out I could tell the Navigator when we crossed the 100 fathom mark as the vibrations disappeared at that point (this was at high speeds, of course)."

On 2 November, after a brief period in port at Boston, the *New Jersey* entered Casco Bay for the first time. One of the junior officers in the secondary battery fire control division during operations off Maine was Lieutenant (junior grade) Les Heselton. His impressions of the time and place were similar to those of many in the crew. He described Maine in late 1943 as "the coldest spot on earth—cold, damp and windy." When the ship was anchored at night, the practice, as previously, was to put out picket boats to report the approaches of boats or swimmers— essentially anti-sabotage patrols. The men on watch in the picket boats wore so much protective clothing, said Heselton, that they were too hot at first and then "practically frozen" by the end of a watch. Ensign Bill Coyne also stood boat watches and remembered the penetrating cold and the frequent showers of spray that turned to ice almost immediately. The most threatening thing Coyne sighted during his boat duty was a floating log or two.

It was also cold on liberty in Portland, Maine, but men went over anyway, even though they had to endure long boat rides. Petty Officer Leonard Jung was struck by the way men huddled over the engines of the motor launches, because any source of heat was welcome. When the men stepped ashore in Portland

The *New Jersey*'s dance band performs at a club ashore in Portland, Maine, in the autumn of 1943—prior to the ship's departure for the Pacific. These men are already combat veterans, having been members of the heavy cruiser *Northampton*'s band at the time of her sinking off Guadalcanal on 1 December 1942. After survivor leave, they reported to the commissioning crew of the *New Jersey*. *Courtesy Leonard J. Jung*

for the first time, they were herded into a corral and had to wait until enough men were on hand for a lecture about proper liberty decorum. Apparently, previous Navy men on liberty there had created a poor image for the service, so the crew of the *New Jersey* was warned to follow strict standards. Both Jung and Fireman Russ Brown remembered the precise instructions to have white hats square across their foreheads and all buttons on the heavy blue peacoats buttoned. For both men, the thing to do on liberty was to head for a restaurant and a good steak dinner. Some men holed up in hotel rooms to rest and share a bottle.

For Seaman Bob Westcott, who had a wife at home and couldn't afford a hotel room, an overnight liberty in Portland was a particular trial. After the movies ended at 9 p.m., there was little to do except wait for the next boat back to the ship. One night he crawled into a railroad station luggage rack and wrapped himself in newspaper to try to keep warm. Another night he went to a fishery and chatted with the night watchman, because it at least gave him a warm place to kill time.

In November, the members of the *New Jersey*'s crew began to have the benefit of a ship's newspaper, the editor-in-chief of which was Lieutenant Julius Edelstein. For the first few issues, the paper was known as *Clean Sweep Down*, and crewmen were invited to submit nominations for a permanent name. The incentive for the winner was a prize of ten dollars, which represented about two weeks' pay for some of the most junior men on board. In early 1944 the title became *The Jerseyman*.

The initial issues of *Clean Sweep Down* offered profiles on the ship's senior officers, with Captain Holden featured in the first one and Commander McDowell in the second. The paper's front page featured a snorting animal labeled "N. J. Bull," which may or may not have been intended as a comment on the contents. Each issue was a compendium of news tidbits about the various divisions that comprised the ship's company. Featured often were items about engagements, marriages, and births of children. Cartoons, poems, and jokes (frequently feeble) dotted the paper. There were interesting pieces of information; for instance, the crew ate twenty-seven hundred pounds of turkey on Thanksgiving that year.

Along with the times at anchor, the *New Jersey* was also under way a fair amount during November and the first half of December. She operated with destroyers in Casco Bay and fired both her main battery and antiaircraft guns to keep the crew in practice. The cold weather had an effect on the shooting, along with everything else. Gunner's Mate Ellis Mamroth of turret three was impressed by the layers of ice that built up on the 16-inch gun barrels, including the recoil slides that retracted into the turret proper upon firing. When the guns were fired in Casco Bay, good-sized sheets of ice flew through the air after they'd been knocked off the slides.

On Thanksgiving morning, Thursday, 25 November, Ensign King G. Brandt attended a Protestant church service in the mess compartment on the second deck aft. "All of a sudden," he remembered, "there were these terrific vibrations. We couldn't imagine what was going on, but it almost drowned out . . . the minister." It turned out that the *New Jersey* had been operating her OS2U Kingfisher scout planes that morning. When one of them came back in to hook up to the stern crane, the aviation radioman attempting the hookup, Clinton A. Hanscom, was knocked off the plane by a wave and fell into the sea.

His expected survival time in the frigid water was quite short, so Captain Holden immediately kicked up the speed and began turning the ship in order to recover Hanscom. One of the planes got to the chilled radioman, but his waterlogged flight suit made him too heavy to pull aboard the plane. He stayed on the plane's float until a motor whaleboat launched by the *New Jersey* picked him up. As it turned out, the heavy leather flying suit that kept the plane from rescuing him had helped ward off the effects of the cold. Even so, he was already turning blue by the time he got

This is the second edition of the ship's newspaper *Clean Sweep Down*, published in November 1943. The large animal in the upper left bears the title "N. J. Bull." The contest to rename the paper brought a ten dollar award to Private First Class Carl W. Ritner of the ship's Marine detachment. His winning entry, *The Jerseyman*, was used on the issue dated 1 January 1944 and thereafter. *Courtesy William Dugan*

back on board the battleship. He was warmed up in the sick bay by a combination of rubbing and doses of medicinal alcohol. After a day in sick bay he was up and about and soon recovered. What's more, Captain Holden's stock with the crew went even higher because of his demonstrated determination to save one of his men.

When the month of December reached mid-term, the mission of the *New Jersey* and her accompanying destroyers as a fleet-in-being to counter the German fleet-in-being came to an end, and the ships headed south. From the sixteenth until the twenty-eighth, the battleship moored at the South Boston Annex of the Boston Navy Yard for last-minute maintenance attention and a period of Christmas leave for crew members.

Unexpected Christmas presents came to the men of the battleship from the newly formed State Society of the Battleship New Jersey, spearheaded by New Jerseyite Gill Robb Wilson, who was a reporter for the *New York Herald Tribune*. Each man received a "buddy bag," which was a small ditty bag containing such items as a harmonica, shaving gear, socks, and comb. Each bag contained the name and address of the person who had packed and donated it, so the recipient could write and thank his benefactor. It was a nice touch that helped build a relationship between the ship and the state for which she was named.

Tight security concerning the ship's plans was in force as the old year ended. Crew members were deliberately not told where the *New Jersey* would be going. Seaman Second Class Roger Faw, fresh out of boot camp, was ordered to catch a ferryboat and train from Norfolk to Boston to join the ship, even though Norfolk was the *New Jersey*'s next destination—something he specifically was not told. Another shipmate, Seaman Second Class Bill Hartley, went through the same routine and remembered that his Christmas dinner consisted of sandwiches and coffee on the train northward. Had he known at the time of the ship's schedule, he would have much preferred to spend Christmas with his family in Washington, DC, and then meet the ship at Norfolk.

For one *New Jersey* officer, the period in Boston was the end of the line—far sooner than he wanted to leave. Executive officer Pete McDowell had been on board only seven months from the time of commissioning and very much looked forward to going with the ship to the war zone so he could see the results of his psychological testing and assignment of personnel. But his personality had clashed on numerous occasions with that of Captain Holden, so when the news came through that McDowell had been selected for the rank of captain, he was reassigned right away. On 23 December, McDowell reluctantly turned his job and his spacious shipboard quarters over to Commander Rufus E. Rose, the gunnery officer. Rose celebrated the promotion and the holiday by having his wife and son come on board for Christmas dinner. He made it a point to visit all the messes and observed that the cooks had done an excellent job.

One *New Jersey* officer for whom the Boston stop proved especially memorable was Ensign Bill Coyne. Years later, he wrote,

> I do remember very vividly having some Boston friends aboard for dinner one evening and walking back to their car with them following the movie in the wardroom. It was a clear moonlit night, and when we were some 200 yards from the ship we turned and looked back. There broadside, silhouetted against the night sky, was that magnificent ship. We stood there, silent, for several minutes, drinking in the beauty, the strength and awesome power of the NEW JERSEY. Many years later I again visited those same friends in Boston. They could still remember the sight of that beautiful ship and the lasting impression it had made on them. It also made a lasting impression on me.

Shortly after Christmas, the *New Jersey* headed south for Norfolk, which also was cold. The year 1943 ended with the battleship taking on 324 16-inch high-capacity projectiles while at anchor in Hampton Roads. The first day of January was spent taking on new men and transferring some who had been on board since the commissioning. For nearly all in the crew, their destination was still a mystery, especially because men had been ordered to equip themselves with long underwear and other cold weather gear. They had even been inspected to make sure they complied.

At 1:37 on the afternoon of Sunday, 2 January, the ship got under way from her anchorage and began standing out of Hampton Roads. The captain, exec, navigator, and pilot were on the bridge, and Lieutenant Rosy Mrozinski was officer of the deck. Lieutenant John Rossie of the engineering department thought the ship was getting under way just so she could move to another anchorage; instead, she took up station in column two thousand yards astern of her sister ship *Iowa* and began heading south for the Panama Canal. Rossie remembered, "They were trying to fool somebody; they sure fooled me."

Later in the afternoon, when the battleships were clear of Hampton Roads, four destroyers joined the heavy ships and fanned out ahead to provide an antisubmarine screen. Up ahead in the *Iowa*, the officer in tactical command was Rear Admiral Olaf M. Hustvedt, commander of the newly formed Battleship Division Seven. As the six ships headed steadily to the south, they were on wartime footing—showing no lights at night and zigzagging to foil potential submarine attack. Such precautions were still prudent, although no longer so vital as in 1942 and 1943 when German U-boats posed a much greater menace in the Caribbean and along the Atlantic seaboard than in 1944.

With the warming of the weather, the men of the *New Jersey* began to gain a better idea of their destination. In the meantime, they had to put up with the discomfort of storm-tossed seas in the traditionally rough Cape Hatteras region off the Carolina coast. On 4 January, for instance, Seaman Second Class James V. Grimm received a fracture to the upper part of his left arm when heavy seas washed him against the shield of a 20-mm gun mount on the fantail. The battleships had to slow down, because the destroyers could not keep up in the rough weather.

Friday, 7 January was a long day for the *New Jersey* as she made her laborious way through the locks of the Panama Canal. She had been designed so she would barely fit through those locks, and now her dimensions were put to the test for the first time. She had less than a foot of clearance on each side. After passing into the Pacific for the first time in her career, she stopped overnight for liberty in Balboa, Panama Canal Zone. For the vast majority of the ship's crew who had been ashore in a foreign country only in Trinidad, the experience in Panama was quite a revelation. For Philip Fuller, a member of the *New Jersey*'s band, "Getting into the city of [Balboa] and seeing the conditions there at that time, I think, opened a lot of our eyes to the fact that all the world isn't like America."

The men of the *New Jersey* went on liberty at the same time as those of the *Iowa*, and a rivalry sprang up that was to last for quite a while. The two sister ships had gone into active service within a few months of each other, and the men from each battleship felt that theirs was the better one. Seaman Second Class Roger Faw observed that the men of the *New Jersey* and *Iowa* "were constantly at each other's throats." Almost anything could start a fight. One barroom brawl erupted when the men of one ship felt that a Panamanian woman performing in the bar had been mistreated by some of the men from the other ship. Even so, that fight was an exceptional one, according to Faw, because, "I guess that was the only fight I can remember seeing and knowing what started it." In most cases things broke loose merely because the men of the *Iowa* and *New Jersey* were together. For Seaman Rafael De La Maza, who was in the *New Jersey*'s fourth division along with Faw, his ability to speak Spanish was a boon to his shipmates. He was able to serve as interpreter and keep his friends from getting cheated in transactions with local ladies.

The stop in Panama afforded the last opportunity for the *New Jersey* to take on fuel before her long transit to the South Pacific. Even so, she wasn't supposed to fill the fuel oil tanks above the waterline, explained Lieutenant John Rossie, the auxiliaries division officer, because of fleet practice. The feeling was that oil above the level of the water was more likely to catch fire than that below. The Panama fueling facilities delivered the heavy black oil at well over one thousand gallons a minute, a considerably faster pumping rate than the *New Jersey*'s fueling gang was used to.

Each fuel tank was equipped with a vent pipe routed to an overboard terminal point. The vent served two purposes, as an escape path for the air in the tank that was displaced during the filling and as a relief pipe to prevent overpressure in the case of overfilling. For some reason, one of the ship's tanks did get too much oil that night and, inexplicably, the vent pipe from the tank led not overboard but to a small storeroom adjacent to the tank. The storeroom was fitted with a duct connected to the exhaust ventilation system of the A division berthing compartment.

The oil from the overfull tank quickly filled the storeroom, which was sealed off by a watertight door. The fuel then continued up the ventilation duct to the A division compartment and rained down upon sleeping men. Machinist's Mate First Class William Chambers, in a bottom bunk, awoke with the odd sensation of finding himself awash in fuel oil, because it covered the deck of the compartment to a depth of a foot or more. Wearing only his skivvy shorts and a coating of oil, Chambers scrambled along the deck, falling into the black pool at one point. He managed to get up a ladder and to the quarterdeck with the urgent message that pumping should be stopped, which it was.

Lieutenant Rossie remembered that Chambers' quick thinking may well have averted a much worse problem. In addition to flooding the berthing space, a considerable amount of the fuel was drawn through the vent by an exhaust fan and found its way to one of the boiler uptakes. Uptakes are spaces above the firerooms from which blowers pull air for combustion. When the cleanup crew opened the uptake space sometime later, they found the deck covered with oil to within a few inches of the top of the protective coaming surrounding the air intake openings to the boiler that was steaming for auxiliary purposes. Had the pumping not been stopped when it was, the fuel oil would have topped the coaming and flowed into the combustion air intake and then into the operating boiler, possibly causing an explosion and fire.

Late the next morning, Saturday, 8 January 1944, the *Iowa* got under way from Balboa, and the *New Jersey* followed shortly past noon. In appearance, the two sister ships traveling together were a marked contrast. The *Iowa* was painted in a crazy-quilt "dazzle" camouflage pattern of gray, black, and white—a confusing mixture of shapes designed to minimize detection and determination of the direction in which the ship was headed. For a submarine seeking to set up a torpedo firing solution, the target's course was important. The *New Jersey* was painted all over in a dark bluish-gray. The intent of that particular camouflage scheme was to make the ship blend with the sea, especially when viewed from above or from a distance. The teakwood decks had been painted over so that the light color of the planking would not stand out against the dark sea when viewed from the air.

During the next two weeks, the *Iowa*, *New Jersey*, and their destroyers maintained a course that was nearly west-southwest, with a speed generally around twenty knots or slightly higher. The battleships could easily hold that pace with half their boilers on the line. Each day the *New Jersey* held practice general quarters drills; for Seaman Roger Faw the drills were a useful means of breaking the monotony of the transit. Other than that, there was an endless round of chipping, painting, cleaning, swabbing decks, and standing watches.

A device that was useful both for keeping the men busy and for preparing to handle their coming combat duties was the loading machine on the 02 superstructure deck between the two smokestacks. It was a mockup of part of the machinery inside each 5-inch gun mount and provided training for the gun crews through the use of dummy projectiles and powder cases. The loading crew took the ammunition out of the loading machine hoist, loaded it into the breech of the barrel-less "gun," then hit a lever to ram projectile and shell casing into position. The repeated practice developed speed, coordination, and perspiration. Seaman Second Class Bill Hartley said of loading machine drill in the equatorial regions, "I'll guarantee that would bring the sweat out of you."

One of the normal traditions of the Navy was dispensed with during that January transit because of the urgency of getting the battleship out to the war zone. Customarily, the ceremony associated with crossing the equator included much hijinks and merriment. The pollywogs who had never been across the line before—and that included nearly everyone in the *New Jersey*—would have been the victims of playful mischief on the part of the shellbacks who had been across already. There was no such ceremony when the *New Jersey* crossed into the South Pacific for the first time on 13 January. Instead, the men were all handed wallet-sized cards that executive officer Rufus Rose signed on behalf of "Davey Jones" and "Neptunus Rex."

With their arrival at Funafuti Atoll in the Ellice Islands on 22 January, the battleships and their escorts entered a lagoon filled with ships—the battleships *Washington* and *North Carolina*, aircraft carriers, supply ships, tankers, and transports. Seaman Rafael De La Maza was awed by the sight of all the naval vessels: "When we went there and we anchored, I never, never in my life had seen so many ships together. I never will forget that. That was tremendous."

The preliminaries were over at last. The USS *New Jersey* had joined the fleet that was fighting Japan.

CHAPTER II

WORLD WAR II—
EVERYTHING EXCEPT A BATTLESHIP
January 1944–August 1945

The *New Jersey*'s main engines scarcely had a chance to cool at Funafuti Atoll before she was off and running again. The Central Pacific offensive against Japan—built around amphibious landings and carrier air strikes—was moving into high gear. Soon after arrival at Funafuti, Captain Holden reported to Rear Admiral Frederick Sherman in the carrier *Bunker Hill*. Joining Holden at the pre-operation conference for the Marshall Islands invasion were Rear Admiral Olaf Hustvedt, commander Battleship Division Seven, and Captain John McCrea of the *Iowa*. Commander Roland Dale, the carrier *Bunker Hill*'s air group commander, got the impression that the battleship officers expected their ships to win the war. As Dr. Clark Reynolds wrote in *The Fast Carriers*, combat veteran Sherman soon set them straight by saying, "I don't care whether or not you can shoot your 16-inch guns, but you'd better know how to use your antiaircraft batteries." Aircraft carriers were now the top dogs.

Radarman Third Class Joseph McGowan and many of his shipmates stayed up long into that night of 22–23 January to bring supplies on board. Radio technicians (later known as electronics technicians) were also busy because of problems with the SG surface search antenna. The repairmen finished

Battleship Division Seven—*Iowa* in the foreground and *New Jersey* beyond—approaches Funafuti Atoll on 22 January 1944. Soon they would be on their way to support the invasion of the Marshall Islands. *Courtesy Erling Hustvedt*

In the foreground are two 40-mm quad mounts on board the division flagship *Iowa*. In the background, the *New Jersey* prepares to turn to port to follow the *Iowa*. *Bureau of Aeronautics 256596 in U.S. Naval Institute photo archive*

about daylight and were met by Lieutenant August Cook, the colorful radar material officer described by another member of the *New Jersey*'s wardroom as a "capricious genius."

Cook took the men to his stateroom and telephoned the wardroom for four glasses and four cans of pineapple juice. He then broke out some bottles of alcohol he had smuggled on board in Philadelphia by telling the officer of the deck they were radar repair parts. He conveniently disregarded the prohibition against alcoholic beverages on board U.S. Navy ships, although the bottles did have a connection—as reward—with radar repair. After the technicians finished their drinks, Cook told them, "All right you bastards, don't say nothing to nobody. Just go up and go to sleep."

Fewer than twenty-three hours after her arrival, the *New Jersey* was under way. She and the *Iowa* soon joined Sherman's Task Group 58.3. Included, besides the flagship *Bunker Hill*, were the light carriers *Monterey* and *Cowpens*, the heavy cruiser *Wichita*, and nine destroyers. Altogether, four such task groups composed Task Force 58 under Rear Admiral Marc Mitscher. As the force steamed northward, Captain Holden told the *New Jersey*'s crew members their destination. Kwajalein Atoll was considered the heart of the Marshalls, though not the most heavily defended part.

About 3 a.m. on 29 January, the men of the *New Jersey* were roused from their bunks, given coffee and sandwiches, and sent to general quarters. Joe McGowan described the scene in a letter written shortly afterward: "My battle station was Air Defense aft so I was able to see everything. It seemed funny, everybody was quiet and you said so long to your friends and went at it." In the darkness that morning, some seven hundred planes took off to attack Kwajalein; they achieved complete surprise. No Japanese planes came within sight of the *New Jersey*.

Once control of the air was achieved, battleships principally old ones—began giving the boomerang-shaped Kwajalein Island a "Spruance haircut," named for Vice Admiral Raymond Spruance. As commander, Central Pacific Force—which was designated as the Fifth Fleet—he was in overall command of the operation. The murderous gunfire mowed down palm trees, buildings, and Japanese.

Task Group 58.3 then steamed west; an enemy scout plane trailed during the night, until daybreak on Sunday, 30 January. The battleship's crew took the plane's presence as the precursor of a large attack. From the thirtieth until 1 February, the day of the amphibious assault on Kwajalein, Sherman's task group operated between Bikini and Eniwetok in the Marshalls. Carrier planes pounded the latter with bombs to keep Japanese forces there from threatening the Kwajalein landings.

The Marshalls campaign turned out to be as close to a textbook operation as possible. The Japanese Combined Fleet chose not to contest it, and the U.S. Navy ended up in possession of a new fleet base in the Marshalls. Majuro Atoll, 250 miles southeast of Kwajalein, had a large, protected anchorage, much closer to the scene of future operations than was Funafuti. The *New Jersey* arrived at Majuro late on the morning of 4 February and anchored. The gathering of ships was even bigger than that at Funafuti, and now there was a chance for liberty of a sort. Landing craft borrowed from amphibious forces present came alongside to ferry men ashore for beer, barbecue, baseball, and swimming.

The stay at Majuro also brought the battleship her first embarked flag officer, Vice Admiral Spruance. Shortly after his arrival, a message received in the *New Jersey*'s radio central brought the news that President Franklin Roosevelt had just nominated Spruance for promotion to four-star rank. Spruance was a lean, taciturn individual known for his shrewdness. Ensign King Brandt of the *New Jersey*'s communication staff remembered that in radio messages the admiral "could say more in about ten lines than any other naval officer I ever ran into." The admiral was not one for oral small talk either, as Lieutenant Commander Bill Abhau of the ship's gunnery department discovered. Once, it fell to Abhau to escort Spruance to a movie about to be shown on the fantail. Abhau said, "I quickly learned that all he wanted to hear from me was, 'Good evening, Admiral.'" Of the methodical flag officer, Abhau observed, "When Spruance was in command, everything happened just the way it was laid down in the plan. Somehow, the Japanese always conformed."

There was, however, at least one exception. In the first two years of the war, Truk in the Caroline Islands was considered an impregnable stronghold for the Japanese Combined Fleet. Now it had to be neutralized so the Fifth Fleet could proceed with its plans to capture and occupy Eniwetok. Admiral Mitscher's task force was assigned to attack by air, and Admiral Spruance elected to lead a surface task group against Japanese warships escaping from Truk Lagoon.

Late in the morning of 17 February, a task group consisting of the *New Jersey* and *Iowa*, heavy cruisers *Minneapolis* and *New Orleans*, and four destroyers assembled under the tactical command of Admiral Spruance and began a counterclockwise circuit about Truk. The events of the day were mostly anti-climactic, because the bulk of the Japanese fleet had fled shortly before. Even so, the day brought plenty of excitement, not least because it marked the first time the *New Jersey* fired her guns in anger.

At midday, a Zero fighter plane dropped a bomb that came close to the *Iowa*'s bridge. The *New Jersey* took the plane under fire, but it got away. During the course of the afternoon, the *New Jersey* fired at more aircraft; sank the trawler *No. 15 Shonan Maru* at close range; shot at the destroyer *Maikaze*, which was later finished off by the cruisers; barely escaped being torpedoed by the light cruiser *Katori*; and then was involved in a long-range stern chase in which 16-inch projectiles from the *New Jersey* straddled the fleeing destroyer *Nowaki* before she escaped. The battle against the trawler was pitifully one-sided. She was only a few thousand yards away from the *New*

A small Japanese trawler pours out smoke after being hit by 5-inch projectiles from the *New Jersey* during the Truk strike on 17 February 1944. Soon afterward the exploding ship disappeared in a large cloud of smoke. *From the* New Jersey's *after-action report, courtesy Naval Historical Center*

Jersey, so she was dispatched with the ship's 5-inch and 40-mm guns.

Before the *Katori* was sunk by the cruisers, she unleashed a spread of torpedoes that passed between the *Iowa* and *New Jersey*. None exploded, and at least one broached after passing through the *New Jersey*'s wake. Radio Technician Robert Parmelee recalled that "when those torpedoes went by us, I was right next to that 16-inch magazine, and I wasn't scared too many times, but that was one damn time I was scared."

Spruance's biographer, Commander Thomas B. Buell, recounted in his book *The Quiet Warrior* that the admiral's chief of staff, Captain Charles J. Moore, was mortified that the torpedoes came close to hitting the *New Jersey*. Spruance's staff was used to making strategic decisions rather than tactical ones, so Moore wasn't quick enough to realize that torpedoes were being fired at the *New Jersey* and to take appropriate action to get the formation out of the way. Normally, a fleet commander would have passed tactical command to a subordinate, such as Rear Admiral Hustvedt in the *Iowa*. Buell wrote, "It had been a near thing, and the torpedoes had missed the battleships through luck alone." In a sense, Truk was the Japanese equivalent of Pearl Harbor, so Spruance's command of the task group may have been his way of flaunting the dramatic growth in American naval power since December 1941. It also gave him a chance to act, in essence, as a battleship division commander in combat.

The day of battle was still not over because of the fleeing *Nowaki*. Only the two forward turrets were used, because the *New Jersey*'s progress would have been impeded by turning to fire turret three. As it was, recalled turret two officer Oscar Gray Jr., the ship weaved back and forth about ten degrees either side of a true trailing course to avoid the shock damage to the raised bow that might have resulted from shooting directly over it.

Turret two opened with a salvo of three projectiles, followed shortly by a salvo from turret one. The latter knocked the SG surface search radar out of commission but didn't affect the Mark 8 main battery fire control radar. Lieutenant Commander Abhau of the gunnery department was impressed by the latter, because the signal on the radar scope was so precise that fire controlmen could see the splashes of the 16-inch projectiles falling near the target. Overall, the *New Jersey* fired for nine minutes as the destroyer's range opened from 32,200 yards to 35,000. She unleashed eighteen 16-inch shells; they came close but not close enough. On the morning of 18 February, the *New Jersey* rejoined Task Group 58.3 to resume her role of conforming to the movements of the carriers. That less-than-glamorous duty continued until she anchored in Kwajalein Atoll on 19 February.

The five-day stay at Kwajalein was the first time that most of the men of the *New Jersey* encountered the effects of war at close range. The guns of the old battleships had devastated the island, and the rifles of American soldiers had created many, many corpses. When Lieutenant Roman "Rosy" Mrozinski went ashore, he saw an American soldier sitting among the corpses and flies, happily eating a can of captured Japanese pineapple. The soldier offered some, but Mrozinski hadn't much of an appetite at that point. Lieutenant Gray saw a Japanese pillbox heavily damaged by naval gunfire, so he went inside for a closer look. He came face to face with a detached Japanese head suspended from the top of the pillbox.

One other event at Kwajalein was Spruance's formal promotion to full admiral on 21 February. That was the first time he had an opportunity to take the physical exam required for promotion. Once he passed the physical, he was able to wear on his khaki shirt collar the four-star insignia made for him in the *New Jersey*'s machine shop. His blue and white four-star flag was hoisted high in the ship.

On 25 February, after a brief trip from Kwajalein, the *New Jersey* anchored at Majuro, where she spent much of the next month awaiting ensuing stages of the Central Pacific campaign. Admiral Spruance was absent for nearly a week, having been summoned to Pearl Harbor to be briefed by Admiral Chester Nimitz, commander in chief, Pacific Fleet, on Joint Chiefs of

Spike, mascot of the ship's Marine detachment, sits atop a hatch on the forecastle. *Courtesy Mrs. Frank Reagan*

Admiral Raymond A. Spruance, *left*, commander, Fifth Fleet, with his flagship captain, Carl F. Holden, 8 April 1944, at Majuro Atoll. The two are standing near the turret two barbette. *Naval Historical Center: NH 62516*

Staff decisions concerning future strategy. Spruance's forces were to bypass Truk and capture the Marianas Islands to the north to provide the Army Air Forces with bases for long-range bombing of Japan.

While Admiral Spruance was away, the *New Jersey* and *Iowa* went out for a practice session that proved unexpectedly hazardous. It was intended strictly as a training session at bypassed Mili Atoll in the southern Marshalls. The two battleships, still new to the war zone, would get their first opportunity to practice shore bombardment against live targets. Rear Admiral Willis A. "Ching" Lee Jr. was on board the *Iowa* in overall command of the Mili striking group, while Rear Admiral Hustvedt remained in the same ship and had command of the two-battleship bombardment unit. The striking group arrived off Mili on the morning of 18 March. With Spruance away, the *Iowa* was again temporarily senior ship, so she had the honor of opening fire first with her 16-inch guns. The two battleships proceeded methodically to send 1,900-pound high-capacity projectiles toward defense installations on Mili. The *New Jersey*'s three turrets were firing in rotation as the range closed, giving her gun and ammunition handling crews practice against a supposedly easy target.

In the *New Jersey*'s lower handling room, near the bottom of the ship, Seaman First Class Robert Knoll had the job of taking powder bags out of the flameproof passing scuttle and carrying them over to put on the hoist up to the turret. In an adjacent magazine, other men took the bags out of the aluminum containers in which they were stored. They caught whiffs of the ether used as a preservative and put the bags into their side of the scuttle so they could go through to Knoll. The handling room and magazines were separated by a stout bulkhead to confine the effects of a possible mishap.

All went well until the two ships closed in to 19,000 yards. Then, more than two hours after the battleship bombardment started, pinpricks of light began flashing on the beach. The Japanese had waited until the American ships were within range of their 6-inch guns and then opened fire themselves. Splashes were soon straddling the *New Jersey*. The Japanese guns had the right bearing but were off in range. Storekeeper Third Class Willard Bartusch was standing on one of the *New Jersey*'s superstructure decks when a Japanese projectile went over the ship from port to starboard. Said Bartusch, "I felt the heat, but I didn't realize what it was until somebody said that was a shell that hit the water on the other side."

Inside turret two Lieutenant Oscar Gray had his periscope trained forward on the *Iowa* when he saw two flashes as enemy projectiles hit the sister ship, causing minor damage on her port side. Up in the *New Jersey*'s exposed air defense station, Lieutenant Commander Bill Abhau watched the enemy shore batteries through binoculars. While his eyes were fixed to the binoculars, he said something to a Marine lieutenant stationed with him but received no answer. Abhau turned around to look; when he found the lieutenant behind the foundation of the main battery director, he asked, "What are you doing back here?"

The lieutenant replied, "You just can't dig a foxhole in these steel decks." Abhau admitted he was not feeling comfortable himself at that point, especially because the two battleships continued to stay within range of the enemy guns, even while the Japanese were peppering away at them: "We didn't turn, we didn't change speed, and . . . the pair of guns that was shooting at us had too good a [fire control] solution. They managed to keep one short and the other one over the whole time. But it would have been a lot more comfortable if we'd turned or done something."

The situation on board the *Iowa* was unusual. Even though Admiral Lee was senior to Admiral Hustvedt, he did not have tactical command. Years later, in his oral history reminiscences, Hustvedt said, "I should like to record here my appreciation of the fact that Admiral Lee, although he was a very interested observer of the operation . . . never at any time interposed anything which could be interpreted as an interference with the plan which I had issued in my short operation order nor with the movements as they were executed by the forces under my command." Frank Pinney, the *Iowa*'s assistant gunnery officer, remembered differently—that Lee told the ship's captain that he should clear out to save his ship and ammunition. The damage during an easy practice run led Lieutenant Harry Reynolds of the *New Jersey* to summarize the operation, "We looked silly at Mili."

On Sunday, 19 March, the day after the Mili bombardment, the *New Jersey* anchored in the lagoon at Majuro Atoll. Admiral Spruance returned from Hawaii, and so the *New Jersey* was once again fleet flagship. Upon the *Iowa*'s return to port, her skipper, Captain McCrea, received a message from the fast battleship *Alabama*'s commanding officer, who asked the cause of the hole in the side of the new ship. Captain McCrea puckishly replied, "Rats."

The next targets were the Palau Islands in the Western Carolines. The objective was two thousand miles west of Majuro and more than one thousand west of Truk. After it escaped Truk, the Japanese Combined Fleet moved to Palau. There, it would be in a position to harass Army General Douglas MacArthur's planned April landings on the north coast of New Guinea. During the long journey westward, Task Force 58 was seen and reported by Japanese search planes, so the element of surprise was lost. The date of the carrier strike, which was also to include aerial mining to bottle up ships in Palau harbor, was changed from 1 April to 30 March.

On the night of 29 March, the *New Jersey* encountered her first night air attack of the war. Surprisingly, the first warning of the incoming raid came when her main battery fire control radar detected Japanese planes at a range of 30,000 yards. The SK air search radar picked them up a minute later. Shortly before 9 p.m., the 5-inch battery opened fire. The secondary battery fire control radars indicated that one plane was shot down. Although no explosion was visible in the sky, the bursting 5-inch projectiles could be seen on radar in the vicinity of the plane, and then there was no more blip for the plane. Another aircraft

Having shed his shirt, a crewman takes some sun in front of the two forward turrets. Note the rifling at the muzzle end of the right gun of turret one. A wartime censor has removed the radar antenna atop the forward fire control tower. *U.S. Naval Institute photo archive*

turned away and disappeared when the first was apparently shot down. The *New Jersey*'s 20-mm and 40-mm guns were also chattering away during the enemy raid.

On 30 March, Admiral Mitscher's aircraft went after their targets and achieved considerable success, both in bottling up ships with their mining and in destroying enemy aircraft and small vessels. Alas, as at Truk, the big ships, including the Combined Fleet flagship *Musashi*, had been tipped off and were able to escape. The Palau operation provided the crew of the *New Jersey* with yet more knowledge of the ways of a battleship in a carrier war. Radio Technician Bob Parmelee recalled that some of the officers in the FA division carried with them for too long the notion that the most important part of a Mark 37 antiaircraft director was its optical rangefinder. However, as the attack on 29 March demonstrated—and as many more would during the war—radar-controlled gunfire was effective, and at night it was the only way. After a while, he remembered, "If the radar wasn't pluperfect, we caught hell. It was a complete turnaround."

As the Pacific campaign progressed, everyone on board was concerned with sleep deprivation. For Russ Brown, a machinist's mate in the boiler division, the berthing compartment became inconvenient because of all the general quarters drills to which the ship was subjected. To avoid the treks from the berthing compartment to his battle station in forward diesel, Brown remained at his battle station at night. He explained, "You just threw a blanket on the steel grate and slept on that."

For Leonard Jung, a musician in the ship's band, the narrow separation between individual bunks in the four-tiered racks caused problems. They were so close together in some cases that men had trouble turning over, especially if the man above was heavy. Thus, Jung also found sleeping on deck to be preferable. As a pillow, he used his folded-up hat, previously white but dyed dark blue to make detection difficult at night. After a night on deck, his left hipbone was sore in the morning.

The days and nights on the way back to base passed relatively quickly, for the ship was heading away from the threat rather than toward it. On 18 April, at Majuro, the *Indianapolis* came alongside, and on the following day received Admiral Spruance and his staff. They were headed for Pearl Harbor to work on planning for the forthcoming Marianas campaign, and the *New Jersey* would soon be off to support landings at Hollandia, New Guinea.

On 13 April, Task Force 58 left Majuro for New Guinea. As expected, the *New Jersey* didn't get in sight of land, and the aviators of Task Force 58 met little opposition from the Japanese. Because of the effectiveness of bombing strikes on New Guinea by the Fifth Air Force, Mitscher's task force hadn't been needed to support MacArthur, but it was better to be safe than sorry.

Although the trip to Hollandia was not memorable in terms of enemy action, the crew of the *New Jersey* did form lasting impressions of the heat in the equatorial region. The temperatures of more than 100° produced pools of perspiration. Fire Controlman George Teller recalled that Hollandia was the first place where the men of the *New Jersey*

Four members of the ship's fire control gang are gathered in a plotting room on the fourth deck, inside the armored box. Second from right is George Teller. *Courtesy George R. Teller*

encountered Japanese use of flares to illuminate the American ships at night. The crews of these ships, including the *New Jersey*, were then obliged to go to battle stations to be ready for possible attack. Fatigue set in, and as Teller recalled, "You built up a certain numbness after a while."

One consequence of the heat, recalled Rafael De La Maza, a seaman in the fourth division, was that many of the ship's crew members developed heat rash with itching, peeling skin. It was especially uncomfortable around the crotch and between the legs, so sick bay had many customers for a purple ointment that provided some relief and doubtless produced some interesting-looking sailors.

When Task Force 58 was released to leave the area, Admiral Mitscher scheduled another strike at Truk on 29 April. On the afternoon of 30 April, after the air strikes had eliminated Truk as a major Japanese base, the *New Jersey* was released from Task Group 58.2 to join up with other fast battleships. For the first time in the Central Pacific campaign, the recently promoted Vice Admiral Lee had a chance to operate the battle line together. The *New Jersey* and *Iowa* joined the *North Carolina*, *Massachusetts*, *Indiana*, *Alabama*, and *South Dakota*. Ponape, the largest of the Carolines at nineteen miles in diameter, was considered a suitable target because it offered potential as an alternate Japanese air base after Truk was hit.

Altogether, the *New Jersey* fired 90 rounds of 16-inch ammunition and 154 of 5-inch. Air spotters reported that she had caused considerable damage to Japanese barracks buildings. It was the *New Jersey*'s best shore bombardment to date, but one member of the 5-inch gun crew did not participate in the gunnery. Seaman Roger Faw of the fourth division felt abdominal pains when he reported to his general quarters station, so he went to the sick bay for treatment. The ship's senior medical officer recognized the symptoms of an inflamed appendix and proceeded to operate during the shore bombardment. Faw had only a local anesthetic during the appendectomy, so he was alert enough to realize that the doctor interrupted work whenever a 16-inch salvo was coming up.

During the *New Jersey*'s operations with the fast carrier task force, her movements were controlled by a rotation of officers of the deck on the bridge. Captain Holden relied on three lieutenants, all Naval Academy graduates: Rosy Mrozinski and Gene Hayward of the class of 1939 and Oscar Gray from 1940. Later in the year, Lieutenant John Sullivan, Gray's classmate, moved into the rotation. Sullivan recalled Mrozinski as a stolid, stone-faced man in whom lurked a mischievous sense of humor. He also considered Mrozinski the ship's best officer of the deck, someone who knew tactics thoroughly and was calm under fire. On one occasion, when the captain was sitting in his chair on the bridge and appeared unnerved by the tactical situation, Mrozinski walked over, patted the skipper on the head, and said, "Just relax. Everything's under control." Normally, a senior officer would not tolerate such familiarity, but Holden's future prospects depended on these OODs keeping him out of trouble—and both he and Mrozinski realized that.

The *New Jersey*'s crew was able to rest for about a month when the ship arrived at Majuro on 4 May. On the fourteenth, Vice Admiral Willis Lee, commander, Battleships Pacific, became a new occupant

During most of May 1944, Vice Admiral Willis A. Lee Jr., commander, Battleships Pacific Fleet, was embarked in the *New Jersey* while his regular flagship, USS *Washington*, was repaired following a collision. *Courtesy Donald Siders*

in flag quarters. His favorite flagship was the USS *Washington*, but she had been damaged in a collision with the *Indiana* on 1 February 1944, so Lee had switched to the *North Carolina*. Now that ship was headed to Pearl Harbor for rudder repairs, and Lee moved again, to make his home in the *New Jersey* for the next three weeks. Vice Admiral Mitscher was also in Majuro on board the carrier *Lexington*, so the period offered them a chance to work on the planning necessary for the Marianas. On 30 May the *Washington* stood in to Majuro and later that day embarked Lee and his staff.

Two members of the *New Jersey*'s supply department found an interesting pastime during the period the ship was at anchor. Seaman Third Class Wesly Krstich and Seaman Second Class James Russo wrote a letter to the New Jersey state chamber of commerce to propose a pinup contest in which photos of girls who lived in the state would be forwarded to the ship for posting on bulletin boards. An excerpt from their letter was published in the 17 May edition of the *Newark Evening News*. Altogether, more than seventy photos arrived. Among them was a beguiling shot of five-month-old Harolyn Cheryl Meyer, whose father was an Army Air Forces pilot. He had recently been shot down over Europe and taken prisoner. The photo of baby Harolyn was the overwhelming winner in the crew's voting later in the year. The *New Jersey*'s generous men then pitched in to donate to the baby girl a silver napkin ring and war bonds that would mature to a value of $3,200. Years later, Harolyn used the money for her education at New Jersey's Caldwell College, married shortly after graduation in 1965, and became a schoolteacher and mother.

One advantage of the relaxed pace in port was that it gave the *New Jersey*'s crew a chance to attend regular worship services, uninterrupted by demands of underway watches and frequent trips to battle stations. The ship had a Protestant chaplain, Catholic chaplain, and an unofficial Jewish lay leader. Father James J. Gaffney sometimes found an unconventional approach to be the most effective means of serving the needs of the crew. Musician First Class Leonard Jung was at one of Gaffney's services to provide musical accompaniment, but the singing by the congregation was lackluster. Thereupon, Gaffney said, "For Christ's sake, why don't you guys sing those goddamn hymns?" He continued, "Now I shocked you, didn't I? I'll tell you why. You know, my stateroom is right near the bottom of this one ladder

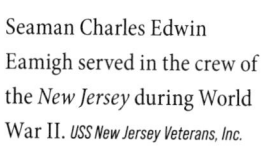

Seaman Charles Edwin Eamigh served in the crew of the *New Jersey* during World War II. *USS New Jersey Veterans, Inc.*

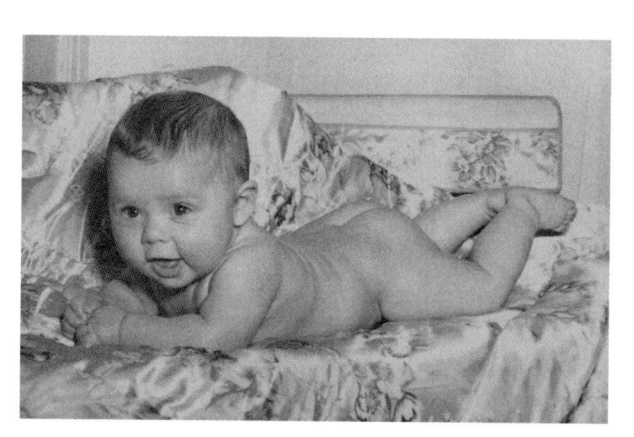

This picture of baby Harolyn Cheryl Meyer earned her election as Miss USS *New Jersey* in the summer of 1944. *Courtesy Mrs. Harolyn Lawton*

Charles Eamigh felt such a connection with the *New Jersey* that his tombstone in Westmoreland County, Pennsylvania, features the name and silhouette of the battleship etched in stone. *findagrave.com*

where a lot of you fellows gather to shoot the breeze. The language I hear all the time is so sickening. How did it sound coming from me?" Fire Controlman J. P. Loughan, who was also at the service, believed Gaffney made his point most effectively.

The stay in port came to an end on 6 June when the *New Jersey* departed as part of Task Group 58.2 on the way to the Marianas. Thirty-two minutes into the new day of 12 June, the persistent bong-bong-bong sound of the *New Jersey*'s general alarm swept through the ship. Crewmen were in and out of bunks that night in response to enemy planes that dropped flares. The *New Jersey* and the carriers, cruisers, and destroyers with her were zigzagging through the June night at twenty knots. Surrounded as she was by friendly ships, the *New Jersey*'s antiaircraft battery was in a "guns tight" condition. Then a Japanese Betty torpedo bomber roared in directly at the starboard beam of the *New Jersey* at an altitude of three hundred to five hundred feet. It dropped a torpedo and then, eight hundred yards from the ship, it turned sharply to the right to parallel the ship's course.

At 4:04 a.m., Gunner's Mate Third Class V. D. Griffin, manning a 20-mm gun on the starboard side, saw the plane and began firing, soon to be joined by three other guns. Within seconds, Lieutenant John Sullivan, on the bridge, saw the Betty's left engine nacelle catch fire. He remembered, "A small glow of orange spread and spread, and the thing crashed in front of us." As the torpedo passed twenty-five hundred yards astern of the *New Jersey*, Sullivan ordered a slight change of course to port to avoid passing too closely to the burning aircraft. The four guns had fired only eighty-one rounds. A grateful Captain Holden promptly advanced Gunner's Mate Griffin from third class to second.

The following day, 13 June, the *New Jersey* and the six other fast battleships under Admiral Lee were withdrawn from the carrier task groups to make a pre-invasion bombardment of Saipan and Tinian Islands, because D-day at Saipan was scheduled for 15 June. Alas, explained historian Samuel Eliot

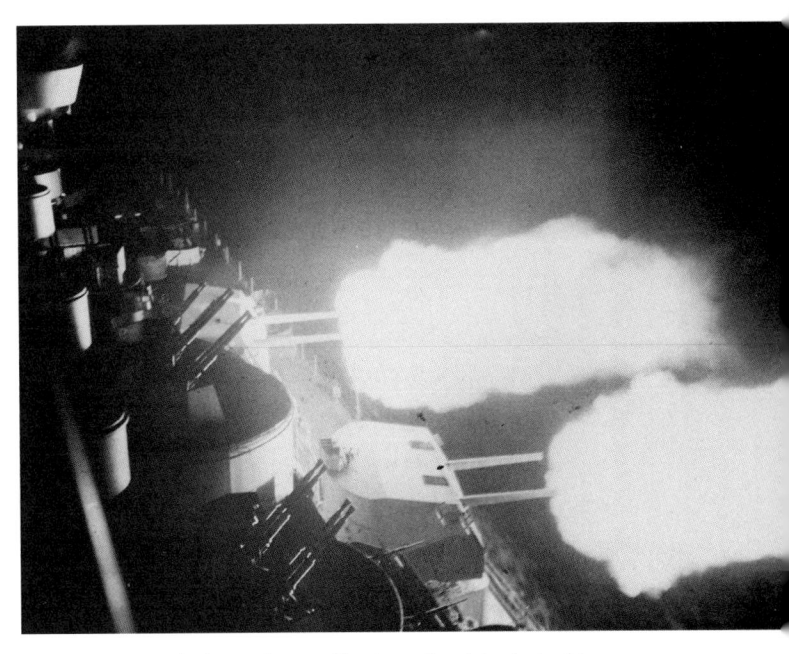

Flashes from the ship's 5-inch guns illuminate the night sky in this wartime view. *National Archives: 80-G-K-4550*

Morison, the bombardment by the fast battleships that day was a failure. Because they had been spending almost all of their time with the fast carriers, they hadn't had an opportunity to practice the slow, methodical approach to sighting in on a land target and then applying corrections until it was destroyed. Heavy 16-inch projectiles were flying all over the place, but they were destroying only such things as farmhouses and sugar mills. Morison endorsed the words of one sailor who wryly observed that the 13 June firing was "a Navy-sponsored farm project that simultaneously plows the fields, prunes the trees, harvests the crops, and adds iron to the soil." The following day, the much more skilled old battleships showed how the job should be done.

For the Marianas campaign, the Fifth Fleet mustered a vast armada of 644 ships. Many of them were amphibious warfare ships and landing craft, and on 15 June they disgorged their cargoes of Marines onto the beaches at Saipan. The Japanese fleet could no longer avoid a fight. The Marianas were too close to the home islands to be lost without a serious challenge to the American invaders. From the Philippines to the west came the First Mobile Fleet, commanded by Vice Admiral Jisaburo Ozawa.

Before the fleets tangled, the men of the *New Jersey* observed mass death in progress. Dr. William Robie, one of the officers in the *New Jersey*'s medical department, looked at Saipan through one of the spotting scopes for the 16-inch turrets and saw Japanese civilians walking off cliffs and plunging to their deaths.

Task Force 58 had two principal objectives during the Battle of the Philippine Sea, as the engagement came to be known. The one considered more important by Admiral Spruance was to protect the amphibious transports of Vice Admiral Richmond Kelly Turner's landing force at Saipan. The second, if possible, was to seek out and destroy the Japanese fleet. On 18 June, the *New Jersey* joined with six other battleships, seven heavy cruisers, and fourteen destroyers to form Task Group 58.7 under Vice Admiral Lee. This was to be the battle line that would stand between the carrier task groups and the heavy ships of the Japanese if a surface battle loomed. One carrier group was assigned to provide air cover for the battle line.

The surface battle never took place. Lee declined Mitscher's suggestion of a gun battle on the night of 18 June. Lee was cautious because his ships had been integrated into the carrier groups for so long that they hadn't had much chance to drill together in tactical maneuvers. Spruance, filled with concern that the Japanese might try an end-around to get at Turner's transports, quickly endorsed Lee's decision. Task Force 58 went eastward on the night of 18–19 June instead of toward the enemy.

The battle that ensued on 19 June is one of the classics in naval annals, known as the "Marianas Turkey Shoot" because American pilots shot down more than three hundred Japanese planes that day. As a result of the overwhelming success on the part of fighter pilots in their F6F Hellcats, only a relative handful of enemy planes reached the battleships. When they came, Rafael De La Maza, a member of the gun crew for one of the 5-inch mounts, opened a hatch to see what was going on. He said, "When you stuck your head out there, the sky was black with explosions. You thought something was coming your way." After that, he decided it was safer and wiser not to open the hatch.

At various times during the battle, the *New Jersey*'s 5-inch, 40-mm, and 20-mm guns were firing at a Zeke fighter, a Jill fighter, and a Tony fighter—nicknames assigned by the Americans so that lookouts and gun crews wouldn't have to struggle with trying to pronounce the actual Japanese names. The *New Jersey* was credited with a "sure assist" for her 20-mm and 40-mm fire in downing a Tony also being attacked by two American planes. The ship also damaged one Zeke and one Tony. Seaman Art Scott, whose job was to elevate and depress the barrel of a 20-mm gun on the port side, felt vulnerable in his exposed position in the superstructure. But the vantage point also afforded a sense of satisfaction. He said, "I guess seeing enemy planes shot down made me feel I was personally doing my share."

For Ensign Val Winkelman there was no question of being able to look up and see what was going on; the problem was trying to hit anything. When the ship was operating at high speed in a formation, the propellers—which were practically underneath his quad 40-mm mount on the fantail—set up such a vibration that it was hard for Winkelman to keep his gunsight on the targets. Unlike the radar-controlled 5-inch guns, the 40-mm mounts depended on the officer operating the director being able to see the enemy planes. Later in the war, Fire Controlman First Class J. P. Loughan was able to rig up a system in which the 40-mm mounts in the center of the *New Jersey* were hooked into the radar-controlled Mark 37 directors that aimed the 5-inch guns. The parallax angle was too great, however, to permit linking the 40-mm mounts on bow and stern.

When the aerial slaughter of 19 June was over, Task Force 58 was released from protecting the transports and was thus free the next day to attack the Japanese fleet. The strikes of carrier planes were launched at long range late in the afternoon. The night of 20 June 1944 became justly famous as the time when Task Force 58 ships, including the *New Jersey*, turned on searchlights to serve as beacons for the returning planes. In the darkness, with gasoline tanks in their planes nearly empty, the American fliers scrambled desperately to get back aboard.

On the morning of 21 June, the *New Jersey*, as part of Admiral Lee's battle line, was detached to proceed westward in pursuit of Admiral Ozawa's fleet but didn't even come close. On 24 June, the *New Jersey* again joined a carrier group, Task Group 58.3 under Rear Admiral John "Black Jack" Reeves Jr. On the twenty-fifth the *New Jersey* got into the air-sea rescue business, an unexpected role for the battleship. That afternoon, Lieutenant W. A. Butt, one of the pilots in the *New Jersey*'s aviation division, landed his OS2U Kingfisher scout plane off the island of Guam, which was still held by the Japanese. He picked up three fliers from a USS *Lexington* plane. While the rescue was in progress, Japanese shore batteries opened up on the Kingfisher, splashing shells nearby but not hitting it. With three extra men on board, the plane was too heavy to take off, so Butt taxied over to the destroyer *Caperton* to drop off his passengers and then flew back to the battleship.

While the rescue of the *Lexington* men presented an unusual hazard, just operating the catapult planes from the *New Jersey* was frequently hazardous enough. The normal procedure called for the Kingfisher to sit at the rear of the catapult and rev up its engines. Ideally, when the plane was to go off to starboard, for example, the launching officer waited until the ship rolled all the way to starboard, then gave a signal to the launching petty officer to yank the lanyard that fired the powder charge underneath the movable sled on which the plane sat. There was a one-second delay between the giving of the signal and the firing of the powder. With a great whoosh, the plane jumped forward. By that time, the ship was on an up-roll, giving the plane a small boost as its 450-horsepower engine clawed the air to gain altitude. The pilot held his hand on the throttle and elbow into his stomach so that he wouldn't inadvertently pull back on the stick when the force of the catapult shot came.

Throughout the remainder of June and all through July, the battleship continued to operate with Task Force 58. During July, the *New Jersey* was under way continuously, except for a few brief stops in Saipan harbor, a sheltered anchorage for providing fuel and stores to destroyers. The *New Jersey* was able to replenish her own supply of fuel from fleet oilers, but her supply of food grew ever lower, for by late July she had been away from Majuro for nearly two months. Chili beans and rice became daily staples in the diets of *New Jersey* men who, until then, had for the most part experienced considerable satisfaction from the mess deck and wardroom. Fresh meats were available for a while after the *New Jersey* had been in a port to stock up, but then her men had to fall back on canned meats such as Spam and Vienna sausages.

A Kingfisher floatplane is hoisted on board in November 1944 at the end of a mission. The *New Jersey* carried OS2Us from the time of commissioning until she returned to the United States in the spring of 1945. *National Archives: 80-G-469922*

Shipfitter William Dugan remembered, "There were times when we had Spam for breakfast, Spam for dinner, Spam for supper. You had it fried, baked, in soup—every way you could think of, we had Spam." Later, when the *New Jersey* pulled into one of the islands to get mail, Dugan received a letter from his wife. He turned to a shipmate nearby and asked, "Hey, Hack, what do you think my wife is sending me? A box of Spam."

Nearly all who served in the ship during the war agreed that the highlight of the food was that from the bakery—freshly made bread, rolls, and pastries. Musician First Class Leonard Jung kept a jar of peanut butter in his locker. Every so often, he explained, the bakery "gave us a hot loaf of bread; it would be so hot you'd have to juggle it. And then I put peanut butter on that, and, oh man, that tasted real good." The long period since taking on stores finally came to an end when the *New Jersey* spent about four hours on 4 August at Eniwetok in the Marshalls. As was frequently the case when stores were brought aboard, large numbers of *New Jersey* men were summoned to form working parties.

The stay at Eniwetok was short, because this time the *New Jersey* didn't have to take on provisions for a long operation. The ship had been ordered to steam to Pearl Harbor for alterations to her flag plot so she could accommodate Admiral William F. Halsey Jr., who was coming on board as commander, Third Fleet. He explained in his postwar autobiography that members of his staff had been shipboard observers during the Marianas campaign and came up with a list of improvements to be incorporated into the *New Jersey* when she was designated to receive the Third Fleet flag. Halsey wrote, "On the basis of their recommendations, the *New Jersey*'s flag plot was extensively altered, and when we put to sea, it was the best in the fleet." All electrical cables were replaced and much new communication equipment put in. Halsey even arranged for the installation of a ladder so that he could go directly from the flag mess on the 02 level to the flag plot one deck above.

For many of the battleship's men, who had been without real liberty for about seven months by the time of arrival on 9 August, Hawaii itself wasn't as important as being ashore in a civilized area. They were mainly interested in wine, women, and song—with precious little emphasis on the singing. By 1944, Hawaii was swamped with American servicemen, so many of them that long lines waited to get into the brothels. Men coming in from the sea went from bar to bar, drinking in good cheer, with headaches to follow.

Rafael De La Maza, a seaman in 1944, had souvenirs of Honolulu for the rest of his life, for he was tattooed there. Marine Private First Class Dale O'Bryen found the Hawaiian culture attractive during his forays ashore, "I listened to Hawaiian music every chance I got. Of course, I had my picture taken with the Hawaiian girls and their grass skirts." Fireman Sherman Brattin went ashore with a religious group that had formed on board the *New Jersey*. The men went to parks and other recreation areas, including

The month is August 1944 as two *New Jersey* Marines check calendar art near a washroom on the second deck. *Courtesy Mrs. Frank Reagan*

swimming at Waikiki and the beachfront Royal Hawaiian Hotel. The latter had been set aside as a haven for submariners between war patrols, but Brattin recalled, "We'd kinda walk around the fence every once in a while and get in on the beach side there, just to say we'd been in there, really."

On 22 August, as the rest and recreation period approached its end, the *New Jersey* took on a large load of ammunition. In the period just before getting under way, she also took on a hefty load of Third Fleet staff personnel. Early in the year, Admiral Spruance had brought with him about thirty officers as the Fifth Fleet staff; Halsey had double that number for the Third Fleet. These were not two dissimilar fleets that had to be administered; they were essentially the same ships but designated differently now that Halsey was in charge. Lieutenant (junior grade) Bill Coyne of the *New Jersey* observed that "Admiral Halsey's staff was not only larger but also noisier and more flamboyant." The chief of staff was Rear Admiral Robert B. "Mick" Carney, who later served as Chief of Naval Operations from 1953 to 1955. One of the *New Jersey*'s newly reported junior officers, Ensign Roland "Bud" Bowler Jr., explained years afterward that the statement "That's what Admiral Carney says" had a way of ending debates.

Bowler, fresh from the Naval Academy, had to put behind him what he'd picked up at Annapolis and learn now about his seagoing job. He began studying the practice of visual communications with Chief Signalman E. L. Wilkes serving as his mentor. In Bowler's view, "The chief was clearly in charge of me. There was no doubt in his mind, and that was okay with me. I was a brand, spanking new ensign, and he just took me under his wing and kept me there for a year. He was happy when he thought I had learned enough to be essentially on my own, and to me, that was normal." Bowler was one of many who came on board in Hawaii, because that was the first convenient place in months to turn over a significant number of personnel. The Hawaii interlude was a time of departure for many of the plank owners who

OS2U floatplanes sit on both catapults as the *New Jersey* steams away from Pearl Harbor on 31 August 1944 to return to the war zone.
U.S. Naval Institute photo archive

had been with the ship since her commissioning fifteen months earlier.

During the cruise west and south from Hawaii, the days fell into a pattern for the new crew members, especially as they were indoctrinated into the ways of the ship. The process was sped by a repetition of the sort of drills that had been the order of the day during shakedown the year before—firing, firing, and more firing of the guns. One of these practices involved repelling simulated night destroyer torpedo attacks from ships of the *New Jersey*'s screen. The battleship fired 5-inch star shells for illumination of the attacking destroyers.

Lieutenant Commander Bill Abhau, the assistant gunnery officer, remembered, "When the star shell spread broke, I could see every one of the destroyers

The *New Jersey* takes water over the bow during operations in late 1944. *Courtesy Eugene F. Hayward*

with the naked eye, didn't need glasses." He checked the radar and the star shells—which were 5-inch projectiles with flares in them—to ensure they were the right distance above and behind the destroyers. The senior officer in the destroyers, however, claimed that the flares had come too close to the ships. Captain Holden was furious and sent for Abhau and Lieutenant Commander Baxter Russell, the gunnery officer. The two of them listened to a tongue-lashing until Russell could take it no longer. He defended his gunners, saying that people were so used to star shells being too far from their targets that when they came down in the right place, they looked too close. Holden decided it was time for Russell to move on to other duty, and Abhau became the department head.

Abhau had mixed feelings about the episode—happy to be promoted but sorry that Russell had to depart for supporting his men when he was convinced they were right. Abhau explained, "I had learned by that time not to try to reason with Holden when he was angry." Interestingly, Abhau recalled that Commander Gerald Ogle, elevated from chief engineer to executive officer a few months earlier, apparently concluded that his promotion chances were not too strong. He was more willing than his two predecessors to stand up to Captain Holden. As a result, he was an effective executive officer for the *New Jersey* and ended up being promoted to captain after all.

On 4 September, the journey out from Hawaii ended when the *New Jersey* and her escorts anchored at Seeadler Harbor, Manus Island, in the Admiralties. The following day, the *New Jersey* was under way again, first with Task Group 38.5, then joining 38.2. The task groups were part of Task Force 38, the Third Fleet counterpart of Task Force 58 with which the *New Jersey* had been during the first half of the year while in the Fifth Fleet.

On the twelfth, the battleship received a contingent of Japanese prisoners from the destroyer *Marshall*. With hundreds of curious sailors and Marines standing around watching, the Japanese were stripped of their clothes, bathed on deck, deloused, given haircuts by one of the ship's barbers, and then dressed in dungarees of the type worn by the crew. Once the Japanese got through their experience

Commander Gilven Slonim, *left*, a Japanese-language specialist on the Third Fleet staff, reviews captured enemy charts with Rear Admiral Robert B. Carney, Admiral Halsey's chief of staff, in December 1944. *National Archives: 80-G-471152*

topside, they were taken down and put in cells of the ship's brig, below and aft of the mess deck.

Private Don Kelly was a member of the ship's Marine detachment who served guard duty. He recalled Commander Gilven Slonim, the Japanese language officer on Halsey's staff, coming down to interrogate the prisoners and reassuring them about their fate. The Japanese were initially fearful, for they thought they had been transferred to the *New Jersey* to be executed. Each day, when no shootings took place, the prisoners smiled more and more. Even though the brig, down near the hot, steamy ship's laundry, was cramped and uncomfortable, the Japanese—according to Kelly "were just smiling all the time, . . . just as happy as could be to be in that brig."

From 12 until 14 September, the *New Jersey* was in Rear Admiral Gerald Bogan's Task Group 38.2 as it conducted air strikes on the Visayan group in the central Philippines, for the reconquest of the Japanese-occupied Philippine Islands was a prime item on the Third Fleet agenda for the upcoming autumn season. The month of September wound down, and the battleship steamed to newly occupied Ulithi Atoll in the Carolines.

Just as the capture of Kwajalein in the Marshalls had enabled Majuro to be taken over as a fleet base, so the conquest of the Palau group permitted the Third Fleet to move into the vast lagoon at Ulithi. It served as the principal base during the coming offensive to recapture the Philippines. After arriving on 1 October and giving the crew liberty at Mog Mog Island of the atoll, the *New Jersey* and other Task Force 38 ships had to sortie on 3 October because of the approach of heavy weather. They returned on 4 October. The postwar cruise book commented that the typhoon "hit like a bolt out of the blue. It was a question of which was rougher—the typhoon, or Mog Mog liberty?"

Landing craft provided trips from the ship to Mog Mog, a place remembered by Fire Controlman J. P. Loughan for the customary routine of "two beers and a fight." Those who didn't drink could opt for sodas

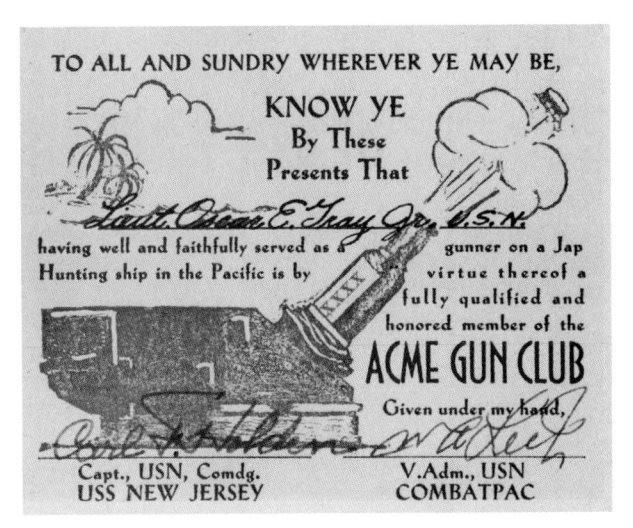

When Pacific Fleet battleships were not operating, they spent time in various anchorages. Once ashore, officers and men were able to drink alcoholic beverages. As the battleships type commander, Vice Admiral Willis Lee was head of the unofficial Acme Gun Club. Here the turret is shooting a cap from a bottle of Acme beer. The membership card is signed by *New Jersey* skipper Carl Holden and Admiral Lee. Lieutenant Oscar Gray was one of the ship's wartime officers of the deck. *Courtesy Oscar Gray*

or else sell their beers to those who were not easily satisfied with only two. Since Loughan was interested in neither beer nor fighting, he often stayed on board ship. The island was also a place for swimming, softball, baseball, and other sports in which the intership games could serve as an outlet for the rivalries that sprang up between various vessels. For Sherman Brattin, a denizen of one of the *New Jersey*'s boiler rooms, the island was a pleasant contrast to the shipboard world of steam and steel. On the beach at Mog Mog, he could get out and stretch his legs by running around its perimeter. Leonard Jung of the ship's band had still another recollection of the island—as a place for high-stakes gambling. He recalled "hundred dollar bills floating around; they didn't have anywhere else to spend it."

Although Ulithi was one place for gambling among the crew, it was far from being the only venue, for the "sport" was widespread on board the *New Jersey* as well. It was taken for granted on paydays, no matter how much against the rules. Blackjack was popular, and so was crap shooting. Both officers and enlisted men participated enthusiastically. The officers had both low- and high-stakes versions; the crew had many games at a variety of levels. Rafael De La Maza recounted his observations in the fourth division living compartment: "They would gamble after lights-out under the red lights that they had in the compartment, set up a blanket and roll dice there all night."

The red lights that illuminated the interior of the *New Jersey* went on when the bugler played taps over the general announcing system and stayed on until another bugler sounded reveille the next morning. The red lights were sufficient at night for those who had to be awake, but not bright enough to prevent sleep. Throughout the night, men such as Shipfitter Bill Dugan regularly patrolled inside the ship. One night, with the red lights showing the way, Dugan approached the machine shop on the second deck. There he was suddenly brought up short when he saw a body strung up to the overhead and swinging to and fro in harmony with the rolling of the ship. He approached ever so cautiously, thinking perhaps one of his shipmates had decided to kill himself. He got up close and shined his flashlight on the body—only to find that it was the dummy the ship's officers threw over the side from time to time so they could practice making man-overboard recoveries. Such dummies are habitually known in the Navy as "Oscar," and on this night "Oscar" had been the pawn in a practical joke.

In October, American forces were to redeem General Douglas MacArthur's famous pledge to return to liberate the Philippines. As at the Marianas, an air battle off Formosa was one-sided. Japanese carrier planes went ashore to help fend off the attacking Americans, and this time the Japanese lost approximately 550 planes. The most striking memory for J. P. Loughan was a night when the American ships were dramatically silhouetted by air-dropped flares. Fortunately, the Betty torpedo planes mistimed their approach and were shot down before the flares could do them any good.

The Battle of Leyte Gulf toward the end of October was a source of great controversy, because—as was the case at the Marianas in June—the U.S. Navy did not score the knockout blow it had been seeking against the Japanese fleet. Unlike the Marianas, this time the Japanese felt compelled to come close and fight it out. They mounted a three-pronged effort aimed at attacking the American amphibious forces at the Leyte beachhead. Vice Admiral Shoji Nishimura's southern force was devastated by Rear Admiral Jesse Oldendorf's old battleships in the Battle of Surigao Strait. Vice Admiral Takeo Kurita's center force, including the giant battleships *Musashi* and *Yamato*, was to approach through the Sibuyan Sea and San Bernardino Strait to attack the transports. Wily Vice Admiral Jisaburo Ozawa, Spruance's adversary at the Marianas, came in with a northern force consisting of one fleet aircraft carrier, three light carriers, and the converted battleship-aircraft carriers *Ise* and *Hyuga*. Since the carriers' air groups had been pulverized in the Formosa operation, Ozawa's role was to act as a decoy so that Kurita's center force could get through to Leyte Gulf. Admiral Halsey, eager to knock out the Japanese carriers, fell for the ploy and charged northward with Task Force 38.

Part of Halsey's plan was that Vice Admiral Willis Lee, the battle line commander, would form Task Force 34—to be composed of fast battleships and supporting vessels in the event of a surface engagement. On 24 October, carrier planes attacked Kurita's ships in the Sibuyan Sea and sank the giant battleship *Musashi*. Afterward, his force headed west, away from the transports at Leyte, so Halsey decided not to activate Task Force 34. During the night, a message from a USS *Independence* scout plane reported that the center force had again turned east and was headed for San Bernardino Strait. Lee considered it prudent to form some of the battleships into Task Force 34 so that they could stay behind and guard the strait. He sent messages to Halsey on board the *New Jersey* to call attention to the new contact report, but he received only acknowledgments from the

Third Fleet staff. Halsey took all the fast battleships with him anyway, thus keeping intact the antiaircraft capability of Task Force 38 for the impending duel with Ozawa's northern force.

Kurita's center force then made its way through the unprotected strait. The only thing standing between it and the American transports was a group of destroyers, destroyer escorts, and escort aircraft carriers. They performed heroically in standing off the Japanese heavy ships. Vice Admiral Thomas Kinkaid, commander of the Seventh Fleet, had expected Lee's Task Force 34 to be at San Bernardino Strait and sent a series of increasingly frantic messages asking for help. Halsey continued north until a radio dispatch arrived from Admiral Nimitz; it asked where Task Force 34 was. It was meant as a nudge and certainly achieved its purpose. Lieutenant John Sullivan was the officer of the deck on the *New Jersey*'s navigation bridge when Nimitz's message arrived. He said that Halsey was so mad that he threw his cap down and stomped on it.

Late on the morning of the twenty-fifth, the *New Jersey* turned south. She was in Task Group 34.5 under the tactical command of Rear Admiral Oscar Badger in the *Iowa*, for Badger had relieved Olaf Hustvedt as commander Battleship Division Seven. The force initially had to slow to refuel the escorting destroyers. As the evening progressed, the task group built its speed to twenty-eight knots. The *New Jersey* and *Iowa* were the only battleships in the Third Fleet that could steam that fast.

During the night, the ship's radar detected a surface contact. Lieutenant (junior grade) Bill Coyne was adjacent to the main battery plotting room forward, where "the atmosphere was tense as all hands watched the target being tracked on the [Mark 8] range keeper. But not a shot was fired; nor did either we or the target alter course and speed. Obviously the decision had been made that our presence in Leyte Gulf was more important." In fact, Admiral Kurita had become concerned. He took his ships back into San Bernardino Strait without ever attacking the U.S. transports. One of the stragglers from Kurita's force, the destroyer *Nowaki*, was sunk by surface gunfire on the morning of 26 October. (This was the destroyer that escaped the *New Jersey*'s salvos at Truk in February.) By the time the *New Jersey*, *Iowa*, and their escorts reached their objective, it was too late. The transports were safe, but the Japanese fleet had escaped.

Historian Samuel Eliot Morison contended that the missed opportunity may well have been providential for the Americans, because a force of only two U.S. battleships would have been outgunned by Kurita's four. During the greatest naval battle in history, the *New Jersey* was the fleet flagship, but she didn't fire a single shot. For her crew the reaction was a mixture of disappointment and relief. Marine Private Donald Kelly said, "We had a great deal of confidence in our gun crews, particularly our main batteries. And we thought, sure, if we had the opportunity, that we would have done a heck of a fine job. So I would say a sense of extreme disappointment that we didn't close with the enemy." Rafael De La Maza, on the other hand, remembered that the married men in the crew were making out their wills and had trouble sleeping during the night of the approach to San Bernardino Strait. They were just as glad that the planned encounter didn't take place.

With the benefit of a great deal of hindsight, we can observe after the battle that the U.S. Navy missed two golden opportunities to eliminate the bulk of the Japanese battle line—because of Admiral Lee's caution at the Marianas in June and because of Halsey's impulsiveness in October while chasing after the decoy carriers and unwittingly leaving San Bernardino Strait to be defended by small boys. In the process, the *New Jersey* was deprived of fulfilling the role for which she was designed and built—to fire her 16-inch guns against the heavy ships of the enemy. Retired Rear Admiral William Abhau, the *New Jersey*'s gunnery officer during the Battle of Leyte Gulf, did a splendid job of putting the ship's World War II experience into perspective: "We were part of the antiaircraft protection. We did a good deal of shore bombardment. We also served as . . . an underway refueling ship and as a hospital ship. In fact, we did everything except be a battleship."

In late October and early November, the *New Jersey* was back to her antiaircraft duties in Task Group 38.2 during air strikes on Luzon, the main island in the Philippines. As so often during the war, the *New Jersey* refueled destroyers in between periods when the task group met up with oilers at a fueling rendezvous. There were also other reasons for destroyers coming alongside, and on the afternoon of 4 November, the USS *Colahan* made an approach on the *New Jersey*'s port quarter for a transfer of personnel and movies. The *Colahan* apparently lost steering control. Her starboard anchor raked the *New Jersey*'s port quarter, tearing loose two chocks, ripping out numerous lifeline stanchions, and sheering off rivets at the deck edge.

The transfer of movies between the *New Jersey* and other ships was a frequent occurrence during the war, for they served as one of the main forms of recreation with the ship at sea. Radio programs, beamed into speakers in the living compartments, were also sources of entertainment. Music was frequently featured, as were news broadcasts put on by some of the ship's officers who read reports received on the radio circuits.

Gunner's Mate Ellis Mamroth remembered playing bridge and Monopoly with FM division members on top of the stable element or Mark 1A computer in the main battery plot. In the turret with his fellow gunner's mates he played hearts, pinochle, cribbage, and acey-deucey. Mamroth's turret three also had a phonograph and record library that included many popular tunes as well as the type then known as hillbilly music and now as country and western.

Another attraction was the "gedunk," which sold soda pop and various forms of ice cream. For Storekeeper Third Class Willard Bartusch, keeping the soda fountain supplied was a chore. Whenever the gedunk was open, there was a line all the way up the port passageway. Sometimes the place ran out of ice cream before everyone could be served. Philip Fuller of the ship's band enjoyed getting chilled pineapple juice from the gedunk and drinking it topside. Of his shipboard relaxation, Fuller recalled, "Some of the most pleasant hours of my life were spent on the *New Jersey*. You'd sit on the fantail at night and look up at the Southern Cross, and it was beautiful. The waves would get that white [cap] as they would crest, the phosphorescence. And you'd watch the flying fish alongside."

While some of the *New Jersey*'s crew members were satisfied with the products available at the gedunk, others wanted stronger stuff. A number of them liberated alcohol used in ship's equipment and then cut off both ends of a loaf of bread and poured the liquid through to strain out impurities. In order to preserve the supply of alcohol, the ship's doctors began mixing it with croton oil, a severe laxative that apparently could not be strained out by bread. Other men tried making their own. The wooden tubs in which shipments of Coca-Cola syrup came to the gedunk were highly prized because empty ones could be used for brewing concoctions such as raisin jack.

Fire controlmen gather in front of the control panel in main battery plot in December 1944. The switches can set up many combinations of directors, guns, and range keepers. *National Archives: 80-G-469932*

For a number of Third Fleet staff officers, and for Admiral Halsey himself, supplies of real liquor arrived in mail bags or pieces of luggage. There were some embarrassing moments, such as the time one of the bags banged against the deck, broke open, and spilled part of its contents. "Scotch whiskey was running all over the deck," said John Rossie, an officer in the ship's engineering department. Admiral Halsey's brand was Black & White, which featured drawings of black-and-white Scottie dogs on the label. On at least one occasion at Ulithi, a number of nurses from a hospital ship were brought to the *New Jersey* in the admiral's barge and were escorted to the flag quarters for socializing with the Third Fleet staff. Some of the crew members resented the nurses, the whiskey, and other things that seemed to come the way of the staff but not the ship's company. On the other hand, many of the *New Jersey*'s men were very much taken with the admiral, because he was friendly and interested in them.

Sometimes Halsey showed up in Gunner's Mate Mamroth's turret. "He just seemed to pop in, sit down, shoot the breeze, have a cup of coffee with the fellows," said Mamroth. "We would have gone anywhere he said, without any question. I mean, just from the standpoint of confidence in what he could do." Sometimes Halsey went to the berthing compartments to say hello to the men. On one occasion this happened when the band had been playing and was changing out of uniform afterward. "Well, what do you do?" wondered Musician Philip Fuller. "Do you salute an admiral when you're in your shorts? But all he did was he stood around and talked to us." When he encountered men out on deck, sunbathing perhaps or just relaxing, Halsey was not one who expected them to jump to attention. He also endeared himself to the crew by going through the mess line from time to time to see that they were well fed.

For a number of the *New Jersey*'s officers, the presence of a staff—especially one as large as Halsey's—was not so popular as with the enlisted crew members. For one thing, the staff took up a

Admiral William Halsey eats holiday dinner with the crew in the Third Fleet flagship's mess deck on Thanksgiving 1944.
National Archives: 80-G-291498

good many staterooms that would normally have been filled by ship's company officers. The latter had to crowd even closer together. At its height during the war, the combination of ship's company and staff personnel was probably around three thousand men.

After a brief stop at Ulithi in mid-November, the *New Jersey* was again under way with Task Group 38.2 late in the month for more air strikes against the island of Luzon. By this time, kamikazes, Japanese suicide planes, were beginning to wreak havoc on the Third Fleet. Previously, Japanese planes had been frequently intercepted and either shot down or driven away by the combat air patrol of fighter planes before they could get within gun range of the big ships. Now, with the normal instincts of self-preservation having been overcome, the pilots of the suicide bombers bored their way through. Much of the time, they aimed for the carriers, both because the carriers' planes were doing damage to the Japanese ashore and because the carriers and their unarmored flight decks were a good deal more vulnerable than the thick-skinned battleships.

On 25 November the *New Jersey* was the guide in the center of Task Group 38.2 when a Zeke fighter dived on the *Hancock* and was disintegrated by a combination of gunfire from the carrier and the *New Jersey*. A section of burning fuselage landed on the *Hancock*'s flight deck. Soon afterward, two more Zekes dived on the *Intrepid*, Admiral Bogan's flagship. The *New Jersey* splashed one that exploded and crashed into the water. The battleship's gunners also hit the second, but it succeeded in crashing onto the *Intrepid*'s flight deck and started large fires. Within minutes, the *New Jersey* also fired on planes going after the *Iowa* and the carrier *Cabot*; a kamikaze crashed into the latter. The *Essex* was also hit during the day. Harry Reynolds, who had been down in main engine control, said, "I went up on the topside after general quarters secured, and there were four carriers burning."

When planes were getting in as close as they did during the kamikaze strikes of 25 November, the dozens of 20-mm guns on board the *New Jersey* were in frequent use. Many of those manning the 20-mm guns were members of the battleship's Marine detachment. Private Dale O'Bryen's job was as loader on a gun near turret two. He remembered that the noise was "terrific" when a lot of guns were firing at once, but then added, "I remember that it would get so exciting that you would forget about the noise and everything else. You would just be interested in the plane you were shooting at. If a plane blew up in front of you, then everybody kind of cheered like a ball game, and you had to make sure you didn't spend too much time doing that."

The Marines and sailors in the *New Jersey*'s crew had a friendly rivalry that included trying to outdo

The deck on the *New Jersey*'s starboard side is drenched from spray during refueling from a fleet oiler in December 1944. Note the battle helmets stored on the 40-mm gun tub at right. *National Archives: 80-G-469975*

one another and also passing jibes back and forth. There was a fair amount of good-natured kidding, remembered Don Kelly, who was a Marine private. He became used to being referred to as a "seagoing bellhop," while the Marines referred to the sailors as "deck apes" and "swabbies." The rivalry extended to their prowess in gunnery, but the Marines won easily when it came to military appearance. Kelly admitted, "Of course, with so much time on our hands, we would just literally spend half our life either shining our shoes or shining our pistol holsters or the brass."

Both Marines and sailors got another shot at Mog Mog liberty in Ulithi before the Third Fleet sortied again on 11 December. With landings on the island of Luzon scheduled for early 1945, the Task Force 38 fighter planes sought to knock out the kamikazes at their fields before they could get airborne, rather than when they were over the American fleet. During the Third Fleet run-in toward Formosa in September, bad weather had been an ally, shielding the fleet's approach until it was time for the strikes to begin. In mid-December, by contrast, weather was a ferocious enemy of the American ships.

The problem was already apparent during the noon hour on Sunday, 17 December, when Admiral Halsey was seated at the lunch table in the flag mess. Through an open door, he could look out and see the difficulties the destroyer *Spence* was having in trying to take on fuel alongside the *New Jersey*. The *Spence* was rolling wildly in the heavy waves and having trouble maintaining steering control. Both fueling hoses to the destroyer parted, and the effort had to be abandoned.

Admiral Halsey was much criticized for persisting in his efforts over the following two days to refuel the fleet and continue the planned schedule of air strikes rather than making escape from the storm his first priority. The *New Jersey* was in a typhoon that grew even worse on the eighteenth, with mountainous seas and winds and spray blasting past at more than one hundred knots. Normally, the battleship was able to plow through seas that treated destroyers as corks, but this time, even the *New Jersey* was rolling noticeably. In his postwar memoir, Halsey wrote that the storm peaked at midday on 18 December, adding, "No one who has not been through a typhoon can conceive of its fury. The 17-foot seas smash you from all sides. The rain and scud are blinding; they drive at you flat-out, until you can't tell the ocean from the air. At broad noon I couldn't see the bow of my ship, 350 feet from the bridge."

Down inside the mighty *New Jersey*, three thousand men were learning firsthand what a typhoon could do to a battleship. Lieutenant Harry Reynolds, eating dinner in the wardroom, was summoned by the engineering officer of the watch to number-three engine room. There, Reynolds heard "the damnedest popping and snapping around the high-pressure turbine.... I went down underneath, in the lower level, and it was the sliding feet of the high-pressure turbine." Normally rock-solid, the turbine was moving back and forth, perhaps an eighth or 3/16 of an inch, in time with the rolling of the ship. Reynolds rounded up a grease gun, gave the zerk fittings on the track a few shots of grease, and the loud noises stopped.

Dan Scanlon, tending a boiler in one of the firerooms, had to take someone else's word for it that the waves outside the ship looked like mountains. He and Russ Brown, who was also in B division, went for nearly a week during the mid-December period without seeing daylight. Crewmen were emphatically warned not to go topside, so they stayed below and kept the *New Jersey* running. Though sleeping was tough on men not used to the storm conditions, eating was even more difficult. The mess cooks didn't even try to set up the spindly legged mess tables. Instead, they just served sandwiches and coffee. People had to hang on just to fill their cups. Warrant Officer Bob Moore went to the 02 deck topside to have a look. There the water stung like a spray of BB pellets when it hit his face.

Gradually, the storm abated, and when it did new troubles were apparent. Some of the 20-mm projectiles had been wrenched loose from their stowage

Admiral William F. Halsey Jr., commander, Third Fleet, sits in his chair on the flag bridge as the *New Jersey* steams toward the Philippines in December 1944. *National Archives: 80-G-471108*

The bow of the pitching New Jersey *plunges into the water in November 1944 as she steams in company with the carrier* Hancock. U.S. Naval Institute photo archive

The silhouetted fleet flagship is prominent in the foreground as the Third Fleet lies anchored in Ulithi Atoll in late 1944. U.S. Naval Institute photo archive

places and were washing back and forth in the waterways alongside the edges of the wood planking on the main deck. Elsewhere, some destroyers had rolled so badly that their masts were nearly parallel to the water before they righted themselves. A few kept on going when they reached that point. One was the *Fletcher*-class destroyer *Spence*. Her inability to fuel from the *New Jersey* on the seventeenth was apparently compounded by a decision on the part of her commanding officer not to take on saltwater ballast. When the roll was called by voice radio after the storm, the *Spence* was no longer around to answer, and neither were the older destroyers *Hull* and *Monaghan*.

On Christmas Eve, after a period of normal steaming in the wake of the storm, the *New Jersey* pulled into Ulithi Atoll and anchored. That morning, the ship's Marines, including Private Dale O'Bryen, were gathered on the stern, aft of turret three, to pose for a group picture. Then, all of a sudden, the Marines started to break ranks, because they saw 5-inch projectiles landing around the ship. Ships in one of the carrier task groups were practicing antiaircraft gunnery against drone targets as they approached Ulithi.

When 5-inch projectiles went up and didn't explode, they had to come down somewhere. One went through the main deck on the *New Jersey*'s fantail, not far from where the Marines had been standing. The projectile also went through the second deck and finally rattled around inside a head on the third deck before coming to rest in a wash basin. Seaman Second Class Robert Clower received a number of wounds in the leg from the wayward shell, and two other men sustained superficial injuries. Lieutenant George Van Vleck, the *New Jersey*'s bomb disposal officer, tossed the projectile over the side after a fire hose cooled it.

Later in the day, Chester Nimitz, recently promoted to the rank of five-star fleet admiral, flew in to Ulithi for a conference with Admiral Halsey. When Nimitz came on board the *New Jersey*, a five-star flag was flown aloft, the first such occasion in a Pacific Fleet warship. With him, Nimitz brought a decorated Christmas tree for the New Jersey's wardroom. Nimitz's biographer, Professor E. B. Potter, noted that the admiral was disappointed because the battleship's officers preferred an artificial tree the crew had made from nuts, bolts, and scrap metal. Ensign Allen

Fleet Admiral Chester Nimitz's flag is hauled down after being flown on Christmas 1944. It was the first time a Pacific Fleet warship flew a five-star flag. *National Archives: 80-G-295422*

Trecartin, one of the *New Jersey*'s scout plane pilots, had duty as in-port officer of the deck at Ulithi. He recalled that the total number of stars from all the flag officers on board the ship during Nimitz's visit was forty-five.

With the *New Jersey* in port over the holiday period, many sacks of mail came on board and were eagerly seized upon by the crew. When the mail arrived, remembered Fireman Russ Brown, a letter might remark that one he had sent home earlier had been heavily cut up by one of the ship's censors. The result sometimes looked like a doily. The remedy was self-censorship; however, said Brown, "You'd start out, 'I'm feeling fine,' and there just wasn't much else to write about."

Even before the onset of the new year of 1945, the *New Jersey* was under way once more with Task Group 38.2. On 30 December 1944, the Third Fleet carrier force was again on the prowl, conducting air strikes against Formosa and Luzon, then proceeding through the Bashi Channel between Formosa and Luzon and into the South China Sea. Admiral Halsey's foremost goal at that point was to sink the two Japanese half-battleships, *Ise* and *Hyuga*, that had escaped Third Fleet guns at Leyte Gulf because of the turn south on 25 October. The pair got away again this time. However, carrier planes from Task Force 38 struck along the coast of Indochina—later Vietnam—and at Formosa, Hong Kong, and the Chinese mainland.

On 26 January, the day after the *New Jersey* returned to Ulithi, the ship received a new commanding officer, Captain E. Tyler "Slim" Wooldridge. The weather during the change of command ceremony was such that Admiral Halsey was wearing nonregulation khaki shorts and a short-sleeved shirt when he presented Holden with a Bronze Star medal for his command tenure. A day later, Halsey and his Third

Captain Edmund Tyler Wooldridge commanded the ship from 26 January to 17 November 1945. The dolphins insignia above his service ribbons denote his previous duty in submarines. *Courtesy Mrs. E. T. Wooldridge*

Fleet staff were gone as well, because it was time to shift to the Fifth Fleet organization once again. Since Admiral Spruance preferred to have his flag in the cruiser *Indianapolis*, that left the *New Jersey* available for Rear Admiral Oscar Badger, commander Battleship Division Seven. He and his staff embarked on 29 January, because his previous flagship, the *Iowa*, was leaving for overhaul.

Lieutenant John Sullivan recalled an occasion he supervised as the *New Jersey* brought on board 16-inch powder from a merchant ship alongside. Sullivan discovered that some of the powder bags were so rotten that pellets of powder were falling out. Admiral Badger came along to exert his authority. In what Sullivan remembered as Badger's "usual God-almighty way," the admiral told Sullivan that the powder was satisfactory and should be sent to the magazines. Naturally, if something untoward had happened, the responsibility would have been on Sullivan and the ship's crew. As soon as the admiral had departed the scene, the defective bags were once again brought back up and returned to the merchantman.

The *New Jersey* was in Rear Admiral Frederick Sherman's Task Group 58.3 during its wide-ranging attacks against the Japanese from 10 February to 5 March. In this period, planes from the carriers of Task Force 58 struck at the Japanese home islands for the first time. Then they went on north to hit Iwo Jima in the Bonin Islands, and Admiral Badger embarked temporarily in the *Indiana* to command a shore bombardment group. Iwo was to provide a landing spot for American bombers damaged during sorties against Japan. The *New Jersey* was with Sherman's task group northwest of Iwo Jima when the Marines hit the beach on 19 February.

On the way back from the Bonins, the carriers again hit Tokyo, and then the task group headed toward Okinawa so that the carrier planes could conduct photo reconnaissance. After returning to Ulithi on 5 March, the *New Jersey* had a respite of only a little more than a week before she had to be on the go again. It was a time to relax, including watching movies topside on the fantail. On the evening of 12 March, the ship's crew gathered in front of the screen and sat on galvanized buckets that were often used for washing clothes. For movies they were turned upside down to serve as seats. When the word was passed over the general announcing system that an air raid warning was in effect, it didn't faze the men of the *New Jersey*. A plane came up from astern and flew along the starboard side. Commander John McCormick, the ship's engineer officer, saw the bluish flame of the plane's exhaust as it passed. It was a kamikaze that crashed into the stern of the carrier *Randolph*, anchored ahead of the *New Jersey*. It killed twenty-five of her men and injured another 106. When the plane exploded upon hitting the carrier, the fantail of the *New Jersey* was cleared in no time, leaving behind only a sea of overturned buckets.

During that period in Ulithi, a new executive officer reported to the *New Jersey*. Commander Robert Rice was a former submarine skipper who had been picked for the job by Captain Wooldridge, breaking the pattern in which the two previous execs had been *New Jersey* department heads who moved up. When Rice reached the *New Jersey*, he directed that his Marine orderly walk ahead of

The dark gray bulk of the *New Jersey* stands out against the sky as she refuels the *Allen M. Sumner*–class destroyer *Borie* on 16 March 1945. Note the many spectators on board the battleship and the "bloomers" on the 5-inch guns. *U.S. Naval Institute photo archive*

Two members of the wartime wardroom were Captain Frank Reagan, *left*, commanding officer of the ship's Marine detachment, and Lieutenant Leonard Goode, Catholic chaplain. Reagan was a prewar all-American halfback at the University of Pennsylvania and postwar professional football player for the New York Giants.
Courtesy Mrs. Frank Reagan

him—rather than the normal practice of following behind—so he could help the newcomer find his way around inside the huge, much-compartmented ship. If the size of the ship was a bit much at first, so were nightly telephone calls Rice began receiving. When he answered, he was confronted with foul language, presumably from new men who didn't want to be in the war. The callers were also pouring abuse over the phone lines to Captain Wooldridge and Chaplain Leonard Goode, so all three soon had their telephones disconnected.

A few days after departure from Ulithi on 14 March, the *New Jersey*'s Task Group 58.3 proceeded to Kyushu, Japan, for air strikes on 18 and 19 March. On the eighteenth, the battleship's Kingfishers were launched to attempt a rescue of a *Bunker Hill* pilot who had been shot down near Kyushu. One of the OS2Us, flown by Lieutenant W. A. Ethridge, went in and snatched the pilot from heavy seas.

The following day, 19 March, the *New Jersey* was able to refute the charge of having "wooden guns." The ship's air defense officer was Lieutenant Commander Archie "Zeke" Soucek, whose station was on the 011 level air defense platform. He kept a log of events. Beside Soucek were officers to relay his commands to the antiaircraft guns. That morning held favorable conditions for the attackers, because they could dive out of low clouds; gun crews had only a short time to react. At 7:15 a.m. a plane did get through and dropped two bombs on the carrier *Franklin*, which was steaming near the *New Jersey*. At 7:41 a Judy dive-bomber plummeted out of the clouds and flew forward along the port side of the *New Jersey* in an attempt to crash on the *Essex*. The battleship's machine guns knocked off the plane's tail, and it crashed "very close" to her starboard bow.

At 8:13 another Judy came out of the low ceiling and went straight for the *Bunker Hill*; the *New Jersey*'s 40-mm brought the plane down in flames. At 1:21 p.m., a Zeke fighter headed for the *Bunker Hill*. This one was hit by the *New Jersey*'s 5-inch battery, which, in Soucek's words, "turned him into a ball of flame and scattered bits of wreckage all over the ocean." At 2:18 another Zeke passed the *New Jersey*'s stern, headed toward a carrier. The *New Jersey* claimed credit when the plane was knocked down off her starboard beam by 5-inch shell bursts. At 2:31 the battleship fired on another Judy, which was splashed by U.S. fighters. Either by herself or with the assistance of gunfire from other ships, the *New Jersey* shot down more than a half dozen enemy planes that day. When Soucek was able to climb down from his lofty perch at day's end and crawl into bed, he had been on the air defense station forty-one continuous hours.

On 22 March, the *New Jersey* joined Rear Admiral Arthur Radford's Task Group 58.4 for operations in the vicinity of Okinawa. On the morning of the twenty-fourth, she shifted to a bombardment group under Admiral Badger. Also included were five

Seen here in a photo taken from the deck of the *New Jersey* in December 1944 is the *Fletcher*-class destroyer *Franks*. On the night of 2 April 1945 the destroyer and battleship collided, with disastrous results. *National Archives: 80-G-470279*

destroyers and the battleships *Missouri* and *Wisconsin*. The ships shelled the southeast coast of Okinawa. Soon it was back to work in the carrier task groups, first Rear Admiral J. J. "Jocko" Clark's 58.1 and then back to Radford's 58.4. Easter Sunday, 1 April 1945, was the day of the Okinawa invasion. The *New Jersey* continued to operate about fifty to sixty miles off the coast with her task group.

The battleship received a profound jolt on the night of 2 April. At 9:08 p.m., just after the last dusk combat air patrol was recovered, Task Group 58.4 was turning out of the wind and heading south for a fueling rendezvous. The *Fletcher*-class destroyer *Franks* had been serving as plane guard astern of the USS *Yorktown*, Radford's flagship. When released from that duty, she was to return to her normal screen station on the outer circle of the task group.

The *New Jersey* was plowing through the dark, cloudy night at twenty-three knots when her officer of the deck, Lieutenant Gene Hayward, spotted the lights of the *Franks* close ahead, crossing the battleship's bow from starboard to port. At 9:14, Hayward saw that the destroyer was on a collision bearing and shouted "Right full rudder emergency" and ordered the engines to back at full power. Had he not done so, the mammoth dreadnought might have cut the *Franks* in half. The destroyer frantically sounded her whistle, and at 9:15, the two ships sideswiped each other, port to port. The *New Jersey*'s huge anchor, high above the water, ripped through the bridge of the *Franks*, sending the captain and officer of the deck crashing down onto the main deck and injuring both badly. The *New Jersey* continued her turn to starboard while the destroyer sent showers of sparks into the air, rolling back and forth and banging into the solid side of the battleship with each roll to port. Hayward then shifted the rudder to left full to swing the *New Jersey*'s stern clear of the passing *Franks*.

On board the destroyer, Quartermaster First Class Mike Bak thought his ship had been hit by either a torpedo or mine. Wearing only his undershorts, he made ready to abandon ship. Fortunately, the hull of the *Franks* was intact. She stayed afloat, and Bak stayed on board. Robert Huff had just climbed into his bunk on board the *Franks* when he heard the emergency alarm and felt heavy vibrations. He jumped out of bed and ran topside. There, he said, "all I could see was the enormous hulk of the *New Jersey* looming above me." In the *New Jersey* Russ Brown saw one of his shipmates writing a letter with a pen that he dipped into an open bottle of ink. When the crunch of collision came, the fellow was so unnerved that he spilled his ink and started running. Lieutenant John Sullivan went to the bridge from the wardroom and there found OOD Hayward beside himself because he hadn't been able to avoid the collision. It would comfort Hayward afterward to realize that he had prevented the incident from being much worse.

On board the battered destroyer, the commanding officer, Commander David R. Stephan, was so badly injured that he died two days later as a result of fractured ribs having punctured his left lung. His officer of the deck, Lieutenant (junior grade) Bob Numbers, was injured but survived. Ensign Mark Lillis,

Drooping from its normal position is a gun tub on the port side of the *Franks* after her collision with the *New Jersey*. To the right is the repair ship to which the destroyer moored while being patched up sufficiently to return to the United States. *Naval Historical Center*

This badly mangled 40-mm gun mount shows the effect of its encounter with the *New Jersey*. *Naval Historical Center*

the junior officer of the deck, recalled that Stephan ordered the destroyer's engines to back when she got within about one thousand yards of the *New Jersey*. Hayward, recounting the event from a perspective nearly forty years afterward, believed that the smaller ship might have made it safely across the *New Jersey*'s bow if she had kept going. The *New Jersey* sustained negligible damage from the encounter.

On 7 April, the planes of Task Force 58 went after the Japanese battleship *Yamato* and her consort of a light cruiser and eight destroyers that were steaming west of Kyushu. This was a ship version of the kamikaze effort and proved not nearly so effective as the airborne type. Though Admiral Spruance would have preferred to sink the Japanese giant with his battle line, Admiral Mitscher's planes could do the job more quickly, and so they were sent in and executed the kill.

The next day, the *New Jersey* shifted once again to Task Group 58.3, but her activities in support of the Okinawa campaign were nearly finished. On 14 April, Captain Wooldridge announced to the crew that the battleship was going back to the United States for overhaul, and the men were understandably enthusiastic. On 16 April, the *New Jersey* arrived at Ulithi, where Admiral Badger gave a farewell talk to the crew. Two days later, he transferred his flag to the *Iowa*.

The *New Jersey* made the journey to Pearl Harbor in company with the heavy cruiser *Minneapolis*. The stay in Hawaii was a brief one, fewer than twenty-four hours, and then the battleship resumed her journey eastward. The man in the captain's sea cabin during the voyage to Bremerton, Washington, was making the trip reluctantly. Captain Wooldridge would have much preferred that the *New Jersey* remain in combat, because he was on board her to get the big ship command experience he needed for promotion to rear admiral.

Edmund Tyler Wooldridge was a supreme gentleman and a brilliant officer. He was known for his expertise in the field of personnel and was a highly capable administrator. Indeed, he went on to three-star rank. On the other hand, he lacked a number of the qualities possessed by Carl Holden, whose highest active duty rank was rear admiral. While both were ambitious officers intent on doing fine jobs on board the *New Jersey*, Holden had a special relationship with the crew that Captain Wooldridge was never able to achieve. The commissioning skipper had a feeling and sensitivity for the men's wishes and needs that his successor did not. Wooldridge probably suffered in the crew's eyes because he was not Carl Holden, the man they had come to love because he cared about them and in whom they had developed a great sense of confidence.

When it came to the matter of enforcing regulations, Holden had started off as strict when he took command, because that was the way he had been brought up in the Navy. Gradually, though, as the ship got into steady combat, things had eased up, because combat itself was demanding enough. When Wooldridge came on the scene, he resumed the strict enforcement of regulations. The trouble was that the crew wasn't starting at the same point as Captain Wooldridge was, and so they saw the tightening as an unfortunate contrast.

Captain Wooldridge was an abstraction to the enlisted men at large, for they didn't get to know him personally. One who did was Marine Private First Class Dale O'Bryen, who served as Captain Wooldridge's orderly, summoning people to see him, handing him his binoculars and coffee and so forth. O'Bryen observed that Wooldridge had a physical condition in which his hands shook so noticeably that he could take only a half cup of coffee at a time. As O'Bryen, Commander Rice, and others close to the captain realized, the condition didn't affect the captain's ability to think or act, but word of it still got around among the crew and reinforced their impression of him.

On 6 May, the *New Jersey* arrived at Puget Sound Navy Yard, Bremerton, Washington. The shipyard period was to be long enough to allow the crew to go home on leave in two installments. For the half not on leave at a given time, there was enjoyment to be had in Seattle, where there were USO-sponsored dances and other attractions. One member of the first leave group was Fire Controlman First Class J. P. Loughan. He rode trains for four and a half days to Boston to be married. The Pullman car going to Chicago was occupied entirely by *New Jersey* crew members on leave. Loughan remembered, "We were able to persuade the porter to leave the bunks made up, and we just slept when we felt like it. So it wasn't all that bad. It's just that we were anxious to get home." He was married within a few days of getting home and then had a nine-day honeymoon in New York City. The toughest part was leaving to head back to the ship, especially since he had no idea when he would see his bride again.

Roger Faw, then a seaman first class, was in a delegation of *New Jersey* men who went to Seattle by ferryboat. They remained all in a group until they had bought their train tickets. He recalled that those in charge "were afraid that we would probably get on the beach, get drunk, lose all of our money, and wouldn't have fare home. And they were absolutely right." As it was, Faw lost his wallet, identification card, and leave papers. The shore patrol in Chicago fixed him up with temporary papers and sent him on his way to home in Washington, DC. There he

Captain E. Tyler Wooldridge cuts a birthday cake in May 1945 to celebrate the second anniversary of commissioning. *Courtesy Archie H. Soucek*

received a telegram from a Bremerton barmaid who had found his wallet and later mailed it to him. Once he was back on the West Coast, he gave her a carton of Lucky Strike cigarettes every time he went on liberty until the ship departed.

For married officers such as Lieutenant Commander Archie Soucek and Lieutenant Bill Coyne, the leave period was a time to be reacquainted with their families, eat their wives' cooking, and spend some time with their children. For Soucek that included Archie Jr., who had measles. Coyne and his wife went to Vancouver, Canada, for two weeks of vacation and then settled into a government-owned cabin in Port Orchard, Washington, for the duration of the overhaul. "The cabins were sparsely furnished," he explained, "with a wood stove for cooking and heating, but after 18 months at sea it was a welcome change. The overhaul was completed in record time . . . and all too soon we were heading back to the war zone."

As for the ship herself, there was a fair amount to be accomplished in a relatively short time to get the *New Jersey* ready to go back out to finish the job against the Japanese. Probably of foremost concern was overhauling the engineering plant, because it had logged many thousands of miles of demanding, high-speed steaming. The *New Jersey* also received a new, roomier, square-front bridge in place of her rounded one. The new one was of the same type that was built into the *Missouri* and *Wisconsin* during original construction and added to the *Iowa* as part of her early 1945 navy yard period.

Inevitably, the work wrapped up, and it was time to go again. Many of the *New Jersey*'s men treated their last night in port as if there would be no tomorrow—at least not one for on-the-beach "steaming." The town of Bremerton was not big enough to contain that boisterous, rowdy last night, which included much drinking and destruction of property. Typical was an incident in which someone took a stuffed moose head down from a tavern wall and followed it out through a front window.

A spaghetti-like tangle of hoses fills the slim forecastle of the *New Jersey* on 24 June 1945 at Puget Sound Navy Yard. *National Archives: 19-N-94339*

The rebuilt square-front bridge can be seen in this 24 June 1945 view at the Puget Sound Naval Shipyard. It was constructed to the same design as the original bridges of the *Missouri* and *Wisconsin*.
National Archives: 19-N-94340

The ship went under way for sea trials on 30 June. She anchored to take on ammunition, and only the officers and chiefs were able to have liberty. Captain Wooldridge had a busy time of it while the ship was at anchor on 2 July, handing out a fistful of punishments at mast and informing the crew that he'd received too many reports on their foul language in Bremerton. Roger Faw, who hadn't returned to the ship on time because he was with a woman, stood before the captain at mast and was awarded a punishment of restriction to the ship. "Now do you think it was worth it?" asked the captain.

"Yes, sir," replied the undaunted Faw, so the captain increased the severity of the punishment and repeated the question. Faw still thought the woman had been worth it, so then Wooldridge asked if Faw thought she was worth a court-martial. No, she wasn't, and so Faw ended up with his restriction to the ship. That was really no punishment at all with the *New Jersey* about to head back to the war and not much liberty in sight anyway.

On leaving the Pacific Northwest area, the *New Jersey* proceeded south to San Pedro, California, in company with the light cruiser *Biloxi* and destroyer *Norris* to undergo a period of refresher training that would bring the crew back up to speed. Again, the men were kept on board, because the captain didn't want anyone jumping ship at a time when he was determined to get her back to excel in combat.

Before leaving the United States, about a dozen men were dropped off and left behind when Commander Rice, the exec, discovered that there was a group of homosexuals on board the ship. He explained, "The Navy had a very stern policy with respect to that sort of thing, and I think quite properly so. It detracts from other interests, such as duties." (The situation has changed dramatically since 1945. Gay and lesbian individuals now serve openly in the U.S. armed forces.)

On 19 July, with the crew training completed, the *New Jersey* stood out of San Pedro harbor and

A Japanese projectile splashes off the port bow during the *New Jersey*'s 8 August 1945 bombardment of Wake Island. *Courtesy Robert H. Rice*

headed west for Pearl Harbor, an intermediate stop on the way back to the war. On 8 August, still farther west, the *New Jersey* stopped near Wake Island long enough for a practice bombardment. The island had been seized by the Japanese soon after the beginning of the war in December 1941, but by 1945 it was so far beyond the drawn-in Japanese defensive perimeter that it was more liability than asset. Still, it provided a live target for the guns of the battleship and got her men into the spirit of combat again. As at Mili in March 1944, the Japanese were spirited enough to send some shells zinging out at the *New Jersey*. The four salvos fell between two hundred and twenty-five yards short, and Captain Wooldridge quickly conned the ship out of harm's way. One of the ship's spotting planes—SC-1 Seahawks now in place of the old Kingfishers—had its main pontoon and wing float damaged by enemy fire, but the other planes were unhit.

At 4:30 p.m., after shooting much of the day except for a lunch break of sandwiches and coffee, the *New Jersey* gathered up her escorts—the light cruiser *Biloxi* and four destroyers—and began steaming southwest.

CHAPTER III

POSTWAR DOLDRUMS
August 1945–June 1948

As the *New Jersey*'s heavy anchor chain rattled out through the hawsepipe at Eniwetok Atoll on the evening of 9 August, plans called for the Third and Fifth Fleets to support the invasion of Japan's home islands. Admiral William F. Halsey Jr. was scheduled to arrive at Eniwetok in the *Missouri*. There he would transfer his Third Fleet staff to the *New Jersey* for what was expected to be the final campaign of World War II. After supper that evening, as members of the crew chatted, the air was buzzing with rumors that the war was nearly over. U.S. B-29 bombers had dropped atomic weapons: on Hiroshima, Japan, on 6 August, and three days later, on Nagasaki. The noose had reached the choking point, and Japanese leaders were scrambling to find a formula for peace.

At 5 a.m. on the eleventh, Captain Wooldridge was awakened and presented with what he described as "two startling pieces of information. One was to the effect that Japan had made proposals to surrender provided the emperor was left in power and, second were urgent sailing orders for the *New Jersey* to proceed to Guam." The captain sent his orderly to summon the ship's navigator, Commander Myers Keithly, so he could prepare to get the ship under way. Later that morning, the *New Jersey* and five escorting destroyers began their journey, which ended two days later in Apra Harbor. Guam had become the forward headquarters of Fleet Admiral Chester W. Nimitz, commander in chief, Pacific Fleet and Pacific Ocean Areas. He was conferring with Admiral Raymond A. Spruance, commander, Fifth Fleet, and his staff concerning the coming landings in Japan.

As the *New Jersey* bided her time, diversions were provided for the war-weary crew. A boxing ring was set up on the fantail for intramural matches, and on one occasion the fantail was a concert setting as the Pacific Fleet band played from an impromptu stage atop turret three. Meanwhile, the rumor mill continued to grind. The Japanese cabinet accepted surrender terms on 14 August. Reaction on board the *New Jersey* was subdued. The crew was still far from home and apprehensive about what lay ahead. In a letter to his wife on 15 August, Captain Wooldridge explained, "We still don't trust the Japs and realize that all opportunities for treachery will probably be used; this means that we will remain on a complete war footing until we have actually disarmed the Nips."

With World War II just over, men of the *New Jersey* relax topside at a Pacific anchorage. *Courtesy Robert H. Rice*

On 16 August, with the fighting ended, Admiral Spruance and his staff embarked in the *New Jersey*. Admiral Halsey would remain in the *Missouri* and be responsible for receiving the surrender of the Tokyo area and northern Japan. Spruance would take over western Honshu and the islands of Kyushu and Shikoku. Many in the crew believed that their ship deserved to be the site of the formal Japanese capitulation, but then came word that President Harry S. Truman had chosen the *Missouri* instead. She was named for his home state, and his daughter had christened the ship. The *New Jersey*'s men harbored a feeling of disappointment for some time.

The next stop after Guam was Manila, in the Philippines, where the *New Jersey* arrived on 21 August. The ravages of war were much in evidence. The city itself was 85 percent destroyed, and the harbor was littered with wrecked Japanese ships. Some were completely underwater, while the masts and stacks of others protruded above the surface as a menace to navigation. In heavy rain, Wooldridge, navigator Keithly, and a harbor pilot gingerly threaded their way through the maze to bring the *New Jersey* to her anchorage.

The captain and navigator, both of whom spent much of their time on the bridge when the ship was under way, had formed a bond. Both were qualified submariners. Wooldridge had specifically requested a former skipper, concluding that someone who had commanded his own vessel would have an appreciation of the kind of information a captain expects from his navigator.

While in Manila, Admiral Spruance held planning meetings with General Walter Krueger, whose Sixth Army had been designated to occupy the Japanese islands of Kyushu and Shikoku, as well as the western part of the main island of Honshu. Also involved in the meetings was General of the Army Douglas MacArthur, who was to be supreme allied commander for the surrender.

As the officers and men of the battleship walked the streets of Manila, which was feeling the effects of the hot summer sun, their nostrils were invaded by the sweetish smell of rotting human flesh. One young *New Jersey* officer was struck by the great sadness he encountered. Bud Bowler, then an ensign, explained later that the local inhabitants "were still battered and bedraggled and sad—and obviously undernourished. I didn't see any happiness at all among the Philippine people. That was kind of startling. You would have expected a great deal of exuberance to carry them over any remaining hard times, but they were just beat to a pulp, from my observation."

After staying at Manila from 21 to 28 August, the *New Jersey* steamed to Buckner Bay, Okinawa. There she remained for two weeks while Admiral Spruance's occupation fleet assembled. Halsey's Third Fleet was already in action against the Japanese when the surrender came and thus available to move into Tokyo Bay. Sufficient ships were now available for both the Third and Fifth Fleets to exist simultaneously, but it still took time for Spruance's to come together.

On 2 September, while the surrender ceremonies were taking place on board the *Missouri*, Admiral Spruance was hundreds of miles away, because Admiral Nimitz had directed him not to be present. One logical explanation is that the Americans were still concerned about the possibility of last-minute Japanese treachery and so didn't want to have all the top U.S. naval commanders in one spot.

The stay at Okinawa afforded the opportunity for high-ranking visitors to confer with Admiral Spruance. One was a khaki-clad Army officer, General Joseph "Vinegar Joe" Stilwell, who had earned fame fighting the Japanese in the China-Burma-India Theater. He had taken command of the U.S. Tenth Army on Okinawa and would be in charge of accepting the surrender of all Japanese forces in the Ryukyus Islands. Yet another guest soon after the war's end was Rear Admiral Carl F. Holden, the previous commanding officer. When he stepped onto the quarterdeck, he remarked to Captain Wooldridge, "What a beautiful deck. How did you get it like that?" He was used to seeing it covered with camouflage. Getting the paint off after the war's end had been a real chore. The men of the deck force had to scrape holystones back and forth over the wood until the layers of paint were removed—a back-straining job.

When the battleship left Buckner Bay on 13 September, she was able to steam toward Japan at a leisurely sixteen knots, and to operate with her running lights burning brightly—after some 200,000 miles of Pacific steaming at darkened ship. As the *New Jersey* approached Japan, she was greeted by a touching and symbolic event. Her destination was the port of Wakayama at the eastern entrance to the heavily mined Inland Sea of Japan. Pulling out after loading hundreds of just-released Allied prisoners of war was the USS *Sanctuary*. As the hospital ship passed on the *New Jersey*'s starboard side, the ex-prisoners let forth a cheer for the battleship, and the men of the *New Jersey* applauded the newly liberated POWs.

The Fifth Fleet flagship arrived at Wakayama on 15 September and left the following day. She reached Tokyo Bay on 17 September, slightly more than two weeks after the surrender signing, and moored to a buoy at the former Japanese naval base in Yokosuka. At that point, Admiral Spruance took command of

An SC-1 Seahawk floatplane from the *New Jersey* flies near a Japanese volcano in the autumn of 1945. The pilot was Allen Trecartin. *Courtesy Allen Trecartin*

Pilots of the ship's aviation detachment gather in front of an SC-1 floatplane in October 1945. *Left to right*: L. Harlan Goodpasture, Allen L. Trecartin, Glenn Harris, and G. E. Percival. *Courtesy L. Harlan Goodpasture*

all U.S. naval forces in Japan. In addition to keeping control of the islands already assigned to the Fifth Fleet, he took over eastern Honshu from Admiral Halsey and Hokkaido from Vice Admiral Frank Jack Fletcher.

The Fifth Fleet's staff operations officer, Captain Edward M. Thompson, noticed that Admiral Spruance seemed not to be adjusting to the fact that he was no longer a combat commander. Even though it might have made more sense, for example, to set up the fleet communicators ashore in Japan, Spruance insisted on keeping them on board the *New Jersey* so that the fleet wouldn't be robbed of its mobility. Though thousands of American servicemen were headed back to the United States, the *New Jersey* herself would not be going home right away. Because of her overhaul at Bremerton, she had been to the States most recently of the available battleships and so was tapped as flagship for the occupation forces.

To the *New Jersey*'s crew the occupation role offered an opportunity to see firsthand the land of their recently conquered enemies. The feared Japanese treachery did not come to pass, but *New Jersey* men were still wary about the reception they would encounter. Hank Kubicki, one of the buglers, remembered that the Japanese "were more stand-offish than anything. I think they were afraid of us as much as we were apprehensive of them." For the most part, the people were docile but understandably reluctant to warm up to their conquerors, although there were exceptions. In part, relationships grew out of the generosity of the Americans who were willing to share food and other items. Barter also took place as a result of the widespread American desire to take home souvenirs, particularly Japanese swords. Seaman Harry Fagan of the *New Jersey* tried to obtain the sword of a Japanese policeman, who was reluctant to give it up. Fagan finally desisted when someone explained to him that a policeman's sword constituted his badge of authority.

Kubicki and several shipmates visited a local bathhouse, where they saw that Japanese of both sexes were in the tub. The Americans doffed their uniforms and got into the water, although they did keep on their skivvy shorts as a matter of modesty. Afterward, Kubicki got a massage as a young Japanese woman walked on his back with her bare feet. "That was one of the most relaxing moments of my life," he remembered. "Her heels and toes going up and down your spine—it was just absolutely gorgeous."

The officers of the fleet were accorded liberty privileges not given to enlisted men. Groups of them were able to go off for a few days' leave in Japanese resort hotels in an undamaged part of the country. Commander Zeke Soucek, the gunnery officer, went with a group that included Commander Bernard F. Roeder Jr., who relieved Commander Rice as exec. Their jeep took them over rocky, bumpy roads and included a picturesque view of the Japanese countryside.

Certainly there were aesthetic experiences. During her time in Yokosuka, the fleet flagship was frequently in view of beautiful Mount Fuji, the snow-capped volcano that is much revered in Japan. Ensign Charles Mathias, an officer from the occupation fleet, recalled, "I must say that the morning watch [4 to 8 a.m.] was one of the most beautiful experiences I ever had, to watch the sun coming up on Fujiyama and

Snow-capped Mount Fuji is in the background as the *New Jersey* lies at anchor in Yokosuka harbor in the autumn of 1945. She is the flagship for Admiral Raymond Spruance as the occupation of defeated Japan gets under way. *Courtesy Robert H. Rice*

see it change color from just being a gray shadow on the horizon, and then to have the sun touch the top of the mountain and turn it first to a sort of gold and then to pink and finally, pure white."

Although life on board the *New Jersey* generally fell into a routine of maintenance work, watch standing, and liberty, two of the ship's officers found the autumn of 1945 to be anything but routine. Lieutenant Commander John Sullivan and reserve Lieutenant John Yeager were detached for three months' duty ashore in Japan. When General MacArthur's occupation troops had moved into the country, some inadvertently detonated Japanese naval weapons, such as mines and torpedoes. Thus, naval ordnance officers were called for, and Sullivan and Yeager got the job. Assigned to help them were a couple of Japanese—a former Imperial Navy captain who had been educated in the United States and was fluent in English, and a kamikaze pilot who didn't get into action before war's end. Yeager managed to commandeer an Army jeep as their transportation, and the group traveled widely.

On Thursday, 8 November, the *New Jersey* received a new occupant in her flag quarters. Raymond

Spruance was relieved as commander Fifth Fleet by Admiral John H. Towers, who had become the Navy's third aviator more than thirty years earlier. Spruance was piped over the side and rode away in a barge en route to relieve Admiral Nimitz as commander in chief, Pacific Fleet. When he left the *New Jersey*, Admiral Spruance was concluding the last seagoing assignment in a naval career that stretched back nearly to the turn of the century.

The departure of Admiral Spruance led to the ship receiving a new captain. Captain Wooldridge had been selected for rear admiral. He couldn't hold that rank as the ship's commanding officer, but he was eligible for the promotion as soon as a vacancy occurred. The fleet operations officer, Captain Thompson, went to Spruance with the suggestion that Wooldridge could take the place of a cruiser division commander whose flagship was also in Yokosuka. Thompson volunteered to command the *New Jersey*. Spruance and Thompson were not on the best of terms, and so the admiral turned down the proposal. As soon as Spruance was relieved, however, Thompson presented his plan to Admiral Towers. Towers agreed and sent off a message to the Bureau of Naval Personnel, which also approved. On 17 November, only nine days after Spruance's departure, Wooldridge left also.

In November 1945 Admiral Raymond Spruance, *second from left*, and Admiral John Towers, *second from right*, receive congratulations from visiting officers during the Fifth Fleet change of command. National Archives: 80-G-355329

The crew, already beginning to decline in numbers, gathers on the fantail on 8 November 1945 at Yokosuka for the Fifth Fleet change of command. Thomas Buell collection, U.S. Naval War College

The new commanding officer presented a contrast to the old in his manner of operating the ship. Wooldridge, a former submariner, was perhaps awed by the great size and bulk of the *New Jersey*, for he was timid in conning her. Thompson, on the other hand, was inclined to be bold. He had the added advantage of having been conning officer of the fast battleship *Massachusetts* while serving as executive officer when she was first commissioned. In 1942, during the Allied invasion of North Africa, he had kept the *Massachusetts* away from enemy gunfire and torpedoes as she dueled with the French at Casablanca.

Commander Myers Keithly, the navigator who had been brought on board by Captain Wooldridge, remembered Thompson as "a very bold man," likable, outspoken, and abrupt. He was not aloof, which Wooldridge had been in dealing with subordinates. Near the end of the month, on 28 November, the *New Jersey* was to get under way for the first time since arriving in Yokosuka. Thompson concluded that one means of winning the crew's confidence was to put on a bold display of ship handling. The ship was moored to a buoy near the berth of the Japanese battleship *Nagato*. Rear Admiral Wooldridge, as senior officer for the maneuvers that would follow, offered tugboats to help the *New Jersey* move away from the *Nagato*. In order to demonstrate his self-confidence—and

This view of Yokosuka on 30 December 1945 depicts the *New Jersey* at left. Just beyond her is the *Nagato*, the last surviving Japanese battleship. *National Archives: 80-G-265872*

possibly to show up his cautious predecessor—Thompson declined the tugboats and twisted the *New Jersey* clear with her own engines.

Several officers who served under Captain Thompson in the *New Jersey* offered their assessments of him. One called him "a wonderful skipper . . . a very, very fine officer, and he let you do your job." This same individual added, in speaking about Thompson, "He was a little on the heavyset side. He didn't present quite as clean a military appearance as some of the other officers, but as far as being an all-around good officer, it was a pleasure to work under the gentleman." Gunnery officer Soucek remembered that Captain Thompson "was well-loved on board; we all liked him, and we had good camaraderie with him, enjoyed him very much. But when he got angry, by golly, he'd get angry, and his face would get red, and boy, he didn't mince any words. He'd tell you what was what, but he was still very well liked."

During her first three days at sea under Thompson, the *New Jersey* spent a lot of time training—exercising at general quarters, maneuvering in company with Rear Admiral Wooldridge's flagship *Pasadena*, and firing her antiaircraft guns. The crew was already turning over, because experienced men were leaving quickly now that the war was over. Performance suffered, including a foul-up between ships. At one point, recalled Zeke Soucek, the *New Jersey* got so close to the stern of the *Pasadena* that "I could have thrown a potato and hit that ship."

During the entire time Captain Thompson was in command of the *New Jersey*, the ship didn't have a single opportunity to fire the main battery, but he did enjoy the rare occasions, such as this, to fire the antiaircraft guns. By this time the battleship was already so undermanned that Soucek had to pool his men in order to assemble gun crews. One of the newly arrived gun crew members was Seaman Harry Fagan, who remembered that some of the shots nearly hit the aircraft flying past instead of the target sleeve it was towing. The pilot reported afterward that he didn't want to work with the *New Jersey* until her gunnery improved.

Several reasons explain the letdown in crew performance during that period. First, there was no longer a war. It provided a built-in self-preservation instinct that improved men's shooting. Second, there was considerable loss of experience. Finally, the two-month layoff while in port might have dulled the edge of even a wartime crew.

Discipline had to be tightened up during this period, because the beginning of peacetime had brought some slackness. Strict standards were still largely in place, but crew members no longer felt the previous incentives to observe them. A number of men were just biding their time until they could be discharged and return to civilian life. Even when punishment was necessary, however, Captain Thompson dispensed it reluctantly. He explained years later that "a perfect day for me was to have the chief master-at-arms come up and say, 'No men at mast today.' . . . I hated to hold mast, [but when he did hold it] I always went on the assumption 'hit 'em hard and hit 'em quick.' Three days' solitary confinement on bread and water, administered on the spot, is a damn sight more effective than thirty days' loss of pay submitted two weeks later."

Throughout the autumn of 1945, crew members left in droves to return to the United States for reassignment or discharge. The manning problem was rampant in most other ships as well. Rear Admiral Charles Wellborn Jr. was then on board as chief of staff to Admiral Towers. He recalled the period as a time when the battleship served principally as a hotel and communications facility for the fleet commander.

The *New Jersey* spent the months of December 1945 and January 1946 mostly at a buoy in Yokosuka. That routine was interrupted for a brief period each month by operating at sea with the *Pasadena* and accompanying destroyers. Some new men reported to beef up the crew slightly and to compensate for the many who had been detached. One such was reserve Ensign Dan Duffy, whose case illustrated the disorganized state of naval personnel in the year after the war. He had previously served in the heavy cruiser *Louisville* and then was in San Francisco following VJ Day. A personnel officer on duty there seemed to think Duffy was having too much fun, so he was sent out to join the crew of the *New Jersey* for a trip to—of all places—San Francisco.

Admiral Towers' two-month stay in the *New Jersey* ended on 18 January as he relinquished command of the Fifth Fleet to Vice Admiral Frederick C. Sherman. Sherman's stay was brief; on 28 January, he shifted to the USS *Iowa*, swapping flagships with Rear Admiral John W. Roper, commander, Battleship Division One. Hundreds of passengers reported to the *New Jersey* for transportation to the United States. Among them was the man with whom Admiral Spruance had conferred in Manila, General Walter Krueger. The old warrior and his staff were going home, and that would justify cranking on a few more knots than permitted under normal postwar economies.

The great day came at last on Tuesday, 29 January 1946. At 1 p.m., the crew was mustered at quarters, and the master-at-arms force searched the ship for stowaways. At 1:58, the battleship was under way for San Francisco. General Krueger explored the giant dreadnought and learned something about her operations. On one occasion, he was chatting with the navigator, Commander Keithly, who sought to explain to him the sextant used in measuring the angle between the horizon and various stars for celestial navigation. The general cut short the conversation by saying, "I was surveying the west coast of

The ship's Marine detachment poses in front of turret one on 4 January 1946 at Yokosuka.
Courtesy Mrs. Frank Reagan

Luzon with a sextant before you were born." A serious concern was operating the *New Jersey* during the return transit after she had lost so many experienced people, including nearly all the qualified helmsmen. Keithly and a chief quartermaster shared the steering duties until they could break in replacements.

The ship also needed new officers of the deck. Before his departure, Captain Wooldridge had sought to hang on to his turret officers as OODs and junior officers of the deck. But they were being swept out in the demobilization, and so a new group of men came under instruction. One of them, Lieutenant (junior grade) Bob Moore, found it a new experience after serving in a fire control division throughout the battleship's wartime service. His training was enhanced a month later with the arrival of a new senior watch officer. The white-haired lieutenant, Bob Pearson, had spent the war piloting newly constructed tank landing ships (LSTs) down the Mississippi River and had much useful ship-handling experience to pass on to his new shipmates.

When the *New Jersey* reached San Francisco on 10 February, she steamed beneath the Golden Gate Bridge, timing her arrival for the high tide. Some families of crew members were on hand to welcome the long lines of sailors standing on the main deck. Among those sailors was Fireman Russ Brown, who remembered that the ship was welcomed by a boat with a band on board; included in the tunes played for the crew was "Jersey Bounce." As a whole, though, this was a much more subdued celebration than greeted the bulk of the fleet upon its return the previous autumn. By February, the freshness of victory had worn off, and so the *New Jersey*'s arrival was anticlimactic.

Despite the letdown, the men were still thrilled to be back, particularly the passengers who had been overseas for a long time. Hundreds of them were disgorged at San Francisco, along with still more crew members to be discharged from the service. Fewer than six hours after anchoring in San Francisco Bay, the ship was under way once again, to Long Beach in Southern California. This, for a time, would be the *New Jersey*'s base. Men could become accustomed to stateside liberty again, including such simple pleasures as eating fresh food. Zeke Soucek remembered the enjoyment he had by gorging himself on salads and fresh milk upon reaching California. During the next few months, the doldrums from the time in Yokosuka became even worse in Long Beach. Still more men left for discharge, and the ship lay anchored for weeks at a time. Boredom became a shipmate of the crew, for the *New Jersey* had no real purpose.

On 26 March, after having been anchored in port for a month and a half, the ship went under way long enough to move to a pier at the naval shipyard in Long Beach. A beneficial side effect of the long time in port was that it allowed the crew members to go away on leave for extended periods. One was Seaman Harry Fagan, who rode by train to his home in Brooklyn. After an enjoyable stay of several weeks, he bought a bottle of whiskey, which he planned to use as part of a birthday celebration once he returned to the *New Jersey*. He and several shipmates were on the westbound train. In the evenings, the other men repeatedly implored Fagan to share a shot of the liquor with them to help them get to sleep in the day-coach seats in which they were riding. He turned them down, he remembered, jealously saving his treasure for a party.

On the night Fagan and his mates returned to Long Beach, they stepped up to the quarterdeck and saluted the officer of the deck to ask permission to return on board. The OOD, one of the officers from the ship's Marine detachment, informed the men that he was going to inspect their luggage. Fagan quickly decided to return ashore and throw his bottle away, because it was better to do that than to be punished for trying to smuggle liquor on board ship. The Marine had been kind to Fagan by giving him the chance to get rid of the bottle rather than searching him on the spot. On the other hand, Fagan had to face the rebukes of his buddies from whom he had kept that bottle night after night on the train.

During those months in Long Beach, the personnel turnover continued. When the ship did get new men, they were frequently inexperienced seamen second class, straight from boot camp. They were given some training about the ship, but there were precious few knowledgeable petty officers left to do any training. For the officers as well, life was a desultory affair. To escape the boredom of the ship's routine, Ensign Duffy applied for training in Navy schools. He had already been to firefighting school, but he went again, if only because it gave him a chance to visit relatives nearby. He passed up a course in recognition of Japanese planes, which surely had outlived its usefulness, and applied instead for one in ice cream making. Alas, that one was canceled.

In late April, the pace of activity picked up, although only temporarily. Late that month and through early May, the *New Jersey* was under way frequently in the area off Long Beach to train with the *Iowa*. Rear Admiral John Roper, as commander, Battleship Division One, was embarked in the *New Jersey* for the local operations. There were steering exercises, man-overboard drills, launching of planes from the fantail catapults, fire drills, seamanship drills, gunnery drills, underway replenishment practice, antiaircraft practice, navigation and ship handling drills, and a surprise military inspection to test readiness. For Captain Thompson, the training period was an all-too-rare chance to operate the ship, but it still had limited value, because the *New Jersey* was so pitifully undermanned.

A task that fell to the ship's new supply officer, Hank Kretz, was an assignment that turned out to be a mirage. He was to prepare the *New Jersey* for duty as host ship for VIPs at the atomic bomb tests scheduled for July at Bikini Atoll in the Marshall Islands. The ship had understandably been stripped down for wartime, in large part to remove fire hazards. Now her roomy flag quarters could get new carpeting and furnishings. Provisions for the trip were put into storerooms. But once the ship had been made nearly ready to go to Bikini, her participation in the tests was canceled. She would go into deeper hibernation instead. The *New Jersey* and *Iowa* got under way together from Long Beach on 29 May to proceed to Puget Sound Naval Shipyard. There they would sit beside a pier, because they no longer had enough men to operate.

En route, the two ships anchored on 1 June at the naval ammunition depot at Bangor, Washington, and unloaded the tons of powder and projectiles that had been on board since war's end. During the process, which lasted two days, the *New Jersey*'s magazines and projectile flats were unburdened of more than one thousand 16-inch projectiles and more than 11,000 of 5-inch. There were more than 100,000 rounds of 40-mm antiaircraft ammunition and more than 85,000 of 20-mm. It was a big job, and in competition with the *Iowa*'s crew, the men of the *New Jersey* finished slightly sooner.

Once the ammunition was offloaded, the two battleships reached the shipyard on 4 June. As if she hadn't already lost enough, the *New Jersey* then gave up still more of her men, these to be assigned to cruisers. Lieutenant (junior grade) Roy Lee Vaught had reported as electrical division officer in February. At the time, his division numbered about 140, because the ship still had to generate her own power when she was anchored. Upon arrival at Bremerton, the battleship hooked up to power cables from the shore, and so the division soon melted from 140 to about 30, and even that left the E division better off than some. The wartime crew of nearly 3,000 men had been reduced to around 400. The battleship was manned with a crew little bigger than a destroyer's.

The rest of 1946 was a time of drabness. The *New Jersey* lay moored the entire time, much of it alongside the *Iowa* until that ship returned to more active service in late October and departed Bremerton. Rear Admiral Roper was relieved of his duties as commander, Battleship Division One, on 23 June and left two days later. Commander, Battleships Cruisers Pacific Fleet, with headquarters in Long Beach, also took on the duties of division commander.

Boatswain's Mate Second Class Rafael De La Maza, *right,* supervises the painting of a lifeline stanchion during the ship's enforced idleness at Bremerton in 1946. De La Maza was one of only thirteen crew members who served on board during the entire 1943–48 period in commission. *Courtesy Roger Faw*

Captain Leon J. Huffman, at the microphone, takes command of the *New Jersey* on 5 August 1946. The outgoing skipper, *at left,* is Captain Edward M. Thompson. The latter was a fine ship handler, but the battleship operated so little during his tenure that he seldom was able to use his skills. *Courtesy Archie H. Soucek*

Months passed, and on 5 August, the dormant *New Jersey* received a new commanding officer. Captain Thompson had maneuvered to get command the previous fall, but the *New Jersey* turned out to be a hollow prize. This officer who took such delight in bold ship handling ended up with few opportunities. There had been little to do during the long transit from Japan or the long in-port periods at Long Beach and Bremerton. Only the couple of dozen days of training maneuvers had given him a chance to practice his craft, and even then the battleship wasn't able to fire her big guns. Captain Thompson's command tour was a short one, only eight and a half months, and the satisfactions were few. As he put it, "If it had been active and operating, it would have been something else, but just to be tied up to a damn dock at Bremerton was no fun."

The new skipper was a handsome submariner, Captain Leon J. Huffman. Nicknamed "Savvy," he finished high in his class of 1922 at the Naval Academy, standing 27th of the 539 graduates that year. Hyman G. Rickover, who later became famous for developing nuclear submarines, stood 106th in the class. There are few recollections of Huffman from his time in the *New Jersey*, because the period of hibernation offered little chance for the crew to see him in action. He is generally remembered as being an able and eager athlete—bowling, golfing, and playing softball, among other things. A junior officer who served in the *New Jersey* during that period describes Huffman as "sort of reserved, austere, very nice-looking, always in good physical shape, always in perfect uniform."

Sports provided one outlet for the crew, which had little of real consequence in the way of military duties to pass the time. There were too few men to operate the *New Jersey*, so they did their best to keep the ship reasonably clean and rust-free, but even those efforts were only partially successful because of the shortage of manpower. Electronic gear and fire control equipment were kept going, but help was required there. Lieutenant Commander Noble C. Harris, combat information center officer, sometimes had to depend on manufacturers' representatives to take care of electronic gear, because he didn't have sufficient qualified technicians as part of the crew.

In midsummer, a new batch of ensigns reported from the Naval Academy, and they were assigned make-work duties. One of the new ensigns was Elmer Kiehl, who recalled that the ship had three brows, or gangways, while she was at Bremerton. At most other times, she had two brows, one for officers and the other for enlisted men. The third one was installed for the carrying of ship's garbage to the pier, and that brow was assigned for watch standing by the ensigns.

Kiehl remembered that one of the few occasions for contact with the commanding officer came during inspections of the ship. Kiehl said that the crew felt a sense of excitement—a mixture perhaps of anticipation and apprehension—when Captain Huffman was due to come around. There was still a considerable gulf between officers and enlisted men, and the captain was a remote figure at the top of the officer pinnacle. Kiehl said, "I can remember being on one of the ammunition-handling platforms, in the lower part of the barbette, when he came sweeping through, and everybody was excited that he was coming. Everybody was anticipating, and, of course, he swept around, and he found a couple of things wrong and a couple of things good and sort of patted everybody on the head, and went sweeping out again. Did it very well, as I remember."

During the forlorn months in Bremerton, some watches were still necessary, meals cooked, clothes washed, and the ship kept reasonably clean. But the clear sense of purpose that had invigorated the *New Jersey* during the war was no longer in evidence. As a result, there was an inevitable concern about morale. Commander Kretz, the supply officer, sought to keep some of the men in his department interested by instituting a storekeepers' training course that would be beneficial in preparing them for advancement. Training on radar in the combat information center was one of the few useful pursuits available for eighteen-year-old Seaman Second Class Harold Gill, fresh out of school. After reporting to the ship, he wrote, "I spent the next 3 or 4 months . . . learning about plotting and running the gear since there were very few of us [and] not much to do."

Recreation was another means of keeping men interested, and that didn't always mean hanging out in bars or engaging in the shipboard crap games that sprang up on paydays. A duck-hunting club was established on the nearby Hood Canal for the benefit of the *New Jersey*'s men. The crew built several rafts, which were towed out into the canal and used as duck blinds. To supplement the rafts, Hank Kretz requested two used boats and outboard motors from the shipyard's supply department. He got a negative reply, so he sent a message to the Bureau of Ships in Washington, explaining in detail why he wanted the boats and motors. Within forty-five minutes, Kretz remembered, he received an information copy of a message from the Bureau of Ships to the Puget Sound Naval Shipyard. The yard was directed to provide the ship with two brand-new boats, instead of the old ones he asked for, and four outboard engines instead of the two he requested. The recreation project turned out to be a huge success.

By autumn of 1946, the Navy had decided to put the *New Jersey* in mothballs. In October, Lieutenant Commander Ernest William Dobie Jr. reported to take over as main battery officer and principal assistant to Commander Soucek, the gunnery officer. Dobie wrote that the assistant did not have "exciting prospects since the ship was already commencing its first inactivation.

The Gunnery Department personnel level had been drawn down to about 100 souls, from a normal complement of about 900. We barely had enough bodies to handle all of the 'mothballing' procedures required. The work was hard, not too exciting—more like being a mechanical embalmer." Because the ship was preparing for the reserve fleet, Dobie stepped up to become the gunnery officer, a department head.

The remainder of the year dribbled out in the frequently rainy Pacific Northwest, and the process of inactivation moved beyond the preparatory stage of conducting inventories and making up work lists. Soon after the beginning of 1947, on 11 January, the *New Jersey* was dry-docked and subsequently underwent an InSurv (inspection and survey) visit to determine in detail her material condition. Before the inactivation could get well under way, however, the Navy found a mission for the *New Jersey*. She would be part of the Navy's first overseas midshipman training cruise since before the war.

The inactivation was halted, and the process was reversed. In three months, the crew doubled in size, to approximately eight hundred. These men didn't even constitute a normal peacetime allowance, but they would permit the ship to steam and shoot, and there would be hundreds of additional men in her bunks once the midshipmen arrived. All told, the midshipman squadron was to embark more than two thousand students from the Naval Academy and various NROTC units. Gunnery officer Dobie observed that the buildup was helpful in numbers, but even so, many of the men were woefully short of experience in battleship gunnery and procedures. He recalled the time as an exciting challenge for a thirty-year-old gun boss who didn't have nearly the wealth of talent to draw upon that his predecessors enjoyed. Finally, about two weeks before the *New Jersey* was due to leave the shipyard, a turret captain arrived. He was a lifesaver for a crew with virtually no experience in firing 16-inch turrets.

The work of putting the ship back together continued in all departments, and on 12 March she emerged from dry dock. On St. Patrick's Day, she took on a full load of fuel oil, which made her ride about a foot lower in the water, and in early April she loaded enough ammunition to increase her draft a good deal more. She also took on provisions for the forthcoming voyage. Supply officer Hank Kretz remembered of the job, "I think every cigarette company in the United States sent two or three representatives in order to be sure that their brand of cigarettes was going to be exposed in the best possible way to the midshipmen."

An incident on the morning of 2 April 1947 was vivid for those present. The ship was moored alongside a pier at the naval magazine at Bangor, Washington. Shortly after 5:30 a.m., the loading of ammunition began. After about six hours came a mishap during which 2,700-pound, 16-inch armor-piercing projectiles were loaded from a barge alongside. Then a set of slings lowered the projectiles to the appropriate places inside the barbette of turret two.

Ensign Robert C Peniston, who was in charge of loading that turret, recalled the incident years later. As Peniston described it, the loading was proceeding satisfactorily when the ship's fire control officer came along and said things were moving too slowly. Despite Peniston's protests, the officer ordered the quick-release yard sling used, and it wasn't long before an accident occurred. The sling hit a hatch coaming, the projectile came loose, and it landed about five decks below inside the barbette.

As the ensign looked down into the ammunition-loading hatch, he saw the big splash of blue dye from the projectile. (Projectiles carried dye in them for use when shooting against other ships. The idea was that when a number of battleships were shooting simultaneously, they would use different colors of dye and thus would know which ship's shots were falling closest to the enemy.) Lieutenant Commander Dobie, the gunnery officer, had directed that the projectile be raised and then transferred ashore for examination. Instead, in Peniston's recollection, the turret two division officer put the projectile on a dolly. To avoid the shell becoming a possible time bomb, he rolled it over to the edge of the deck. He then dropped it overboard, thus producing a big plume of water. Lieutenant Commander Dobie was understandably disturbed by the turn of events, but Peniston remembered Captain Huffman as being surprisingly placid about the whole thing, "rather than raise hell like you would expect."

The story had a sequel. In the years that followed, both Peniston and the *New Jersey* went their separate ways. Twenty-two years later, they were reunited. In August 1969, Captain Robert C Peniston was ordered to command the ship in which he had served as an ensign. As part of the process of refamiliarizing himself with her, he climbed down to take a look at the spot where the projectile had landed in 1947. The dye was long since gone, but he could still see a 16-inch half-moon shape embossed into the steel of the deck.

Once the ammunition loading was completed, the *New Jersey* got under way from Bangor on 5 April for a journey down the West Coast. A two-day stop at Long Beach on 8–9 April was marked by a departure inspection conducted by commander Cruiser Division 13 and two of his ship captains. Once they had satisfied themselves, the *New Jersey* was on her way south to the Panama Canal. Her all-day trip through the canal on 20 April marked her return to the Atlantic for the first time since 1944.

Test-firing of the antiaircraft guns was a nearly daily feature of the trip, because the new men needed lots of practice. Finally, the turret crews got their opportunity. When the 16-inch guns opened up on 21 April, they were doing so for the first time since the end of the war. The big guns got more of a workout as the ship practiced shore bombardment in the Caribbean, part of an overall refresher training program conducted with the *New Jersey* operating in and out of Guantanamo Bay, Cuba. Day after day was occupied with steaming and shooting. The training effort culminated on 8 May in a mock battle problem. The following day, the ship headed north. When the *New Jersey* arrived at Bayonne on 13 May,

New Jersey governor Alfred Driscoll observes as Captain George Menocal, *right*, prepares to relieve Captain Leon Huffman, *left*, as commanding officer. The event took place on 23 May 1947, the ship's fourth birthday. *Courtesy Mrs. George Menocal*

it marked her first visit to the state for which she had been named.

The fourth anniversary of the ship's commissioning was celebrated with a flourish on 23 May. New Jersey governor Alfred E. Driscoll attended the ceremonies, as did former governor Walter E. Edge. Rear Admiral Carl F. Holden, who had put the ship in commission as skipper four years earlier, flew up from Norfolk to attend. As he spoke to the assembled guests, he held in his arms three-and-a-half -year-old Harolyn Meyer, the ship's pinup girl during the war.

The most substantial event of the day was the ship's change of command. Relieving Captain Huffman was Captain George L. Menocal, who had been head of the foreign languages department at the Naval Academy following a variety of destroyer duty during World War II. He would do much in the succeeding months to put his imprint on the ship and the crew. A short man, he was a Naval Academy classmate of Huffman, but he finished well below him in the 1922 class standings.

The day after the change of command, the *New Jersey* headed south for Hampton Roads. She spent several days at Norfolk and took on board a number of Naval Reservists to help fill out the crew. She needed these men for her coming cruise to northern

Commander J. Wilson Leverton, *left*, initially served as the ship's executive officer. When Captain George Menocal, *right*, departed without a four-stripe relief, Leverton was the last commanding officer during the ship's first period in commission. *Courtesy of J. Wilson Leverton*

European waters. Reserve centers were canvassed, and a number of men volunteered for a temporary return to active duty. One who did so was Ensign Charles Mathias Jr., a reservist who was drilling at Baltimore while attending law school. He later served as a U.S. senator for the state of Maryland.

An enlisted man is prepared for a highline trip from the *New Jersey* to the oiler *Chemung* during refueling off the Virginia Capes on 8 June 1947. *Courtesy Dudley J. Kierulff*

The *New Jersey* anchored on 3 June in Annapolis Roads. A rainy mist was in the air on 7 June as a procession of motor launches plied back and forth between the Naval Academy seawall and the squadron of ships anchored offshore. Up the accommodation ladders came 518 Naval Academy midshipmen of the classes of 1948 and 1950. The former had but one more year before graduation; the latter had completed only one year. The men of 1948 would dress and be treated much like junior officers. The new sophomores, known as "youngsters" in Naval Academy jargon, would live in similar fashion to the junior enlisted men. The only distinction was that the white hats of the midshipmen carried dark blue stripes around the rims to distinguish them from crew members.

Two of the prospective members of the class of 1950, Midshipmen William J. Aston and Alexander G. B. Grosvenor, wrote of their time in the *New Jersey* for a later issue of *National Geographic* magazine. Of their arrival in the berthing compartment, they wrote: "Our pipe bunks—and they were comfortable too—were stacked in tiers of four, lining the bulkhead (walls or ship's side) and grouped compactly in columns, fore and aft, two tiers wide, but with enough room to scoot out quickly. We were each assigned a locker, so tiny it left us skeptical. How could we cram all the gear in our two bulging bags into that small space? Nevertheless, after much refolding and rolling, our 'white works,' 'skivvies,' etc., were squeezed in."

For the midshipmen, many of whom had probably never been to sea, the cramped nature of shipboard living spaces was an education in itself. It was nothing like the three-man rooms they had known in Bancroft Hall at the academy. In fact, part of the purpose of this indoctrination cruise was to give the midshipmen—both those of the Naval Academy and the approximately two hundred men from the Naval ROTC units of various universities—an idea of what life was like for the enlisted men who would eventually be working for them once the midshipmen became officers.

Shortly before 10 a.m. that day, the *New Jersey*'s anchor chain was heaved in, and the ship was under way in company with the *Wisconsin* to rendezvous with the rest of the ships in Task Force 81, the training squadron. The *New Jersey* dutifully followed fifteen hundred yards astern of the other battleship, because the *Wisconsin* was carrying Rear Admiral Heber H. McLean, commander, Battleship Division One. BatDiv One had for all practical purposes gone out of business in 1946 when the *New Jersey* was tied up pier-side at Bremerton. Now that the ships were steaming, the division was reactivated.

The two battleships joined the remainder of the ships off Cape Henry, Virginia, and set course for Rosyth, Scotland. With them were two fleet carriers, the *Kearsarge* and *Randolph*; the destroyers *O'Hare*, *Cone*, *Stribling*, and *Meredith*; and the dock landing ship *Fort Mandan*. The latter, an amphibious warfare vessel, was included so that her covey of landing craft would be available to provide liberty boats in European ports.

The Atlantic crossing was made at a leisurely pace to give the midshipmen and reservists plenty of time for underway training, and it is also likely that the new crew members were receiving indoctrination as well. Commander J. Wilson Leverton Jr. was the executive officer, and he particularly remembered the ship being overpopulated with chief petty officers, to the point of having to expand the chiefs' quarters to accommodate them. The chiefs were there in disproportionate numbers, because these were career Navy men, not war-enlistment people. Since quite a number of them had been in the service since before the war, they now enjoyed a good deal of seniority. And even for those who had left to join the reserve, a cruise such as this was a strong lure. The upshot of the skewed manning was that a number of chiefs wound up doing relatively menial jobs, because there were not enough junior people to do them.

The officers' wardroom was a curious amalgam as well. The division officers were largely "mustangs"—former enlisted men. There were few Naval Academy graduates in the crew; of the academy men who were there, the preponderance were ensigns not long out of Annapolis. These two groups were from far different social and educational backgrounds, but the mustangs had the advantage of being senior to the academy ensigns and were not hesitant about reminding the new men that they had been out fighting the war while these ensigns were still hitting the books at Annapolis. Moreover, the mustangs were sorely needed in the talent-depleted ship for their technical expertise in such specialized areas as gunnery and engineering.

Leverton recalled that the ex-enlisted men weren't the well-rounded types of officers who could be assigned to the Pentagon, for example, but they were top-notch in their specialties. Even so, throwing the two groups together in the wardroom probably made both a bit uncomfortable. Senator Mathias remembered that Commander Leverton was "distressed, because the mustangs had imported a number of the customs from the chiefs' mess to the wardroom. One of the most obvious was a big bowl of toothpicks on the wardroom table."

A clever cartoonist in the *New Jersey*'s crew depicted the skipper's reaction after being dive-bombed by a passing seagull. On the back of the drawing Captain Menocal wrote, "This happened to me on the bridge of the N.J. G.L.M." *Courtesy Mrs. George Menocal*

Down in the crew's mess, conditions were less elegant than in the wardroom. In 1947 Ted Kosmela was a seaman striking for quartermaster. After he had served in a small, rocket-armed landing ship during World War II, the *New Jersey* was for him the epitome of what Navy life should be. The mess deck was roomy, even if the benches and tables, with their spindly, fold-up legs, had to be set up for each meal and put away in between times. Since they weren't fast to the deck, as the mess tables would be later in the ship's career, things got a bit hectic on the occasions when the big ship was in heavy seas.

Even though Kosmela served in the *New Jersey* for only a few months, the experience was a vivid one, and even years later he could still recite a good many details. The bulkheads were painted green and the decks gray, although the most heavily traveled portions of the passageway decks were left as bare steel to save wear and tear. During the war, decks and bulkheads were routinely left unpainted to prevent paint from adding to fire hazards.

Senior petty officers lived in the same compartments as the rest of the men in their division. They served a valuable function as leaders; said Kosmela, "You learned by watching those old salts with the hashmarks on their arms. If they didn't like something, they were quick to let you know about it. If somebody was dirty, or the sacks weren't made up right, or the compartment was dirty, they were after you." Besides being disciplinarians, petty officers were advisers, teachers, and perhaps father substitutes for young sailors who had left home not long before.

Being a quartermaster was a delight for Kosmela, because the duty of winding the ship's clocks gave him a legitimate reason to roam the ship to an extent permitted to few enlisted men of that time. At night, when he was quartermaster of the watch, he enjoyed going down to the bakeshop to get some fresh bread or rolls, telling a white lie that the food was for officers. At other times, he enjoyed standing out on deck at night, listening to the sounds as the ship made her way through the dark sea, watching the play of moonlight on the huge gray smokestacks aft of the bridge. Some days, to escape the usual routine, he would invent an excuse to walk up to the bow. There he would peer down through the hawsepipes, high above the water, and enjoy a time of quiet solitude. "All the noise was behind," he explained, "and then you'd turn around and you'd look at that big, beautiful ship."

There was no chance for quiet solitude on the morning of Sunday, 8 June, when the *New Jersey* broke from her training routine long enough to take a drink from the fleet oiler *Chemung* during the voyage to Scotland. The midshipmen who were topside that June morning saw the *Chemung* up ahead, linked by heavy black fuel hoses to the *Wisconsin*, which was on the oiler's port side. The midshipmen writing for *National Geographic* reported, "A veteran officer told us that even in wartime simultaneous refueling of two battleships was as rare as 'sun off Cape Horn.'"

The midshipmen had an enforced training regimen that acquainted them with operations throughout the ship. They stood watches on the steering wheel (although certainly not while alongside the oiler), life

On 16 July 1947, the oiler *Chemung* simultaneously refuels the *Wisconsin, left,* and *New Jersey, at right. Photo by Alexander G. B. Grosvenor © National Geographic Society*

buoy watch on the rail, lookout watches high up in the air defense station, and engineering watches. They learned seamanship and navigation, engineering, ordnance, and gunnery; included in the latter were taking apart and cleaning a 40-mm antiaircraft gun. Lieutenant Commander Noble Harris, combat information center officer, set up a duplicate CIC in the flag plot and arranged for midshipmen to send their own radar reports to the bridge by sound-powered telephone. In this capacity they served as a backup for the ship's radar gang.

One event that gave the midshipmen a feel for the way enlisted men lived was the field day set aside for cleaning the ship thoroughly. The day began at 5:30 a.m. when the boatswain's mate of the watch passed the word over the ship's announcing system, "Reveille! Reveille! Heave out and trice up." On came the normal lights in each berthing compartment, and off went the red lights that provided the only illumination during the night, because they wouldn't interfere with the ability of the eyes to adapt quickly to darkness.

After reveille had hauled sailors and midshipmen from their sleep, the men got dressed and went up on deck. With scrub brushes they went carefully over the wooden decks, their feet bare because a man with a hose was close behind. When holystoning was called for, large GI cans were filled with a caustic solution of bleach, saltwater soap, water, and boiler compound. (Ted Kosmela remembered the solution as being "so powerful it almost smoked.") In addition, sand was sprinkled on the wooden decks to add still more abrasiveness when the holystones, which were made by drilling holes in boiler bricks, were scraped monotonously across the wood.

Inside the ship, other men were sweeping and swabbing, cleaning the tops of lockers, and reaching into tight corners to clean out accumulated grime. Others were polishing up mirrors, sinks, urinals, and shower stalls. When all were finished, the decks were clean enough to sleep on, and the men of the *New Jersey* were famished.

Midshipmen use squeegees to wipe away excess water after hosing down the teakwood deck. *Photo by Alexander G. B. Grosvenor © National Geographic Society*

By the time the battleship had been at sea for two weeks, the midshipmen had received sufficient training and practice to man the guns. While firing at drones and target sleeves, the antiaircraft guns were operated entirely by midshipmen, with officers in the mounts only as safety observers. Gunnery officer Bill Dobie remembered that it was useful to have Naval Academy staff members on board from the departments of seamanship and gunnery to provide advice to the none-too-experienced ship's crew.

In charge of the training detail from the academy's faculty was Commander John D. Bulkeley, who had received a Medal of Honor early in World War II for his exploits in PT boats in Philippine waters. His boat successfully evacuated General Douglas MacArthur from beleaguered Corregidor in 1942 and took him on the first leg of a trip toward safety in Australia. Some of the *New Jersey*'s officers and enlisted men got the impression that Commander Bulkeley mentioned his wartime heroics a bit too often. He was overbearing in pointing out infractions and usually managed to work into the conversation something along the lines of, "I was there in the big war; where were you?"

On the bright Sunday morning of 22 June, Task Force 81 steamed past the sheer cliffs of Scotland's

The *New Jersey* approaches the cantilevered Firth of Forth Bridge shortly before her arrival at Rosyth, Scotland, on 23 June 1947. *Courtesy Neville T. Kirk*

Cape Wrath and then to Dunnet Head and the sometimes-turbulent waters of Pentland Firth, which separates Scotland from the Orkney Islands. Scotland was green and lovely, with the fields coming right down to the water's edge. The scene was on the dismal, rainy side the following day when the task force entered the Firth of Forth and passed ships of the British Home Fleet at Rosyth, Scotland. The ships of both nations rendered honors to one another as they passed. Ensign Mathias was out on deck to take in the scene. He said, "The bands played the national anthems, and there were gun salutes; it was one of the most thrilling moments in any sailor's life—this whole experience of these two great fleets passing."

Although a battleship as large and powerful as the *New Jersey* was a joy to handle in the open sea, with room to roam and stretch her sea legs, things were more difficult when she reached constricted waters. Whenever the ship got into a situation that required close-in maneuvering, Captain Menocal frequently dispatched his Marine orderly to a stateroom far down in the ship so he could summon Lieutenant Commander Dick Peek to the bridge.

Peek was a Naval Reserve officer from Buffalo, New York. During the war he had gained a good deal of ship-handling experience as commanding officer of a destroyer escort, so the captain called on him to conn the *New Jersey* through tight spots in the midshipman cruise.

As the ship made her approach to Rosyth, there were already indications of the hospitality to come. The U.S. task force steamed through a group of fishing boats, and as the ships and their thousands of sailors passed, an officer on board the *New Jersey* overheard a reaction. A Scottish voice from one of the boats remarked, "It'll be a hot time in Edinburgh tonight." When the *New Jersey* passed under the great cantilever railroad bridge across the Firth of Forth at Rosyth, her mast barely cleared the lower span. From that span, as recounted in the *National Geographic* article, "five hooky-playing Scottish children leaned out and waved a large American flag."

During the trip across the Atlantic, the *New Jersey* had had to bring up the rear as far as the battleships were concerned because of the rear admiral on board the *Wisconsin*. The situation was dramatically reversed when the task force reached Scotland. Soon after the anchor chain had been made fast to the mooring buoy at Rosyth, Admiral Richard L. Conolly's four-star flag was hoisted on board the *New Jersey*. He was commander, U.S. Naval Forces Eastern Atlantic and Mediterranean, normally headquartered in London. For the duration of the ship's visit to Northern Europe, he became a seagoing flag officer and took considerable pride in showing off the *New Jersey*.

The arrival of the training squadron was the signal for an outpouring of goodwill on the part of the Scots. Commander Charles K. Duncan, executive officer of the *Wisconsin*, was on that ship's forecastle to help supervise mooring. He recalled years afterward that "immediately after we were shackled up [to a buoy], someone handed me a program of events about two inches thick. They contained the most meticulous detail of such items as to what cars would meet our people, how many were to go, and where they were to go. I found when I opened it that three events had already passed." He added, "It nearly killed me, not the hospitality, but trying to get the midshipmen where they were to go, because the people opened their homes. We had invitations that could not be filled. Particularly after about the third day I had to order people on lists to go to parties because the people of Scotland were so hospitable."

The same sort of quota system was set up on board the *New Jersey*, involving both the ship's company and the midshipmen. As the cruise went on, it became a rather demanding ritual. Lieutenant (junior grade) Bob Moore tried to hold back and hope the invitations would be filled up before his name was called, because he needed a chance to recover from all the kindness that had been showered upon him and his shipmates.

Ensign Mathias was invited to a party at the home of Rear Admiral Frederick Dalrymple-Hamilton, the senior officer at His Majesty's Dockyard in Rosyth. (As a captain, Dalrymple-Hamilton commanded HMS *Rodney* during her famous encounter with the German battleship *Bismarck* in 1941.) The party was, Mathias remembered, almost like a Gilbert and Sullivan event, highlighted by Scots in kilts doing a sword dance, pipers, and "lots of gin, lots of gin." The admiral's wife had an extraordinary social faculty, even though blind. Mathias explained, "Although hundreds of people went through the receiving line, she could then call you by name later in the evening just from recognizing voices."

The Scots were so generous in their hospitality for the visiting American Navy men that they gave until it hurt. On one occasion, a group of U.S. officers went into a pub for a drink and absently asked if there was something to eat as well, although they had surely been well fed on board ship. After some conferring, the Scots broke out a can of potted meat and made sandwiches for their guests. In so doing, they were sharing from their own scarcity, for they had not yet recovered from the food rationing of the wartime years.

Since taking over as skipper of the *New Jersey*, Captain Menocal had been terribly demanding about keeping the ship clean and squared away. Junior officers feared his wrath if he found something amiss while they were on watch. He was also a stickler for the observance of proper honors and ceremonies, and there were plenty of them with a four-star admiral and his staff embarked. Ensign Elmer Kiehl stood officer of the deck watches on the quarterdeck when the ship was in port. He said, "It was like going into battle, practically, to go out there and have the deck during that period, for fear that you would make some gross error and have the whole world come crashing down on you."

An important individual on the quarterdeck was the ship's bugler. There was a set of rules for these honors and ceremonies, but it seemed that every admiral and every consular official had his own special variations. Kiehl well valued the bugler's contribution:

> The rules were not so specific that anybody knew exactly what to do. The officer of the deck didn't know; the receiving captain didn't

know. They knew the general outline of the ceremony, ruffles and flourishes and a certain number of side boys and everything, but there were little details.... The bugler—that was his profession; he'd been up there all his life, watching people come and go, and he wasn't a dumbbell. He had figured out what to do in situations... when the arriving personage violated the rules. He knew how to handle it and make it look like it was all pro forma.... If you, as an ensign, understood that he knew better than you what to do, and you somehow or other transmitted that information on to him, he would protect you to some degree. If he thought you were a super jerk and conceited, he would not protect you.

The visit to Rosyth lasted six days, and then the *New Jersey* and *Wisconsin* were off to Oslo, Norway, marking the first time big ships had been there since the war. Other ships from the training squadron went to ports in Denmark and Sweden. Sightseeing, dances, and parties were the order of the day, as well as shopping expeditions on the part of the prosperous Americans. To a degree, this prosperity sparked resentment and coolness on the part of the

The *New Jersey* steams in company with the aircraft carrier *Kearsarge* during the cruise. *The Mariners Museum*

Catholic divine service on the ship's fantail on 27 July 1947
National Archives: 80-G-279895

Norwegian men. They were interested in seeing the American ships and the technology they incorporated, but they did not like the well-heeled visitors barging in and dating their girlfriends. The midshipmen writing in *National Geographic* told of one Norwegian mother "who insisted that a midshipman date her son's fiancée while the poor lad remained home!" It's no wonder some of Norway's young men physically attacked midshipmen ashore.

Because of the far northern latitude and the time of year, it was daylight or at least dusk almost around the clock. That was the occasion for all-night partying by some of the Americans, and it led to an embarrassing incident. Norway's King Haakon VII, who was raised in a naval tradition, was quite taken with these wondrous modern warships that were visiting his land, so Admiral Conolly invited him to the flagship.

The rail-thin king, wearing the uniform of a Norwegian admiral, boarded the *New Jersey* by accommodation ladder and proceeded on a guided tour,

As they pass by the ship's Marine detachment on board the *New Jersey* on 2 July 1947 at Oslo are, *left to right*, King Haakon of Norway; Admiral Richard Conolly, commander, U.S. Naval Forces Eastern Atlantic and Mediterranean; Rear Admiral Heber McLean, commander, Battleship Division One; and Captain George L. Menocal, the ship's commanding officer. *U.S. Naval Institute photo archive*

evincing a good deal of interest in the things he saw in the way of weapons and mechanical equipment. Then, because he had been accustomed to the quarters in smaller, older ships, he asked to see an officer's stateroom. Eager to please, Admiral Conolly led the king to a room and flung open the door. The occupant, Commander Bulkeley, had been one of those out much of the night, and now he was recovering with a peaceful snooze. One who was on board the *New Jersey* at the time remembered of the slumbering officer that "if it had not been for the fact that he had the Congressional Medal of Honor strapped firmly around his neck, I think he would have been picked up bodily by the admiral and stuffed through the porthole."

Seaman Kosmela, the quartermaster striker, also recalled Conolly's time on board, because the admiral was pleased with the appearance of the flagship's bridge during an inspection tour. The painting and polishing to make it what Captain Menocal referred to as "my jewel box" had been successful, although there was a price to be paid for the sparkling look. A number of *New Jersey* officers remembered that Menocal was ready to chastise for the slightest infraction of procedure or appearance of sloppiness. The captain could be charming and courtly with visitors, then suddenly turn and inflict his temper on a ship's officer for a stray cigarette butt or some grease leaking from a lubrication fitting. The captain took a more kindly approach toward the enlisted men and was more popular with them than with the officers.

To move between ship and shore, the *New Jersey*'s sailors rode liberty boats. The going and coming presented marked contrasts. When leaving, liberty parties were carefully inspected to make sure that their uniforms were impeccable—hair cut, faces clean-shaven, and shoes brightly polished. Each man stepped up to the officer of the deck, saluted, presented his liberty card, asked permission to go ashore, and then filed down into the waiting boat. During the ride to the boat landing, petty officers enforced a strict regimen. Each man had to sit in his place, being careful to keep his hands and arms off the boat's gunwales.

Hours later, when it was time for the return trip, many of the men were drunk, white hats pushed to the back of their heads, shoes scuffed, and demeanor much less military than before. Ted Kosmela said of the men of the master-at-arms force, "They were just happy to get everybody back on board." Sometimes even that was difficult. One time, in the early hours of the morning, a boat was returning to the *New Jersey* with a load of drunken midshipmen and sailors. The coxswain misjudged the running of the tide, and when he tried to go around the bow of the ship, he was set down on the anchor chain. The boat rode up the chain and ended up in an almost vertical position before gravity took effect and returned it to the water.

The next stop was England, following a transit marked by rough seas. The men of the *New Jersey* received the red carpet treatment once again, particularly because of the reservoir of goodwill Americans had built up during the war. At Portsmouth

Crowds of Navy men line up to visit Lord Horatio Nelson's flagship *Victory* during the stop at Portsmouth. *Photo by Alexander G. B. Grosvenor © National Geographic Society*

When Britons went on board the *New Jersey* at Portsmouth, they were impressed by the ship's availability of food. They had been living on short rations throughout World War II. *Courtesy Mrs. George Menocal*

midshipmen visited Lord Horatio Nelson's famous flagship *Victory* from the Battle of Trafalgar. Twenty midshipmen were lucky enough to be invited to a garden party thrown by King George VI at Buckingham Palace. Princess Elizabeth had recently become engaged to Prince Philip, and the two of them filtered through the crowd.

One of the future officers described the event:

Our midshipmen's group had long since dissolved, each seeking to get the closest view of the royal party. While elbowing my way into the path of the slowly advancing group, I noticed our captain had caught the eye of an ushering Air Force officer. This unexpected opportunity of meeting the Princess and her fiancé was not to be lost because of the intervening crowd. By a bit of fancy dodging and ducking and numerous apologies, I was soon standing nervously with two other shipmates, waiting to be introduced to Elizabeth and Philip. After the presentation their naturalness and friendly nature quickly put us at ease. Soon we were chatting gaily and even joking as if with an old acquaintance. Philip seemed extremely interested in the Academy, and we swapped a few tales of Dartmouth and Annapolis. . . . Our talk, which lasted for 10 to 12 minutes, was finally interrupted by the fidgeting ushers, who realized that we had more than tripled the usual allotment of time. With words of congratulation and good luck, we moved off into the crowd.

There were also some touching encounters with British commoners. While the *New Jersey* was tied up at the royal dockyard jetty in Portsmouth, a number of local people were invited to come on board to eat a meal in the wardroom. A mother and a boy about five years old were sitting with Commander Dudley Kierulff, the supply officer. Kierulff was startled when the boy pointed to butter and bread on the table near him and asked, "Mum, what is this?"

"Why, that's butter."

"We don't have that at home," he said. "And look—white bread. Ours is dark."

As Kierulff observed, "It sort of wrings your heart. We had excellent bakers aboard and when we left Portsmouth, we left many loaves of 'white' bread ashore at the officers' mess for delivery to the needy."

Lieutenant Commander Neville Kirk, a Naval Academy professor who made the cruise in the *New Jersey*, had a similar experience. When he went by train to visit relatives in Leeds, he took along a substantial box lunch prepared on board ship so he wouldn't have to deprive the British. At noontime during his ride, he broke out his meal and noticed a little girl looking on with wonder at his hefty ham sandwiches and thick slice of dessert cake. He shared with the people in his compartment who were "pathetically thankful" for the food. During his trip, he visited an uncle who put him up for the night and then served him a breakfast of synthetic oatmeal. To Kirk, it tasted like sawdust, so he flushed it down a toilet when his uncle wasn't looking.

On 18 July, after thousands of British citizens had visited the *New Jersey*, Admiral Conolly's flag was hauled down, and Task Force 81 departed. This time the midshipmen and crews of the training vessels were headed south for Guantanamo Bay, Cuba. Within a week, they were soaking up tropical sun and watching hundreds of flying fish skimming along the Gulf Stream. There were daily gunnery drills, and the usual watches to stand, but nightfall brought moments of relaxation as the mids had a chance to watch movies on a screen set up in the open air on the fantail.

The *New Jersey* reached Guantanamo Bay on 1 August. Following that stop in Cuba, the ship set sail for Culebra, a small island near Puerto Rico. The island was raked by the 16-inch and 5-inch guns. It was the first time during the cruise that the big guns had fired, and they blasted old Army tanks ashore with devastating accuracy. Despite the inexperience of his crew, gunnery officer Bill Dobie and his senior petty officers had trained their people well. Alas, such capability was to be short-lived, because the ship's days of active service would soon be over.

As the cruise wound down and the ships of the task force headed home for the United States, night gunnery and submarine warfare were the main themes of the training. At night target sleds towed by tugs were used to sharpen the battleships' gunnery against enemy vessels, in contrast to the land targets they had fired at on Culebra. The *National Geographic* description said, "These night-firing exhibitions were spectacular and, in fact, enjoyable once we got used to the roar of the 16's and the ear-splitting cracks of the secondary battery. Barrages began with the 5's firing star shells to light up the targets. Then, its turrets trained, the main battery let go with 2,700-pound calling cards. These weighty shells are sped by brilliant orange flames flashing 30 feet beyond the muzzles. Instantly, light vanishes, and the ship is left in darkness. As your ears recover, you hear the shells cleaving the distant atmosphere. The sound resembles the swoosh of a jet plane. Long after firing has ceased, you remember the shell's weird moan."

The days and nights at sea came rapidly to an end. On the night of 25 August, the first classman with the lowest class standing (known as the "anchor man") followed tradition by going to the *New Jersey*'s forecastle to knock open the pelican hook with a hammer and send the anchor to the bottom of

Shortly before the *New Jersey*'s departure from Portsmouth, England, in mid-July 1947, members of her crew watch the U.S. passenger liner *America* leave for home. At left is a Mark 37 director for the battleship's 5-inch guns. On top are the Mark 22 radar antenna and the parabolic "orange peel" Mark 22 height finder.

Photo by Alexander G. B. Grosvenor © National Geographic Society

Chesapeake Bay off Annapolis. With the coming of the following dawn, motor launches came out to take the midshipmen ashore, and the *New Jersey* was soon on her way again.

She arrived on 28 August at New York City, where several thousand visitors came on board. Then the ship proceeded to an anchorage in Gravesend Bay and began offloading her ammunition, much of it left from the laborious loading at Bangor, Washington, earlier in the year. Once the ammunition was removed, the *New Jersey* went on 3 September to moor at the Naval Supply Depot in Bayonne, New Jersey, just across the harbor from New York City.

The new lease on life offered by the cruise to Europe had merely delayed the inevitable. Now the inactivation could be put off no longer. It was a result of the very heavy cutting of the national defense budget. Navy manpower was drastically reduced, and that meant there would not be enough bodies to keep the *New Jersey* going even in a reduced status. The *Wisconsin* was also to be decommissioned, and the *Iowa* would follow a year later.

On 3 September 1947, the very day she arrived at Bayonne, the process of taking apart the *New Jersey* began when the large SK-2 radar antenna was removed from her foremast to facilitate her trip two days later to the New York Naval Shipyard at Brooklyn. The radar antenna would not have safely cleared under the Brooklyn Bridge. On 12 September, Rear Admiral McLean, the division commander, shifted his flag from the *Wisconsin* to the *New Jersey* and remained until 27 October.

One afternoon, Admiral McLean's official car pulled up at the ship's forward brow as Machinist's Mate Third Class William Tiernan was leaving the *New Jersey* to go on liberty. When the petty officer saw McLean emerge from the car, he snapped to attention and saluted, whereupon the admiral instructed his driver to take Tiernan to the navy yard gate because a heavy rain was imminent. Remembered Tiernan, "The downpour started, and we approached the Gate with the Admiral's flags still flying. A Marine guard opened the car door and smartly saluted, and out stepped a Third Class Petty Officer. I was rather amused, but the Marine remained impassive."

In the days and weeks at Brooklyn, the process of mothballing the battleship continued, accomplished mainly by the crew, with some technical assistance from shipyard personnel. It was done at a fairly leisurely pace, because the decommissioning date was not to be until the end of the following June. In the interim, dehumidification equipment was installed in the interior of the ship to prevent rust. Plastic cocoons were lowered over the 40-mm antiaircraft guns to protect them from the elements. Exposed equipment was covered over with a framework of tape in crosshatch squares, and then a plastic preservative substance was sprayed over the tape to form a watertight shield. Storerooms were inventoried to make sure spare parts were on hand for possible reactivation. Cosmoline preservative was put into piping to keep moisture from building up. In the wake of World War II, the scientific mothballing of ships had been perfected, and the process was used hundreds of times as the vast wartime fleet shrank to one more suited to the era of Pax Americana. When it was time for the *New Jersey* to join the other mothballed war veterans, the process had been well set down in available publications.

For the crew, inactivation led to a workaday existence, much like any another job, and certainly without the excitement and differing experiences of the summer cruise. To provide some incentive for the chief petty officers, Commander Leverton set up a procedure whereby specific divisions were assigned certain spaces to inactivate in a given amount of time. If they finished before then, the men of the division were given open gangway for liberty ashore.

The new year of 1948 arrived, and in the following weeks there was a brief interruption to the period in the shipyard when the ship steamed out again to Gravesend Bay to pump off her supply of aviation gasoline and to offload the rest of her ammunition.

While the *New Jersey* was making her approach to the assigned spot for dropping the hook, Captain Menocal ordered the anchor party on the forecastle to "let go." Commander Jim Dyer, the ship's first lieutenant, called up by sound-powered telephone to the bridge and said the order was premature, because the ship was still going too fast. Twice more, he was ordered to drop the anchor, and on the third such order, he finally did, ordering the forecastle cleared as he did so. Because the ship still had so much way on, the anchor chain came up out of its storage locker at a much faster rate than it should have and was undulating about three feet off the deck as a result. Fortunately, nothing untoward happened.

Captain Menocal's days in command of the *New Jersey* were rapidly coming to an end. By this time, he had perhaps concluded that he was not going to be selected for rear admiral, and there was certainly no more future for him on board the *New Jersey*. He put in his papers for retirement and then began holding a round of farewell lunches and dinners in his quarters on board ship. On Valentine's Day, Commander Leverton relieved Captain Menocal as the *New Jersey*'s commanding officer.

Following Menocal's departure, the short, slender, good-natured Leverton continued to perform pretty much the same duties he had as exec. A ship captain's job is to operate the ship, and that role was eliminated by the *New Jersey*'s moribund status. About all that was left was internal administration of the battleship, which is what an executive officer does normally. The biggest change was that Leverton no longer had to serve as a buffer between Menocal and the ship's other officers. He no longer had to find a way to remain loyal to the captain on one hand and protect the junior officers on the other. Even years later, Leverton remained loyal to Menocal, saying of him, "He was a nice, lively type, and he was a good ship's captain. . . . He used to get the whole crew out and tell them about smartness and shipkeeping. . . . If you've got a ragged pennant flying, everybody in the Navy can see it and know you've got a ragged ship. . . .

Tugs move the *New Jersey* from the New York Naval Shipyard to Bayonne, New Jersey, on 29 June 1948. *Ted Stone photo courtesy of Howard Serig*

If you take care of the little things, you take care of the big ones at the same time."

As more and more of the battleship—by now riding high in the water with her ammunition removed—was closed up, the crew moved off and into a barracks vessel. The floating accommodation craft was alongside the *New Jersey* until late March when the ship was moved into dry dock for further inactivation, including the sealing up of the underwater openings in the hull. More and more, this once-active dreadnought was becoming an inert hulk. She came out of dry dock in late April, and once more took up position alongside a pier in the shipyard. On 29 June, all her shoreside connections, including electricity and fresh water, were cut loose. The berthing vessel was taken away, and a group of tall-stacked, steam-powered tugboats came alongside to shepherd the lifeless *New Jersey* across the harbor to the state for which she was named. Again, she tied up at Bayonne, now to be her mothball fleet berth.

The fiscal year ended on Wednesday, 30 June 1948, and so also did the first period of commissioned service for BB-62. Just a little more than five years after the ship went into commission, only thirteen

The *New Jersey* is decorated with signal flags during her decommissioning ceremony. *Thomas Kinkaid collection, Naval Historical Center*

The decommissioning ceremony was at the naval supply depot in Bayonne, New Jersey, on 30 June 1948. *Thomas Kinkaid collection, Naval Historical Center*

members of the original crew were still part of ship's company. They had a place in the first row as various speakers honored what might, under some circumstances, have been the *New Jersey*'s final passing from the Navy. After the national ensign was lowered, it was cut into thirteen pieces, recalled Boatswain's Mate Rafael De La Maza. Each of the thirteen plank owners, including De La Maza, received a piece.

In his remarks that day, before reading the decommissioning orders and directing that the flag be hauled down, Commander Leverton said, "I must confess that this occasion is, in many ways, a depressing one. To me it is depressing because I am being instrumental in retiring this wonderful ship from active service. We are indeed fortunate that our country does not need to retain in active service this mighty and proud ship. She has no potential foes worthy of her steel. Lesser ships are able to maintain the inviolability of our shores and sea frontiers."

He need not have been depressed. All too soon, the *New Jersey* would again have "potential foes worthy of her steel."

CHAPTER IV
KOREA, MIDSHIPMEN, AND KOREA AGAIN
September 1950–July 1953

With each passing day she sat idly at Bayonne, New Jersey, the battleship bearing the state's name took on more of the dismal appearance of her surroundings. She was moored alongside the Bayonne Naval Annex, a concrete peninsula jutting into New York harbor. In the midst of an industrial area, the *New Jersey*'s paint faded, and she took on a patina of grime. Fortunately, the effects of time, weather, and pollution were soon reversed.

During the ship's time in the mothball fleet, the world at large kept turning, and war broke out once more. The communist North Koreans launched an invasion of South Korea in late June 1950. An ambitious secretary of defense, Louis Johnson, had gone on a cost-cutting spree to eliminate fat from the nation's budget. In his hacking, though, Johnson went well beyond fat. Thus, by the time war came, the U.S. Navy was down to one active battleship and only a few aircraft carriers in commission.

In the wake of the North Korean attack, the U.S. Navy scrambled to reinforce the Western Pacific. The sole battleship, the USS *Missouri*, was hurriedly pulled from midshipman training and steamed to Korea, where she began shore bombardment in mid-September. Within a few days, the Department of Defense announced the reactivation of a battleship from the reserve fleet. On 26 September 1950, workmen boarded the *New Jersey*. Cranes removed igloos that protected 40-mm gun mounts. Crowbars produced screeching sounds as they pried away a framework of wood from around lifeboats. Seals were removed from around hatch edges and from the recoil mechanisms of 16-inch guns. Covers were

The *New Jersey* is gradually moving toward recommissioning in this shot of the forward turrets, taken 3 October 1950 at Bayonne, New Jersey. All Hands *magazine*

taken from radar antennas and winches. Divers examined the underwater hull to look for covered-up openings. In the engineering spaces, men examined lines and joints. During the weeks that followed, more progress was made, including removal of dehumidification machines.

By October, a new crew was being assembled. The Naval Reserve was called upon, in large measure. In many cases, the recall to active duty was an unwelcome surprise for World War II veterans who had settled into comfortable civilian jobs and begun raising families. Even for those who were single, it was quite a change from the routine.

Seaman Joe Brooks was a Navy storekeeper in the closing days of the previous war. By 1950 he worked for the telephone company in Washington, DC, and drilled in the Naval Reserve. He thought, "They'll never get me." But one night he came home and discovered a registered letter telling him to get his affairs in order and report for processing at the naval station in nearby Anacostia. About ten days later, he saw his name show up on the *New Jersey* list and headed for Bayonne. In Bloomfield, New Jersey, Gunner's Mate First Class Bob Storm received his letter and was on board the battleship about a week later. He had just gotten a good job and moved into a new home, so the transition was abrupt and unsettling. His Navy pay would be a good deal less than the civilian salary that was to be the basis for his monthly mortgage payments. By law, the mortgage couldn't be foreclosed in such circumstances, but he would have to make up the difference once released from active duty. That obligation, said Storm, turned out to be "a bitch on wheels for a while."

Officers soon came as well. Lieutenant (junior grade) Ben Conroy was a regular officer who had been on active duty since his graduation from the Naval Academy in 1947. He quickly grew tired of hearing complaints from the *New Jersey*'s reactivated reserve officers who talked about how much more pay they were making in civilian life. Conroy had been drawing low Navy pay all along, so he felt little sympathy.

Enlisted men David Rupp and Eugene Duncan of York, Pennsylvania, reported to Bayonne after brief stops in the Washington area. Geographic proximity played a large part in the early call-ups. Many of those reporting were from New York, New Jersey, Pennsylvania, Massachusetts, and Ohio. George Hill, a seaman, was recalled from his home in Maryland.

Hill and other men were given bunks in the escort carrier *Mission Bay*, moored forward of the *New Jersey*, until the battleship's berthing compartments were ready. Seaman Rupp remembered that paint flaked off bulkheads and tumbled to the deck when the sealed and dehumidified compartments were opened to the atmosphere. New paint was applied, and the reactivation teams went from space to space

On 3 November 1950, more than three weeks before recommissioning, the galley is already activated and serving meals. *National Archives: 80-G-421955*

to make them livable. In the weeks that followed, the galley was reactivated, and the ship again served meals.

During the mothballing, equipment was cleaned and often given a coat of a gummy preservative known as Cosmoline to seal out moisture. Gunner's Mate Storm had particular difficulty removing the material from hydraulic lines in turret one. He and other men removed it a little at a time by pumping hydraulic fluid into the lines, running equipment, and pumping the fluid out. The insides of the gun barrels had also received preservative coating. Here the solution was to shoot out the Cosmoline when the guns were fired for the first time.

Commander Charles Coley was ordered in from the Naval ROTC unit at Cornell University to become the *New Jersey*'s executive officer. He was the senior man in the prospective crew for several weeks before the commanding officer, Captain David Tyree, reported. In choosing a captain for the first battleship reactivated for Korea, the Bureau of Naval Personnel took into account Tyree's postgraduate education in ordnance, battleship duty in the old *West Virginia*, and service as gunnery officer of the heavy cruiser *Salt Lake City* at the outset of World War II.

A hardy crowd is gathered on the fantail for the frigid recommissioning at Bayonne on 21 November 1950. *NavSource USS New Jersey*

Soon after he reported, Tyree found a welcome source of information in Carl Holden. By 1950 the ship's first skipper was a rear admiral and commander of the nearby New York Naval Base. He was delighted to show Tyree his scrapbooks and tell him about preparing the "Lovely Lady" for the earlier war. Holden, however, declined an invitation to attend the recommissioning ceremony at Bayonne on 21 November, perhaps because he didn't want to upstage the new captain and perhaps because he didn't trust his emotions.

One benefit Holden received by staying away was that of avoiding the windy, bitterly cold weather. Robert Plumb wrote for the *New York Times*, "A gale was blowing across Upper Bay, whipping a white meringue on the moss-green water." The *New Jersey*'s enlisted men stood and shivered on the main deck aft, wearing their white hats and navy blue peacoats, many with their collars turned up. The members of the Marine detachment wore heavy coats also and had chin straps tucked securely to keep hats from blowing away.

The principal speaker was Fleet Admiral William F. Halsey Jr. His five-star personal flag blew stiffly at the main truck during his speech, which was delivered with chattering teeth and cut short because of the cold. Mrs. Charles Edison, clad in a fur coat—as she had been during both the launching and first commissioning—was also among the assembled dignitaries. Both she and her husband made a warm impression on a cold day.

The day after the *New Jersey* went back into commission, she returned to Brooklyn, where she had

Principals are bundled up for the recommissioning ceremony. *Left to right*: Captain David Tyree, commanding officer; Governor Alfred Driscoll of New Jersey; Fleet Admiral William F. Halsey Jr.; and Vice Admiral Oscar Badger. Halsey and Badger used the *New Jersey* as flagship during World War II. *U.S. Navy*

Captain David M. Tyree commanded the *New Jersey* from recommissioning on 21 November 1950 to 17 November 1951.
National Archives: 80-G-1032611 via Naval History and Heritage Command

undergone part of the inactivation process in 1948. Her engineering plant was not yet ready, so she was towed on 22 November to the New York Naval Shipyard by a collection of sixteen tugboats. Within a few hours, she went into dry dock.

In the waning days of the year, as the ship moved closer to being ready for action, her crew did also. Dozens of men went to damage control school at Philadelphia and antiair gunnery school at Dam Neck, Virginia. The *New Jersey* became more and more shipshape as compartments and equipment were declared ready for active service and checked off. A limited amount of new equipment was installed for radio communication, but essentially the mission was to restore the battleship to her 1948 condition.

On 16 January 1951, the *New Jersey* made the short trip back to Bayonne, and she did so under her own power this time. Soon she was off to Norfolk, her new home port. A year earlier, the *Missouri* had run aground in the Hampton Roads area. It took two embarrassing weeks before she was refloated. Shortly before Captain Tyree was to take the *New Jersey* into Norfolk, one of his seniors in the chain of command warned, "Whatever you do, don't run that damn ship aground. The Navy's gotten a black eye already, and you don't want it to happen again." Tyree was cautious in handling the *New Jersey* throughout his command tenure and especially so that first trip.

After two weeks in Norfolk, during which the *New Jersey* took on supplies and ammunition, she headed south for Guantanamo Bay, Cuba, to begin a shakedown period for the crew. The days were long and the work hard as the fleet training group put the men through many drills and practice sessions. The antiaircraft guns were tested, including 5-inch, 40-mm, and 20-mm. Only a few remained of the latter.

On 23 February, for the first time since recommissioning, the *New Jersey* fired her 16-inch guns. When Seaman Joe Brooks, high up in the Spot 1 forward fire control station, had his initial chance to aim a 16-inch barrel, he was understandably nervous. He recalled, "I didn't know whether to fire on the uproll of the ship or the downroll of the ship or when. I think my first one wound up in the water...."

A crane on deck hoists 16-inch projectiles on board the *New Jersey* on 29 January 1951. *Courtesy B. C. Abernathy*

But they didn't get upset; they knew it was all new to us." He was supposed to fire at the peak of the uproll, when the ship was steady for just an instant before beginning to roll the other way.

The main battery fired against a towed sled and conducted shore bombardment against the island of Culebra, not far from Puerto Rico. Other tests were engineering casualty drills, a mock battle problem, and a simulated response to a type of weapon then still relatively new. The signal "Prepare for defense against atomic attack" was passed to the crew on 1 March. The procedure called for men to take cover if a blast occurred and to shield themselves as much as possible for ninety seconds. Once the immediate danger was past, teams from the damage control division would go out with Geiger counters and mark off areas considered contaminated. Men with fire hoses would then wash the contamination off the ship, and those crewmen who were found to be contaminated would go for ten-minute scrubdowns. After the shakedown ended, the *New Jersey* conducted a thirty-two-knot full-power run on the way north.

The battleship arrived at Norfolk on 19 March, and the crew welcomed a period of liberty after the full days of training. Boatswain's Mate Charles Jacobus discovered Norfolk's disadvantage as a liberty spot. He said that there were "too many sailors and not enough women." As a result, Navy enlisted men congregated in a series of bars that lined both sides of a four- or five-block section of Norfolk's East Main Street. Jacobus tried to have a beer in each place. He remembered, "You'd be going back and forth across the street; you just wouldn't make it to the end, because you couldn't stand up at the time."

The time originally planned for the post-shakedown shipyard availability at Norfolk was extended as a result of a casualty in turret one during the shakedown. The powder hoist for the turret's center gun "completely disintegrated," in the words of Gunner's Mate Bob Storm, and fell all the way to the bottom of the barbette. At the shipyard in Portsmouth, Virginia, one section of the turret's roof had to be removed so a new hoist could be installed.

The *New Jersey* came afloat in her dry dock on 6 April and remained there several more days during dock trials before going out for a speed run. After a stay at the naval operating base, the ship left for Panama to relieve her sister ship *Missouri*, due in from

On 16 March 1951 the *New Jersey* makes a thirty-two-knot full-power run from Guantanamo Bay, Cuba, to Norfolk. Catapults for floatplanes have been removed from the fantail, and a helicopter is among the ship's boats. The high speed throws up a "rooster tail" of spray in the ship's wake. *U.S. Naval Institute photo archive*

Korea. As in 1945, the men of the *New Jersey* again had the feeling that the *Missouri* would get the lion's share of the publicity, no matter how well their ship performed.

Seaman David Rupp went all the way to the top of the *New Jersey* for sightseeing on the way through the Panama Canal on 20 April. He had to shield himself as the temperature reached 92°. Down on the main deck, members of the gunnery divisions didn't have the luxury of getting out of the sun. Boatswain's Mate Leo Meyer was supervising the placing of fenders made of manila line down between the ship's sides and the nearby walls of the locks. As the *New Jersey* went into each lock, fenders went over the side one by one, and each man stayed with his fender. As the ship moved farther forward, a continuing string of men put in still more fenders, with some of the earlier ones being pulled out and carried forward when they were no longer needed at the stern.

Going through Gatun Lake in the center of the canal offered the *New Jersey* a rare opportunity for a freshwater washdown without the need to use water from the evaporators. Fire hoses came out, and deck sailors began the process of spraying the topside and each other. Some of the sailors in the crew seized upon the opportunity to inflict some mischief on their Marine brethren. Joe Brooks observed someone saying, "Let's go get the Marines and bring them topside." That was all some men needed to inspire them to go below and drag out a number of the Corps' finest. "They were like sacrificial lambs," said Brooks. "The deck divisions proceeded to wet them down something fierce. So from that point, there was no love between the . . . deck divisions and the Marine detachment."

The *New Jersey* stayed overnight at Balboa on the Pacific side of the Panama Canal Zone, and then the *Missouri* arrived the next morning for turnover briefings. Officers from the *New Jersey* went over to learn from their opposite numbers as much as they could about operations in the Far East. Captain Tyree learned, in talking with the *Missouri*'s Captain George Wright, that the harbor pilot in Sasebo, Japan, was extremely capable and could be relied on to take the ship in and out through a tricky channel beset by currents.

On the last day of April, the *New Jersey* arrived at Pearl Harbor. Some of the crew headed for the local dives. Those with more expensive tastes, such as Seaman Joe Brooks of the FM division, spent their time drinking at the Royal Hawaiian Hotel. The time available for drinking was brief. The *New Jersey* was soon on her way to a fleet operating area near the Hawaiian island of Kahoolawe so the officers and men could do one additional session of training. Both the main battery and antiaircraft battery fired. One of the ship's motor whaleboats put a shore fire control party on the island to spot gunfire, and the ship's helicopter went aloft to provide aerial spotting as well. (By this time, the floatplanes of the 1940s and their accompanying catapults were gone from the fantail. In their place, the battleship now had one Sikorsky HO3S-1 helo.) On 4 May, the ship departed for Japan.

Captain Tyree was widely perceived among the officers and crew as both a gentleman and a gentle man. He reinforced that perception as the *New Jersey*

The "Jersey Cats" perform during the Korean War period.
Courtesy Boatswain's Mate Charles Jacobus

steamed independently on her journey westward. Charles Jacobus was boatswain's mate of the watch one night when the sea was unusually smooth. The bridge was illuminated with dim red lights, and Jacobus was taking it easy when he heard the familiar cry "Captain on the bridge" and sprang to attention. Once Tyree had been briefed on steaming conditions, he sent down to the galley for a fresh pot of coffee and a supply of cups. Then he and the boatswain's mate went from man to man in that night's watch section, Jacobus carrying the coffee and Captain Tyree, the cups. As each man received coffee, he also received a tangible sign that the captain knew of his contribution and cared enough to show appreciation.

On 12 May, the *New Jersey* reached port in the Far East, mooring to a buoy in the harbor of Yokosuka, Japan. The conning officer on the bridge lost sight of the buoy long before the ship came close because of the vessel's long, sloping bow. So Commander Coley, who had previously commanded a destroyer, went to the bow and maneuvered the ship from there, passing orders to the bridge by phone while keeping an eye on the buoy below. Once the ship was in position, a wire went out, and then an anchor chain followed so it could be hooked onto the eighty-pound shackle atop the cylindrical buoy.

The day after arrival, the *New Jersey* embarked the Seventh Fleet commander, Vice Admiral Harold M. Martin, and his staff. On the fifteenth the *New Jersey* was under way in company with the carrier *Philippine Sea*, light cruiser *Manchester*, and three destroyers, heading for a rendezvous with Task Force 77 off the east coast of Korea. The role was to provide antiaircraft protection if needed. The task force, built around *Essex*-class carriers, was the principal striking arm of the Seventh Fleet and was roughly comparable to one of the several task groups that constituted Task Force 38/58 during World War II.

On the evening of 19 May, the *New Jersey* and two escorting destroyers were detached from Task Force 77 and sent to bombard shore installations in North Korea. It was a pattern of operations that

The slender prow of the *New Jersey* is evident in this 12 May 1951 photo taken in Yokosuka, Japan. The anchor chain extending down from the bullnose is to be used for mooring to a buoy. The 20-mm twin mounts on the forecastle are for possible use against floating mines. *All Hands magazine*

Kimono-clad Japanese dancers welcome the *New Jersey* to Yokosuka on 12 May 1951. *National Archives: 80-G-429451*

would be followed throughout the remainder of the war—alternating periods of shore bombardment and steaming with the aircraft carriers. The first firing mission for the 16-inch guns came on the morning of 20 May, when the *New Jersey* commenced bombardment at 5:00 at Kansong. It was a city not far north of the famous thirty-eighth parallel that divided North and South Korea. After firing for an hour and a half, the ship moved north and hit Kosong. The goal in both places was to interdict the movement of enemy supplies from north to south.

After the second mission, the *New Jersey* moved still farther north to an enemy stronghold, Wonsan. It was a center of transportation for the North Koreans. In the evening of 20 May, the ship anchored in Wonsan harbor. At 11:10 p.m., she began firing her 16-inch battery and continued well past midnight. Shortly after 3 a.m., a fire started in one of the 40-mm mounts after burning particles from one of the 16-inch guns ignited oil that had splashed from an open can onto life jackets and canvas ammunition covers. One 40-mm shell exploded in the fire, and several others were thrown over the side. Within minutes, a repair party had extinguished the fire.

About 9:30 a.m. on 21 May, some of the men topside noticed splashes in the water on the port side of the ship. The splashes were walking progressively closer to the *New Jersey*; at 9:32, one of the enemy's guns—probably 4- or 5-inch—found the range. Inside turret one, Gunner's Mate First Class Bob Storm was looking through his periscope when it suddenly went blank. One of the enemy projectiles hit the port side of the top of the turret and broke into pieces. One of the pieces shattered the periscope. Others inflicted superficial damage, and still others landed in the water on the port side. Encased in the turret's heavy armor, Storm didn't hear or feel a thing.

Up on the bridge, Quartermaster Third Class Roff Grimes quickly called down to main control to tell the engineers to be ready to stand by for engine orders. The shrill, urgent voice of an undoubtedly upset boatswain's mate of the watch rang out through the ship on the announcing system: "All hands, man your battle stations! The Reds are firing back at us!" Within seconds, the *New Jersey* was a surging mass of men. Among them were Seaman Robert Osterwind and Seaman J. H. Dezekon. Both were on the port side when an enemy shell exploded near them and sent fragments toward the ship. Pieces of shrapnel ripped through Osterwind's life jacket and pierced the left side of his chest. Another piece went into Dezekon's left arm. Boatswain's Mate Leo Meyer was nearby and directed a man from his division to send word for medical help. Osterwind was already dead by the time he reached the wardroom casualty treatment station. He was the only man ever killed in action on board the *New Jersey*.

Seven minutes after she was hit, the *New Jersey* was firing back at the enemy gun battery. It was in the mouth of a cave on a rocky peninsula named Kalma Gak that jutted into the harbor. Seaman Joe Brooks was in a plotting room on the fourth deck when general quarters sounded. His battle station was in Spot

The heavy rubber "bloomer" is torn away from gun turret one as a result of enemy shore fire at Wonsan, North Korea, on 20 May 1951.
Courtesy Robert J. Storm

1, up on the 010 level. Once inside the pointer's chair for aiming the 16-inch guns, he explained, "I was winded. I was hot, and my face was radiating heat." His gun sight soon fogged up, so he turned on a fan to clear it. As the sight was clearing, the main battery officer, Lieutenant Commander Robert Beadle, told Brooks and the man in the trainer's position next to him where the target was on Kalma Gak. Brooks was able to see gun flashes still coming out of the cave's mouth. The trainer got the guns lined up in bearing, and Brooks cranked hand wheels that set the proper elevation. Firing one projectile at a time, the *New Jersey* was first too short, then off to the right. Then, said Brooks, "The third one went right in the cave, and that has got to be the biggest all-time thrill I have ever had in my life."

Both 16-inch and 5-inch guns were involved in the bombardment. While it was in progress, turret three was trained as close as possible to the superstructure so it could bear on North Korean positions. Boatswain's Mate Meyer recalled that two *New Jersey* enlisted men were wounded by gun blasts from the turret when they were climbing a ladder they shouldn't have. The *New Jersey*'s counter-battery fire silenced the enemy, scoring a direct hit on the gun emplacement and direct hits on two other caves. After about six or seven minutes, the battleship ceased fire and finally got under way shortly after 10 a.m. to leave the harbor. It was the last time the *New Jersey* fired in Wonsan while at anchor.

Throughout the ship, there was an air of disbelief. Seaman George Hill could see a difference in men's faces after the incident, adding that "everybody got a deep concern then that we were in war." Joe Brooks, despite the triumph he felt over scoring a hit on the enemy's gun emplacement, was a troubled young man that night of 21 May. He and many other men had the shakes. As he put it, "Here we are over there for two days, and we've lost one man already. What the heck do we have to look forward to?" He couldn't fall asleep in his bunk, so he went to the ship's post office on the second deck for a chat with the chief postal clerk, a fellow reservist Brooks knew from home. When Brooks arrived, he told the chief, "I'm having one heck of a time. I can't go to sleep."

"I think I've got just the thing," replied the postal clerk. He fetched a bottle of soda and mixed up a drink for Brooks with a miniature bottle of liquor from a supply he had smuggled on board.

"I drank that," remembered Brooks, "and went back to my compartment and slept like a top."

Not everyone slept in berthing compartments; some had bunks in the 16-inch turrets. A number of void spaces had bunks. Sleeping in the turrets gave crewmen a head start in getting equipment turned on and warmed up when general quarters sounded. During the early part of the deployment, the equipment didn't need to be warmed up. The weather off Korea was so chilly that pointer motors, trainer motors, and so forth kept running to provide some warmth for the turret inhabitants, because the regular heaters were not working. Gunner's Mate Bob Storm estimated that probably a dozen men slept in

Gunner's Mate First Class Bob Storm, a reservist recalled to active duty, poses by the breech end of the turret one 16-inch gun he serves.
Courtesy Robert J. Storm

turret one; his bunk was in the right gun room. The turret also contained a small hiding place for a coffee pot and hot plate.

Throughout the rest of May, the ship fired against Yangyang in North Korea. Her big guns dropped a bridge span, destroyed three large ammunition dumps, and annihilated a large number of enemy troops. Near the end of the month, the *New Jersey* headed for Sasebo, Japan, to take on ammunition. It was a frequent port of call for the ship during her two tours off Korea. Handling the heavy 16-inch projectiles and accompanying powder was difficult at best, so it was considered safer for the battleship to take on ammunition in port rather than under way.

Quartermaster Roff Grimes steered the ship in and out of port. He, as did Captain Tyree, developed a great admiration for the Japanese harbor pilot, whom he remembered as having been a high-ranking officer and battleship skipper during World War II. The pilot, who gave his commands to Grimes in English, handled the ship beautifully. The harbor entrance was surrounded by high, craggy rock formations and had a twisting course through a channel swept free of mines. The pilot knew the points of reference on land and used them to indicate which courses to steer and when to turn. Captain Tyree was grateful to be able to trust the pilot who had the conn. Years later, Tyree recalled of the Japanese officer, "He knew just when to put that rudder over and just how close he could come to that bank and so on. It was the most marvelous piece of ship handling I ever saw. . . . I can't remember how many times we went in and out, but every time we did, he was the one that had the conn. I would no more have been able to do that than fly a kite, because he knew that channel, every inch of it."

On board during the next venture to Korea were Admiral Arthur Radford, commander in chief Pacific Fleet, and Vice Admiral C. Turner Joy, commander, U.S. Naval Forces Far East. They were treated to a bombardment of Wonsan. In time, a number of the ship's officers and men adopted a cynical view of the

An HO3S helicopter lands on the fantail to deliver a high-ranking guest. *John Hastings photo*

routine when high-ranking visitors embarked. Lieutenant (junior grade) Ben Conroy was assigned to the ship's combat information center. He recalled, "We could almost lay odds that once we picked up this particular VIP or group of them we'd be back up to Wonsan again."

After Wonsan and sending the visitors off by helo, it was back to steaming with Task Force 77. On 7 June, the *New Jersey* took on provisions at sea from the stores ship *Graffias*. The battleship's wartime complement of some twenty-four hundred—augmented by the officers and enlisted men of the Seventh Fleet staff—had a large collective appetite. Among the many items that came over by highline that day were 990 pounds of spaghetti, 2,016 pounds of sauerkraut, and twenty-nine gallons of Worcestershire sauce.

The *New Jersey* also refueled that day, taking on a supply of oil from the USS *Ashtabula*. It was time for oil king Frank Oliver, a boilerman first class, to take over. His station was the oil shack on the third deck, close to amidships. From there he used a set of phones to direct the disposition of incoming fuel. He told the oiler when to start pumping and when to stop, and he also kept in touch with men throughout the ship to tell them how much fuel should go into

Fresh bread was always popular with the crew. *John Hastings photo*

which storage tanks. The men responded by opening and closing various valves in sequence.

During normal underway steaming operations, Boilerman Oliver had a crew of men who went around the ship each night at midnight to take soundings of the fuel tanks. The practice was to empty each storage tank only down to the waterline so there would still be liquid to absorb the impact if that area of the ship were hit by a torpedo. When the battleship got down to about 65–70 percent of her capacity of two and a half million gallons, it was time to schedule another replenishment and start the whole cycle again.

During June, the *New Jersey* operated for a while under the tactical command of Rear Admiral Arleigh Burke. As commander, Cruiser Division Five, he was embarked in the heavy cruiser *Los Angeles*. Burke, who became Chief of Naval Operations four years later, had a reputation from his World War II destroyer days as an officer with a great deal of zest and dash. When he was transferred to the *New Jersey* by highline for a conference with Vice Admiral Martin, Commander Coley saw him come over and later described the event, "I remember his grinning and kicking his feet during the transfer, as if he was really enjoying the transfer, and I believe he did." Nearly all other dignitaries arrived by helicopter when the *New Jersey* was at sea.

The port of Yokosuka offered a number of pleasures for the *New Jersey*'s crew when they arrived on 15 June after nearly a month of Korean operations. George Hill enjoyed the boat ride from ship to shore, because it gave him a chance to glance back at the graceful, majestic-looking *New Jersey* and to feel a thrill of pride in being part of her crew. On arrival at the naval base, he often went for a boxing workout in the gym, had dinner, and went to the base library afterward. "After that Wonsan harbor," he explained, "I thought I'd get a little closer to God, and I did a lot of Bible-reading." Boatswain's Mate Meyer found solace of a different sort. He and a number of shipmates preferred to ride trains to Yokohama, which they considered cleaner than Yokosuka. They liked Japanese beer and Japanese nightclubs, particularly because the latter had a touch of elegance. In those days before air-conditioning became commonplace, large blocks of ice with flowers frozen into them were put in the middle of the nightclub floor. Fans blew on the ice to distribute its cooling power. For Boatswain's Mate Charles Jacobus, Japan was alluring because of its "accommodating women" who offered "Stateside beds" rather than the customary tatami mats.

Being in port also meant standing quarterdeck watches. Seaman Joe Brooks particularly enjoyed duty with big, handsome, spit-and-polish First Lieutenant Claude Kirk Jr. of the ship's Marine detachment. Kirk, who later served as governor of Florida from 1967 to 1971, had a good-natured side, which probably helped his political career. Brooks, for example, told Kirk that where Brooks came from, Arlington, Virginia, Marine lieutenants were messenger boys in the Pentagon. Kirk didn't take offense

Two of the *New Jersey*'s officers during the 1951 deployment: Lieutenant (junior grade) Ben Conroy, *left*, and Marine First Lieutenant Claude Kirk. Kirk later served as governor of Florida from 1967 to 1971. *Courtesy Benjamin J. Conroy*

and was willing to joke with the enlisted men on watch with him.

When the *New Jersey* was in port, she had two brows or gangways. The forward one was used by the ship's officers and visiting VIPs. The after brow, where the officer of the deck stood watches, was used by the enlisted men for coming and going and was also the place from which the ship's routine was dictated by announcements and bugle calls. Jacobus considered the Marine bugler exceptionally proficient: "just a pleasure to listen to, very good." For the young Jacobus, the end of the day was a moment of quiet satisfaction as he lay in his bunk and thought about the pleasures of being part of a great ship. At 9:55 p.m. he heard the notes of the bugle call "tattoo," a five-minute warning. At 10:00 the bugler sounded the traditional taps, and another day ended.

After the stop in Yokosuka, the *New Jersey* was off to Sasebo and then again to Wonsan. During the course of July, the *New Jersey* continued to alternate between shore bombardment and periods with the carrier task force. A bombardment on 6 July near Kansong was in support of United Nations troops who were conducting a limited push against the enemy. As she did customarily during her Korean War operations, the *New Jersey* flew the United Nations flag in addition to the U.S. national ensign. Captain Tyree considered close support of friendly troops to be the most difficult and satisfying of the ship's achievements during the 1951 deployment. It required greater precision than other types of bombardment because of the danger of injuring friendly forces, but it also offered the opportunity to save the lives of allies close to the enemy.

Lieutenant Kirk was often above in a helo to act as spotter during the fire support missions. Other times it was an Army or Marine spotter in an aircraft, and still other times the firing was spotted and corrections sent by a shore fire control party on the ground. Even before the first round was fired near friendly troops, Captain Tyree insisted that the navigator, combat information center, and plotting room all have the same solutions on the bearing and range of the target from the ship. "If any one of them showed a discrepancy," said Tyree, "we would stop and find out why. And, as a result, as far as I know, we never hurt any of our own people." After the opening ranging shot, the spotters pulled the fall of shot closer and closer to the front lines between friend and foe, the place where the exploding 16-inch projectiles could do the most good.

This sense of caution was typical of Tyree throughout his tour in command. Boatswain's Mate Charles Jacobus recalled that Tyree often had a troubled look on his face while on the bridge. Ensign Bob Watts, who stood junior officer of the deck watches during the deployment, observed that the captain was "pleasant but nervous." He chain-smoked cigarettes, and Watts was fascinated to see that the ash on the captain's cigarette often reached an inch and a half before the skipper knocked it off into one of the butt kits on the bridge. To the junior officer, the skipper didn't appear comfortable enough to enjoy his time in command.

Few of the *New Jersey*'s men had the opportunity to observe Captain Tyree at close range. One who did was executive officer Coley, who offered another facet of the skipper's personality: "Captain Tyree was a soft-spoken individual, not demanding, with a genuine concern for the crew and officers in the order given. He was not an outgoing individual, but after knowing him, you soon discovered his sincere concern and capabilities. He used the public address system to keep the crew informed. In short, he had their welfare at heart and made every effort to see that their needs were met. As a ship handler, he was about average."

On 16 July, while the battleship was operating at high speed with the carriers, a shortage of feedwater developed in the tanks serving boilers seven and eight. In a compounding chain of events, one problem led to another. Because of the low water problem, the boilers were shut off, which stopped the supply of steam to main lubricating pumps in number four engine room. That, in turn, led to the loss of lubricating oil pressure to number three main engine, and the loss of main steam also prevented the immediate stopping of number three propeller shaft. Because the shaft kept turning for two or three minutes without lubricating oil, bearings were wiped in both high- and low-pressure turbines, and other damage was done as well. The shaft was locked as soon as possible, and the *New Jersey* dropped out of formation to work on the problem.

Examination revealed that engineering personnel had not taken corrective action quickly enough when trouble developed and failed to recognize conditions that indicated potential casualties. It could well be that the problem was a consequence of the ship's relative newness back in commission. Training on how to deal with propulsion plant casualties had evidently not been sufficient for those on watch that morning.

Fortunately, the solution was at hand in Yokosuka, where the shipyard workforce was almost completely Japanese. The *New Jersey* didn't need to go into dry dock; she was repaired while moored to a buoy in Yokosuka harbor. The irony of the situation struck Captain Tyree when he went down to observe the work in progress by the Japanese. He explained, "It hadn't been so awfully long before that we were all trying to kill each other." He recalled that a lot of the work accomplished by "swarms of people" was done by hand. "They knew what they were doing, and they did an outstanding job. We weren't there very long."

Afterward the *New Jersey* was again off to Korea. In late August, she fired at enemy troop concentrations and North Korean transportation facilities. Targets hit included Kansong, Sapyong-ni, and Changhang-ni. Major General Edward M. Almond of the Army Tenth Corps praised the *New Jersey* for the devastating effect on enemy morale. The thanks and congratulations received by the ship were typical of many such messages that expressed gratitude for her accurate and effective shooting. To Commander Coley, they were the best sort of reward for the work the ship was doing. Messages from ashore indicated that the *New Jersey* was able to accomplish destruction that aircraft had not been able to.

When the *New Jersey* was out of range of enemy guns, the firing was often carried out at Condition III by whichever of the three sections had the watch. These watches, with only part of the guns manned, sometimes went on both day and night, and the latter caused problems for those trying to sleep. Lieutenant (junior grade) Ben Conroy had a stateroom in the superstructure, with only a bulkhead separating him from a 5-inch gun right outside. It took some time before he was able to sleep through the repeated sharp cracking of the 5-inch guns.

During the first Korean cruise, the *New Jersey* had two chaplains. The Protestant was Commander Chester Hults, and the Catholic was Lieutenant Peter Brewerton. In his capacity as the chaplains' yeoman, thirty-year-old Seaman David Rupp sometimes prepared the answers to incoming letters and sought only the signatures of his bosses. In many cases, this

The library aft of the mess deck provides magazines, books, and a comfortable place to relax while off duty. In this September 1951 photo, the man second from right is Seaman David Rupp, ship's librarian and the chaplain's assistant. *New Jersey State Archives*

was easy, because the same types of letters arrived often. They were frequently about problems back in the States—a missing allotment check or a pregnant woman trying to locate her baby's father. When a member of the family of a *New Jersey* man died, Rupp set the paperwork in motion to arrange for emergency leave. Sometimes, members of the crew used Rupp as a sounding board on what to say to the chaplains. For instance, a Catholic sailor who had just had his first sexual experience with a woman wanted Rupp's advice on whether to confess to the priest.

On Sundays Rupp set up for chapel services, and every morning he arranged the library to serve as chapel for early mass. It was convenient, because Rupp's bunk was in the library. On Friday nights, Rupp turned the library into a mini-synagogue, complete with gefilte fish and matzos, so the supply officer, Commander Herman Strock, could conduct Jewish services. Rupp even accommodated a group of crew members he termed "holy rollers" who had their own church. That group's organ music and accompanying vocal efforts became so loud that their particular brand of religion had to be terminated in the *New Jersey*.

As the ship's librarian, Seaman Rupp kept the library stocked with the latest issues of periodicals, as well as books supplied by the Navy Department. As often as possible, the ship received copies of *Stars & Stripes*, a daily newspaper published in the Far East by the Defense Department. Members of the crew were particularly interested in sports. The paper enabled them to keep track of that year's National League pennant race. Bobby Thomson of the New York Giants won it with a ninth-inning home run at the Polo Grounds. George Hill remembered that the recalled Naval Reservists in the crew were especially eager to get news of progress in peace negotiations with the communists. They wanted the war to end so they could go home. Hill estimated that two-thirds of the men recalled from civilian life were unhappy with their lot and would just as soon have been elsewhere.

Among other diversions during the deployment was the perennial favorite—gambling. In his role as disciplinarian, Commander Coley was concerned about the pernicious effects the pastime could have in the crew. He couldn't prevent the wagering but did try to limit its ill effects. One tactic was to deputize different masters-at-arms just before paydays so that gamblers wouldn't always know whom to be on guard against. Coley recalled that a prime concern was the welfare of the gamblers' families. One report came to him that about $600 had been stolen from a petty officer; he said it was a bonus for reenlisting. He had been planning to send it home to his family, but a shipmate had taken it from him. Coley then checked the ship's post office and discovered that a money order had recently been sold for just about the amount of the missing money. The buyer was hauled up and asserted he had won the money from the newly reenlisted man in a dice game. The loser had invented his story, because he didn't want his family to know what had really happened.

Fire Controlman Joe Brooks remembered that it was standard practice to play records on the fantail during those evenings when movies were shown. One night, while Vice Admiral Martin was embarked, a

Turrets one and three are trained toward the rugged mountains of North Korea as the *New Jersey* patrols her shore bombardment station off the coast during the summer of 1951. *Courtesy T. E. Shireman*

tune played while the crew gathered before the show included the playful lyrics "The admiral's daughter is down by the water; she's out to get your dinghy." Admiral Martin was due to watch the show that night, and an officer from his staff apparently considered the song to be in poor taste. He picked the record off the machine and hurled it over the side. Brooks said word of the officer's action got back to Admiral Martin, and the officer was disciplined for unauthorized destruction of the crew's property.

Sometimes the crew's off-duty time contained a useful measure of training. Boatswain's Mate Charles Jacobus gathered men together after ship's work ended and taught them various aspects of marlinspike seamanship, such as knots and splices. Several became skilled enough to be able to tie eye splices and back splices blindfolded. He taught them how to make pieces of line into quoits, which were then tossed at sawed-off pieces of swab handle in a game similar to horseshoes.

As summer turned to autumn, the *New Jersey* continued her superb shooting. On 5 October, while the ship was operating in the Hungnam-Hamhung area off North Korea, Lieutenant George Tuffanelli, a *New Jersey* helicopter pilot, rescued Lieutenant H. C. Engle Jr., a flier from the carrier *Bonhomme Richard*. Engle had been shot down in a river ten miles south of Wonsan. Thanks to cover provided by spotting planes from Task Force 77, Tuffanelli and his crew were able to brave heavy small arms fire by the enemy and pick up the grateful Engle. The injured pilot was brought to the *New Jersey* for medical treatment.

Two guns of turret two send projectiles on their way during a bombardment of Hungnam, North Korea, on 22 October 1951. *Philadelphia Naval Shipyard*

The demands of plotting targets, firing the guns, and looking out for hostile fire from ashore in such places as Hungnam and Wonsan were such that simply steaming with the carriers seemed easy by comparison. In one of his letters home, Lieutenant (junior grade) Ben Conroy wrote, "When we're in Task Force 77, it's like a vacation." He had earlier received another sort of relief from the normal underway duties when he and Radarman First Class Arthur Fowler went ashore to spend several days with the Army. Their mission was to coordinate gunfire spotting missions between ship and shore and to encode radio messages going to the ship. The men were in an area in North Korea known as the "Iron Triangle" of Pyonggang-Kimhwa-Cheorwon, south of Wonsan. For Conroy, the time ashore provided a revealing glimpse of how the other half lived. Coming from the ship, where alcohol was prohibited, Conroy was surprised to find that the Army officers always seemed to have a good supply of liquor and beer. One Army officer advised Conroy to open a can of beer and leave it by the cot in his tent overnight. When Conroy woke the next morning with a bit of a headache, the warm beer seemed to do the trick in getting rid of it. The young naval officer developed an admiration for aerial spotters when he flew over enemy areas in an Army helicopter. There was great visibility, but virtually no protection against gunfire from the ground. One of his most vivid memories of the time spent living with the Army was that of being close enough to the enemy lines to hear Chinese bugles in the distance.

Toward the end of the deployment, turnover occurred in the *New Jersey*'s crew. Included was the release of some reservists who had been recalled from civilian life. At the same time, new crew members were arriving. One of them was a big bear of a man—6-foot, 6 inches and probably in the neighborhood of 250 pounds. He wasn't assigned any specific duties at first, so he wandered throughout the ship to see what was where. One morning he pulled on a navy blue knitted watch cap and a khaki uniform without insignia and then proceeded down to the engineering spaces. After emerging from the long, long third-deck passageway known as "Broadway," which opens onto the engine rooms and firerooms, the new man found a ladder and climbed up to the mess deck. He got himself a compartmented aluminum tray and pushed it along the serving line, where it was filled with breakfast.

When the big fellow sat down at a mess table and began eating, curious crew members started passing the time of day with him. "Chief, how long you been aboard?" one asked.

"I just got here a couple of days ago," said the fellow in khaki.

"Are you going to stay long?"

"I don't know. You know the Navy. I don't know whether they'll let me stay very long or not."

Fairly soon after that, someone came along and recognized the big man as Captain Francis D. McCorkle, who had reported on board on 1 November to prepare himself to take over command from Captain Tyree. He welcomed a period without duties or responsibilities to explore the ship at his leisure to find out what made her run, what the men were like, and a host of information that would be useful to him as commanding officer. The Tennessee-born McCorkle had enough down-home informality that he enjoyed the opportunity to pretend he was a chief petty officer rather than immediately demanding all the honors and perquisites that went with his rank.

In early November, with McCorkle along for the ride, the *New Jersey* went to bombard such places as Iwon, Tanchon-Songjin, Chongjin, and Kansong. Targets included bridges, tunnels, buildings, railroad yards, rail junctions, bunkers, caves, gun emplacements, and enemy troops. Lieutenant (junior grade) Conroy felt "pretty damn cold" because the ship was operating up near the Siberian border. Splashes and airbursts came near the ship but no hits.

The five-day interdiction mission ended on 6 November. Then the *New Jersey* headed to Task Force

Snow squall off North Korea, December 1951 *Courtesy John Hastings*

Chief Aviation Photographer's Mate Patrick Cady took this spectacular photo while flying over the *New Jersey* as she unleashed a nine-gun salvo at Korea on 20 November 1951. Notice the blast effect on the water. *National Archives: 80-G-435681 in U.S. Naval Institute photo archive*

77 for a short interval and on to Sasebo, Japan. On 13 November, the *New Jersey* used the spotting services of planes from the Australian light carrier *Sydney* while firing on enemy targets in the Changsan Got peninsula. That particular bombardment put the battleship's total of 16-inch rounds fired during the Korean deployment past the three thousand mark. During World War II, she had fired fewer than one thousand of her big projectiles in anger.

The next stop was Yokosuka. Captain McCorkle relieved Captain Tyree as commanding officer on 17 November, and Vice Admiral Martin used the ceremony as an occasion to pass out a fistful of medals and other awards to the men who had made a success of the *New Jersey*'s deployment.

Four days later came the event that the men of the *New Jersey* had been waiting for. The *Wisconsin*, fresh from recommissioning and a midshipman cruise to Europe, arrived to take over as Seventh Fleet flagship. The navigator who brought her into Yokosuka was Lieutenant Commander Elmo R. Zumwalt Jr., future Chief of Naval Operations. On 22 November, a *New Jersey* signalman hauled down Admiral Martin's three-star flag, and its twin went fluttering up on board the *Wisconsin*. Captain McCorkle quipped that the *New Jersey* rose about 15 inches out of the water when the fleet staff transferred to the other battleship. There was no longer a need for officers to fight for seats in the wardroom or enlisted men at movies. Ben Conroy used two terms to describe the departing guests: "staffbastards" and "flagbastards," all run together, just as inhabitants of the Old South used to refer to "Damnyankees."

On 24 November, the ship was under way, and Captain McCorkle poured on the speed going through the submarine nets guarding the entrance to Yokosuka harbor. He had to squeeze the 108-foot beam through a 200-foot gap in the net and decided that the best way was to rush right through so there would be less chance for the current to swing him into the net. The *New Jersey* formed a column with the heavy cruisers *Toledo* and *Helena* and headed for Hawaii. She was able to arrange an overnight liberty for the crew there on 1–2 December, then took on a

Captain Francis D. McCorkle commanded the *New Jersey* from 17 November 1951 to 20 October 1952. Before taking over, he roamed the ship incognito for a few days to get a feel for the crew. *Courtesy Francis D. McCorkle*

Storekeeper Third Class Edward Coletti adds up the prices of ship's store purchases made by Sal Cusumano. *National Archives: 80-G-437222*

load of VIP passengers for the next leg of the voyage, to Long Beach, California.

Included in the group was Colonel Wilburt S. "Bigfoot" Brown, described by executive officer Coley as "one of the most colorful characters in the long history of the Marine Corps." McCorkle decided that Brown, as the senior officer on board, rated Admiral Halsey's old cabin, and the other guests, including the president of the University of Hawaii and other educators, had suitable accommodations elsewhere.

Captain McCorkle and the visitors gravitated to Colonel Brown's quarters, because he was an entertaining storyteller. One of the educators surveyed the opulent surroundings in the flag suite and made a speech directed at Brown and McCorkle, "Oh, you fellows have got it good in the Navy. I got in the wrong business. Just look over there at that mahogany table. Look at this deep rug. All air-conditioned. Now, when you get ashore, you've got PXs, you've got movies, you've got a commissary. This is a wonderful life."

Bigfoot took it all in for a while, then responded, "Doctor, it certainly gives me encouragement to think that a man of your intellectual caliber could so appreciate the fine life we live in the military. Now, I haven't seen my wife in two years; she's back in Mississippi. And yes, there is a movie; there is a commissary; there is a PX in New Orleans, but all that is five hundred miles away from her. I've tried to explain to her all the things you're saying. I just wish you could talk to her; maybe you could persuade her."

The *New Jersey* stopped briefly at Long Beach on 8 December to give part of the crew liberty. The ship arrived back in Norfolk on 20 December to be home in time for Christmas. For some reason, the use of Norfolk as home port continued for all the battleships during the Korean War, even though the ships could have saved about three weeks' travel time on each deployment had they been based at Long Beach, the traditional battleship home port prior to World War II.

Captain Francis McCorkle, seen from the rear at left, and Rear Admiral Ray Thurber, *right*, commander, Battleship Division Two, inspect the ship's Marine detachment on 2 February 1952. *Courtesy Mrs. Richard Donovan*

The Christmas season was a time of great change in the *New Jersey*'s crew. Many of the recalled reservists were going home, and other crew members were transferring to different duty. Captain McCorkle felt he was being robbed of a good deal of talent, especially since the ship was being drawn down to overall numbers that were more in keeping with her peacetime allowance than her wartime complement. On 4 January, Rear Admiral H. Raymond Thurber and his Battleship Division Two staff moved on board. The division had been activated to provide an administrative home for the battleships now that enough of them had been brought out of mothballs to join the *Missouri*.

On 11 February, the *New Jersey* entered the naval shipyard at Portsmouth, Virginia. The two remaining 20-mm gun mounts were removed from the forecastle. The large rounded splinter shield, which had been painted with an outhouse in 1943, was removed from the bow also, replaced by a much smaller shield just above the bullnose. At the top of the ship, the circular, dish-like antenna for the SK-2 air-search radar was removed and replaced by a smaller, rectangular one for the SPS-6.

As the *New Jersey* went through the overhaul, she had a new executive officer. Commander Paul Joachim brought to his capacious shipboard cabin a tankful of fish and the palette of a skilled oil painter. One of the enlisted men was also a quite talented artist. Quartermaster First Class P. H. Stevens executed a drawing of Seaman Robert Osterwind. He presented it to the dead sailor's parents in a solemn ceremony on board ship shortly after the *New Jersey* returned to Norfolk.

In early 1952, the ship's library near the mess deck received a number of new books. Included was

Captain Francis McCorkle, *right*, plays with his dachshund, Heiny, while Rear Admiral Ray Thurber watches from a couch in the ship's flag cabin. *Courtesy Mrs. Richard Donovan*

Ship's Servicemen John Nelencamp, *left*, and Charles Manley contend with a mountain of laundry in January 1952. *National Archives: 80-G-437215*

Herman Wouk's bestselling novel about the World War II Navy, *The Caine Mutiny*, which contained a passage set on board the *New Jersey*. There were some removals from the library shelves as well, because this was the time when Senator Joseph McCarthy of Wisconsin conducted congressional inquisitions in an attempt to expose communists, real and imagined. In that Red-hating atmosphere, the Navy Department apparently decided it should be above reproach, so David Rupp, the ship's librarian, received a visit one day by a woman with the Navy's library service in Washington. She spent two mornings going through the *New Jersey*'s collection, throwing into boxes books that were by communist authors or deemed to be subversive for some other reason. Rupp went along as part of a working party that included a Marine and two sailors as they carried the boxes of books to the Portsmouth city dump. The only proscribed book that stuck in Rupp's mind was a dictionary of slang and unconventional English. Subversiveness was in the mind of the beholder.

The battleship left dry dock on 16 April and then, except for sea trials and the loading of ammunition, spent much of the remainder of April and May alongside a pier at the naval operating base in Norfolk while preparing to steam once again. By early May, the crew was down to 1,920 officers and men, nearly 85 percent of whom were from east of the Mississippi River. The crew comprised 1,754 Navy enlisted, 103 Navy officers, 61 Marine enlisted, and two Marine officers.

The ship headed south to Guantanamo Bay for refresher training. It was a time for new officers of the deck and many other men throughout the huge ship to receive concentrated training in their duties and to experience battle problems and casualty drills. Lieutenant Donald Poe of the battleship division staff appreciated the fact that Admiral Thurber and Captain McCorkle let the junior officers sit in on discussions of professional topics. McCorkle would have preferred to spend the time with his own officers and men and have the staff anywhere other than on board the *New Jersey*. This was especially the case in regard to Admiral Thurber's preferred anchorage near the Guantanamo officers' club. Once, when leaving that anchorage, the captain had to give perhaps as many as one hundred engine-order changes to twist the giant *New Jersey* around and on her way out of the bay. The next time McCorkle was in that spot, he told Admiral Thurber he was going to back the ship out, and he did, because it was much easier.

The big captain with the big ship relished the opportunity to maneuver her, and he was extremely good at it. The same enthusiasm with which he handled the steel monster came through in his approach to the crew. During the short time in which Commander Coley served as McCorkle's exec, he observed that the skipper had a number of qualities one associates with a politician. The captain had a gregarious nature and was eager to "press the flesh" with his shipboard constituents. Just as he had done when he first reported on board, McCorkle liked to wander all over the ship and see things for himself. He learned the names of men, where they were from, and what they did in the overall scheme of things. The approach was similar to that of an old-time political boss; it was also highly effective.

While in Guantanamo, Captain McCorkle donned his white service uniform, complete with white gloves and high, choke collar. Then the entire crew lined up at division parade, and he went up and down the ranks, noting the military appearance of the men. He remarked that shoes here might need more work, and a haircut there had gotten a bit too shaggy. McCorkle was, however, especially impressed when he came to Dick Molinaro—the 6-foot, 5-inch fireman was one of the few crew members he didn't have to look down to see. The skipper was so struck by the appearance and military bearing of the A division sailor that he called him "the best looking man on the ship." Extra liberty back in the States would be the reward for the fireman's efforts while preparing for the inspection.

The Caribbean liberty ports were not so inviting as those the *New Jersey* was to hit during a coming midshipman cruise, so it was a relief for many in the crew to put this phase of training behind them. The ship headed for home after a round of gunnery drills that involved firing the main battery at towed targets and at the island of Culebra. The *New Jersey* reached port at Norfolk on 3 July, just in time to full-dress the ship with signal flags from stem to stern in honor of Independence Day.

The mission for the summer of 1952 differed greatly from the previous venture off the coast of Korea. The training cruise began on 19 July after the ship had taken on 731 midshipmen from the Naval ROTC units of twelve colleges and universities. The *New Jersey* steamed in company with the light cruiser *Roanoke*, oiler *Severn*, and seven destroyers. It was her first trip across the Atlantic since the midshipman cruise of 1947.

During the voyage, Boatswain's Mate Third Class Charles Jacobus enjoyed the idea of having the third class midshipmen working for him as if they were nonrated enlisted men. Jacobus told the half-dozen or so midshipmen assigned to him that they would have two minutes after reveille to get topside to their morning cleaning stations. The first morning, both the midshipmen and ship's company deckhands were slow in meeting his requirement. So he put it to them, "Tomorrow morning, I want you up here before me." The next morning, the midshipmen hurriedly pulled on their dungarees. They raced topside, and there was Jacobus, who had slept up there overnight just to play a trick on them. He didn't have any trouble after that in getting them to their stations promptly.

On 30 July, the *New Jersey* and her consort of destroyers approached the English Channel. All was going routinely down in the combat information center. Then a radarman announced that he was tracking a surface contact headed toward the *New Jersey* at about forty knots. One of the watch officers announced that it had to be an air contact, because no ship could go that fast. After some double-checking, the watch officer finally became convinced that it was a surface ship and relayed the word to the officer of the deck on the bridge. More incredulity surfaced there, until finally the realization came that this must be the new passenger liner *United States*, which had set a transatlantic speed record during her maiden voyage earlier in the month. The radar also showed another large contact, probably a liner, tracking along near the *United States*.

The next concern for the battleship was getting past the two oncoming ships, because there was not much room to maneuver, and the *New Jersey*'s escorting destroyers were fanned out ahead in a bent-line antisubmarine screen. Ensign Bob Watts, the officer of the deck, became increasingly concerned during that evening watch, because a turn in either direction would bring the *New Jersey* and her screen into the path of the oncoming ships. The Battleship Division Two staff had tactical command. Watts kept calling flag plot on his squawkbox to alert the staff, but he received no results. He finally called Captain McCorkle, who came charging out of his sea cabin. Once McCorkle was aware of the problem, he sent out an impromptu signal by voice radio to the destroyers: "All small boys take cover on Onrush." "Onrush" was the *New Jersey*'s voice call sign and thus a quick means of identifying her to the destroyers.

Like chickens following the directions of a mother hen, two of the destroyers scooted out into a line ahead of the battleship and two fell in astern. Thus, the *United States* and the other ship would have to pass only a single column of ships rather than go through the pickets of a naval fence. Out of the night roared the mammoth *United States*, nearly one thousand feet long and lit from stem to stern so that she appeared as a seagoing city. She passed close aboard on one side of the *New Jersey*, and the second liner went past on the other side. The sea giants passed quickly in the darkness, and then they disappeared astern.

Years later, McCorkle reminisced about the event and said he took comfort during the unexpected meeting because he knew that the liners would be

The British passenger liner *Queen Mary* arrives at Cherbourg, France, on 4 August 1952 and prepares to moor astern of the *New Jersey*. *Courtesy Mrs. Richard Donovan*

handled correctly by their officers when speeding past at distances measured in hundreds of yards. Said McCorkle, "You knew damn well those ships were run by professionals that were good." The liner captains could have said the same of him.

The *New Jersey* arrived off Cherbourg, France, on the last day of July and was guided to her berth alongside a dock. Four days later, RMS *Queen Mary* arrived and moored astern of the *New Jersey*. The French were trying to increase the flow of commerce through Cherbourg, and having two such large ships in at the same time was a dramatic way of showing off the port's capability.

Almost as soon as the *New Jersey* arrived, crewmen and Battleship Division Two staff members were off on tours that had been set up through American Express. The Paris tour, for example, had a package price of $36.50 for midshipmen and officers and $30.00 for enlisted men. A special train took the men to Paris, and then they could both go sightseeing on their own or take tours in buses with English-speaking guides. For $6.50 they could take buses from Cherbourg to see the island of Mont Saint-Michel. Naturally, the tour brochure provided by American Express advised the Navy men that they should be sure to protect their funds with travelers' checks.

From Cherbourg, the *New Jersey* went on to Lisbon, Portugal, staying from 11 until 15 August. Lieutenant Poe of Admiral Thurber's staff was particularly impressed by Commander Eugene Fluckey's preparations for the visit. Fluckey was a World War II Medal of Honor recipient as a submarine skipper. By 1952, he was U.S. naval attaché in Portugal, and he pitched in with enthusiasm and thoroughness in setting up parties and other events for the benefit of the midshipmen and the ship's crew. There were more tours through American Express, and people from the battleship also went to Lisbon's Campo Pequeno Arena for a bullfight.

After five days in Portugal, the inevitable postliberty disciplinary cases followed. On some occasions at captain's mast, the skipper sent men to Ship's Serviceman First Class Mike Danese for chastening in the *New Jersey*'s laundry. Danese was a giant of a man, about as tall as McCorkle and a good deal broader amidships. With a cigar in his mouth and tattoos on his forearms, he was not the sort whom a young enlisted man could take lightly. Laundry temperatures as high as 120° were such that men often had to work in their skivvies.

En route from Lisbon to Guantanamo, the *New Jersey* ran into heavy seas. The weather was so bad, remembered Fireman Allan Frank, that, "There were lines going into the head to throw up. The stench of the head, plus the humidity and the heat below decks, was unbearable." There were lifelines through the mess decks to help men keep their balance. Water was on the decks, sucked in through ventilators even when hatches were closed. One of the midshipmen told Frank he was going to get out of the Navy as soon as he could get back to his university's NROTC unit to resign.

Captain Charles L. Melson commanded the *New Jersey* from 20 October 1952 to 24 October 1953. *U.S. Naval Institute photo archive*

Once the seas had calmed somewhat, Midshipman Roger Taylor gloried in the weather. He took pleasure in going up on the slender "long snout" of the bow as the ship plunged into head seas. There, looking out at the turbulent water and then back at the main part of the ship, he had a feeling almost as if he were on the long bowsprit of an old sailing ship. He recalled, "You felt that the vessel following you was a huge juggernaut that the sea couldn't hurt."

When in Guantanamo for the second time in a few months, the *New Jersey* carried out more training maneuvers. Before her return to Norfolk, the *New Jersey* took on board Captain Warner Edsall. He was destined to command the *Missouri*, but she was undergoing overhaul at the Norfolk Naval Shipyard, and he wanted to spend some time getting the feel of a ship of the class. While spending time on the 04-level bridge, Captain Edsall discovered that it was different from that of the *Missouri*, and he preferred the *New Jersey*'s setup. McCorkle explained to the visitor that the 04 level had been altered during the overhaul earlier in the year, and he summoned the navigator, Lieutenant Commander Ray Wilhite, to provide a thorough tour.

After arriving in Norfolk on 4 September, the day Captain Edsall took command of the *Missouri*, the *New Jersey* had a brief stand-down to give married men time with their families. She spent the latter part of September and much of October in training exercises, largely in the lower Chesapeake Bay and in the Virginia Capes operating area of the Atlantic. From 21 September to 4 October, the *New Jersey* played the role of training ship for a group of Naval Reservists.

Much of the *New Jersey*'s training that autumn involved various competitive exercises and drills prescribed by the Navy for determining relative rankings among ships in the category of battle readiness. Some of the mid-October training was for the benefit of Captain Charles L. Melson, who arrived to relieve Captain McCorkle. McCorkle let his successor take the conn to become familiar with the ship. And when she was going in and out of port, several other officers, including operations officer James Darroch and navigator Ray Wilhite, handled the ship so Melson would be reassured that he had capable subordinates. Melson relieved McCorkle on 20 October and had the responsibility on his own shoulders.

On 8 November, Rear Admiral Clark Green relieved Admiral Thurber on board the *New Jersey*, and that same day the ship went under way the first time under Captain Melson's command. Years later, in recording his oral history with the U.S. Naval Institute, Melson said,

> The first time we got under way, everything went along nicely. We started down the channel. The only trouble was the channel didn't seem to be wide enough. It looked to me like we were wider than the channel. These were all first impressions. We went to sea and operated for about a week, came back in, and again that channel didn't look big enough, particularly

when something else was coming down the channel, coming out when you were headed in.... Actually, I guess all these impressions were exaggerated, because it was my first time that it was my sole responsibility. I'd seen the same thing happen under McCorkle, but it didn't impress me the way it did when I was the one that had to give the orders.

Elsewhere in his oral history, Melson said he never developed a great deal of confidence during his tenure as skipper. He had a tough act to follow in the area of ship handling. He got the job done, though not with the same flourish.

In November, while operating in rough weather off the Virginia Capes, Captain Melson was impressed by the *New Jersey*'s ability to plow through the water "as steady as she could be." On one dreary weather occasion, the *New Jersey* was in company with the aircraft carrier *Coral Sea*. Fog set in while the carrier's air group was in the air, so the task group began steaming around at high speed in search of a patch of clear sky through which the planes could be brought back on board. The task group went into relatively shallow water so that the combination of shallowness and speed sucked the *New Jersey*'s stern downward. At one point, observed Melson, "the geyser at the stern was higher than my bridge." The planes were recovered, and the incident ended.

Much of December was spent at anchor in Hampton Roads after the operations ended, and then the *New Jersey* arrived at the naval operating base at Norfolk for the holiday season. An impressive array of Christmas lights decorated the battleship, including each of the big guns outlined with lights. A Christmas tree was on top of turret two and a lighted cross in the superstructure. Chief Machinist Pervy F. Parrish portrayed Santa Claus. He was the hit of a party in the after mess deck on Christmas Eve. It was for the benefit of some seventy children of *New Jersey* crew members. The event began with cartoon movies for the children, and then Parrish arrived to have the kids sit on his lap. First the youngsters received stockings filled with candy and nuts. Then came the big presents, paid for by the ship's welfare and recreation fund. For the boys there were games, trucks, tractors, and fire engines. Girls received dolls, dollhouses, and other toys and games. Ice cream and brownies completed the celebration.

As the new year of 1953 began, Captain Melson settled in as skipper. He was widely viewed by the *New Jersey*'s crew as a very friendly man. He was smoother and less flamboyant than McCorkle. Both men impressed their subordinates as fatherly types to be liked and trusted, but the men still couldn't get too close to the new captain. To Fireman Jacob Brown of the interior communications shop, Melson was "somebody you felt like you could turn to for counsel rather than a game of cards."

On one occasion, Brown had to repair the telephone in Melson's sea cabin. It was right next to the skipper's bunk so that officers of the deck could reach him easily. Brown thought the most convenient way to fix the phone was to lie in the bunk, and he soon was so comfortable that he fell asleep. The next thing he was aware of was Captain Melson shaking him by the shoulder and asking, "Are you done with the repair, son?" Brown was finished and soon on his way out, but the captain wasn't reproachful. In fact, Brown thought the skipper seemed amused by the whole thing.

In mid-January, during a training period off Cuba, the *New Jersey* was put through an operational readiness inspection by Admiral Green, commander, Battleship Division Two. Previously, Admiral Thurber had been unsuccessful in attempts to have the division commander and his staff serve in combat. Instead, the job remained that of working on the East Coast to prepare the battleships for duty overseas. Green's operational readiness inspection (ORI) was, in effect, grading the crew on how well it had learned the lessons imparted during several trips to Guantanamo Bay over the preceding months.

Commander Bill Braybrook, the gunnery officer, was especially eager to show off the results of the thorough job of realigning the gun batteries the previous summer. Braybrook remembered that the ship had saved eighteen target projectiles for the 16-inch guns and built the ORI salvo plan around the eighteen. The ship fired six salvos of three guns apiece, using one gun from each turret per salvo. Shooting at a towed target sled, the *New Jersey* scored eighteen hits, and the 5-inch guns performed beautifully as well.

It was useful to have such tests before sending the ship back to the combat zone because of the high turnover of personnel since the last time she had been to Korea. For men such as Seaman Apprentice Roland Blanchette, new to the ship in November 1952, the repeated training periods were essential as a means of working into the crew and providing practice at his battle station. In fact, he rotated among several stations in a 5-inch mount, including serving as hot shellman and pointer. The hot shellman stood behind the breeches of the mount's two barrels, and he wore a pair of long asbestos gloves. In most cases, the hot brass shell casings were ejected automatically from the mount when the guns fired. However, when the barrels were at high elevations for shooting at aircraft or sleeves, the hot shellman had to reach in, pull out the hot shell case, and toss it out through a scuttle at the rear of the mount.

The *New Jersey* reached the Norfolk Naval Shipyard on 26 January and remained there nearly a month. On 24 February, Admiral Green transferred his flag to the *Iowa*, and the next day the *New Jersey* moved to an anchorage in Hampton Roads to load ammunition. The time in the Norfolk area before heading overseas provided a study in contrasts as far as liberty activity was concerned. Seaman Apprentice Blanchette had saved a couple of hundred dollars to buy a 1950 model Ford. As a result of having wheels and being able to stay with a Norfolk family when he was off duty, he enjoyed some of the advantages of home.

Seaman Apprentice Don Hood, fresh from training at Bainbridge, Maryland, resembled many of his shipmates in frequenting the establishments on East Main Street. He explained, "The sailors were lonely and away from home, so they'd go to a bar and get drunk." Ensign Rodion Cantacuzene, the assistant navigator, concluded that many of the people who ran downtown businesses that catered to Navy men were parasites. Sailors hocked watches and other items to get money, and it was soon gone. Merchants sold a variety of wares, especially jewelry, that put sailors into debt. If a man missed an installment payment, the merchant repossessed the item and started the process again with someone else.

When he was on board ship instead of ashore, Seaman Apprentice Hood was attached to the *New Jersey*'s "dog" division, "dog" being the word for the letter D in the phonetic alphabet then in use. Essentially, the men in that division were the ship's side cleaners, responsible for cleaning and painting the hull from main deck to waterline. Usually they worked from a scaffold hung over the side of the ship, sometimes from floats alongside, and occasionally from boatswain's chairs. During that period in early 1953, the side cleaners painted the ship's hull number 62 on both bow and stern with much larger numerals than used previously. The Navy as a whole was changing to large white numerals shaded in black, so the *New Jersey* followed suit.

The stay in Norfolk was broken up by an enjoyable ship's party. Half the crew went on 20 February and the other half the following night. Beforehand, a crew's committee investigated no fewer than fourteen possible locations before settling upon the spacious Norfolk Municipal Auditorium. The most important considerations were capacity, ability to serve beer and liquor, and willingness to accommodate the entire crew—both Black and White. Bandleader and saxophonist Tex Beneke's group provided the entertainment. The party was quite successful, and even Commander Joachim, the executive officer, got into the swing, taking over the string bass for a while and playing with Beneke's group.

Once crewmen had kissed wives, sweethearts, and other interested parties goodbye, the *New Jersey* got under way from Norfolk at 10:19 a.m. on 5 March. She spent nearly all that month under way without escort, going through the Panama Canal on 9 March, stopping from the seventeenth until the nineteenth at Long Beach, California, and then heading for Pearl Harbor. The visit in Hawaii lasted only two days, because the *New Jersey* had business ahead in the Far East. The stop was long enough for Fireman Jacob Brown of the IC gang to make his first attempt at riding a surfboard; it was a disaster.

The Hawaii stop gave Captain Melson a pleasant opportunity to attend a reception given by Admiral Arthur Radford, commander in chief, Pacific. Melson also spent time with staff officers in Radford's operations section to be briefed on the situation in Korea. On 26 March, the *New Jersey* departed Pearl Harbor with Captain Melson at the conn. After the ship passed the sea buoy, which marked the end of the channel out of the harbor, Commander Joachim came to the bridge to show Melson a radio message that had arrived just before the ship went under way. It reported that Captain Warner Edsall, a Naval Academy classmate of Melson's back in 1927, had just dropped dead on the bridge of the *Missouri* while conning her into Sasebo, Japan. He had suffered a heart attack and died instantly. The executive officer delayed the message, because he didn't want Melson to have to think about his friend's untimely death while in the midst of maneuvering his own ship.

On 5 April, the *New Jersey* arrived in Yokosuka and was met by a U.S. Navy warrant officer who would serve as pilot to conn the battleship into the harbor and bring her alongside the *Missouri*. Quartermaster Second Class Roff Grimes, the sea detail helmsman, was at the wheel as the *New Jersey* followed the pilot's directions while putting her starboard side along the port side of the Seventh Fleet flagship. As he got in close, the pilot cut the *New Jersey*'s speed, and pusher boats gradually eased her over next to the *Missouri*. Then lines went over, and the *Missouri* used her winches to reel in the dreadnought to port. "It's easy to tie up alongside somebody who's tied to a dock," explained Grimes, "but when you've got somebody anchored and your movement moves them, it's a little bit more difficult."

On 6 April, the Seventh Fleet commander, Vice Admiral Joseph J. "Jocko" Clark, shifted his flag to the *New Jersey* to continue the fleet's direction in the effort against Korea. Clark was aggressive, eager, and ready to take matters into his own hands if he wasn't satisfied with the way things were going. In his oral

Sister ships are moored side by side at Yokosuka, Japan, as the *Missouri* prepares to relieve the *New Jersey* as Seventh Fleet flagship at Yokosuka on 6 April 1953. By this time large hull numbers on bow and stern have replaced the smaller ones in use previously. *Courtesy William M. Braybrook*

Seaman Arthur G. Longley, *left*, and Gunner's Mate First Class Henry P. Castles use a power-driven rotating capstan and a piece of line to parbuckle a projectile across one of the flats in the turret two barbette on 9 April 1953. *National Archives: 80-G-K-16313*

history, Melson said, "I'd heard many stories about Jocko Clark. Some of them made me wonder what kind of life I'd live as flag captain, but I say here and now I never dealt with a more pleasant individual. The whole time he was on board the *New Jersey*, he never once corrected me or told me how to do anything. He said, 'Do this or do that,' and that was it. I saw a lot of him, and I found him a very interesting individual and a very competent officer."

Within a few days, the new fleet flagship was off to Sasebo and soon after that joined up with Task Force 77. For the small percentage of *New Jersey* men who had been on board in 1951, there was considerable similarity in the pattern of operations—steaming with the carriers and bombarding the shore. At 5:15 on the morning of 13 April, the *New Jersey* went to general quarters, and at 6:24 her main battery started pumping out shells at targets in the Chongjin area. She steamed on courses parallel to the coast, usually staying eleven to thirteen miles offshore to avoid mined areas. One floating mine was spotted close to the battleship's port side, so the destroyer *Laws* was summoned to sink it with rifle fire. Aircraft from Task Force 77 provided spotting services for the *New Jersey*, and other planes from the carriers alternated their air strikes with the battleship's bombardment in a coordinated attack. Among the targets for the first main battery mission were a telephone headquarters building, a suspected enemy telephone exchange, a weather station, and a warehouse. That day, the *New Jersey* fired 104 rounds of 16-inch high capacity ammunition, all with full powder charges.

As the deployment proceeded and the crew became more comfortable with steaming closer to the shore, many of the missions were fired with reduced powder charges because they produced less wear on the gun barrel liners. On occasion, that would be a problem. Lieutenant Stu Sadler, the fire control officer, was surprised once when the aerial spotter didn't see the fall of shot at all. Sadler then discovered that the man operating the Mark 8 range keeper in the plotting room had set the equipment for reduced charges and thus had the barrels at near maximum elevation for a target about twelve to fourteen miles inland, which was about as far as the reduced charges could propel a projectile. Unfortunately, the turret loaded full service charges, sending the 16-inch projectiles much farther inland than the spotter was prepared for.

Other problems could happen near those 16-inch powder bags, as Seaman Apprentice Don Hood learned in one of the magazines. Safety rules dictated that men remove their shoes, rings, belts, and anything else that might cause a spark. Hood vividly remembered the day when "we were all sitting around there, and it was hot. Nobody's talking. This one sailor pulled out a cigarette lighter, and he was playing with it, clicking the top back and forth, back and forth. Nobody really sensed what he was doing at first, and then, when it hit everybody, we liked to kill him. If he'd struck that cigarette lighter, we'd all been gone."

Despite the occasional foul-up, the *New Jersey* was again doing some spectacular shooting, as she had in 1951. On 15 April, the target was in the Kojo area. Two days later, it was in the area between Hungnam and Songjin. On 20 April, it was back to potent Wonsan, which still had an inexorable attraction for U.S. warships. Ensign Rodion Cantacuzene, the assistant navigator, was on the secondary conning station with the executive officer and two bearing takers—a team prepared to take over if the bridge personnel were disabled. The young officer, who hadn't even bothered to strap on his helmet or tie up his life jacket, noticed that Quartermaster First Class Sam Delvecchio, one of the bearing takers, had a dogging wrench in his pocket. "What's that for?" asked the ensign.

"Just in case somebody gets excited," Delvecchio told him. Cantacuzene was still calm at that point, gazing over at the enemy coast of Korea through his binoculars. The next thing he knew, a shell whizzed overhead, making a sound like a truck. Cantacuzene heard a lot of movement down below on the bridge. Soon Lieutenant Commander Wilhite, who was navigating on the 04 level, noticed that no one was standing up except himself and helmsman Grimes. Captain Melson was in the pilothouse, cautiously giving steering orders and standing up from time to time to look through the narrow viewing slits.

During his 14 April 1953 visit to the Seventh Fleet flagship, President Syngman Rhee of South Korea is flanked by the *New Jersey*'s skipper, Captain Charles Melson, *left*, and the fleet commander, Vice Admiral Jocko Clark. *Courtesy John Hastings*

Shells were soon falling on both sides of the *New Jersey*, and when Cantacuzene had a chance to take stock at one point, he discovered that he had strapped on his protective gear without being conscious he had done so. Seaman Roland Blanchette was in a 5-inch mount on the starboard side. His mount captain, Gunner's Mate Third Class D. E. Klotz, had a hooded opening at the top of the mount so he could see outside. He invited Blanchette up for a look. The seaman saw splashes and asked, "What the hell is that?" When Klotz told him they were enemy projectiles walking their way toward the *New Jersey* Blanchette ducked back down into the mount and concluded that being shot at wasn't so comfortable as being on the delivering end.

During April, the *New Jersey* went briefly to the South Korean port of Pusan, and the crew manned the rail when President and Mrs. Syngman Rhee came for a visit. It was one of several times the flagship paid that honor to the president of the Republic of Korea. May was spent much as April had been, with more and more shore bombardment. By 1953, the likelihood of air attacks on the carriers was deemed much less than it had been in 1951, so the *New Jersey* spent most of her time firing at Korea's east coast. This was especially the case after the communists launched a vigorous offensive in mid-May in an attempt to strengthen their bargaining position during armistice negotiations. In late May, the *New Jersey* went around into the Yellow Sea off Korea's west coast. On 25 May, she bombarded targets near Chinnampo, within range of communist MiGs based in Manchuria, but she was not attacked.

Her firing concentrated on enemy gun emplacements in caves on Amgok Peninsula. The *New Jersey* operated in concert with the U.S. destroyer *Chauncey* and two British ships, the heavy cruiser *Newcastle* and the aircraft carrier *Ocean*. Aerial spotters reported the results of the *New Jersey*'s bombardment as "good to excellent" and a news service reported the bombardment being temporarily interrupted by etiquette. According to the Associated Press, the *New*

In this May 1953 photo, radiomen listen to Morse code on headphones and turn it into messages with typewriters in front of them. *National Archives: 80-G-K-16289*

Jersey was firing away when the two British ships passed near her. She suspended bombardment long enough to render the customary whistles and salutes, "and then, etiquette taken care of, let fly again at the Reds."

Along with the gunnery missions, the *New Jersey* continued to be, as she had been in 1951, a gigantic admiral's barge for the Seventh Fleet commander. There was a small airfield ashore designated K-18, and it was frequently the *New Jersey*'s lot to crank on the steam and get into a position from which Clark could take a helicopter ashore to confer with Army and Air Force commanders. Ensign Cantacuzene thought it would be preferable to have a destroyer deliver the admiral and leave the *New Jersey*'s bombardment uninterrupted. As he bent over a chart one day on the way to K-18, the assistant navigator said to Chief Quartermaster W. M. Brown, "I wonder who the goddamn fool was that thought this up."

Cantacuzene then heard a good deal of scurrying and breath being sucked in, and he heard a voice saying, "I was." He turned slightly, peered under his arm, and all he could see was a blue uniform with one broad gold stripe and two narrow stripes on top.

It was Admiral Clark, who continued, "Young man, why am I goddamn fool?" Cantacuzene proceeded to put forth his theories about the lower fuel consumption rate of a destroyer and the battleship's usefulness in responding to fire missions on the bomb line. Clark then explained the reason for taking the *New Jersey* and added, "Son, do your course and keep your nose clean. And if you get promoted to vice admiral, you can do it your way. But in the meantime, we're going to do it my way." (The admiral's way meant less time away from the action for him.)

Cantacuzene answered with a meek "Yes, sir," and Clark walked out of the charthouse. Just as he was leaving, Captain Melson was coming in, so Clark said, "Charlie, I haven't been called a goddamn fool in fifteen years." The assistant navigator noticed a very shocked look on his captain's face at that moment.

In the midst of the high-level maneuverings, the enlisted men of the *New Jersey* were following

Three crew members stand watch in an engine room, operating the throttle and relaying orders by sound-powered phones to other engine rooms. *Left to right*: Fireman John M. Hernandez, Fireman James Cronin, and Machinist's Mate Fireman Robert E. Plank. *National Archives: 80-G-K-16325*

off-duty routines that often had to do with food. Fireman Allan Frank was once in a working party when his fireroom crew was called upon to help break out provisions from a storeroom. As was so often the case, some of it never made it to the galley storerooms. The boilermen and machinist's mates had discovered that the void spaces above the boilers were crosshatched with a checkerboard pattern of metal slats. These were ideal for storing canned goods and other nonperishable items. If the crew became hungry during a watch, the men broke out their information sheet to see that such and such an item was so many spaces over and so many back.

Seaman Roland Blanchette had grown uncomfortable in the confined spaces of a 5-inch mount, so he requested transfer to the S-1 division, where

Empty brass powder cases litter the ship's deck after firing the ship's 5-inch mounts in the spring of 1953. *National Archives: 80-G-K-16303*

This remarkable photo displays both the advantages and disadvantages of the *New Jersey*'s berthing compartments. We see a good deal of camaraderie but also an obvious lack of privacy. *National Archives: 80-G-K-16306*

Chief petty officers engage in two favorite Navy pastimes, drinking coffee and playing acey-deucey. *National Archives: 80-G-K-16287*

New Jersey signalmen communicate with another ship by flashing light on 18 April 1953. At right an officer uses "big eyes" binoculars. *National Archives: 80-G-K-16323*

he served first as a butcher and then as a baker. The bakers were popular throughout the ship and could trade their wares for head-of-the-line privileges at the ship's store, free ice cream concoctions at the gedunk, and other things. And they freely gave away their pastries and bread. At one point, however, the chief commissaryman decided that too much of a sweet tooth wasn't a good thing for the men of the *New Jersey*, and so he decided to eliminate between-meals snacking. The cutoff produced a good deal of unhappiness in the crew, and so it was up to the E division to rectify matters. The electrician's mates suddenly concluded that it was just the right time of year for the annual inspection of the bakeshop fans, so they were all removed. Naturally, a bakeshop without fans can be uncomfortably warm. Within a day or two, the chief commissaryman surrendered, and the flow of pastries resumed.

In the middle of May, more than 250 *New Jersey* crew members went ashore for a three-day rest and recreation period at Japanese hotels in the Yokosuka area. The highlights were top-quality food, the chance to sleep in real beds instead of crowded berthing compartments, freedom from the demanding shipboard routine, and a variety of forms of recreation. The hotels, which were run by U.S. armed forces special services, offered such things as boating, sailing, fishing, golf, horseback riding, and sightseeing. In addition, each hotel held nightly dances for the men.

The tenth anniversary of the ship's commissioning was observed on 23 May 1953, when Captain Melson pulled out his sword and cut a birthday cake. Ten days later, on 2 June, there was a celebration of a different sort when the *New Jersey* was at Sasebo, along with the British carrier *Ocean*. It was the coronation day in London for Queen Elizabeth II, and her subjects around the world wanted to honor her. A few of the *New Jersey*'s men ashore on liberty that day took exception to the laudatory remarks, and the inevitable row ensued.

A number of the *New Jersey*'s officers were invited to festivities on board the *Ocean*. Cantacuzene

Captain Charles Melson celebrates the tenth anniversary of the ship's commissioning by cutting into a ship-shape cake on 23 May 1953. At left is big Mike Danese, major domo of the ship's laundry. At right is Radioman Third Class W. J. Parmalee. *Charles L. Melson Collection, U.S. Naval Academy Library*

observed afterward, "I have never had such a serious bout of drinking in my life. I prided myself on being a Seventh Fleet sailor, but I'd never seen anything like that in my life. We ended up playing leapfrog, and that was pretty rugged, because you were leaping over people and heading toward a steel bulkhead to see who got there first. I didn't win. I didn't even try to win, because I wasn't about to bang my head. But the Brits did, with gay abandon. We all came back feeling miserable, but I felt we had a great deal to do with Her Majesty being coronated properly."

In mid-June, back in Korean operations, the *New Jersey*, heavy cruiser *St. Paul*, and aircraft carriers worked together to support U.N. efforts to recapture the Anchor Hill area, which the enemy had taken a month earlier. This followed a period of several days earlier in the month when the *New Jersey* had been frustrated in her efforts to provide shore bombardment because of poor visibility. Admiral Clark later recounted in his autobiography, *Carrier Admiral*, that he considered unobserved battleship gunfire to be essentially wasted, and so shooting was curtailed

The crew mans the rail at Inchon, South Korea, on 23 May 1953. The occasion was a visit by South Korea's President Rhee. *Charles L. Melson Collection, U.S. Naval Academy Library*

when it wasn't possible for spotters to get the shells on target.

Early on the morning of 16 June, Lieutenant Henry J. Airey, flying an F4U-5 Corsair night fighter from the USS *Philippine Sea*, was returning to his ship after a close-air-support mission ashore. His engine died, and his radio was already deceased as well, so he decided to land near friendly ships offshore to eliminate the need for a prearranged rendezvous. His Corsair's hydraulic system was in bad shape, and he couldn't get his flaps down, so he made a high-speed ditching near the *New Jersey*. Lieutenant (junior grade) W. H. Williamson was aloft almost instantly in the battleship's helicopter "Jersey Bounce." Along with his crewman, Airman J. L. Spahr, Williamson hoisted Lieutenant Airey into the hovering helicopter at 7:07 a.m. and carried him back to the waiting deck of the *New Jersey*.

As she had in 1951, the *New Jersey* again made Sasebo her most frequent logistic support base. One such replenishment took place on 21 June, when the ship made a dawn arrival. As she approached the Japanese port, Ensign Cantacuzene saw what he had come to expect—fishing boats from horizon to horizon. Initially the ship slowed down so she wouldn't swamp any of them, but then she maintained course and speed, because it was easier for the boats to get out of her way than vice versa. It even seemed to be a game as the boats zipped in close under the bow of the giant gray battleship, being lost from sight for a time to those on the bridge. Then they popped up again on the other side, their skippers hoping they had transferred any evil spirits that might have infested the boats onto the arriving behemoth.

Cantacuzene's boss, navigator Ray Wilhite, enjoyed the Sasebo stops as a rare interlude from the demanding periods off the bomb line when he got little sleep because of the need to spend so much time on the navigation plot when close to shore. Thus, he spent most of his time at Sasebo asleep. On 21 June, the *New Jersey* took on 650 tons of ammunition, 130 tons of fresh provisions, 83,000 gallons of fresh water, and 33 bags of mail. The ship's post office was at the same time sending out an estimated 100,000 letters and 35 bags of parcel post. Shortly before sunset, the *New Jersey* hoisted anchor and again stood out to sea, headed back to Korea.

When the members of the crew weren't busy writing all those letters, many of them took advantage of the hobby shop on the 02 level or worked on projects they'd picked up while in port in the Far East. Another diversion during the war was the system of remote broadcast outlets in messing and berthing compartments throughout the ship. In those days before closed-circuit television, radio station WRNJ had three different channels that Jerseymen could choose from during the hours of station operation. Seaman Apprentice Danny White hosted a "hillbilly hour" that featured both records and his singing, Chief Boilerman D. E. Stuber had a sports show, and Seaman Apprentice Nait McIntire and Seaman Gene Muir played disc jockey and responded to crew requests. The armed forces radio network supplied tapes of popular music, hit radio programs of the time, and sports events. In some cases news and sports programs were beamed live into the ship's berthing compartments.

After a time, remembered navigator Ray Wilhite, Admiral Clark changed the method of operation for the ship around Wonsan, observing that the destroyers that went into the harbor weren't fired at from ashore if the *New Jersey* was around to cover them. The enemy might shoot at the *New Jersey* if she was firing, but there was no fire from ashore if the battleship was present but not shooting. So the ship went to Wonsan more and more to keep the enemy quiet. Then Wilhite persuaded Captain Melson to have the *New Jersey* sit outside the harbor, because she could still strike back at the enemy, and her own vulnerability was reduced. As the navigator said to the captain, "If you're going to go in a room with a stick that's twice as long as the other guy's, you don't close to the length of his to make it a fair fight."

June and July were months during which the *New Jersey* fired more and more rounds at a variety of targets ashore, supporting friendly troops, bombarding enemy facilities, and continuing to try to interdict the flow of supplies and transportation to those waging war against the United Nations forces. A comparison of the pace of the *New Jersey*'s two Korean deployments can be seen in the number of 16-inch projectiles fired. From May to November of 1951, the total was slightly more than three thousand rounds in six months. In 1953, from mid-April to late July, only about three and a half months, the *New Jersey* put out slightly more than four thousand 16-inch rounds. The shooting was especially hectic in late July, recalled fire control officer Stu Sadler; it was a deliberate attempt to put pressure on the negotiations at Panmunjom. Round after round was fired at certain targets until they were reduced to piles of molecules or became gaping holes in the ground.

The Seventh Fleet flagship made things lively right up to the end. Late on the night of 25 July, she sent an armed spotting crew ashore in a motor whaleboat. The boat proceeded to a point just offshore so that the men could detect an approaching train if one came. The idea was to hit the train while it was moving to see if the battleship could knock it off the track. No trains came along, so the boat returned to the ship at 1:22 a.m., and the battleship sent a few 16-inch calling cards ashore to blast a tunnel entrance and adjoining railroad track.

An hour after reveille that same morning, the *New Jersey* arrived off Wonsan and at 8:34 began blasting away at gun emplacements and bunkers. She ceased firing at 12:30 p.m. after putting out 191 rounds of 16-inch. That was the Korea swansong, for at Panmunjom the negotiators finally worked out their differences sufficiently to sign an armistice at 10:01 a.m. on 27 July with Admiral Clark present to witness the ceremony. The war was finally over after thirty-seven months of fighting. The guns of the *New Jersey* had helped to hasten the process of transforming the Korean War from a news story to an entry in history books still to be written.

CHAPTER V
THE IN-BETWEEN YEARS—
PEACETIME AND LIBERTY PORTS
July 1953–August 1957

With the last stroke of a pen on the armistice documents at Panmunjom, the role of the *New Jersey* changed dramatically. She was no longer fighting a war—nor would she for another fifteen years. The ship's routine became different almost immediately, particularly for those who had been standing long hours of watch. A case in point was Lieutenant (junior grade) Bob Watts, an officer of the deck. He felt fatigued almost from the time the ship reached Korea and then "stayed bone-tired until the armistice." Photographer's Mate John Hastings was taken aback when he went topside at night. After months of operating darkened during wartime, the *New Jersey* and other vessels were displaying peacetime lights.

On 27 July 1953, the day of the armistice, the *New Jersey* was back with the carriers of Task Force 77. The next day she arrived at Sasebo, Japan, and her crew spent two days loading ammunition. From 20 to 27 August, the crew enjoyed a port visit in the British crown colony of Hong Kong. Because of her deep draft, the *New Jersey* anchored in outlying Junk Bay rather than in the picturesque inner harbor often seen on postcards. The Seventh Fleet flagship became an object of scorn in local newspapers. Hong Kong residents indicated that their civic pride was wounded.

If the ship wouldn't come to the people, they would go to the ship. Residents of Hong Kong were invited to visit on the afternoon of 26 August if they provided their own transportation. Commander William M. Braybrook was command duty officer and had the dubious distinction of presiding over

Pandemonium engulfed the *New Jersey* when hundreds of Chinese visitors scrambled on board to tour the ship at Hong Kong on 26 August 1953. *Courtesy William Braybrook*

mass confusion. Of the early afternoon, he wrote: "The water was black with boats, hundreds of them! All in a race to be first alongside. You've never seen a 'horde' until you've seen a bunch of [Chinese]! The boats came crashing toward us. When the first few got alongside, the others merely jammed into them and the people started walking toward the accommodation ladder from boat to boat. Soon there were literally hundreds of them jammed together.... In a short time there was a steady stream,... including women and children, streaking up the ladder."

Fortunately, some English-speaking visitors served as interpreters in an effort to keep the situation at least somewhat under control. Lieutenant Stu Sadler, the fire control officer, had the duty that day, and his biggest

A close-up of Chinese boats milling about during visiting day at Hong Kong. *U.S. Naval Institute photo archive*

problem was removing the visitors. The Chinese were determined to leave in the same boats in which they came. It had been a free-for-all as people stampeded on board, but they weren't about to stampede off. Sadler had to match the right group of people at the top of the accommodation ladder with the right boat at the bottom. The problem finally eased as both the number of people on board the ship and the number of waiting boats grew smaller.

Much more pleasant were the experiences of the crew members who toured such exotic sites as Tiger Balm Gardens and availed themselves of the vast array of merchandise for sale. Some merchants even came on board and set up shop on the fantail. To Seaman William Hunt, a radioman striker, it looked like a "farmers' market" with all sorts of trinkets and wearing apparel on sale.

Fireman Jacob Brown was struck by the diversity of cultures. Hong Kong was one of the fabled outposts of the vast British Empire, which in those years still held considerable sway. In contrast were the Chinese of many different social strata. Fireman Allan Frank of B division observed the gulf between squalor and luxury. Years later, he reflected, "I guess when you're a young kid, the splendor and the glory are what stand out. As [I] got older, [I] realized that while I was having a good time . . . there were people probably starving over there that I never even thought about."

After Hong Kong was a trip to the island of Formosa, now known as Taiwan. An important part of the mission of the U.S. Seventh Fleet was to provide support for the island, so the *New Jersey* spent some time off the coast on 28 August. Captain Melson was part of the welcoming committee for what he recalled in his oral history as "the midshipmen of the Nationalist Chinese Naval Academy and what must have been all the officers of their navy. I'd never seen so many. They came out in destroyers alongside and boarded. We made a short trip up and down the coast during the day and fired some guns for their benefit, and then sent them home."

After stops in Japan, the fleet flagship arrived on 15 September at Pusan, a port at the southeast corner of South Korea. The following day, the crew manned the rail for a visit from President and Mrs. Syngman Rhee of the Republic of Korea. The occasion was the presentation by Rhee of the Korean Presidential Unit Citation to the U.S. Seventh Fleet for the period from July 1950 to July 1953. Vice Admiral Clark accepted the award on behalf of the fleet.

A twenty-one-gun salute to South Korea was obligatory. Commander Bill Braybrook, the gunnery officer, had to keep his fingers crossed over the performance of the saluting guns, which dated from the Spanish-American War. Of one such occasion, Braybrook wrote, "During a 21-gun national salute, we fired 22 guns! I was standing on the 01 deck forward. I was counting. After the 22nd round went off, I looked casually toward the flag bridge [and] the navigation bridge to see who was sending for the gun boss. But nobody said a word. Only the gunner and I were counting."

The lack of reaction was probably symptomatic of something Lieutenant Commander Ray Wilhite, the *New Jersey*'s navigator, noticed while serving as majordomo of honors and ceremonies. The ship had been doing so well for so long that excellence was taken for granted. She had had a great deal of practice in her role as fleet flagship, and Wilhite and the Marine detachment skipper, Captain Joe Odenthal, had the ability to adjust as necessary to just about anything as they coordinated side boys, band music, announcements on the public address system, boatswain's pipes, and so forth.

With the winding down of the Far Eastern deployment, the weekly issues of *The Jerseyman* published maps of the Pacific that showed the progress of sister ship *Wisconsin* as she made her way westward to become fleet flagship. The newspaper's issue of 9 October carried a front-page cartoon that showed a grinning *New Jersey* alongside a scowling *Wisconsin*. The former was about to head home, while the latter's period in the Far East was about to start.

The long-awaited day came on 13 October when the *Wisconsin* loomed out of the mist at Yokosuka and gingerly came alongside. Three days later, the *New Jersey* was freed from both the *Wisconsin* and from her mooring buoy in order to steam to Pearl Harbor. The ship was jammed with passengers as she transported men home after the war's end. They had a chilly ride during that late October trip. In addition, it was rough because of heavy seas through which the ship passed. Relief came on the fourth day, off Wake Island.

Before the storm abated, Yeoman Third Class Jack Cruppenink went high in the ship to avoid being hit by flying water. When he looked out upon the angry seas, the escorting destroyers were going up and down so much that he thought of them as submarines—now you see them, now you don't. One member of his division didn't leave his bunk for several days because the *New Jersey*'s rolling made him so nauseous. Cruppenink and other helpful shipmates brought food to their living compartment to keep the unhappy man going.

Fortunately, most *New Jersey* men didn't have such tender stomachs. They found the cruise a pleasant one, especially after the seas flattened, because they had been released from their wartime responsibilities. Fireman Jacob Brown recalled that the trip homeward "was a very jubilant time for us. It was the least military of all the time that I was aboard. There were not as many drills as usual, and the atmosphere was more relaxed."

In this view of the combat information center on 20 September 1953, Radarman Seaman E. E. Lockley marks a position on the transparent vertical plotting board. Radarmen became adept at writing backward so the display could be read correctly by those at the radarscopes. *National Archives: 80-G-629468*

Captain John C. Atkeson commanded the *New Jersey* from 24 October 1953 to 18 March 1955. *Courtesy John C. Atkeson*

The journey from Yokosuka ended when the *New Jersey* arrived at Pearl Harbor on Friday, 23 October. The next day was Captain Melson's last in command of the *New Jersey*. The new skipper, Captain John C. Atkeson, embodied the qualities most valued in a destroyer man. During the World War II Battle of the Komandorski Islands in the Aleutians, Atkeson commanded the destroyer *Bailey*. He took her in close to launch torpedoes against Japanese cruisers, even though they were hitting his ship with heavy projectiles. His courage earned Atkeson the Navy Cross.

The *New Jersey* was under way again on the morning of 26 October. Captain Atkeson practiced ship handling during the trip. He hadn't served in battleships since he was a junior officer. The carpenter shop constructed a large wooden raft for him to use as a reference point for maneuvering the ship in the open ocean. He spent several hours figuring out rudder and engine combinations and becoming comfortable with the *New Jersey*.

As Atkeson was settling into his new duties, the ship had a relatively new executive officer as well. He was Commander Fred Chenault, whom one officer recalled as "a brilliant guy, really a sharp individual. . . . He knew everything that was going on on board ship. He ruled much like Captain Atkeson in that he would tell you what to do and expect you to do it and left you pretty much alone unless things got fouled up." The exec used psychology effectively. Lieutenant Commander Ray Wilhite, the navigator, observed that Chenault was a very intelligent officer who "hid behind the pose of a dumb country boy. . . . He would get the department heads in and make them think of what he wanted done in the first place. And since they thought of it themselves, they thought it was a great idea. When I accused him of it one time, he said, 'Don't tell them.'"

Commander Chenault also impressed Ensign Rodion Cantacuzene, who was himself moving into a new job in the *New Jersey* with the arrival of peace. During the operations off Korea, Cantacuzene had served as assistant navigator under Wilhite. Now he was taking over the third division and turret three because Lieutenant (junior grade) Bob Watts was due to leave shortly. Watts taught him the value of crane room coffee in exercising leadership. The space below the fantail contained the machinery for operating the crane, a holdover from World War II. The boatswain's mates of the third division gathered there each morning to drink coffee and plan their day. Said Watts, "You knew you were accepted by them when they invited you down to have coffee with them."

Cantacuzene carried on the tradition in third division. When the bugler blew reveille, the new division officer was up in short order to enjoy the fresh morning breeze. But more than that, he was topside to drink a cup of coffee with his leading boatswain's mate and to show his men that if they had to get up early, he would get up early as well. He showed his concern in other ways. When the Marine detachment held marching practice on the fantail and made black marks on the deck by grinding in the rubber heels of their boots, Cantacuzene got the Marines to help out with holystoning for a while so they could see how hard it was to clean the marks off. After that, the Marines were much more careful in their stepping.

Besides running the fantail, Cantacuzene had to learn his turret three duties. There he relied on Gunner's Mate First Class Bob Moore. The new division officer termed Moore the "finest gunner's mate I've ever known, and I've known some neat ones." Cantacuzene did have to do some things himself. About once a quarter he got into the breech end of each gun of his turret and lay on a canvas sled with a piece of line attached. Crewmen then pulled him slowly through the length of each barrel so he could use a flashlight to inspect the lands and grooves of the rifling to check for cracks, erosion, and the buildup of copper. In addition to pulling Cantacuzene's whole body on the canvas sled, the men of the turret crew sometimes pulled just his leg by joking that they were going to take a coffee break and leave him stranded for a while partway through a barrel.

With each reveille and daily swabbing of the teak decks, the *New Jersey* moved closer to Long Beach. She arrived on 30 October and stayed only a day. To make up for the months overseas, the crew was broken into various leave parties, the first of which left from California. The next stop was Panama, where the ship went through the canal on 9 November. In the process, because of low water, the ship was stuck for a while and scraped against the walls of a lock.

From there the ship was scheduled to steam to Norfolk, but Captain Atkeson decided to stop first in Cuba, on 11 November. He recalled, "I requested permission to go into Guantanamo so I could clean the sides from rubbing against the side of the canal. I didn't say anything about my brother being down there." The skipper's elder brother, a rear admiral, was commander of the naval base at Guantanamo. When he approached the anchorage at the Cuban base, the new skipper relied too much on his small-ship experience. He wanted to make a snappy approach—barreling in, backing down quickly, and dropping the anchor. He didn't take into account the huge ship's momentum. Irrepressible Quartermaster Second Class Roff Grimes was on the helm as the *New Jersey* sped in. He recalled hollering out to Atkeson, "You better back the damn thing down."

By the time the backing bell did take effect, it came within a whisker of being too late. Lieutenant Stu Sadler was on the bridge, and as he looked over the side, he noticed that the ship was still moving forward at a good clip after the anchor was dropped. The anchor chain acquired considerable momentum and was jumping high off the deck as it sped out. The ship's boatswain ordered the forecastle evacuated, and he climbed over the lifelines, ready to jump some thirty feet down into the bay if he saw red-painted links of chain coming toward the hawsepipe. That would mean the chain was near its end. The end might have ripped loose from its mooring in the chain locker below and possibly killed anyone still up on deck when it whipped overboard at high speed. The reversing of the ship's giant propellers finally arrested her forward motion. When she came at last to a stop, yellow anchor chain was up on deck; the red links were not far behind. On the bridge, recalled Grimes, a chastened Atkeson apologized to those around him and then went off to visit his brother.

The *New Jersey* was under way for Norfolk later the same day after crewmen painted over the canal scrapes. Down in number two fireroom, Fireman Allan Frank, a Naval Reservist, was standing watches, as he had been for the nearly two years since he joined the crew. An important part of Frank's watch routine was to make sure that everything sounded right. He had stood so many watches that his ears told him when something was amiss. Every hour on the hour, he walked around, read gauges, and recorded his findings.

On 14 November, the *New Jersey* brought Frank and his shipmates back to their home port. As usual, Quartermaster Grimes was at the helm on the way in, using his skill to keep the ship out of the mud on the long approach up Thimble Shoal Channel to Norfolk. So little water was under the keel that he had to steer something of a sinuous course, putting the rudder five degrees to the right, then shifting to five degrees left as soon as the rudder took effect. The deep-water part of the channel was narrow, and the mud had a suction effect that might have pulled the hull against the bank if Grimes hadn't used the constant-helming technique.

At long last, the *New Jersey* cleared the channel and moored to pier seven. Rear Admiral Clark Green, commander, Battleship Division Two, welcomed Captain Atkeson to Norfolk. The crew had already welcomed the new skipper. The ship's communication officer was Lieutenant Commander Jim Pringle. He said, "By the time we reached Norfolk on our return from Korea, all hands conceded that Captain Atkeson was the finest officer that they had ever served under.... I have never served in an organization with such outstanding morale."

Part of Captain Atkeson's popularity lay in the swashbuckling spirit he brought from his destroyer days. Then, too, he had a sort of rumpled look and an outwardly gruff manner that gave him the air of a salty sea dog. In truth, the gruffness was mostly a facade. His department heads liked him because he left them alone to do their jobs. If something important needed correcting, he raised hell about it. But he didn't hound people about details. His job was leadership; he left the managerial side to subordinates.

Christmas on board the *New Jersey* at Norfolk in 1953 was much the same as it had been a year earlier. During much of January 1954, the ship was in the Caribbean for training. Embarked was Rear Admiral Green, who had shifted his flag from the *Missouri* two days after the *New Jersey*'s arrival in mid-November. One event of the January cruise was a practice firing of the main battery, held at Culebra Island for the benefit of Green and his boss, Admiral Lynde D. McCormick, commander in chief, Atlantic Fleet. McCormick was an old battleship hand, having commanded the USS *South Dakota* during World War II. On 30 January 1954, shortly after the *New Jersey*'s return to Norfolk, the ship served as the site of the division change of command when Rear Admiral George R. Cooper relieved Green.

On the nights of 8 and 9 February, the crew had its annual ship's party at the Norfolk municipal auditorium. Many of the battleship's men enjoyed Chick Ciccone's dance band and the various floor show acts. In addition to putting away a large buffet spread, the men of the *New Jersey* did a good deal of drinking as well. One officer who attended was Commander Edward "Tex" Winslow, who had relieved Commander Braybrook as gunnery officer. Some thirty years after the event, Winslow called it "truly, a party to end all parties. There are probably some old stiffs still lying around."

The size of the crew had been reduced when the *New Jersey* returned from the Pacific, as it had after the first deployment to Korea in 1951. With the war over, the battleship's manning came back down to its peacetime allowance, and there was a good deal of turnover as well. One cold night in February, Ensign Louis Ivey reported for duty after being commissioned through the Naval ROTC unit at Pennsylvania State University. Ivey was the first Black officer to

In February 1954 Ensign Louis Ivey reported on board as the *New Jersey*'s first Black officer. He later became a noted surgeon.
Courtesy Louis Ivey

serve in the *New Jersey*. He soon received evidence that President Harry Truman's executive order 9981 of July 1948 requiring "equality of treatment and opportunity" in the armed services was not always observed. When Ivey woke after his first night in one of the officer staterooms, he discovered that the man who had been in the room left during the night. Then the roommate reasserted his claim, and Ivey had to move twice before settling into a junior officer bunkroom he remembered as the "ensign locker."

Ivey, who later left active duty and became a successful surgeon, moved cautiously in establishing relationships with his shipmates. He was assigned initially to the boiler division and later became division officer for the *New Jersey*'s radiomen. He decided to concentrate on doing his professional duties well. He gained respect as a naval officer and then established social relationships only as they grew naturally with some of the friendlier junior officers.

Norfolk was still highly segregated in the mid-1950s. Since Ivey wasn't accepted at the places White officers frequented, he had two alternatives. One was to spend time with the small circle of Black naval officers in the area, and the other was to stick largely to the naval base in Norfolk. The latter was federal property and thus integrated by law. Later, when the ship went overseas, conditions were easier, especially in Mediterranean ports, so Ivey was able to go ashore with his shipmates. Even so, he had to pick his friends carefully, because a number of officers let him know, in a variety of ways, that they didn't welcome his presence. One of the ship's doctors told Ivey that his upset stomach was probably the result of having "a tough time adjusting to White man's food." Ivey recalled that he was able to shoot back rejoinders to some digs of that sort. He kept things within bounds so that differences didn't have to be resolved by more senior officers.

The ship's Black enlisted men especially welcomed Ivey, because they viewed his arrival as a tangible manifestation of progress. They sometimes came to him to talk about problems in their workplaces, because they felt more comfortable with him than with their own division officers. Ivey's most frequent contact was with the Black stewards in the wardroom. They made things as easy for him as they could, because they knew that his relationships were not always friendly with his fellow officers.

In February and March, the *New Jersey* was in and out of Norfolk to train her new crew and dozens of visiting Naval Reservists. While at sea, the ship's supply of fresh water—both for boiler feed water and for human use—was produced by evaporators maintained and operated by the A division. Their function, as the name suggests, was to evaporate seawater, draw off the resulting steam, and condense it to make fresh water. The salt was collected in tubes in the evaporators and disposed of.

In late March, the *New Jersey* arrived in Norfolk and began a great deal of preparation to serve as the site of the Atlantic Fleet change of command ceremony on 12 April. Lieutenant Commander Richard

Admiral Robert B. Carney, Chief of Naval Operations, inspects the ship's Marine detachment while on board on 12 April 1954 for the Atlantic Fleet change of command. Carney was Admiral Halsey's Third Fleet chief of staff during World War II. *Courtesy John C. Atkeson*

Brega, who had taken over from Ray Wilhite as navigator, went through a lot of "planning, sweat, and worry" to get the ship ready for all the hoopla. The Atlantic Fleet staff, with headquarters at Norfolk, provided a good deal of guidance on protocol. On the day itself, the battleship's crew mustered on the fantail. Hundreds of guests were on hand as Admiral McCormick turned over the fleet to Admiral Jerauld Wright. The Chief of Naval Operations, Admiral Robert B. Carney, was present. As a rear admiral in 1944–45, Carney lived in the *New Jersey*'s flag country while serving as Admiral Halsey's chief of staff.

A week later, it was back to routine business as the *New Jersey* went under way in company with her sister ship *Iowa* and two destroyers for the 1954 Atlantic Fleet group landing exercise. The ships provided simulated naval gunfire support for an amphibious exercise off Onslow Beach, North Carolina. Then, in mid-May, the *New Jersey* was off to New York City as the featured naval attraction for Armed Forces Day. Captain Atkeson took the ship past the Statue of Liberty and up the Hudson River. She moored at pier eighty-eight on Manhattan's west side.

On Saturday, 15 May, the *New Jersey* sent a contingent of officers and men to march in an Armed Forces Day parade down Fifth Avenue. Marching aside, any *New Jersey* man who didn't have fun that weekend wasn't trying very hard. Seaman Ray Nelson of the seventh division found enjoyment in the music of such New York clubs as Birdland and Basin Street. Storekeeper Second Class Jim Sullivan toured Times Square, watched a couple of movies, and attended a rehearsal for Ed Sullivan's *Toast of the Town*, then the most popular variety show on television. Electronics Technician Third Class William Wright went to the Empire State Building; his only gripe was that the taxi fares were too high. Seaman Jim Donovan of Q division was in Times Square after dark and found it "like a huge carnival with all those lights."

Sunday, 16 May, was a beautiful warm spring day. Tens of thousands of people—both tourists and local residents—were out to enjoy the pleasures of the

The tugboat *Dalzelloch* eases the *New Jersey* into a berth at pier eighty-eight on the west side of Manhattan Island. The ship visited New York City in mid-May 1954 as an attraction during Armed Forces Day. The battleship's crew had enjoyable liberty opportunities in the big city. *Courtesy John C. Atkeson*

season. Seven thousand of them found that pleasure in touring the battleship. Other thousands, including *New Jersey* crewmen, were at city baseball parks. Half the National League teams were on display that day within subway hailing of the *New Jersey*. The New York Giants, featuring Willie Mays, split a doubleheader with the visiting Milwaukee Braves at the Polo Grounds. Over at Ebbets Field in Brooklyn, the Dodgers split a doubleheader against the Cincinnati Redlegs. Yeoman Third Class Jack Cruppenink was delighted by the seats he had for ball games that weekend and liked the price. The generous ballclubs admitted servicemen in uniform free of charge.

The men of the *New Jersey* were understandably reluctant to leave on Monday morning when tugboats backed their ship away from the pier for her trip to Newport, Rhode Island. In Newport, Fireman Charles Huntington of A division had an enjoyable visit with his brother, who was in the crew of the destroyer *Black*. His brother twitted him by casting an eye at the anchored battleship and saying smugly, "I think we can sink it." Then the two of them went off to see the latest in monster movies, *Creature from the Black Lagoon.*

Meanwhile, Captain Atkeson was making his ship available for a baker's dozen of flag officers who were on board for an Atlantic Fleet type commanders' conference. Some thirty years later, Atkeson asked plaintively, "Can you imagine having thirteen admirals aboard at the same time?" There were other guests as well. Clarence Williams and his ten-year-old grandson toured the ship and ate in the recently established first class petty officers' mess. In 1913 and 1914, Williams was in the crew of the coal-burning battleship *New Jersey,* which was commissioned in 1906, decommissioned in 1920, and sunk in 1923 by Army bombing tests conducted by Brigadier General Billy Mitchell.

After Newport, Norfolk, and Annapolis, on 7 June the *New Jersey* was under way to begin the summer midshipman cruise in company with the battleship *Missouri,* heavy cruisers *Macon* and *Des Moines,* escort carrier *Siboney,* the fleet oilers *Nantahala* and *Allagash,* and a covey of destroyers. With the Korean War over and the Seventh Fleet flag having moved from the *Wisconsin* to a heavy cruiser, there was a rarity that June day with all four ships of the *Iowa* class in one place. As commander, Battleship Division Two, Rear Admiral Cooper realized that this was probably the only opportunity for all four ships to operate together. Because of wartime commitments, it had never happened before, and it wasn't likely to take place again, because the impending decommissioning of the *Missouri* had already been announced.

Admiral Cooper took his request for such an event to the *New Jersey*'s former skipper, Captain Melson, who by now was chief of staff to Rear Admiral Ruthven Libby, commander, Battleship Cruiser Force Atlantic Fleet. Libby was designated as task group commander for the upcoming midshipman cruise. Atkeson recalled that Libby was disgruntled by the suggestion but eventually consented. Thus for several hours on that sunny Monday, the four dreadnoughts gathered for formation steaming, photo taking, and maneuvering drills. Midshipman Joe Ballou, just finished with his first year at the Naval Academy, found it an extremely impressive introduction to life at sea. He recalled that the *New Jersey*'s general announcing system made the crew aware of the historic nature of the occasion. When the exercise was over, the *Iowa* and *Wisconsin* steamed back to port, and the *Missouri* and *New Jersey* joined up with the midshipman task group.

With the oiler *Allagash* in company for the slow cruise to Europe, it was convenient for the *New Jersey* to go alongside for a drink. At his customary station at the wheel was Quartermaster Second Class Roff Grimes. He admired Atkeson's approach style, coming alongside the oiler quickly and smartly. He also liked the captain's willingness to change course during replenishment if sea conditions called for it. This could be difficult, because both the oiler and the battleship had to maneuver in tandem while linked by wires and hoses, but it was sometimes necessary in rough seas.

Grimes congratulated himself for his ability to steer the ship within fine tolerances during replenishments, a judgment confirmed by the officers who served with the quartermaster. Grimes preferred a course that put the sea on the starboard bow during replenishment, for the oiler was invariably to starboard. As he stood in the pilothouse, Grimes looked out through the narrow viewing slits in the front, but also frequently out the open side hatch of the armored conning tower. He did so to keep an eye on the movement of water between the battleship and oiler and also the markings shown on the distance line rigged between the ships. While the captain was out on the starboard wing of the bridge sending in orders to the pilothouse, Grimes was relying on what he called an innate gift—a sixth sense, perhaps—that enabled him to anticipate the order the skipper would give him. It took time for the captain's order to be repeated by the phone talker on the wing of the bridge. By the time the order reached Grimes, he was usually already carrying it out. His mind had been working in tandem with the captain's, so the conditions that dictated a steering command on the part of Atkeson had already dictated the same thing to Grimes, and he reacted accordingly.

Grimes particularly admired Atkeson's ship handling skill when it came to the *New Jersey*'s 19 June arrival at the port of Vigo, Spain, on the Atlantic coast, just north of the border with Portugal. The United States and Spain had recently concluded an agreement for use of Spanish bases by U.S. military forces, and the *New Jersey*'s visit was part of the process of implementing the agreement. It was, however, the first time in more than twenty-five years that a U.S. battleship had visited the port, and certainly no previous battleship there had been so large. The Spanish simply weren't prepared. As Grimes remembered, "When we were going into Vigo, they sent out a little one-lunger tug, and it couldn't even have moved one of the hawsers." With the little tug pushing mightily but getting nowhere, said Atkeson, he took the conn for the *New Jersey* and "worried it alongside the dock." He got the ship reasonably close by using the rudders and engines.

She was still too far away for the normal practice of throwing over light heaving lines first and letting people ashore use them to pull in the mooring hawsers. In this case, boats carried the ends of the mooring lines to the dock. They were attached to bollards, and the shipboard ends were put on winches and capstans. Then the ship essentially pulled herself alongside the dock. The entire feat won for Captain Atkeson the admiration of the *New Jersey*'s crew. Several days later, when it was time for the battleship to get under way, the winch trick obviously couldn't be used in reverse. Instead, a towing hawser was delivered to a nearby U.S. destroyer, which pulled the *New Jersey* away from the dock until her own engines could take over.

The bright side of the unusual landing was soon apparent to the crew. The deep water right up to the dock had enabled the *New Jersey* to moor in the middle of town. There was no need to anchor out and endure the long boat rides that were customary in nearly every overseas liberty port the battleship visited. Midshipman Joe Forest was struck by the warmth of the welcome extended by the town of Vigo, saying, "We were berthed alongside the quay and were met by bands and dancing groups and many senoritas, all of whom were well chaperoned."

After the five-day visit to Vigo, the *New Jersey* spent 3 to 10 July in Cherbourg, France. Crew members took tours to London, Paris, and elsewhere. Ensign Lou Ivey and fellow junior officers Ron Esper and Bob Nishman had a rollicking good time on the four-day tour of Paris, which cost only $42.25 for train transportation and for lodging. They bought *Lady Chatterley's Lover* and other books that were still forbidden in the United States. Once in Paris they went from night spot to night spot. Ivey recalled, "It was just amazing the things that we saw that were not customary back home [such as topless dancers], . . . and for that very reason, we couldn't close our eyes. We stayed up all night almost, drank champagne. We had a tremendous time."

Yeoman Second Class Conrad Johnson said of his experience in the French capital: "It was something wonderful, and all men who were given the opportunity should have taken it. The night life in Paris is fabulous. There were many things to see and it was a holiday for photobugs." Johnson was one of several who provided his recollections for the next week's edition of *The Jerseyman*. Each week the staff assembled an issue averaging six pages. About half was devoted to the ship and her crew, and the other half comprised news and features supplied by the Armed Forces Press Service.

The paper printed news on defense developments, a great deal of sports news, cartoons, crossword puzzles, and the inevitable two cheesecake photos of women each week. Many were starlets known only by family and friends. An exception was a Texas beauty named Kathryn Grandstaff, who was pictured in a June 1954 issue of *The Jerseyman*. When she appeared in the paper later in the year, her name had been changed to Kathryn Grant, and still later it was changed to Mrs. Bing Crosby.

When the *New Jersey* reached the Caribbean, she did her only firing of the 16-inch guns during the cruise. High on the 011 level, where he was watching the firing, Midshipman Joe Forest was knocked backward by the enormous concussion. Being assigned to the *New Jersey* that summer was a particular pleasure for Forest. He was the son of the officer, Lieutenant Commander Francis Forest, who was hull superintendent during the *New Jersey*'s construction at Philadelphia. He explained, "It was a great thrill for me to sail in that wonderful ship, especially after having watched her construction and knowing that my father had been instrumental in her design."

Included in the training at Cuba was a landing exercise involving the ship's Marine detachment, commanded by Captain Harry Randall. The Marines from the *New Jersey* and the other ships in the task group were sent ashore in landing craft after climbing down the sides of their ships on nets. Once ashore, remembered Sergeant Sal Triola, the Marines were marched a number of miles into the Cuban jungle, ending up in the wee hours of the morning. Squad leaders such as Triola were given a map and compass and told to lead their men to a tower on the beach around daybreak.

Despite the play-acting elements of it, the operation was realistic enough for Marines who had been on board ship for months and hadn't been able to practice their land-warfare specialties. Reaching the tower, said Triola, was "a glorious occasion." The whole thing was something less than that for Photographer's Mate Third Class John Hastings who went along to take pictures of the operation. It was a far cry from running the ship's darkroom.

On the last day of July, after the Marines had rejoined, the *New Jersey* got under way for home. After offloading her ammunition from 9 to 12 August, she arrived at the Norfolk Naval Shipyard in Portsmouth on Friday the thirteenth to begin her first large-scale overhaul since being recommissioned. This one,

which would include a dry dock period from 23 September to 2 November, was more extensive than the shorter overhaul in the same shipyard in early 1952. For one thing, she received a beefed-up after mast with an SPS-8 height-finding radar antenna on it. In the area of radio communications, teletypes were installed to copy fleet broadcasts, so as not to have to depend on the old CW (continuous wave) Morse code transmissions that had been the norm for so many years. Jim Pringle, who was then the ship's communication officer, recalled it as the "beginning of the end for the old time radioman."

Besides the changes in the *New Jersey*'s electronics setup, there was a renewal in the most basic equipment of all—the big guns. The ship received a new set of liners for her 16-inch gun barrels. The gunnery officer, Commander Tex Winslow, learned from shipyard workers of excessive wear at the breech ends of the rifled barrels. In some cases the insides tended to be elliptical rather than round. Heavy firing had extruded portions of the liners beyond the ends of the barrels, and the extra metal had to be shaved off. The fact that metal was coming from the muzzle ends meant that there was less back down the rest of the barrels. As Winslow put it, "Only the skillful use of the very flexible fire control system compensations allowed good shooting." There is a limit to such flexibility, so in late September all nine gun barrels were lifted out by crane and taken ashore. The old liners were extracted and new ones installed. It was the first regunning of the *New Jersey*'s main battery since her commissioning in 1943.

One task that fell to the gunnery department during the overhaul was preparing for a potentially expanded capability for the 16-inch battery. Projectiles were developed to accommodate atomic warheads. Such weapons were tied up in the great interservice rivalry with the Air Force. Being able to fire atomic projectiles from battleships would give the Navy one more arrow in its quiver. The ones under development were built in prototype form and tested ashore. Lieutenant Commander Ray Peet relieved Commander Winslow as gun boss during the overhaul. Peet, who eventually retired as a vice admiral, recalled that members of the *New Jersey*'s crew were given special weapons clearances and sent to schools to learn about the new projectiles. The former gun boss added, "To my knowledge, we never had one on board, but we had the dummies, and we were all prepared to receive the nuclear projectiles." In the end, they lost out. Fissionable material was still scarce at the time, and gun-type weapons required more of it than did air-dropped bombs. Furthermore, battleships were already on the endangered species list.

Shortly before the beginning of the overhaul, Commander Richard Pratt reported as the *New Jersey*'s new executive officer. To him the five months in the shipyard "seemed like an eternity and it was hard to see such a beautiful ship torn to pieces, as is always the custom in a yard." The new exec quickly formed impressions of Captain Atkeson. Pratt was amused, for instance, by the skipper's practice of driving a "disreputable old jalopy" and parking it in the commanding officer's reserved spot next to the brow.

On 14 December, the *New Jersey* left the shipyard and went out for full-power trials the next day to test the overhaul work in her engineering plant. The newly overhauled battleship built up to thirty-one knots during her trials on 15 December. With the holiday season at the end of 1954, crew members were granted leave. As soon as the second leave party returned, on 3 January 1955, the *New Jersey* left the shipyard at Portsmouth and went out to Hampton Roads to anchor and reload ammunition.

Shortly past noon on Monday, 10 January, the battleship headed to warmer weather at Guantanamo Bay, Cuba. That first night at sea was a rough one. In the early hours of the eleventh, the barometer dropped steadily. The wind kicked up to forty knots and gusted to fifty-five. Photographer's Mate Striker Chuck Hamilton, newly on board after shore duty, suffered mightily. He couldn't have had a much worse beginning. "I thought I was going to die,"

The *New Jersey* is seen from the beach at Guantanamo Bay, Cuba, during post-overhaul shakedown training in early 1955.
Courtesy Charles Hamilton

remembered Hamilton, who then added, "I knew I was going to die."

The shakedown in Cuba was in many respects similar to the training in early 1951 following reactivation. This time, however, the crew contained a nucleus of holdovers, so the crew wasn't starting from scratch. The normal battleship command tour during the 1950s was about one year. In Atkeson's case, the tour lasted about a year and a half so he could provide his experience in leading the rest of the crew through the shakedown.

The *New Jersey* reached Guantanamo Bay on 13 January. Lieutenant Commander Peet, the new gun boss, was pleased with the ship's shooting performance during the shakedown. He gave much of the credit to Lieutenant Commander Joe McGinnis, the assistant gunnery officer, who provided the continuity in that department. McGinnis, recalled Peet, was a former enlisted man who "was outstanding in training gun crews."

The fleet training group in Guantanamo imposed all sorts of casualty control drills and battle problems to improve the crew's ability to react in emergencies. Lieutenant Commander Jim Pringle devised a means of outwitting the training team. The *New Jersey* had received some walkie-talkies, and by chance Pringle discovered that they could be used to communicate between the bridge and after steering as long as the antennas were fairly close to the sound-powered telephone system. Thus, when the fleet training group people imposed simulated casualties at the same time to both the steering system and the sound-powered phones, the walkie-talkies were whipped out and steering orders sent by that means. As Pringle explained, "It worked beautifully but got a 'low horrible' from [the fleet training group] because it wasn't according to the book."

On Saturday, 12 February, the *New Jersey* ended her training period for the week with main battery shore bombardment qualification at the island of Culebra. Next was a visit to the port of Ciudad Trujillo in the Dominican Republic. The purpose was to give the crew some liberty and to demonstrate support for a U.S. ally in the Caribbean. The crew went on liberty on Sunday, and the next day the ship hosted an official visit from President Hector B. Trujillo and from his brother, the head of state, Generalissimo Rafael Leonidas Trujillo. The president arrived in civilian clothes, while the general was wearing a uniform heavily encrusted with gold.

Pleased with the visit, General Trujillo invited the *New Jersey*'s officers to a banquet ashore. The officers scrambled to get into their dress whites and catch buses to the large gymnasium where the fete was held. No drinking was permitted before Trujillo arrived. Finally the skipper and dictator showed up, and the more junior officers quenched their thirsts after waiting an hour and a half. Commander Joe Parsons, the operations officer, was struck by the fact that during the meal the general had an official food taster to check things before he would partake himself. When it got down to the eating, wrote Jim Pringle, "I don't recall what was served but I do recall hearing the amazed gasps of our officer hosts when the Generalissimo clapped the Captain on the back and roared with laughter and the Captain returned the clap on the back with equal gusto. It was a fine party but the next morning was quite painful and there was no loud talking in the wardroom."

A new member of the *New Jersey*'s wardroom who had a special degree of rapport with Captain Atkeson was Ensign Ted Walker, a supply officer. His father was a contemporary and friend of the skipper. One of Ensign Walker's chores was to deliver the captain's pay, either on the bridge or in his cabin. Atkeson once asked Walker how things were going, and the young supply officer began ranting about his problems. The captain replied, "Now, Ted, I want you to understand. You only have two or three really good fights in your lifetime. Save it for something that's important. The Navy's been going to hell for almost two hundred years, but it's not there yet. And you probably are not going to make it go any faster or slower."

In late February, the *New Jersey* returned to Norfolk. On 1 March, a new flag officer reported, Rear Admiral William B. Ammon. He had just relieved Admiral Cooper as commander, Battleship Division Two, on 28 February. The stay was a short one, lasting only until 18 March, when Ammon shifted his flag to the *Wisconsin*. The same date marked the end of Captain Atkeson's tenure. It rained steadily, so the change of command ceremony was held in the ship's wardroom. The rain did stop by the time Captain Atkeson was ready to depart. Instead of the enlisted men who normally serve as side boys on such occasions, this time the double row of men at the end of the brow was composed of the battleship's department heads and assistant department heads. Captain Atkeson went down the row shaking hands with the officers who had served under him. When the time came at last for Atkeson to go, remembered Jim Pringle, "There wasn't a dry eye in the whole line-up when he was piped over the side."

Captain Edward J. O'Donnell, the new skipper, reported from a tour of duty as assistant superintendent of the Naval Gun Factory in Washington, DC, where the *New Jersey*'s guns had been manufactured more than ten years before. Though the turnover

Captain Edward J. O'Donnell commanded the *New Jersey* from 18 March 1955 to 31 May 1956. *U.S. Naval Institute photo archive*

period with Atkeson was brief, O'Donnell knew that the previous skipper had left things in great shape for him. The *New Jersey* was in fine material condition as a result of the recent overhaul, and the crew was in a good state of training because of the shakedown at Guantanamo. With those concerns taken care of, remembered O'Donnell, all he had to do was run the ship, and he had a talented group of enlisted men and officers to accomplish that.

The change of command was on a Friday, and the new skipper was due to get his feet wet in a hurry. Early the next Monday morning, 21 March, the *New Jersey* was under way for a battle problem that included her sister ship *Wisconsin*. Captain O'Donnell's new command returned to Hampton Roads on 28 March. Since the ship was anchored out, crew members had a boat ride of some forty minutes to the fleet landing. Captain O'Donnell took his gig when making the trip, and as soon as he arrived he stepped out and went off to conduct some business. There to meet the boat were the wives of two *New Jersey* officers who were in the duty section, Lieutenant Commander Jim Pringle and Ensign Ted Walker.

The women were going to ride out to join their husbands for dinner, so when they saw a *New Jersey* boat arrive and a tall gentleman in civilian clothes step out, they didn't give it much thought. They jumped in the boat and ordered the coxswain to take them to the ship. Since Captain O'Donnell was so new, the wives didn't recognize him, and the gig's coxswain was apparently too awed by their tone of voice to tell them that he was supposed to wait at the landing for the captain. When the gig pulled up alongside the *New Jersey*, Lieutenant Commander Pringle, as command duty officer, was there to meet it and was aghast to see that the captain wasn't in the boat and his own wife was. He had time to contemplate the possible penalties for hijacking a captain's gig. Back ashore, Captain O'Donnell had to cool his heels until the gig returned for him. He understood the situation when it was explained, and the two officers involved got off with no more than a case of temporary anxiety.

In early April the ship went to Mayport, Florida, for a port visit and open house at Easter weekend. When the *New Jersey* arrived on 8 April, a Florida congressman was due for a visit. Dick Pratt, the exec, had been recently promoted to captain. He was keeping an eye on the pier as the brow was being put in place so that he could spot the arrival of the distinguished visitor. Instead, he saw an attractive, scantily clad woman who was either a stripper or prostitute and was doing a bit of advertising for the crew. Pratt rushed down the brow to tell her to get out of sight before the congressman and other guests began arriving. The sight of the exec rushing frantically to reach the woman created an interesting scene for men all over the ship.

A local organization in Mayport arranged for unmarried *New Jersey* officers to have a pool of women to date during the weekend's social affairs. All the women were White, but the person who organized the gathering approached Ensign Lou Ivey and said, "We knew you would be coming. If you'd like a date, we have made arrangements to call someone, and she will come and meet you. But we didn't want to be so presumptuous as to have one standing here for you." As it turned out, remembered Ivey, the woman standing by in the wings was "very, very attractive, very elegant, very super." That, however, was the only time in his *New Jersey* experiences any organization made such a special effort for him. Everywhere else the ship went, he was on his own.

On Monday, 11 April, the *New Jersey* got under way. Two days later, Rear Admiral Clarence Ekstrom, commander, Carrier Division Six, and his staff were ferried by helicopter from the carrier *Ticonderoga* to the *New Jersey*. He remained for two days of operations, including a spectacular firepower demonstration for the benefit of VIPs on board the carrier. Ekstrom wanted the *New Jersey* to put a salvo of projectiles just aft of the carrier. Captain O'Donnell told him, "I'm game if you're game." Gunnery officer Peet relished the challenge. It was something he enjoyed working on with the skipper, because both were ordnance specialists. Peet knew that if the 16-inch barrels were pointed at the carrier at the time of firing, there was no danger of hitting her, because the ships were on parallel courses. The speed of the carrier and the time of flight would cause the projectiles to drift astern. The carrier was nearly over the horizon when the *New Jersey* fired, and the nine projectiles landed in a tight pattern in her wake. It was a "very impressive" demonstration, remembered O'Donnell.

In the spring, with another midshipman cruise coming up, crew members from the New York area wanted to head for home while they had the chance. The ship chartered buses for them. William Hunt, who was a seaman in the communications division, recalled that men going on the chartered buses were given early liberty on Fridays as an incentive to keep them from driving and facing the possibility of being involved in wrecks or coming back late for some other reason.

One man who frequently took advantage of the bus rides was Seaman Ben Mehling. He spent weekends seeing his family and friends in New York. Then he and the other men from the ship gathered at the port authority bus terminal in midtown Manhattan on Sunday evening for the ride that would get them back to the ship in time for quarters on Monday morning. The men brought beer, sausages, olives, and other items to eat and drink. They all shared what they had brought. Once the meal was out of the way and the bus had moved south a number of miles, said Mehling, "The lights would go out, the jumpers would come off, and everybody would go to sleep. They'd be sleeping on the floor and they'd also be sleeping, believe it or not, on the baggage racks."

In contrast with the streetwise New Yorkers, other crew members were from the interior of the United States. One was Wayne Amend from Wisconsin, who had joined the *New Jersey* back in May 1952, when he was eighteen years old. As did many others while on board the ship, Amend evolved from a boy to a man. As time passed, Amend gained experience and confidence. In 1953 he was advanced to interior communications electrician third class. As a petty officer he had enjoyed the pleasure of overnight liberties in Japan rather than the back-by-midnight "Cinderella liberties" that were the lot of the nonrated men in the crew. In 1954, Amend went still another rung up the ladder, to petty officer second class. Now he found that he was one of those individuals to whom newcomers were looking for guidance, and, yes, for those sea stories that are an inextricable part of the baggage that a sailorman carries with him.

On 31 May, the *New Jersey* arrived at Annapolis for another training cruise to Europe. Now that the Korean War was over, the battleships settled into a regular routine of training the future officers. Because the *Iowa*-class ships no longer had either their wartime crews or their wartime missions, they were well suited to train some seven hundred midshipmen apiece each year.

On the evening of 18 June, the crew settled in for a boxing and wrestling smoker, with the smokes donated by the welfare and recreation fund. Ensign Ted Walker got final proof of just how pungent Captain Atkeson's cigars were. Walker said, "If they tasted half as bad as they smelled, they were just terrible." Once Atkeson left, the market for his brand evaporated. The ones he didn't take with him were marked down in the ship's store to a nickel apiece and then a penny, but no one bought them. The last straw came when the supply department took boxes of Atkeson's brand out to the fantail and tried to give the cigars away—still no takers.

The first stop on the liberty schedule was Valencia, Spain, which the *New Jersey* visited from 20 to 27 June. Before being turned loose on the Spanish populace, the men received a generous number of lectures on the importance of protecting themselves against venereal disease. Some houses of prostitution were okay, but others were declared off-limits. It was up to the shore patrol to enforce the prohibition. Photographer's Mate Third Class Chuck Hamilton did not welcome shore patrol duty. It was relatively easy to go up and down streets and warn men against going into certain places, but he also had to go inside at times and interrupt sailors and midshipmen in their encounters with the women. As Hamilton said, "You've got to get these guys out of the rooms, and that's not the easiest thing to do."

Because the Spanish organize their days and nights in different fashion from Americans, the *New Jersey* had to adjust her daily shipboard routine to accommodate local customs. What with dinner often not beginning until late in the evening—by American standards, that is—Captain Pratt put taps an hour later than usual and let the men of the battleship wait until 7 a.m. before hearing the first strains of reveille.

The *New Jersey* arrived at Weymouth, England, on the morning of 4 July, and at noon that day the ship fired a twenty-one-gun salute to honor Independence Day. The British were good sports; HMS

A midshipman first class samples chow cooked in a huge vat during the cruise. *Courtesy Charles Hamilton*

Maidstone, a nearby submarine tender, answered with a twenty-one-gun salute. The people of Weymouth were extremely hospitable to the visiting Americans. Dances were held on two evenings for U.S. enlisted men, and the local people frequently invited the Americans into their homes after meeting them during chance encounters in town.

One reserve officer who made the cruise was Commander Neville Kirk, a Naval Academy history professor who had also been along on the *New Jersey*'s 1947 midshipman cruise to Europe. This time Kirk observed that the lusty morning appetites of the midshipmen seemed best satisfied by the big breakfasts available in British hotels. They filled up on such things as finnan haddie, sausages, bacon and eggs, fried tomatoes, and kippered herring. All that was far from the continental breakfast of rolls and juice they might have had elsewhere. It was an even farther cry from the disturbing food shortages Kirk had observed when he and the *New Jersey* visited Britain in 1947.

After the visit ended on 11 July, the *New Jersey* and other ships were once again under way, this time for Guantanamo—the traditional wrap-up port for the midshipman cruises before returning to the States. Commander Kirk experienced a challenge one day when he tried to present a lecture to a group of midshipmen on the fantail. Things were going along fairly well until the ship picked up speed, which had two unfortunate side effects. The relative wind increased dramatically, and so did the vibrations of the propellers. Kirk, who was known for his captivating classroom manner in Annapolis, was essentially a contortionist during this lecture. He tried simultaneously to keep the microphone and lectern from bouncing all over the place, to prevent his notes from being blown over the side by the wind, and to shout to be heard above the noise of the wind and vibration.

In late July, the 1955 rear admiral selection board announced its results. Captain Charles Melson, the *New Jersey*'s commanding officer in 1952–53, was on the list, but his successor, Captain Atkeson, was not. Atkeson was one of the few *New Jersey* skippers not selected for flag rank, and the news came as both a shock and disappointment to the crew. Ray Peet, the gunnery officer, remembered that a feeling of sympathy for the former skipper "just permeated the whole ship."

It could well be that Atkeson was the victim of poor timing. When the Naval Academy's class of 1927—of which both he and Melson were members— came into the zone for possible promotion, Charles Thomas was the new Secretary of the Navy. He had already selected Arleigh Burke, a junior rear admiral, as Chief of Naval Operations, and he charged the selection board to go for younger officers than had been the norm. Atkeson might have made it under the rules in effect the year before. Captain Atkeson had an aversion to duty in Washington, DC, and the workaholic pace expected there. That may also have weighed against him, but the men of the *New Jersey* had found him a success at the essence of the naval profession: commanding a man-of-war at sea.

Atkeson's successor, Captain O'Donnell, had the task at the end of the 1955 midshipman cruise of summarizing his observations in a report to the cruise commander. O'Donnell declared that the training regimen imposed on the midshipmen was too onerous. In particular, he said that the cruise journals—consisting of questions to be answered concerning every shipboard department—were unrealistically difficult. O'Donnell wrote, "The first classmen [seniors] were required to complete two assignments per day at sea. To accomplish this, after a full day of watches, drills, and instruction periods utilized all the free time of the conscientious individual."

A number of members of the Naval Academy football team, including all-American end Ron Beagle, were among the midshipmen in the *New Jersey* that summer. The players had to get back to Annapolis to begin fall practice. They were transferred from the battleship to a destroyer by highline and thence ashore. When the first of the football players made the trip in a chair suspended from the highline, the pages from his cruise journal fluttered in the air and were borne away by sea breezes. Presumably he couldn't be graded on his notebook and would have to be given special consideration because of the accident. By curious coincidence, as man after man made the trip to the destroyer, notebook after notebook came open, and the sea swallowed hundreds of pages.

On 3 August, the *New Jersey* and other ships of Task Group 40.1 arrived at Annapolis to offload midshipmen. She next proceeded to Hampton Roads, then went under way on the ninth and joined the *Iowa*, *Des Moines*, and *Macon*. The four heavies steamed together for several days, sometimes in diamond formation, while evading Hurricane Connie. When she returned to port, the *New Jersey* stayed only a short time, getting under way again from 16 to 19 August to steam with the *Iowa* while avoiding the effects of Hurricane Diane. Between them, the two East Coast storms killed more than four hundred people that summer.

As soon as the *New Jersey* returned to Hampton Roads, Captain Richard Pratt was detached, having been relieved as exec at sea on 18 August by Commander Charles Conway "Connie" Hartigan Jr. Lieutenant Pierre Vining, who was then the *New Jersey*'s main propulsion assistant, observed that the arrival of Hartigan to join Captain O'Donnell meant that the ship had "a tall, smiling Irishman for skipper and a short, smiling Irishman as exec."

Without exception, those who served with O'Donnell remembered him for his pleasant disposition. Dick Brega, who was the navigator, recalled the skipper as having a commanding manner and air of dignity, yet not pompous or overbearing; he had time to be friendly with those who worked for him. In ship handling, Captain O'Donnell was inclined to be more cautious than Atkeson. O'Donnell's specialty was gunnery, which is why he spent a good deal more time with the gunnery officer than his predecessor had. And O'Donnell shone in human relations as well. Seaman Ben Mehling was up on the bridge chipping paint one day when he was summoned to the captain's cabin by O'Donnell's Marine orderly. O'Donnell told him to sit down and offered him a cup of coffee, which was even more unexpected than the invitation. O'Donnell then told young Mehling that he had received a gift from the seaman's mother and wanted to tell the sailor of his gratitude. He also encouraged the youngster to write home more often.

When he did send letters home, Mehling probably didn't go into much detail about what he did on liberty in Norfolk. As was the case with many others, he frequently made his way to bars. A favorite was the Savoy on East Main. The proprietor knew that the crews of various ships had their favorite hangouts, so he put a big picture of the *New Jersey* on one wall. It worked; as Mehling said, "If you were going to meet a *Jersey* sailor, anybody from the 'Big Jay,' you went to the Savoy." Dick McDowell, a seaman in the *New Jersey*'s fifth division, was another of the many who went there. The customers were drawn in part by the owner's willingness to make no-interest loans to *New Jersey* men to tide them over between paydays. It was a change from the loansharking practices of some of the Norfolk predators who lent money at high interest rates. The idea of the loans without interest was to build up goodwill and, of course, to keep men coming back time and again.

On 23 August, Rear Admiral Edward N. "Butch" Parker shifted his flag from the heavy cruiser *Des Moines* to the *New Jersey*. Parker had previously commanded the heavy cruiser *Newport News* and was involved in a succession of destroyer billets before that. He was skipper of the four stacker *Parrott* as the U.S. Asiatic Fleet was undergoing its death throes in early 1942 and then commanded the USS *Cushing* when she was sunk by Japanese battleship fire in the Battle of Guadalcanal in November 1942.

The *New Jersey* was about to begin a tour with the Sixth Fleet in the Mediterranean; it was the first of her career. She would be taking a cruiser's place in the deployment rotation, so it was appropriate that Parker, who was commander, Cruiser Division Six, should be embarked. The cruise began on Wednesday, 7 September, as the *New Jersey* left Norfolk. On the seventeenth the battleship pulled in at Gibraltar and anchored for a stay that lasted until the twentieth.

From 22 until 28 September, the *New Jersey* visited Valencia, Spain; it was her second trip there in a short time. Valencia was the place where Photographer's Mate Chuck Hamilton had the duty of chasing men out of the brothels while on shore patrol. This time he had difficulties of another sort, but at least they were connected with his rating. One of the battleship's chaplains asked him to provide photo coverage of a religious service that members of the crew would be attending. Hamilton himself had to remain on board ship because of other duties, so he sent Seaman Apprentice Jimmy Barnes, who had been in the engineering department until a short time before.

Rear Admiral Edward N. "Butch" Parker, commander, Cruiser Division Six, poses with the Marine orderlies on his staff while embarked in the *New Jersey* in the autumn of 1955. *Courtesy Rear Admiral Edward O'Donnell*

Hamilton had been shorthanded, so he recruited Barnes for the photo lab, even though Barnes's only "qualifications" were a desire to help and the fact that both he and Hamilton were from Baltimore. During the religious service, Barnes apparently got rattled, because when he got back to the ship, he had what Hamilton recalled as "the clearest, blankest film you ever saw in your life. That's the first time I ever got chewed out by a chaplain. I didn't know chaplains talked like that, but he sure did."

After leaving Valencia, the *New Jersey* joined up with the Sixth Fleet. Since there was no war at the time, the ship's role was to remain ready if needed and to demonstrate that readiness to Mediterranean nations. Certainly, the usual aircraft carriers were on station with the Sixth Fleet, but a battleship added still more muscle. As O'Donnell explained, "It seems to me that there has not been a sufficient appreciation of what's involved in the gun as part of your essential firepower. When you can use it . . . it's the cheapest and most effective, the most satisfying to the customer, way of going."

In terms of economy of resources to get the job done, that was also a concern of the engineering department. It was reflected in the department's annual standing in the Battleships and Cruisers Atlantic Fleet (BatCruLant) type command fuel efficiency ratings. In fiscal year 1954, the *New Jersey* finished in sixteenth place of the sixteen ships in BatCruLant. Now, with Commander Fred Bitting having taken over as chief engineer and determined to run the ship more economically, she had pulled herself all the way to fourth. Bitting's philosophy included the use, for instance, of only as many generators as were needed for the ship's power requirements, rather than always having extras operating just for good measure. Especially important was the sparing use of fresh water, because that was more of a variable than fuel for propulsion. Each gallon of fresh water made by the evaporators required that much more use of fuel oil. One of Commander Bitting's tactics was to plug up most of the holes in shower nozzles in the officers' heads. When the fiscal year 1956 engineering results were published a year later, the *New Jersey* had moved up a notch to third place in the type command standings.

While the officers were dealing with minor irritants such as shower nozzles, they had a quite pleasant existence in the ship's wardroom mess. Lieutenant (junior grade) Dick Abrams enjoyed the atmosphere with the silver service, white tablecloths, folded cloth napkins, and meals served by stewards. The atmosphere contained a degree of formality. Since Captain O'Donnell had his own mess, Commander Hartigan, as exec, was president of the wardroom mess and sat at the head of the senior table. The places for the rest of the officers were determined by their seniority. The ensigns had their own tables. One of those ensigns was Ted Walker, who years later said facetiously, "You really didn't want to be promoted to jaygee or lieutenant, because then you had to go up and be polite."

One officer who was getting the feel of the *New Jersey* during that cruise in the Mediterranean was Commander Clyde Anderson, who reported in August as operations officer. The son of a chief petty officer who joined the Navy in the nineteenth century, Anderson had been used to seeing battleships since he was a boy in the 1920s. Now he made a close acquaintance with the *New Jersey* and initially expressed a sense of "surprise that any ship so massive, so solid, with such a sense of permanence, could still be so beautiful." He discovered her comfortable handling characteristics as well as her appearance and had the experience a number of times of taking her alongside replenishment ships in the Mediterranean. Because the Sixth Fleet was a highly mobile one, not tied to fixed bases, the *New Jersey* depended a great deal on taking on fuel, stores, and ammunition from other ships while under way.

The *New Jersey*'s time in the Mediterranean was a pleasant period in which fleet operations alternated with enjoyable port visits. One of the latter came between 5 and 13 October at Cannes on the French Riviera. Some crew members did the beach routine, while others went by bus to the town of Valberg in the French Alps. Seaman Dick McDowell learned to ski on a beginners' slope opposite the hotel where he and other *New Jersey* men stayed. Others went ice skating, and there were also toboggan rides available. Seaman John Evans had a good time taking pictures until he lost his light meter in the snow.

Between port visits, the *New Jersey* and other Sixth Fleet ships gradually worked their way eastward across the Mediterranean. A number of them anchored briefly in Souda Bay, Crete, on 19 and 20 October, and the *New Jersey*'s sailors had a swim call. Sure, there had been plenty of chances to go swimming on the beach at Nice when the ship was in France, but this was a sort of bonus—liberty while on board ship. Marines armed with rifles went out in a boat to keep watch over crew members as they swam. Seaman Evans found out why the Marines were there soon after he dived into the water from a 5-inch gun mount. He remembered, "I dove, and I just kept on going down and down and down, and I saw a shark. I turned around and I came back up. There's no way that Marine could have helped me out."

The Marines in the crew, of course, had many other duties besides protecting against shark attacks. Corporal John Walsh, for example, regularly drew guard duty outside the brig. Men were confined there for two principal offenses, unauthorized absence from the ship and fighting. The latter usually took place after too many drinks ashore. Sometimes those in the brig were on bread and water, in which case they were only exercised, not made to work. The prisoners on regular rations were put on work details so their days wouldn't be completely wasted.

Sergeant Sal Triola served as sergeant of the guard, and every fifth day he had duty as the ship's bugler. His duty period ran from reveille to taps, and he used a microphone to send his musical messages throughout the *New Jersey* and thus to regulate the ship's routine. On the days between his stints, Navy members of the crew did the bugling. Triola really considered bugling secondary to his other duties and was most proud of his role in helping to train others.

For instance, when Captain Lemuel C. Shepherd III, the commanding officer of the detachment, wanted to set up a classroom deep within the ship, Triola helped. Some members of the ship's crew

Captain Lemuel C. Shepherd III and Master Sergeant Michael Rodosovich Jr. preside at a ceremony on 22 September 1955 as William Gentry is promoted to staff sergeant. *Courtesy Lemuel C. Shepherd III*

During a course on map reading, a member of the Marine detachment uses a pointer to make comparisons between the terrain model in front of him and the map on the bulkhead. *Courtesy Lemuel C. Shepherd III*

had been apprehensive prior to Shepherd's arrival, because his father was then commandant of the Marine Corps. Men were concerned that Captain Shepherd might try to wear his dad's stars, but that didn't prove to be the case. As Triola put it, "He was just a human being, and he was concerned about his people.... He was a magnificent man." Shepherd was friendly and approachable and treated his men as any other Marine captain would.

From 22 until 27 October, the *New Jersey* was anchored in Phaleron Bay, the port for Athens, Greece. Captain Shepherd's Marines always had a prime role to play in the ceremonial aspects of port visits. Because of the diplomatic mission of the ship and her men, the Marines assigned to shipboard detachments were carefully chosen. They weren't fresh out of boot camp but had some seasoning so that the ones that went to the *New Jersey* and other ships were, in Shepherd's words, "for the most part, very good Marines." In essence, he said, ship detachments were "gold-plated," taking out potential troublemakers so they couldn't cause embarrassments overseas.

Admiral Parker thought there must have been an additional qualification for some—that they be more than six feet tall. The routine for visiting a port was that Admiral Parker would go ashore and call on senior dignitaries in the area, and then the dignitaries were invited to come on board. The ship visit was frequently timed so the guests could have lunch in the flag mess. The Marines were almost invariably taller than the visitors and so helped create a psychological impression about the strength and power of the United States. It was an impression that was reinforced in no small measure by the imposing strength and majesty of the *New Jersey* herself. As Parker explained, "This was a period of time when we were trying to do things to put iron in the back of some of those people under pressures from the Soviets. So the bigger we could make the United States appear, the more likely they would feel that we could help them."

Tall Marines could be helpful in other ways as well. Perhaps the most magnificent physical specimen in the detachment was Sergeant Don Henderson, who was 6-feet-2-inches or so, had broad shoulders and a slim waist. It was he who had the duty of serving as payroll guard when Ensign Ted Walker handed out money to the crew on paydays. That was still a time when men stood in line and stepped forward with pay chits made out for the amount of money they were due. Each chit was signed and marked with the fingerprint of the man's right index finger as protection against someone claiming another man's pay. There were numerous pay lines with a supply officer at each, but it took several hours to pay the entire crew, especially since there had to be lines for watch-standers and stragglers. When a man stepped up with his pay chit, Walker counted out the amount of cash indicated, and then a petty officer recounted it as a double check before the money was handed to the recipient. Then, in the case of the Marines, recalled Walker, the amount of money immediately started diminishing. A number of senior Marine noncoms were standing by to take a dollar for Marine Corps relief, a dollar for Red Cross, a dollar for the Marine Corps ball, and so forth. With tongue in cheek, Walker said, "The kid didn't have any money left when it was over."

Sergeant Henderson, a Black man, was highly thought of by his *New Jersey* shipmates. Private First Class Walsh and Sergeant Triola were embarrassed that they couldn't go on liberty with Henderson in Norfolk because of segregation laws. Walsh had grown up in New England and said, "It was hard for me, as an individual, to understand that." In the home port, the White Marines left the ship with Henderson, and then they had to go their separate ways. Overseas, it was different. Sal Triola described Henderson as "the most superb guy I've ever met in my life. . . . I walked on liberty with that man through all of Europe."

In the diplomatic realm, the *New Jersey* was evenhanded in her visits to two nations whose people had long harbored feelings of animosity toward each other. On 27 October, the battleship weighed anchor in Greece and steamed to Istanbul, Turkey, where she arrived the following day and rendered a twenty-one-gun salute. One effort at international relations was marred, though not seriously, by an amusing miscue. The mayor of Istanbul, an especially short man, came to the ship and inspected the Marine detachment, each member of which had a rifle with a chrome-plated bayonet attached. When one Marine brought his rifle smartly to the port-arms position, the silvery bayonet knocked off the mayor's top hat and startled him until he realized what had happened.

Three members of the *New Jersey*'s crew have a snack while on liberty in the Mediterranean. At left is Photographer's Mate Third Class Charles Hamilton. *Courtesy Charles Hamilton*

An individual who redeemed himself in Turkey was Seaman Apprentice Jimmy Barnes, the hapless photographer who came back with blank film in Spain. In Istanbul the assignment was to go to the local USO and photograph an exhibition of belly dancing put on for visiting American sailors. Once again, Chuck Hamilton, the leading photographer's mate, briefed Barnes on using the Speed Graphic camera. Barnes was evidently inspired, because, said Hamilton, "He did the best job of shooting belly dancers I've ever seen. I mean, the detail was perfect." Barnes' photos later showed up in both *The Jerseyman* and the cruise book for the *New Jersey*'s 1955 operations. That cruise book was marked by an imaginative touch. The staff invited the leading cartoonists of the day to submit drawings that tied in the *New Jersey* with such characters as Dick Tracy, Li'l Abner, and Dagwood Bumstead. One cartoon showed a grizzled chief petty officer saying to his men, "There's been a security leak—every time we hit a liberty port there's my wife."

On 3 November, the battleship left the Dardanelles and refueled the next day from the oiler *Mississinewa*. On the fifth, the *New Jersey* began operations with a carrier task group built around the USS *Lake Champlain*. On 7 November, the 5-inch and 16-inch guns conducted a firing exercise at Portoscuso on the island of Sardinia. It was one of the few times during the deployment that the big guns fired. Captain Shepherd went to the island as part of the shore fire control party observing the gunfire. Since he hadn't had much training or experience at spotting, he mostly observed the work of the Navy men in the party. One of those naval officers was Lieutenant (junior grade) Joseph Metcalf, a member of Admiral Parker's staff. Twenty-eight years later, in the autumn of 1983, Metcalf was a vice admiral in command of the U.S. Second Fleet. He led the expedition that secured the island of Grenada in the Caribbean.

On 11 November, the *New Jersey* visited Leghorn, Italy. The next stop, from 22 until 28 November, was Trieste, Italy, a port at the northeast end of the Adriatic Sea and long a bone of contention between Italy and Yugoslavia. The visit to Trieste offered the crew opportunities to visit Munich and Venice. The Thanksgiving holiday fell on 24 November, while the ship was at Trieste. Along with the roast turkey and baked ham were shrimp cocktail, oyster dressing, pumpkin pie, mince pie, fruits, vegetables, and other treats. Joining the crew for dinner in the mess deck were Captain and Mrs. O'Donnell. The skipper's wife had come to the Mediterranean to follow the ship during part of the cruise. Seaman Dick McDowell of the fifth division was pleased that the O'Donnells ate with the men and that the captain took time to ask crew members how things were going. If there were problems—then or at other times—the skipper worked through the exec and division officers to get things taken care of.

Trieste brought unhappy news for Admiral Parker, the embarked commander of Cruiser Division Six. He had been having trouble for some time with pain in his left foot and had taken medication for a suspected case of gout. The U.S. consul in Trieste happened to know an Italian doctor who had worked with the U.S. Army there. The doctor indicated that the admiral's trouble was probably cancer. Parker sent off a message to the Bureau of Naval Personnel in Washington to report the tentative diagnosis, and then the ship got under way on 28 November. En route to Cannes, France, a message reached the ship on the twenty-ninth, detaching her from Task Group 60.3. She diverted to Naples, Italy, where Parker reluctantly left his flagship on the last day of November and flew to Washington. At nearby Bethesda, Maryland, the diagnosis was confirmed, and his foot was amputated. Eventually fitted with an artificial leg, Parker remained on active duty into the early 1960s and was promoted to vice admiral.

After the interruption, the *New Jersey* continued westward and made port visits at Cannes, France, and Barcelona, Spain. The latter lasted from 17 December until 3 January 1956. The ship held religious services on board on Christmas Eve, but many of the crew went ashore. Captain O'Donnell and Commander Hartigan led a contingent of three hundred men who marched from the fleet landing to Our Lady of Bethlehem Church for midnight mass. One who went was Seaman John Evans, who had some misgivings about the experience, because many of the townspeople were left without seats when the men of the battleship marched in and sat down. Even though a large number of the Spanish had to stand, they were nevertheless friendly toward the visitors.

Barcelona also stuck in memories for two ship's parties that took place on successive nights. The ship paid top dollar to rent the lavish Rialto nightclub. Department store windows carried notices inviting Spanish women to show up for dinner and dancing, and they could also bring their mothers as chaperones. O'Donnell recalled that the Barcelona police were stationed at the door, and any time they recognized a professional hooker, she was invited to leave.

The first day of January was marked by more than the beginning of the new year, for the ship also received a new flag officer to replace the departed Admiral Parker. The new commander of Cruiser Division Six was Rear Admiral John H. "Savvy" Sides. A highly intelligent officer, he had spent the previous three and a half years in Washington as director of the Navy's fledgling guided missile program.

The first stop of 1956 was at Palma, Mallorca, in the Balearic Islands, some 135 miles southeast of Barcelona. It was the spot for the wetting-down party of three officers in the *New Jersey*'s medical-dental department. Actually, the three had been promoted to their new ranks back in November, but Palma offered the first real chance for a party without interfering with the holiday season. Included were new Captain John Bierley, the senior medical officer; Captain Harold Siemer, the senior dentist; and Lieutenant Jack Gehring of the Medical Service Corps. Cut-rate liquor supplied from Sixth Fleet stores came in handy, because two of the officers involved had objections to possible alternative means of celebration. Dr. Bierley explained, "Siemer objected to candy as a gift because he did not wish to contribute to tooth decay; I, as a physician, had always inveighed against tobacco in all its forms; Gehring objected to nothing."

On the morning of 16 January, after she had stopped for a few days for another visit to Gibraltar, the *New Jersey* left for Norfolk, steaming in company with the heavy cruiser *Des Moines*, which had just been relieved as Sixth Fleet flagship. Captain O'Donnell was highly gratified to receive a message from commander, Sixth Fleet: "Your outstanding conduct record and excellent performance of duty have reflected credit upon you and Sixth Fleet. Goodbye and good luck. Vice Admiral [Ralph] Ofstie." The message was especially welcome because of the emphasis placed since the beginning of the cruise on the importance of good conduct ashore. The men of the *New Jersey* were in a true sense ambassadors for their country.

During the week-long voyage back to the States, the *New Jersey* and *Des Moines* conducted drills, including gunnery exercises. After the arrival in Norfolk on 25 January, Admiral Sides remained embarked in the battleship for three more weeks. He shifted his flag to the command ship *Northampton* on 15 February, the day after the *New Jersey* moved to the Norfolk Naval Shipyard for a brief period of upkeep following her overseas deployment. On 28 February, she began heading south for Guantanamo and the annual Springboard exercise to provide training that prepared the crew for the ship's coming operational readiness inspection.

On 13 March, Rear Admiral Henry Crommelin, commander, Battleship Division Two, came on board from the *Wisconsin* to give the *New Jersey* her annual readiness inspection and battle problem. The *New Jersey*'s crew then had a breather from their training in the form of a weekend visit to St. Thomas in the Virgin Islands from 17 until 19 March. Then it was back to Guantanamo Bay and still more training before returning to Norfolk at the end of the month.

Following just over a week at anchor in Hampton Roads, the *New Jersey* went out for training exercises on 9 April in company with the carriers *Coral Sea*, *Forrestal*, and escorting destroyers. The *Forrestal*, which had just been commissioned the previous October, was the Navy's first "super carrier." She was involved in a training period that was especially intensive because of her status as first of a class. She was, indeed, the Navy's biggest ship up to that time. The skipper of the *Forrestal* was Captain Roy Johnson, a Naval Academy classmate of Captain

Two F7U Cutlass fighters sit on the flight deck of the recently commissioned super carrier *Forrestal* during heavy weather exercises with the *New Jersey* in April 1956. *National Archives: 80-G-670836*

The *Iowa*, *foreground*, and the *New Jersey*, *rear*, flank the *Wisconsin* at Norfolk in the spring of 1956. The *Wisconsin*'s bow is damaged as a result of her collision with the destroyer *Eaton* on 6 May. *U.S. Navy*

The *New Jersey* can be seen at Norfolk through the gash in the *Wisconsin*'s bow. Later the bow from the incomplete sister ship *Kentucky* was transplanted to the *Wisconsin*. *Courtesy Leon Morrison*

O'Donnell in 1929. Johnson wanted to demonstrate that the *Forrestal* could operate in heavy weather and was concerned about the ability of destroyers to serve in the plane guard role in case of a crash. So he asked O'Donnell to use the *New Jersey* as a plane guard, which O'Donnell did.

The ship spent April and May largely in the Norfolk area and operating off the Virginia Capes. In late May, the *New Jersey* offloaded much of her fuel so she could lighten her draft and go through the York Spit Channel on her way up the Chesapeake Bay to Annapolis. While the ship was there, Captain Charles B. Brooks became the twelfth skipper of the *New Jersey*. He took command on 31 May, not far from his old office, for he had been secretary of the institution's academic board since 1953. Brooks had previous fast battleship experience as executive officer of both the *Indiana* and the *Iowa*.

The midshipman cruise began on 5 June; the other heavy ships accompanying the *New Jersey* and a flock of destroyers were the battleship *Iowa* and the heavy cruisers *Des Moines* and *Macon*. The first stop was Oslo, Norway. The *New Jersey* arrived on 20 June, just before midsummer night, which was practically no night at all because the sun set briefly about midnight and then came up an hour or so later. Commander

The crew masses on the fantail for a change of command on 31 May 1956 as Captain Charles Brooks relieves Captain Edward O'Donnell. *USS New Jersey public affairs office*

Captain Charles B. Brooks Jr. commanded the *New Jersey* from 31 May 1956 to 21 August 1957, the date of the ship's decommissioning. *Courtesy Mrs. A. R. Brunelli*

Clyde Anderson joined an Air Force colonel whom he had met at the Armed Forces Staff College and who was now on duty in Norway. They spent the night cruising a fjord in a large boat, stopping at every little point of land. They were invited ashore for a drink at each place, and then they'd go off to find another host and hostess. After a while, many boats converged for a grand picnic, warmed by bonfires on the edge of the fjord. Finally the tired celebrants straggled back to their homes—and in Anderson's case, his ship—at about 7:00 in the morning.

Seaman Dick McDowell was much taken by the beautiful scenery in Norway, the opportunities for sightseeing, and the friendliness of the people. He and other shipmates such as Ben Mehling were taken with the women. They all looked the same—blonde, blue-eyed, and with milky skin. Brunettes and redheads were rare. Mehling was pleasantly surprised by the friendliness and hospitality of the Norwegians, for as he put it, "It was unusual for people to treat you that way, because sailors are not the most welcome persons in the world." He gave the natives tours of the ship when he had the duty and visited in their homes when ashore.

In 1955, the *New Jersey* had spent 4 July in England, and did so again a year later. This time she was at Portsmouth instead of Weymouth. Portsmouth marked the completion of the *New Jersey* tour of duty for Commander Hartigan, the executive officer. His place was taken by Commander Harry McElwain, who came to the job reluctantly. His detailer in the Bureau of Naval Personnel told him that the *New Jersey* was scheduled for decommissioning. The *Missouri* had been decommissioned in 1955, and all too soon it would be the *New Jersey*'s turn.

Another who felt unhappy at the projected turn of events was the new skipper, Captain Brooks. He remarked to some of his officers that even if 16-inch guns became obsolete, the *New Jersey*'s hull, power plant, and armor protection made her highly suitable for adaptation to any new weapons the Navy might develop, especially guided missiles. Clyde Anderson recalled that Brooks was even then thinking of the huge Jupiter missiles the Army was using. As it turned out, the large ballistic missiles were scaled down and found their way into the fleet via the Polaris submarine program.

Captain Brooks bore a physical resemblance to Captain O'Donnell; he also was tall and even more slender. He also had a pleasant smile and friendly manner but was not so outgoing and gregarious as O'Donnell. He had more of the reserve and aloofness traditionally associated with the commanding officers of large ships. McElwain recalled that his relationship with Brooks was excellent. The captain told him, "Okay, Harry, you run the ship internally, and I'll take care of the external part." And that was just the way it worked.

As a seaman, Brooks was competent but not flashy. Lieutenant Pierre Vining was the *New Jersey*'s main propulsion assistant. He remembered Brooks as a man who had "universal respect from people on board." Ben Mehling, one of the quartermasters, saw Brooks frequently on the bridge and considered him "a little sterner than Captain O'Donnell." To Mehling, Captain Brooks' presence was more overtly felt than O'Donnell's had been. Brooks was more likely to get involved in correcting small details than O'Donnell, who put his confidence in trusted subordinates for that function. As Mehling said of Brooks, "He wouldn't yell at people, but he'd make sure it was right." Commander Fred Bitting, the engineer officer, was especially struck by Captain Brooks' sense of loyalty to his officers and crew, backing them in their dealings with outsiders.

The biggest project in the ship's print shop during that summer of 1956 was the forty-eight-page paper-covered cruise book for the midshipmen. Along with pictures of liberty ports and shipboard training were group photos of the midshipmen. The NROTC types were largely from eastern universities, and there was the Naval Academy contingent as well. Among the latter was nineteen-year-old Rich Milligan from Matawan, New Jersey. He had just completed his plebe year at Annapolis. Nearly thirty years later, he became commanding officer of the *New Jersey*.

Back in 1956, Milligan was sleeping in the same four-tiered pipe frame bunks as other crew members and sharing the primitive, trough-type heads that didn't have individual stalls. That was the basis for a shipboard practical joke. The troughs were on an incline so the sluicing salt water could flush them. When young sailors were ensconced on the seats above the trough, some mischievous character put a wad of toilet paper in the trough and set fire to it, then watched with glee as it produced hot seats down the line. Another stunt, recalled Ben Mehling, took place in berthing compartments. A sleeping man often draped an arm out of the bunk, and his not-so-kind shipmates would fill the hand with shaving cream, then tickle his face with a feather. When he scratched or smacked the itch, he got a face full of shaving cream.

After winding up activities in England, the *New Jersey* departed on 10 July for the obligatory trip to Guantanamo Bay to complete the training routine, and then to Annapolis, where she arrived 31 July to drop off the midshipmen. Then she steamed down to Norfolk to spend much of August. On 23 August, the *New Jersey* again became a flagship with the embarkation of commander, Second Fleet, Vice Admiral Charles Wellborn Jr., and his staff. This was a repeat visit for Wellborn. Back in the autumn of 1945, when the *New Jersey* was flagship for the occupation of Japan, Wellborn—then a rear admiral—had been in the ship as chief of staff to Admiral John Towers, commander, Fifth Fleet. In this case, Admiral Wellborn wore his "NATO hat," commander, Striking Fleet Atlantic, for a coming exercise off the coast of Europe.

Fortunately for the crew, there were to be additional liberty ports as part of this last, brief deployment prior to the beginning of her pre-inactivation overhaul. She left the Norfolk naval operating base on Sunday, 26 August. Once the battleship was out

Captain Charles Brooks Jr., the skipper, welcomes visitors during the ship's stay at Greenock, Scotland, in late September 1956. *Courtesy Mrs. A. R. Brunelli*

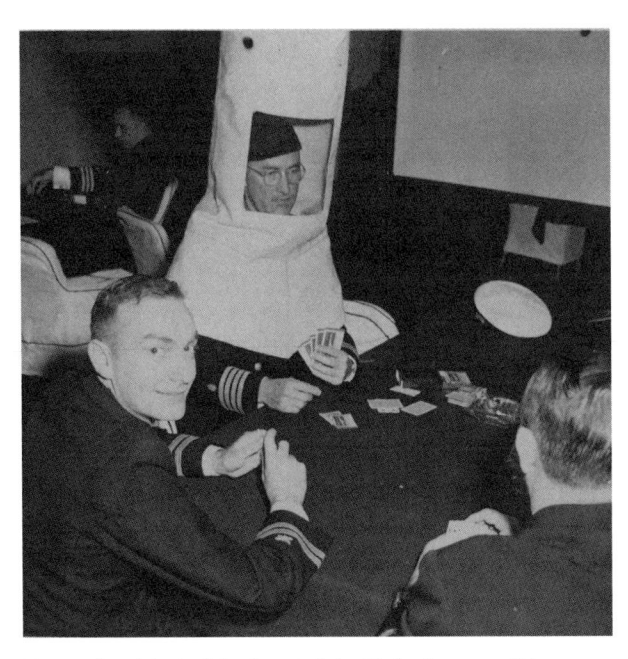

This is a hood devised for Captain John Bierley because of his aversion to cigarette smoke. It attaches to the fresh air vent in the wardroom. *Courtesy John Bierley*

into the Atlantic, she was involved in the communications exercise Gulf Stream from 4 until 8 September as she proceeded toward Lisbon, Portugal. The stop there lasted from the twelfth until the fifteenth, and then she headed north for Scotland. She was at Greenock from 18 to 25 September.

Back on board ship, life became a lot more pleasant for Dr. John Bierley with the arrival of a new first lieutenant, Lieutenant Commander Frank Kalasinsky. Previously, Bierley, who had an aversion to cigarette smoke, had been forced to leave when the concentration got above a certain level in the wardroom. Kalasinsky invented a canvas hood that could be attached to an air duct in the overhead of the wardroom. It flared at the lower end to permit air to escape and had an isinglass "window" through which the doctor could look while playing cards or watching a wardroom movie.

On 25 September, the *New Jersey* departed Greenock for Oslo, Norway, and from the twenty-sixth through the twenty-eighth the Striking Fleet staff on board the ship conducted Exercise Whipback, a simulated air operation off the coast of Norway. It was laying the groundwork for a full-scale NATO exercise the following year. On shore at that same time, the Allied Command Europe was conducting Exercise Whipsaw. The *New Jersey* acted as flagship of a simulated task force of NATO ships, including carriers, cruisers, and destroyers. The role of the "constructive"—imaginary, that is—task force was to support NATO operations in the area of Norway, the Netherlands, and Belgium.

Part of the test was to observe the weather and sea conditions that such a task force would encounter when operating a NATO mission so far north. There was also a hint of something else the NATO ships would encounter. Said Admiral Wellborn, "I recall that at one time during this trip we tracked by radar a 'snooper' plane, undoubtedly Russian, that followed us for some time but was never actually sighted." The *New Jersey*, remembered Harry McElwain, the exec, had an electronic intelligence team on board for the exercise. The team set up shop high in the tower structure above the bridge, listening for radio transmissions and observing when it was likely that the ship was detected on radar.

From 29 September until 4 October, the *New Jersey* was at Oslo, the second such visit in a brief period,

In this magnificent photo, the *New Jersey* is operating near the Arctic Circle during a NATO exercise in the autumn of 1956. *Courtesy John Bierley*

for she had just been there in June during the midshipman cruise. Commander McElwain, the executive officer, observed that the crew was delighted with the prospect of seeing the place again. A number of them took up with the same female friends they'd been seeing during the previous visit. Not all were so lucky. John Evans, then a seaman, recalled, "I looked, but I didn't find her." Admiral Wellborn received an official call from Crown Prince Olav, who had saluted the *New Jersey* and *Wisconsin* during the ships' visit to Oslo in 1947.

In Oslo, as elsewhere, the ship's senior petty officers had a powerful motivational tool to make sure that work got done, uniforms were squared away, and that men carried out the orders they were given; that tool was the liberty card. Each sailor had to have one to go ashore, and so it was a simple matter to withhold the card until things were right. This was part of an informal disciplinary system at the division level. Only relatively serious offenses reached the executive officer and captain's mast. For day-to-day things—including the proper performance of duty—the petty officers had considerable power, either in assigning extra duty or holding back privileges. One of those in charge of seeing that things were done correctly in the E division was Electrician's Mate First Class Arthur Smith. He recalled, "I was a firm believer that if somebody told you to do something, you did it, and then maybe you questioned later on.... But you didn't question [beforehand], because it would be in the back of your mind that if you did, somebody would put a foot up your rear end."

Vice Admiral Wellborn and his staff left the *New Jersey* on 3 October, and on the following day she began the long journey home to Norfolk, arriving on the fifteenth. In the following weeks she was in and around Norfolk, then spent the latter half of November and the first part of December at the Norfolk Naval Shipyard in Portsmouth. On 13 December, the *New Jersey* left for Bayonne, New Jersey, and arrived the following day. There to greet her were two mothballed veterans of the Pacific campaign in World War II, the carriers *Franklin* and *Enterprise*.

On 20 December, tugboats pulled the battleship away from the pier at Bayonne for a planned trip to the New York Naval Shipyard in Brooklyn. The tugs got her too far away from deep water, and she grounded. Her main condensers filled with silt, and the main generators soon kicked off—not the best news for Commander Fred Bitting, the chief engineer. He recalled that the emergency diesel generators then came on automatically, but their intakes soon filled with mud also, and they went off the line. The ship had no propulsive power and no electricity until she could be brought back alongside the dock and hooked to shore power. Bitting recalled that it was a dirty job to open and clean the condensers, and then she was able to go to an anchorage at Gravesend Bay before proceeding on 21 December to the shipyard in Brooklyn.

Soon after the beginning of the new year of 1957, on 7 January, the *New Jersey* again went out to Gravesend Bay, this time to offload her ammunition. She got rid of more than five hundred 16-inch projectiles, more than nine thousand 5-inch projectiles, a commensurate amount of powder, and more than 75,000 rounds of 40-mm ammunition. On 7 January, she returned to Brooklyn, and on the seventeenth her Marine detachment was disbanded—yet another sign of the growing momentum toward decommissioning. This great warship would gradually lose those elements that had made her an active part of the fleet since that cold, windy day in November 1950 when she was recommissioned for service in the Korean War.

The life-draining process would be a two-step affair. The first, which began on 15 January, was a $1 million pre-inactivation overhaul that concentrated primarily on the engineering plant: boiler work, reduction gears, and fuel oil piping and heating coils. After that would be the inactivation itself over at Bayonne. The period at the naval shipyard in Brooklyn ended on 19 April, when the *New Jersey* cast off from her pier and steamed over to the naval annex at Bayonne, where she was put into dry dock. Some of the inactivation process had already started at Brooklyn, and now the mothballing became the main focus of activity.

The *New Jersey* is high and dry while undergoing inactivation at the naval annex in Bayonne, New Jersey, in 1957. *Courtesy Harry McElwain*

This dry dock view clearly shows the underwater arrangement aft. The inboard propellers are at the end of skegs, while the outboard ones are attached to the hull by struts. The light-colored rectangular pieces attached to the rudders are zincs. Their purpose was to absorb electrolytic deterioration rather than having it erode the hull. *Courtesy Harry McElwain*

Because of the electrical equipment and cabling that had to be inactivated throughout the ship, one man who had a large job during the mothballing process was Electrician's Mate Smith. In preserving a motor, for instance, Smith's men completely stripped it down, cleaned it, replaced bearings as necessary, and reassembled it. He was also in charge of batteries and the other electrical aspects of boats, including running lights, wiring, and starters. Other gangs of electrician's mates worked on switchboards, generators, pumps, lighting, ventilation, and the hundreds of other facets of the huge vessel's electrical system.

Elsewhere in the ship, the inactivation process was largely similar to that of nine years earlier, including sealing up the ends of the guns, putting waterproof covers over exposed items, and sealing up holes in the hull while in dry dock. The Cosmoline that had caused so much difficulty during the Korean War reactivation was eschewed in favor of thin film rustproofing. The latter was a liquid that was sprayed on in various thicknesses to seal out moisture. It remained tacky to the touch and could be removed by the use of petroleum-based solvents.

Captain Brooks, who was saddened by having to be involved in the mothballing process at all, was especially unhappy about the requirement to go through the preservation checkoff list on the 40-mm gun mounts. On 13 May he sent a long letter to Captain John Miner, commanding officer of the *Wisconsin*. That battleship was scheduled to go through the mothballing process after the *New Jersey*, and so Brooks wrote to prepare Miner for what he would be up against. In discussing the gunnery aspects, Captain Brooks wrote, "We made a strong effort to get rid of our 40-mm mounts since I feel that they would be one of the first items to come off in case these ships are recommissioned. We were unsuccessful, however, and had to accomplish the normal inactivation procedures for the 40-mm batteries." Brooks's prophecy was fulfilled ten years later. When the *New Jersey* was reactivated for Vietnam, the 40-mm mounts were removed.

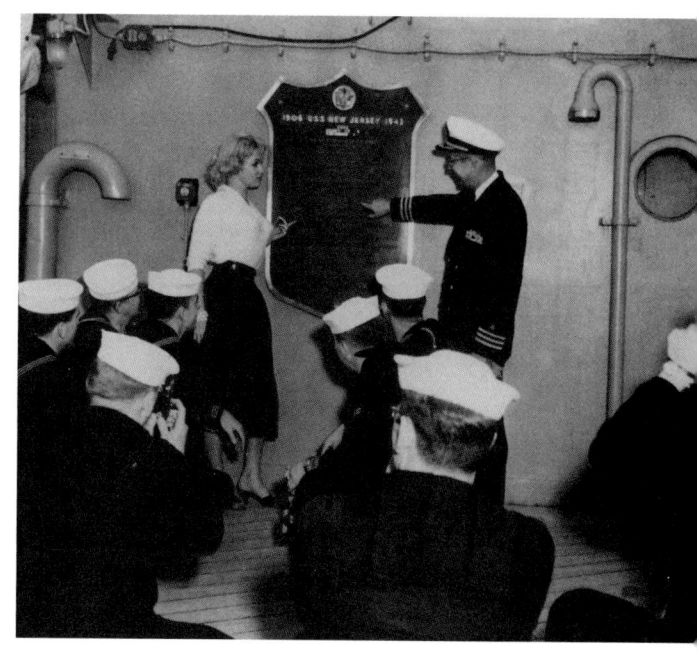

The quarterdeck plaque depicting the ship's battle history is no more than a prop in this 1957 publicity photo. The *New Jersey*'s executive officer, Harry McElwain, is shown with an aspiring starlet for whom the publicity was not sufficient to make her a star.
Courtesy Captain Harry McElwain

There were more mundane concerns, some of which involved the matter of what the crew did when not required to be assisting in the inactivation process. Younger members of the crew frequently went to New York City for liberty. Seaman John Evans sat in free seats whenever he went to big league baseball games. He saw the Dodgers play in Brooklyn during their last summer there before moving to Los Angeles. Lieutenant (junior grade) Charles Mumford, a bachelor officer, made it a point to try to see at least one Broadway show and one off-Broadway show each week. Some were free; others meant he had to be around the cancellation windows at show time. The hardest ticket to get was for *My Fair Lady*, starring Rex Harrison and Julie Andrews.

For more senior members of the crew, especially those with families still in the ship's home port of Norfolk, the weekends were made for commuting back and forth. Lieutenant Commander Pierre Vining noticed that Captain John Bierley, the nonsmoking physician, picked his carpool partners carefully so he wouldn't be gasping for air all the way to Norfolk and back. A couple of warrant officers bought a used car for weekend journeys to Norfolk. Electrician's Mate Arthur Smith observed that it "looked like a typical hoodlum's car, because it was an old Cadillac, and it had side curtains on the windows. They had the concealed places where I guess the mobsters used to keep their guns or something like that."

Commander Ralph Meilandt, the supply officer, had two principal responsibilities during the inactivation—making sure that all the allowance list items were on board the ship and all the "strip ship" items were removed. Equipment and spare parts that would be needed for reactivation were to be on board, but consumables and other items that could be used by other ships were removed. In going through the allowance list requirements with Commander Bitting while back in Brooklyn, Meilandt had discovered that the main shaft bearings called for on the allowance list couldn't be found on board the ship. Accordingly, a requisition was put in for the huge bearings to be fabricated. Later, the engineering department discovered the necessary bearings were on board after all. They had been welded to a bulkhead down in "Broadway," the long third-deck passageway, and subsequently painted over and hidden by other gear. The search had been inspired by the arrival of a new set of bearings, which came to Bayonne on railroad flat cars. Meilandt wrote, "The extra set of bearings were returned to Philadelphia. We weren't entirely surprised to see them again when someone in Philadelphia decided to send them back to us again—the flat cars reappeared alongside the ship a couple of days before our decommissioning. Once more, I sent them off to Philly."

As the time of decommissioning drew nigh, Commander McElwain, the executive officer, found it necessary to make some disposition of the several thousand dollars remaining in the ship's welfare and recreation fund. He wanted to give it to charity, but instead the crew voted for what McElwain describes as "a hell of a big decommissioning party." For one night the *New Jersey* took over a ballroom at

The grinning skipper, Captain Charles Brooks, presents a bouquet to actress Julie Newmar, Miss USS *New Jersey* of 1957, during her visit to the ship. *Courtesy Mrs. A. R. Brunelli*

the Waldorf Astoria Hotel and did things up right. There was even a Miss USS *New Jersey* in the person of actress Julie Newmar, who was appearing in a New York production of *Li'l Abner*. She visited the ship and also attended the party ashore. Speaking of her ship visit, Ben Mehling said, "I remember one time she was going down a ladder. She was going below deck, and I don't think any woman had so many helpers in her life. She was friendly, very friendly."

At the party Mehling discovered there was a good supply of women, and there was also a paddy wagon outside—just in case. He remembered, "It was a happy occasion, yet it was a sad occasion, because every guy was going somewhere else, and you never know when you're going to meet them again."

When it came time for the decommissioning ceremony on 21 August, only a few hundred crew members were left to observe and participate in the *New Jersey*'s passing from the roster of active Navy ships. The mothballing was complete, and the only thing remaining was to hold the funeral service on the fantail. Captain Brooks read the decommissioning order and turned the now-silent battleship over to Captain Charles Hopper, commander of the New York group of the Atlantic Reserve Fleet.

Among the guests that day was Mrs. Pierre Vining, wife of the *New Jersey*'s main propulsion assistant. She found the whole occasion so sad that she vowed never again to attend a ship's decommissioning. Lieutenant Commander Vining himself was philosophical. He and his shipmates had lost their home and indeed the institution that had bound them together for months or even years. Though they would no longer have a physical association with the *New Jersey*, they had the memories of shared experiences that would always remain with them. As Vining said years later, "I don't think I've ever been in a ship that had such a great spirit."

CHAPTER VI

POLITICS AND THE VIETNAM WAR
August 1967–December 1969

Even though the *New Jersey* was designed and built well after the age of sailing ships, she was nevertheless subject to political winds that blew strongly during the 1960s. Her truncated Vietnam career was dictated more by political considerations than military ones. Much had happened on the world political scene in the ten years since her 1957 decommissioning. Cuba acquired a communist regime, the Berlin Wall was built, and the Cuban Missile Crisis raised the chilling specter of nuclear war. Moreover, the United States became increasingly involved in a war in Southeast Asia.

Initially, the battleship remained discarded but not forgotten. In the summer of 1962, as part of a consolidation of the Atlantic Reserve Fleet, she was towed from Bayonne, New Jersey, to the Philadelphia Naval Shipyard. The growing U.S. involvement in Vietnam after the summer of 1964 compelled the examination of possible reactivation of one or more *Iowa*-class battleships. Unlike the *New Jersey*'s quick reactivation for Korea, the process this time was especially long, because Admiral David L. McDonald, the Chief of Naval Operations, was steadfast in his opposition.

Senator Richard Russell of Georgia served on both the Armed Services and Appropriations committees. After 1964, 1965, and 1966 passed with no battleship decision, he said in early 1967, "I will insist on it this year." With his power of the purse, Russell had a great deal to say about paying for the Vietnam War. He got his way. In late May, the Department of Defense announced that it had approved the opening up and inspection of the *New Jersey*. The Navy had already selected her, because she was in better material

In April 1967 three sisters lie side by side as part of the reserve fleet at the Philadelphia Naval Shipyard. *Left to right*: *Wisconsin*, *New Jersey*, and *Iowa*. Of the three, the *New Jersey* was deemed to be in the best material condition because of the overhaul prior to her 1957 decommissioning.
U.S. Navy: 1121518

Movement, both literally and figuratively, came for the *New Jersey* on 11 June 1967, when tugs moved her from the battleship nest to a pier where her reactivation would begin. *U.S. Naval Institute photo archive*

condition than her three sisters, presumably because of her overhaul prior to the 1957 decommissioning.

The so-called inspection actually constituted the opening phase of reactivation—that which would take place during Admiral McDonald's brief remaining tenure as CNO. On 1 August, the same day he retired, the Department of Defense announced that it was going to reactivate the *New Jersey* for Vietnam War duty.

Once the reactivation began officially on 1 August, the Philadelphia Naval Shipyard immediately instituted a three-shift, six-day-a-week working schedule and stepped that up to seven days a week before the month was over. Part of the process involved removing items that were outdated. The 40-mm guns were removed, electronic gear pulled out for replacement, messing and berthing spaces stripped, and so forth.

The resulting clutter was evident when the prospective commanding officer, Captain Richard G. Alexander, reported to Philadelphia. Alexander observed of the *New Jersey*, "That thing was the biggest shambles inside when I arrived six weeks after it had been first opened that I ever saw any ship in, in a shipyard, other than new construction." Alexander was disappointed by what he considered an overlong schedule for the battleship's reactivation. She did not reach Vietnam until some fourteen months after the official start of the shipyard period.

Captain Alexander had extensive experience in destroyers and had compiled a superb record since he graduated from the Naval Academy in 1944. He reported from the Bureau of Naval Personnel and before that had a topnotch tour of duty as skipper of the guided missile destroyer *Semmes*. Captain Bill

Thompson, public affairs officer in the office of the Secretary of the Navy in 1967, observed of the prospective skipper, "Everybody said he had 'flag officer' written all over him." Also on the secretary's staff at that time was Captain Alex Kerr, a Naval Academy classmate of Alexander. Kerr remembered, "He had a reputation of being right in controversial issues, of taking positions that were not in accordance with the common wisdom of the time and having prevailed and been proven right in the end."

In the course of his discussions with officials in Washington and during a trip to ships off the coast of Vietnam, Captain Alexander learned how the battleship was to be employed. She was to support ground troops in South Vietnam, and she was to participate in the Sea Dragon bombardment effort off North Vietnam, shelling enemy coastal supply routes as a means of interdicting the flow of war materials from north to south. These were essentially the same missions the *New Jersey* had performed off Korea fourteen years earlier. In her interdiction role, she would be able to take some of the load off American pilots being shot down in considerable numbers while attacking targets such as the bridge at Thanh Hoa in North Vietnam. In reflecting on the matter, Captain Alexander came up with roles for the battleship that would be potentially even more valuable—effecting a lodgment to neutralize the enemy transportation center at Vinh and enforcing a blockade against the port of Haiphong. The latter would have shut off the arrival of war materials at the source rather than having to attack the flowing supplies after they reached Vietnam. For political reasons, Haiphong was not cut off until 1972, and then it was achieved through the sowing of naval mines.

On board ship at Philadelphia, department heads and other members of the crew were gathering. Captain Robert C Peniston was then involved in making officer assignments at the Bureau of Naval Personnel. He helped assemble a formidable array of talent for key positions throughout the ship. Lieutenant Dick Harris, who had served as a gunfire spotter in

A shipyard period is invariably messy and cluttered. This shot during the early stages of reactivation is an example. In the lower left is the aircraft crane, a vestige from World War II, when the *New Jersey* operated floatplanes. *Philadelphia Naval Shipyard*

The 40-mm mount atop turret two has already been removed in this photo taken 16 February 1968. *Philadelphia Naval Shipyard*

Vietnam, was an exception in that he was assigned to the *New Jersey* on his own initiative rather than being handpicked. Once at the ship, Harris quickly learned that Captain Alexander questioned members of the nucleus crew. The captain frequently knew the answers already, so the questions enabled him to find out whether prospective *New Jersey* men knew the ship and their jobs—and whether they would give him a straight answer if they didn't know something. Fire Controlman First Class Rick Crawford was nearby on one occasion when Captain Alexander was questioning a young enlisted man. Crawford considered the new man overmatched, especially since Crawford—himself a senior petty officer—thought the ship so big and complex that "I was worried about leaving bread crumbs to find my way back."

Even while Alexander was trying to get the ship and her crew ready for duty overseas, his mind was also on another matter—the so-called "Arnheiter Affair." In late 1965 and early 1966, Lieutenant Commander Marcus Aurelius Arnheiter had served for ninety-nine days as commanding officer of the radar picket destroyer escort *Vance*. His overzealous style of leadership and his questionable practices while the *Vance* was off the coast of Vietnam led to his being summarily relieved of command. Alexander took up the deposed skipper's cause. He argued that Arnheiter was removed from his ship without due process and had been undermined by a disloyal group of junior officers. Explained Alexander, "I decided to intervene only when [Rear Admiral Walter H.] Baumberger, [commander, Cruiser-Destroyer Force, Pacific Fleet,] after a thorough review of the case, recommended that Arnheiter be restored to command." Captain Alexander had a private meeting with Secretary of the Navy Paul Ignatius in Washington on 7 November 1967. Soon afterward the captain released to the press copies of a twenty-seven-page statement he had written on Arnheiter's behalf and presented to Ignatius.

Admiral Thomas H. Moorer, who had taken over from Admiral McDonald as Chief of Naval Operations, did not like being bypassed in the Arnheiter case. He considered Alexander's statement "somewhat intemperate" and did not respect Alexander's judgment in releasing his statement rather than pursuing the matter through internal Navy channels. In late December, Captain Alexander was asked to request a transfer from the *New Jersey* to shore duty, and he complied. His once-promising career ended less than two years later when he retired from active duty. He was never selected for the admiral's stars that earlier seemed so likely.

His replacement was Captain J. Edward Snyder Jr. Both he and Alexander were in the Naval Academy's class of 1945, which graduated a year early to get officers out to the fleet during World War II. The new man had a master's degree in nuclear physics and a solid background of big-ship experience. He had served in the battleship *Pennsylvania* and the heavy cruisers *Toledo* and *Macon*. In mid-December, he was about to begin driving across country to take command of the heavy cruiser *St. Paul*. Instead, he reported to Philadelphia the following month to take Alexander's place.

The new skipper had an understandable concern about what effect the change would have on the crew. As it turned out, it was slight. Snyder recalled, "I was concerned to see whether or not the ship had formed any loyalty. I was quickly relieved to realize that there were less than two hundred in Philadelphia, therefore less than two hundred people who even had the opportunity to know Captain Alexander intimately, and that the workload . . . was so strenuous in those days that people didn't have time for sessions and discussions."

An officer who reported aboard with a good deal less fanfare than Snyder was Ensign Chris Reed, who came in wintry February when the *New Jersey* had completed the dry dock portion of the reactivation but was still uninhabited and chilly inside. Reed was struck by the mazelike interior of the ship, which was divided into hundreds of compartments. He recalled, "The cramped interior dimensions of the ship were always a surprise to visitors." His long, narrow stateroom—when he later moved in—seemed to Reed little more than a passageway with lockers on one side and bunks and desks on the other.

One individual who was able to create internal change was Chief Ship's Serviceman Lew Moore. In two previous wars, the ship's store had been a small affair at which customers lined up at a window and bought items such as shaving cream, toothpaste, and cigarettes from the man on duty behind the counter. Chief Moore was involved with the shipyard in constructing a new, much larger walk-in retail store. It would allow crew members to come in and browse as they would in a Navy exchange ashore.

For the return to service, no Marines would be part of the ship's company, which they had been during previous incarnations. Secretary of Defense Robert McNamara put great value on cost-effectiveness and decreed an austere return to service. Captain Snyder was disappointed by the ruling. He was thinking in terms of the Marines' potential value in manning a couple of 5-inch mounts. Familiar with the sort of competition that characterized relationships between Navy and Marine gun crews, he reasoned that the attempts to outdo one another would improve overall performance.

Among the enlisted crew members who reported to the ship at Philadelphia was Seaman Tom Feigley, who had just completed two months of boot camp and six months of gunner's mate school. He was assigned to turret three, the one that Gunner's Mate First Class Bob Moore had served so well as turret captain during the Korean War. By early 1968, Moore had retired from active duty as a chief petty officer and was part of the shipyard crew reactivating the turrets for Vietnam. Feigley and others were there not so much to help reactivate turret three as to learn the workings of the equipment. Supervising the training was the new turret captain, Senior Chief Gunner's Mate George Petrovitz, whom Feigley considered "probably one of the smartest mechanics I ever met, inside or outside the Navy."

Even as the nucleus crew was at work in Philadelphia, another group of *New Jersey* men, known as the balance crew, was undergoing training at Navy schools in San Diego. Fire Controlman Rick Crawford, who had initially reported to Philadelphia, was among those in a fifteen-week main battery school at San Diego. He recalled that the director used in their training was from a light cruiser, the range keeper and fire control radar from a battleship, and the power drives from a heavy cruiser. The instructors were from a previous generation of big-ship fire controlmen who provided both classroom instruction and hands-on drill with the gear.

Walt Migrala and several other ensigns fresh from Officer Candidate School reached San Diego late one week. They were informally attired when they went to the fleet training center to learn the lay of the land and to find out where they would be going when they officially reported the following Monday. Their attempt at getting a jump on the situation backfired. The petty officer on duty at the training center didn't understand that they were on only a preliminary scouting trip. Instead he escorted them in to see Commander James Elfelt, slated to be the battleship's executive officer. Elfelt took a look at the casually clad group and announced, "I don't know where you guys came from, but out here we report for duty in the full uniform of the day. You guys are starting out in a hole." They dug their way out of it by serving as shore patrol officers for a ship's party in San Diego.

Migrala remembered that the training offered in San Diego took into account the many different jobs on board the battleship and the varying skill and experience levels of the prospective crew members. Among other things, men received lookout, firefighting, and damage control training, and practice working with underway replenishment rigs. As at Philadelphia, the training had a secondary effect in getting future shipmates working together and forming associations.

The *New Jersey*'s messing and berthing spaces had been readied just in time for the influx of men from California. One of those reporting with the balance crew was Fire Controlman Second Class Tom Mumpower. When he joined the ship, he was delighted to see that she was air-conditioned and that the FM division berthing compartment had tables usable for letters or playing cards. In time, each living compartment would have a television set also, part of a closed-circuit system donated by the State Society of the Battleship New Jersey. The TV system could be hooked up to an outside antenna for picking up commercial programming when close to land. At sea the setup could be used for showing movies or videotapes.

The ship was, of course, the focus of a great deal of public interest during her reactivation. Ensign Scott Cheyne reported to the ship as public affairs officer and had to cope with the avalanche of interest and attention showered upon the *New Jersey*. Fortunately, he was able to draw on the skills of Lieutenant Commander Brayton Harris, the public affairs officer assigned to the staff of the Fourth Naval District at Philadelphia. Gradually, as Cheyne learned more and became more comfortable in his new job, he was able to take on the load himself. That load included answering letters from both children and adults all over the country. Among them were letters from former crew members who provided advice on various pieces of equipment they remembered and how they should be reactivated.

A media blitz added to the workload. Newspapers, magazines, radio, and television all wanted a piece of this great human interest story. Cheyne and Harris were swamped with requests from reporters who wanted to be on board when the *New Jersey* went out for her first engineering trials in the Atlantic. Because of safety considerations and the need for climbing steep ladders, Lieutenant Commander Harris established a ground rule that the trials could be covered by male newsmen only. Reporters called in to make reservations, and the resulting list included only men's names. Thus, there was considerable surprise when a woman wearing a miniskirt and black

The national ensign on the stern of a Coast Guard cutter frames the *New Jersey* on 26 March 1968 as she proceeds past the Delaware Memorial Bridge en route to the Atlantic for sea trials.
Naval Photographic Center

textured stockings showed up on the morning of 26 March and announced, "I'm Toni Franzolini of the *Courier-Times* in Levittown [Pennsylvania]." Sure enough, a reservation had been made; the person approving the request had mistakenly assumed it was Tony rather than Toni. She was allowed to go on board rather than create ill will. The ship then proceeded down the Delaware River, and Captain Snyder slowed at Wilmington, Delaware, to allow the newspeople to transfer to the Navy tug *Menasha* for the trip ashore.

One man from the news media became a stowaway—sort of. In addition to the male-only ground rule, there was one that stipulated that the reporters had to leave at Wilmington and not stay for the three-day cruise. Photographer Neil Leifer from *Sports Illustrated* stayed with unofficial permission because he was working on a photo book for the *New Jersey*'s crew. When he didn't show up with the group coming back from Wilmington, Lieutenant Commander Harris in Philadelphia sent a message to the ship for Leifer to be removed, but by then the weather was too rough. Despite the temporary embarrassment, Leifer served the ship well. His one book eventually became two: *Dreadnought Returns* and *Dreadnought*

Farewell. Together, they comprise a spectacular pictorial documentation of the *New Jersey* between 1967 and 1969.

The trials themselves went satisfactorily, especially on 27 March when the *New Jersey* conducted a full-power run. The ship built up to maximum speed reported as 35.2 knots in the ship's official history for the year. Ensign Chris Reed formed indelible memories from the trials that day:

> The ship had settled into her taut high-speed transit jiggle, with which we grew so familiar in later months. Because of her great length she pitched very little. At speeds beyond twenty-five knots or so, her slight roll became segmented into one- or two-degree increments so that she made several distinct steps in a full roll cycle. During the test something minor had gone awry with boiler seven or eight, and as we raced through the nearly calm seas we left an impenetrable trail of roiling black smoke. Seven-eighths of the plant was generating the classic light brown haze, but from one of the uptakes in the after stack there boiled up the sooty rebellion of the lone dissenter. The smoke trail was all the more spectacular because there was no wind to disperse it. It continued back to the horizon in an unbroken plume, while directly below it, sparkling rose and gold in the setting sun, the ship's wake arrowed to the same vanishing point on the horizon.

As the ship raced along, her movement created a relative wind that made walking difficult topside. The forced-draft blowers on the air intakes of the giant stacks howled vehemently. Prongs of the radio antenna that sprouted horizontally from the mainmast began vibrating like tuning forks and broke themselves off. The ship's speed built up an inertia that manifested itself dramatically during the most strenuous test of all—going from all-ahead flank to all-back emergency. Underwater, the giant propellers came to a stop, reversed direction, and gradually began to bite into the sea. A crewman threw a smoke float over the side when the engines were reversed. The ship hurtled forward for another two miles before she finally came to a stop and began to go astern.

When the *New Jersey* returned to pier four at the Philadelphia Naval Shipyard on 28 March, she carried a broom on one of the signal halyards to signify a "clean sweep" on her engineering trials. There would be literal sweeping as well, because the world's only operational battleship had little more than a week to clean up for the commissioning ceremony on Saturday, 6 April. In the meantime, two events put a damper on the ship's coming-out party. On 1 April, war-weary President Lyndon Johnson directed that all but the southern panhandle of North Vietnam would be off-limits for bombing and shelling by U.S. forces. He hoped thereby to bring the North Vietnamese to the bargaining table to make peace.

The second event was the assassination of civil rights leader Martin Luther King Jr. in Memphis, Tennessee, on 4 April. Almost instantly a backlash of racial violence erupted in several large U.S. cities. On 5 April, Mayor James Tate of Philadelphia declared a state of limited emergency, akin to martial law. He prohibited public gatherings of more than eleven people and closed bars throughout the city.

The Saturday of the ceremony was a beautiful, warm, sunny early spring day. The disturbances were relatively minor and had more to do with the battleship than with Dr. King. Antiwar demonstrators gathered to stage a protest against a ship that was obviously headed for Vietnam. One group planted a ten-foot-tall "peace tree" about one hundred yards from the naval base; forty-nine protesters were arrested, handcuffed, and hauled away in police vans for violating the ban against public gatherings.

Standing on the deck of the battleship, Ensign Chris Reed heard one of the protesters using a bullhorn to read a prepared statement. At the end of it, the speaker exhorted *New Jersey* men to refuse to serve in what he and his comrades considered an unjust

Thousands of spectators gather for the recommissioning of the *New Jersey* at Philadelphia on 6 April 1968. *Philadelphia Naval Shipyard*

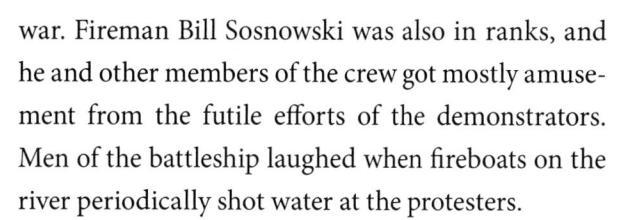

Captain J. Edward Snyder Jr. commanded the *New Jersey* from recommissioning on 6 April 1968 to 27 August 1969. *U.S. Navy*

war. Fireman Bill Sosnowski was also in ranks, and he and other members of the crew got mostly amusement from the futile efforts of the demonstrators. Men of the battleship laughed when fireboats on the river periodically shot water at the protesters.

Even more important were the feelings that the ship herself evoked among crew members—feelings of pride and of being special because such a large crowd had turned out for the show. Captain Snyder soon demonstrated that he was concerned about the crew. When it came his turn to speak, he picked up the podium that had been facing the VIPs and turned it 90° so that he could address the crew members' families on the pier. "Now," he said, "I'm talking to you families out there. And these other people—as far as I'm concerned, they're not even here." It was a grandstand move, and Snyder would make many more of them during his command tenure.

Though he wasn't a psychology major, he might as well have been, for the captain knew how to inspire a crew and make the men feel good about themselves.

Lieutenant Carl Morse was assigned to the shipyard and had a large role in getting the battleship ready for this day. One of his strongest memories was that of Captain Snyder's head-turning and podium-turning speech, "It made quite an impression on the crew and on the families. It was the coolest move he could've ever done."

All too soon the festivities were over, and it was time to get back to work again. More trials were on the docket, this time a check by the Board of Inspection and Survey. On the morning of 15 April, the *New Jersey* eased away from the pier for the eighty-six-mile, eight-hour sea detail trip downriver to the Atlantic. The officer of the deck for the sea detail was Lieutenant Carl Albrecht, a superb ship handler whose primary job was as main battery officer. He had been assigned to the *New Jersey* because of his experience with the 8-inch guns of the cruiser *Macon*. Albrecht remembered that the Philadelphia sea details were made easier by the fact that the Delaware River pilots' association undoubtedly sent its best men.

On the morning of 17 April, off the Virginia Capes, the *New Jersey* began test-firing her guns. Turret one was trained around to a bearing of 110° relative to the bow. As a result, the guns pointed somewhat abaft the starboard beam and would impart the maximum stress to the superstructure. The test was to see how well the ship could withstand the concussion produced by her own guns. It took some forty seconds before the first projectile splashed down in the Atlantic and created a green-colored fountain of spray. A dye-loaded projectile was used to help spot the impact point. Ensign Walt Migrala was manning a secondary battery director in the after part of the superstructure. He had listened with interest as turrets one and two were fired, but when turret three was trained around and pointing forward of the beam, he had the feeling he could almost reach out and touch the barrels. His director wasn't needed for the big guns, so he closed all the hatches and hunkered down inside.

Down in the projectile deck for turret three was gunner's mate striker Larry Pousson. "The first gun we fired," he said, "one or two lights would go out. The second gun, a couple more lights would go out; the third gun, a couple more lights. Then when we loaded up and fired a broadside, a whole bunch of lights went out. It definitely cleaned the dirt out of the overhead." The tests did what they were supposed to do; they demonstrated the weaknesses in the ship's ability to withstand the shock of firing. Some of the new electronic gear was knocked out, fluorescent light fixtures crashed to the deck, ductwork fell, and new plumbing developed minor leaks.

The *New Jersey* fired eighteen 16-inch rounds that day, all with the barrels trained to their limits. For the most part, the ship survived, but Ensign Jack Hayes observed that some yard workmen's tools didn't. The workers, who had come along to continue their tasks on board ship, put their toolboxes inside a circular shield that had once protected a 40-mm gun mount. The muzzles of the guns from one turret were almost directly over the toolboxes when flame and concussion erupted. The muzzle blast crushed the toolboxes around the tools, akin to shrink-wrapping a piece of plastic around an item before displaying it for sale. On 18 April, the *New Jersey* returned to Philadelphia, again wearing a "clean sweep" broom.

The long stay at Philadelphia came to an end on Thursday, 16 May, when the *New Jersey* began the

As part of the loading process, a pallet of 5-inch powder charges lies on a shock mat before being stowed below. *Naval Photographic Center: 1141205*

Seamen in a lower handling room practice transferring canvas-covered powder bags from the passing scuttle at right to the powder hoist car at left. *Naval Historical Center*

long odyssey that would take her to Southeast Asia. As she headed out with her crew paraded on deck in white uniforms, the battleship glided past her still-mothballed sisters *Iowa* and *Wisconsin*. She was saluted by bright red fireboats sending triumphant streams of water into the sky. Her progress down the Delaware River to the sea was filmed by a camera crew for the soon-to-be-released Navy film entitled *The American Dreadnought*.

On Monday morning, 20 May, the *New Jersey* reached Hampton Roads near Norfolk. Her crew spent three reveille-to-taps days taking on some twenty-five hundred tons of projectiles and powder. She went to sea on 23 May, the twenty-fifth anniversary of her first commissioning, to fire dozens of rounds of 16-inch and 5-inch. The shooting a month earlier had been to test the ship structurally. This time the weapons department wanted to calibrate the guns and fire control equipment.

During the weekend of 25–26 May, the battleship was moored at Norfolk. It was the first time she had been there since late 1956. Her nostalgic appeal acted as a magnet during two days of general visiting. Nearly 32,000 people came during the two days. Some of the guests recognized one another and held private reunions. One man who had served in the *New Jersey* during World War II met a Korean War veteran and observed, "Oh, you're a newcomer."

On Wednesday, 29 May, the *New Jersey* headed for Panama. It took five days for the battleship to steam there. She anchored at Cristobal on the morning of 3 June, and the daylong transit occurred the following day. The squeeze was a tight one, as usual. Gunner's Mate Seaman Larry Pousson stood with the toes of his shoes flush with the side of the ship and looked straight down. He said, "You couldn't really tell where the side of the ship ended and the lock itself started." He observed deck seamen using fire hoses to quell the smoke produced when the sides of the ship scraped against the lock walls.

Along the sides of the canal Ensign Chris Reed saw enthusiastic Americans demonstrating their support and encouragement for the giant dreadnought. One woman held over her head a homemade sign that said, "Give 'em hell, *New Jersey*." Reed was not really encouraged, because he and other junior

A tugboat accompanies the battleship during her trip through the Panama Canal's rugged Gaillard Cut. *U.S. Naval Institute photo archive*

In the Miraflores locks of the Panama Canal on 4 June 1968, the *New Jersey* dwarfs a nearby merchant ship. *U.S. Naval Institute photo archive*

Protestant chaplain Harold D. Bodle leads crew members in prayer during a shipboard divine service in the mess deck on 9 June 1968. *USS New Jersey public affairs office, photo by John Cary*

officers thought considerable hazards faced the *New Jersey* in the war zone. In 1967, Egyptian patrol boats had sunk the Israeli destroyer *Elath* with surface-to-surface Styx missiles. The news media had been full of speculation about what might happen to the battleship. Crew members probably were more concerned than they cared to admit.

Soon the ship was in the Pacific for the first time since late 1953. Captain Snyder was interviewed during the northward journey by two Southern California newspapermen, Bob Zimmerman of San Diego and Buck Lanier of the ship's new home port, Long Beach. The captain revealed that the Department of Defense had recently granted his request that more enlisted men be added to the crew, raising the enlisted total from 1,400 to 1,556. The number of officers remained at 70. Austerity has its virtues, but the original manning had been too lean for the ship's intended mission. In his repertoire of motivational tools, Snyder was to dwell on that small crew size—telling the men of the *New Jersey* that they must be twice as good as their World War II predecessors because they could operate the ship with half as many. What he didn't tell them was that the job was smaller this time. The manpower-hungry 40-mm and 20-mm guns were gone, there was no embarked flag officer to support, and the ship no longer had enough engineering personnel to steam at high speeds for extended periods.

On 11 June, the *New Jersey* arrived in Long Beach and was escorted by an enthusiastic group of small craft. She moored at the naval shipyard's huge Pier Echo, near the retired Cunard liner *Queen Mary*, which would be converted to a hotel and tourist attraction. The *New Jersey* steamed to San Diego on 17 June to begin six weeks of intensive training—the equivalent of a shakedown—to prepare the crew for deployment. Gunner's Mate Seaman Larry Pousson considered the crew of turret three well drilled already. Senior Chief George Petrovitz had trained the ammunition handlers slowly and carefully. First they walked through all the movements, emphasizing safety at each step. Only after they had mastered the procedures did they begin to pick up speed. At first it took about two minutes to load a 16-inch round and the associated powder. Gradually the time was reduced to about thirty seconds.

Both Pousson and Fire Controlman First Class Rick Crawford felt that the people from the local fleet training group were at a disadvantage. "We wound up having to teach them," Crawford said. For one practice shore bombardment at San Clemente Island, off the coast of Southern California, the targets were old automobiles that had been painted yellow to make them stand out. Firing from 20,000 yards, the *New Jersey* showered the cars with shrapnel. The weapons officer, Commander Pete Roane, commented dryly in the ship's cruise book, *Dreadnought 68–69*, "I think we've put the yellow cab company out of business."

The battleship returned to port on 2 August to spend a month receiving a final tune-up at the shipyard. The time in home port provided a rare opportunity for the married men to be with their families, and the single men had a good time as well. For some of the ship's chief petty officers, recreation was to be

A crewman pauses in August 1968 for a rest during the stowage of cans containing 16-inch powder bags. *Ralph Wasmer image via Naval Photographic Center*

found as near as the chiefs' club on the naval base adjacent to the shipyard. On Friday and Saturday nights, the chiefs danced with women they met there.

After adding still more ammunition to the supply picked up in Norfolk, the *New Jersey* spent 30 August on a leisurely family day cruise off the California coast. One of the attractions of the day was watching the ship's newly installed closed-circuit television system playing a videotape of one of the summer's practice shore bombardments. Wives, children, and girlfriends saw where their men worked, and all were treated to a barbecue on the ship's broad fantail.

All too soon, the halcyon days of August were over. A huge crowd of families, friends, and well-wishers thronged Pier Echo at Long Beach for the departure on the morning of Thursday, 5 September 1968. After a four-day trip, the *New Jersey* arrived at Pearl Harbor on 9 September. On her bow for entry to the harbor, the battleship carried a colorful lei. The stopover in Hawaii was brief, but there was time for two nights of liberty. Ensign Walt Migrala and another *New Jersey* officer left the ship and were walking along a pier on the way to a good time. In the process, they spotted a ship much smaller than their own. She was 306 feet long and only 37 feet in the beam—DER-387. She was the USS *Vance*, previously commanded by Marcus Arnheiter. Her presence in Pearl Harbor caused Migrala to reflect on what a large role the small ship had played in the selection of the commanding officer who would shortly take the *New Jersey* to war.

On 11 September, the *New Jersey* left Pearl Harbor accompanied by the guided missile destroyer *Towers*. The destroyer would serve as an insurance policy since the *New Jersey* herself was not equipped with antiair missiles. On 17 September, the battleship changed course to swing south of Guam to avoid typhoons Carmen and Della. Later that day, she was overflown by two Soviet Tu-95 "Bear" bombers in a surveillance role. ("Bear" was a nickname applied by NATO.) They went over the battleship and destroyer three times, dropping down to as low as one thousand feet for good photographic coverage.

Captain Snyder hoped that the planes' intelligence-gathering would pick up the fact that he had ordered two of the now-empty 40-mm gun tubs painted light blue inside. One of his stunts was to have these small "swimming pools" topside on the battleship. Many crew members were out on deck during the overflight. Radarman Bob Fulks recalled that sailors were sending quite a few "universal hand signals" skyward. One of the fads of the time for anti-war activists was to raise the old V-for-victory sign but to call it instead a peace sign. In this instance, the battleship's men were giving the Soviets only half of the peace sign.

The *New Jersey* arrived the morning of 22 September at Subic Bay in the Philippines. There she received the finishing touches on her preparations for Vietnam. Departure from Subic Bay was on the twenty-fifth, and the next day the battleship had a final antiaircraft practice. On 27 September, the *New Jersey* rehearsed with a drone antisubmarine helicopter. Certainly she wasn't going into the antisubmarine business, but the ship was equipped to control the small, unmanned craft with the idea that a DASH version with a television camera (known as "Snoopy DASH") could be used for spotting gunfire. (As it turned out, manned spotter planes served the purpose in Vietnam, and the DASH was seldom used.) Also on the twenty-seventh, the *New Jersey* fired one last shore bombardment practice. The targets were barren coastal mountains in the Tabones range in the Philippines.

The *New Jersey* arrived off Danang, South Vietnam, on the morning of 29 September, and nearly three dozen news media people came on board. The media scrutiny manifested itself in reporting on something even before the ship went into action. Under the rules in force at the time, the men of the *New Jersey* would be eligible for an extra $65 apiece combat pay for September since they would be going into action on the last day of the month. Captain Snyder told the crew over closed-circuit television of their good fortune, and the information later showed up in some news stories with the suggestion that the schedule had been so arranged as to give the crew extra money.

Finally, it was Monday, 30 September. The morning dawned gray and choppy. Shortly after 7 a.m., the crew was called to general quarters. The initial target was an enemy supply dump a few miles north of the Ben Hai River that separated North and South Vietnam. The klaxon-horn salvo alarm sounded its warning buzzer three times. At 7:32, simultaneous with the third buzz of the alarm, the right gun of turret two blasted out a 1,900-pound projectile amid a wreath of bright orange flame. Fifty-four seconds later, the shell landed, and the pilot of a Marine Corps TA-4 Skyhawk spotter plane reported that the initial shot landed only a few hundred yards from the intended target—fine shooting. Adjustments were made, and the target was soon eliminated. Later in the morning, the Marine jet came under fire from antiaircraft batteries on the ground. The *New Jersey*'s guns soon silenced them. The appreciative pilot then flew to within close range of the ship, dipped his wings in salute, and radioed, "Welcome to the war."

One of the reporters on board to describe the first day's firing was a retired Marine colonel, Robert Heinl. Being on hand for the first shot was a joyous experience. During World War II, the new fast battleships had operated in support of the carriers, and the old battleships were better at shore bombardment. Now that the *New Jersey* was an old battleship herself, Heinl wrote afterward, she was shooting as well as the old battleships of 1945. He considered that such fine technical performance "could only have come from . . . the highest quality of command of the ship." Lieutenant Commander Albrecht knew Snyder as a demanding skipper, but one whose demands were reasonable. The skipper was not a gunnery expert, but he certainly knew enough about what could be expected of the guns in terms of accuracy—and he meant to get it. Beneath Snyder's sometimes-frivolous exterior was an officer with a technical mind and high professional standards.

For the men of the *New Jersey*, who had been training and drilling for months, the first day on the gun line was—to some at least—anticlimactic. Fire Controlman Crawford remembered it as "just like a day at the office." And, after all the apprehension about possible retaliation, Lieutenant Commander Albrecht felt "a little bit of a letdown" that there had been no reaction at all on the part of the enemy. The enemy did bare its fangs during the ship's second day on the gun line. On 1 October, the *New Jersey* fired at targets seven to twelve miles north of the demilitarized zone (DMZ) that ran between North and South Vietnam. In the process, the North Vietnam antiaircraft artillery hit a TA-4 jet that was on its way to spot for the battleship. The pilot radioed that he was losing fuel and would have to ditch his plane at sea. Chief Radarman MacDonald Shand, down in the ship's combat information center, acted as air controller, giving the damaged plane the course to fly to safety. The Marine plane flew out to the *New Jersey*'s position, where both the pilot and his rear seat observer ejected. They were picked up within a few minutes by the USS *Towers*, the *New Jersey*'s "shotgun" escort.

The *New Jersey* did more shooting north of the DMZ in the days that followed, and on 2 October she had her first underway replenishment off the gun line, taking on ninety-six 16-inch projectiles, 644 5-inch projectiles, and associated powder. She was alongside the ammunition ship *Haleakala* for some four hours. Just as Captain Snyder had demonstrated his confidence in Lieutenant Commander Albrecht by using him as sea detail officer of the deck, he also gave him the conn for underway replenishments. Though Snyder didn't direct the ship's movements personally, remembered Albrecht, the captain was very much in charge. In the case of an underway replenishment, the skipper wanted it done smartly, with the snap and precision that were hallmarks in the destroyer force. Captain Snyder, of course, would have borne the ultimate responsibility had anything gone wrong.

Within a relatively short time after beginning gun line operations, the crew settled into a pattern of firing and rearming. The ship went to general quarters when she was on a firing mission, and those who had to be topside were outfitted with helmets and flak jackets for protection. It was a tiring routine, especially for those who had underway watch stations. During the daytime, jet aircraft were used for spotting, because their speed made them less vulnerable to antiaircraft fire and surface-to-air missiles than were propeller-driven types. Ensign Walt Migrala, the junior officer in turret three, observed that the 16-inch rounds frequently had a time of flight as long as seventy-five or eighty seconds, depending on the ship's range from the target. He explained, "We'd count down so the jet pilot could hear us counting down. Right before the fall of shot, he'd dive down in the plane to see where the rounds landed." By staying high except when it was time to spot the fall of shot, the jets were reducing their exposure to enemy fire.

On the evening of 7 October, a Navy S-2 surveillance aircraft reported a concentration of enemy small craft moving along the coast of North Vietnam near the Song Giang River. In the parlance of the day, these were waterborne logistics craft. The abbreviation, WBLCs, was pronounced "wiblicks" as a kind of oral shorthand. Such craft were considered lucrative targets (abbreviated "LucTars") for the Sea Dragon gunfire forces of which the *New Jersey* was a part. The interdiction strategy sought to choke off enemy war materials on both land and water. Thus the *New Jersey* and her escort *Towers* took the enemy craft under fire with 5-inch guns and destroyed eleven of them before the remainder were able to beach themselves on the coast. The enemy junks showed up as phosphorescent pips on the surface search scopes in CIC and the fire control radars of the Mark 37 secondary battery directors.

Ensign Chris Reed watched radar pips wink and go out, one by one, as the enemy vessels were destroyed. Lieutenant Dick Harris was in one of the 5-inch directors that night; he recalled it as one of the few times off Vietnam when the ship fired a mission by radar control from the directors. Normally, the 5-inch guns were used for shore bombardment, and the mission was run from either a secondary battery plotting room or from the combat information center. That night also marked one of the very few

Port quarter view of the ship in Tonkin Gulf on 6 October 1968
Courtesy Chris Reed

times in the ship's long career that she fired at enemy surface vessels.

The *New Jersey* continued to move her operations farther and farther north up the coast of Vietnam. On 12 October, she fired at targets seventy-five miles above the DMZ, using A-7 Corsair II attack planes from the carrier *America* to spot rounds sent against heavily fortified caves at Vinh. She shot at the caves on the following two days as well, although heavy monsoon rains kept spotters from seeing the targets much of the time. During one of these missions, the heavy rain set off the nose fuze of a 16-inch high-capacity projectile. That led some in the crew to believe that the *New Jersey* had been fired upon from the shore. During the afternoon of 14 October, the *America*'s A-7s were again on the job, and this time the battleship fired for thirty minutes at coastal artillery positions on the island of Hon Matt. The spotter in the Navy plane reported one secondary explosion and the destruction of one artillery position. Then he exclaimed, "You've blown away a large slice of the island; it's down in the ocean." The exploit was widely trumpeted in the world's news media, leading to reports that the *New Jersey* had sunk an island.

In the middle of the month, the world's only active battleship moved south and fired her 16-inch and 5-inch guns in support of friendly ground forces in contact with the enemy. She supported U.S. Army troops in the II Corps area of South Vietnam, providing preparatory fire for a battle from 23 until 27 October. After the *New Jersey* had softened up the area, only seven Americans were lost in the operation, compared with 301 enemy killed.

On 26 October, while the battleship was bombarding targets in and around the demilitarized zone, Machinery Repairman Third Class Bill Sosnowski was on watch in the after diesel compartment. He was all the way in the stern of the ship, at about the level of the waterline. He was assigned to start up emergency diesels if the situation warranted. Unless there was an emergency, however, he had little to do, so he was passing the time by listening to stereo music through

Boiler Technician Earl Williams cleans an atomizer to be inserted into a boiler firebox. The long tube was used to turn the heavy black Navy special fuel oil into a spray that the boiler could burn to produce steam. *Courtesy Howard Serig*

a set of headphones. As a makeshift alarm he put a cylindrical dogging wrench on one of the metal dogs holding the compartment's hatch shut.

When he heard the wrench crash to the deck, that meant the dogs were being opened, and he was about to have company. Thus warned, Sosnowski scrambled to throw the headphones into a hiding place. Soon the hatch opened, and in came Captain Snyder, executive officer Jim Elfelt, and others. Sosnowski stood and saluted, then was told to carry on what he was doing. The officers went to the starboard side of the compartment, which ran from one side of the ship to the other, and asked him, "Did you hear anything?" Naturally, he hadn't heard anything except music, a piece of information he omitted in giving his negative report. The *New Jersey* had just been fired upon for the first time during the Vietnam deployment, and the skipper wanted to know if there was any evidence she had been hit.

Men topside had observed perhaps a dozen splashes in the water; the closest one was about five hundred yards short. Turret three kicked out some retaliatory fire. By the time an aerial spotter was able to get over the enemy position, the mobile artillery piece—which was probably about a 4-inch gun—had disappeared. Radio Hanoi soon claimed that its forces had achieved a direct hit on the *New Jersey*. Captain Snyder was his usual flippant self in reporting the incident to Saigon by radio, saying that it "appeared from the bridge that six to twelve golf balls were driven off Cap Lay in our direction. Next time I will try to get more excited." Snyder recalled that Commander Elfelt was a valuable "balance wheel," restraining some of the wilder messages the captain proposed sending at various times. Even with the exec's calming influence, a number of colorful messages emanated from the *New Jersey* during Snyder's tenure.

On 27 October, Navy Day, fifty men from the Third Marine Division came on board to visit. Some received their first hot showers in thirty days and marveled at the comforts of seagoing life. Staff Sergeant Robert Gauthier spoke to the crew over closed-circuit television, saying, "You are doing more to improve the morale of the men on the beach than anything else in the war. Every time we go on patrol, someone says, 'The big one is out there. Nobody better mess with us or she'll get them.' You are saving lives out here . . . American lives. And we thank you."

On the morning of 1 November, the battleship moved south to a position off Danang for replenishment. Lieutenant Commander Carl Albrecht, who had the conn, noticed that the ammunition ship *Haleakala*'s black boot topping rose steadily higher out of the water as she relieved herself of 417 tons of projectiles and powder. The whole period alongside, including the return of empty powder tanks, took more than seven hours.

During the course of that long replenishment, the *New Jersey* received messages from the Joint Chiefs of Staff indicating that all of North Vietnam was now off limits to U.S. bombing and shelling. Again, political considerations dictated the battleship's operations. Within a few days, Vice President Hubert Humphrey was to face Richard Nixon in the presidential election. Humphrey had been hampered by his support of the Vietnam War, and now President Johnson was making a conciliatory gesture that might aid in the bargaining for peace. Whatever the motivation, the bombing halt put the *New Jersey* out of business in the principal role for which she had been reactivated—bombardment of North Vietnam.

As is often the case with initial reactions, there were many overreactions. The war wasn't being fought for the benefit of the USS *New Jersey*; she was an instrument to be used in executing national policy. However flawed U.S. policy toward Vietnam appears in retrospect, it is unlikely that the use of the *New Jersey* in North Vietnam's southern panhandle during that period would have made a substantial difference to the war's outcome. The *New Jersey* still had a useful role under the strategy being pursued. By firing in support of allied ground troops in South Vietnam, she could do more in terms of the direct saving of American lives than by firing at the supply trail. In the months that followed, *New Jersey* men discovered that there was considerable satisfaction in saving those lives.

For much of the deployment, the ship steered northerly courses. The engines were slowed to bare steerageway, just enough to counter the prevailing north-to-south current and keep the ship essentially stationary. Down in the main battery plotting room, Fire Controlman Second Class Tom Mumpower was frequently assigned to keep the Mark 13 main battery fire control radar locked on a reference point ashore. When there was a call-for-fire mission, the target was plotted by the Mark 48 fire control computer, which solved the trigonometry problem involving the ship, reference point, and target. The Mark 48 computer then fed an offset bearing and range to the Mark 8 range keeper. The latter, in turn, transmitted orders to the guns to put them at the correct bearing and elevation. The higher the barrels were elevated, the farther they would fire—up to an angle of 45°.

To verify the accuracy of the fire control solutions, they were double-checked by the watch team in the combat information center and triple-checked by the team in the command control center, which was the former flag plot on the 03 level. When all the solutions were in agreement, triple C gave the okay. A fire controlman in the plotting room sounded the salvo alarm and squeezed the brass trigger, which sent a projectile on its long flight ashore. When the ship was moving, the Mark 48 computer provided constant updates. When the *New Jersey* was firing at multiple targets or shifting targets, the fire controlmen reacted as needed. They also reacted when given inputs from the spotters, who were either in the air or on the ground.

Another consequence of shifting operations south of the demilitarized zone was that the shipboard routine became a lot easier than it had been. No longer did the whole crew have to go to general quarters when the ship fired. One turret at a time had the duty under Condition III. If it was turret one or two, the topside portions of the forward part of the ship were off limits, but the crew was permitted to go aft for sunbathing or other relaxation. When turret three was firing, the forward part of the ship was available.

Fire Controlman Mumpower remembered, "I used to enjoy the trips topside, onto the fantail. There was a lot of camaraderie after a day on the gun line. . . . We'd go topside—the engineers or weapons types or whatever and bat the breeze back and forth. It was good time. You needed a chance to relax, and you had that opportunity back there." Gunner's Mate Striker Tom Feigley sometimes found it hard to realize that he was in a war at all, because there was little of the excitement or danger that one normally associated with combat. On the other hand, he said, "It's probably the hardest physical work I ever did in my life."

Captain Snyder was aware of the need to keep the crew interested and supplied with diversions. He gave the crew a sense of mission and self-esteem, and he also did something else—he played on the theme that battleship men had more important things to do than be bound by petty rules. In the past, as a flagship for numerous admirals, the *New Jersey* had been a spit-and-polish show ship. Snyder emphasized that she was now a working ship, so he allowed men to go topside without hats; enlisted men could wear T-shirts rather than dungaree shirts. It was a subtle means of thumbing the nose at authority.

In addition to such superficial things, Snyder displayed a genuine concern for his men. Unlike many skippers who spend their underway time glued to the bridge and sea cabin, Snyder was wont to roam the ship. He picked officers of the deck in whom he had great confidence and left them alone to do their jobs. That meant that he could go around and poke his nose into all manner of things. He frequently picked up an aluminum mess tray, filled up on the mess line, and sat down at a table to eat and talk with crew members. Said Radarman Bob Fulks, "He made a special effort to come down and be with the crew, to let them know that he was concerned about the welfare of the crew. He was . . . easy to talk to, a heck of a captain."

Sometimes Captain Snyder did his roaming in a bathrobe. Personnelman Third Class Hank Strub saw the captain in the personnel office late at night at times when Snyder would rather chat than sleep. Or the skipper might be down in the bakeshop at 2 a.m., sampling a freshly baked loaf of bread. And he habitually showed up at the weekly birthday parties in the mess deck. Each week a cake was baked and decorated for all the men who had a birthday that week, and they were given head-of-the-line privileges in the mess line. Snyder remembered that he got awfully sick of birthday cake after a while, but more important was the message he was sending to his men—that he cared about them.

The crew had a couple of ways of keeping up with the outside world during their deployment to Vietnam. One was through news programs that came in on the Armed Forces Radio and Television Service or news reports read on camera by crew members in the television studio. The other was through publication of the *Daily Bugle*, the ship's newspaper named by Ensign Scott Cheyne after a fictitious paper he'd seen in Scrooge McDuck cartoons.

Pete Holste, who was a journalist third class, recalled that members of the newspaper's staff made trips to radio central several times a day to pick up the latest news copy that had come in by radio teletype. Chief Journalist Jim McDonough handled the sports news, always an item of interest, and Holste and Journalist Third Class Bob Schweitzer worked on straight news. The whole thing was typed up as news came in, created in the printshop on the third deck, and then was collated and stapled for distribution to the crew. It was scheduled to come out as officers and enlisted men gathered for movies in the evening.

On 8 November, the *New Jersey* was detached from the gun line and traveled at high speed to Subic Bay to give crew members their first liberty ashore in a month and a half. She stayed there from 10 until 20 November. As for liberty, the tastes of the crew members varied widely. Personnelman Andy Lavella said that he and other chief petty officers spent so much time playing slot machines in the chiefs' club that "you could have scraped the silver off our fingers." Radarman Third Class Bob Fulks thought the U.S. naval base in Subic Bay was fine, but the adjoining city of Olongapo left much to be desired. Warrant Officer Ed Flamboe discovered the unsafe nature of Olongapo one day when he was carrying some money in his shirt pocket. He felt sharp jabs in his ribs, and when he reacted to those, a confederate of the jabbers took advantage of Flamboe's distracted attention to grab money from his shirt.

On the other hand, many of the junior members of the crew took special delight in the pleasures of Olongapo. Ensign Chris Reed observed that, "It was a young sailor's dream come true. . . . Terrific music, plus there was booze, and there were girls. And the girls, by and large, were attractive—better than average . . . and a lot of the sailors just fell in love with the whole thing. . . . It was like a [school] dance, except that you could get drunk, and you could take a girl home." One *New Jersey* petty officer considered Olongapo "heaven." He said, "It was a place where you could go, and you could get drunk. You could get yourself a girl, and she'd [even] feed you, all for under $10.00."

Though he was inclined to make things as easy as he could for the sake of crew morale, Captain Snyder generally showed that he meant business when it came to captain's mast. Ensign Frank Swayze was the *New Jersey*'s discipline officer. He recalled that the skipper often had several dozen cases to deal with when the ship went back to sea after a period in port. Snyder himself said that one tool he found especially useful was what is known in the Navy as a "suspended bust." To "bust" an enlisted man is to reduce him in rate, as from petty officer third class to seaman, for instance. The penalty meted out at mast often depended on the nature of the testimonial the

In November 1968 *New Jersey* crewmen bear a hand to pull in a line from the heavy cruiser *Newport News* as the ships prepare to moor side by side at Subic Bay in the Philippines. *Courtesy Howard Serig*

individual's chief and his division officer made on his behalf. If a man was habitually in trouble, he might well get a stiff sentence. If, on the other hand, he was someone of normally sterling performance who had a one-time misstep, the tendency was to sentence him to a reduction in rate but to suspend the sentence for six months. If he performed well and kept his nose clean for that period, the sentence was not carried out, and he retained his pay grade.

When the *New Jersey* returned to the gun line in Vietnam, she resumed firing mission after mission on behalf of her constituents ashore. Most of the time, the men of the battleship could not see their targets, because they were over the horizon. The only real idea of what was happening at the end of a projectile's long, high trajectory came in the voice radio messages received from spotters. Ensign Chris Reed got the impression that spotters occasionally called in rounds when they didn't really have a legitimate target; they just wanted to see what a big bang looked like.

Ensign Scott Cheyne, the public affairs officer, saw a big bang on one rare direct-fire mission when the target for the 16-inch guns was in sight of the ship. He described the experience: "This mission was such short range—we were shooting against a hillside, some suspected Viet Cong position or something—that you could follow the trajectory of the bullets their entire flight, and you could actually see them impact. The bullets would hit into the hillside, and you could see the shock waves, concentric circles ripple out in the trees. It was the most eerie sight I've ever seen, really strange. The sound, of course, travels slower than light. . . . Several seconds would elapse, and then you could hear the concussion, the shells exploding."

The ship's firing for 25 November was her biggest one-day score of 1968. She fired eight different main battery missions and was credited with destroying 117 structures and 32 bunkers. In addition, she set off eight secondary explosions in enemy storage areas near Quang Ngai, South Vietnam. Her projectiles killed an estimated 40 enemy troops, and spotters gave her credit for damaging 93 structures, tearing up 110 meters of trenchline, and destroying a number of tunnel complexes.

In December 1968 sailors haul seven tons of incoming mail on board ship following an extended period on the gun line. *Courtesy Howard Serig*

On 2 December, forty-five men from the Third Marine Division came on board to spend a two-day rest and relaxation period on board the battleship. Accompanying them was the division's assistant commander, Brigadier General Robert B. Carney Jr., son of Admiral William Halsey's World War II chief of staff. On 8 December, the *New Jersey* fired seven missions in support of Operation "Meade River." When she knocked out an enemy bunker south of Danang, the spotter reported that the resulting crater looked big enough for the foundation for an eight-story building.

Soon, it was time for another trip to Subic Bay, where the *New Jersey* arrived on 10 December and took on ammunition, food, and general stores. On Friday the thirteenth she headed for the equator in company with the destroyer *Towers*. Those who had not already made the crossing would have to undergo an initiation in order to be transformed from pollywogs to shellbacks.

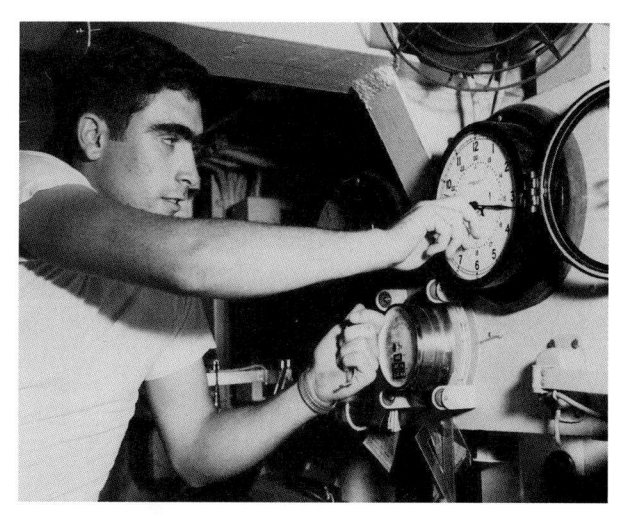

In December 1968 a quartermaster striker sets the time on one of the 139 shipboard clocks he has to wind. *Courtesy Howard Serig*

A reluctant crew member is offered a stalk of celery after crawling through a garbage-filled chute as part of his shellback initiation on 15 December 1968. The ship looped briefly south of the equator in connection with a port visit to Singapore. *Courtesy Howard Serig*

A mock beauty contest is part of the shellback initiation process. *Courtesy Howard Serig*

On 15 December, the day of the crossing, the usual foolishness occurred. Out on deck, Senior Chief Boiler Technician Walt Hosta served as "royal baby" for the initiation, which meant that his ample abdomen was smeared with grease, and pollywogs had to kiss it. Shellbacks lined up from bow to stern with pieces of fire hose to use as shillelaghs to whack the new men as they crawled by on hands and knees. For the most part, the pollywogs who went later in the process felt luckier than their predecessors, because the hose-swinging arms of the shellbacks were weaker and more tired by then.

Fortunately, the line-crossing ceremony was a prelude to a port visit in Singapore from 16 through 20 December. Ensign Chris Reed was struck by the variety of cultures visible. Ensign Ron Kaderli, a merchant ship enthusiast, found Singapore to be a living museum, because some old vessels in the area looked as if they had been around from the time of World War I or possibly earlier. Gunner's Mate Third Class Tom Feigley was one of many who shopped for souvenirs and found that the items for sale didn't have established prices. The system of haggling had been institutionalized and was thus the accepted way of doing business.

On 22 December, after winding up the Singapore trip, the *New Jersey* returned to her station off Vietnam's demilitarized zone. After two days of shooting, it was Christmas, and the men of the battleship celebrated by watching a show presented by Bob Hope and a troupe of entertainers that included nineteen gorgeous women. Featured in the ensemble were Les

K. W. Bowman and Stuart Goldman decorate a Christmas tree in the crew's lounge in December 1968. *Courtesy Howard Serig*

Comedian Bob Hope, famous for his USO tours, provided an entertaining program on board the battleship on Christmas Day 1968. *Courtesy Howard Serig*

Actress Ann-Margret visited the *New Jersey* as one of the bevy of beauties who formed part of the USO show on Christmas. Here she is flanked by Captain J. Edward Snyder Jr. and Gunner's Mate Seaman Wayne Johnson. On 14 January 1969 Johnson saved the life of Seaman Andy Tobias who was being crushed by projectiles inside a barbette. *Courtesy Howard Serig*

The bow of the *New Jersey* is filled with a sea of sailors for the Christmas program presented by Bob Hope and his troupe. *Courtesy Howard Serig*

Brown's band, actress Ann-Margret, and former pro football player Roosevelt Grier. The group arrived by helicopter and presented a ninety-minute show from the top of turret one. Fire Controlman First Class Rick Crawford served as escort for Hope because the younger sailors were all vying to be with the pretty women. Crawford found Hope to be "as funny off the stage as he was on the stage." Among other things,

Hope indicated that his idea of a good time would be to go on a double date with *Playboy* publisher Hugh Hefner and take the rejects. After Ann-Margret told Hope she wanted him both to sing and dance, he said to her, "Okay, but if I require mouth-to-mouth resuscitation, remember—no fellows!"

Having females on board was obviously unusual for a man-of-war, but the crew members proved adaptable. Chief Lew Moore's laundry took care of cleaning clothes for the visitors. He recalled that the women "sent their skivvies and all down to the laundry, and we washed them and sent them right back—no problem." Even more surprising was a request made on behalf of one of the women in the troupe. She had run out of birth control pills, and the "den mother" accompanying the women asked if any were available on board the *New Jersey*. There were, and the request was fulfilled.

Christmas came and went rapidly, and then the ship resumed her firing missions during what little was left of 1968. The New Year's holiday was a time for muted celebration on board ship. This was one night when the rule against consumption of alcoholic beverages on board Navy ships was at least bent. The chief petty officers managed to get a small supply of wine to add a bit of kick to the grapefruit juice punch they concocted in chiefs' quarters. As midnight approached, Chief Personnelman Andy Lavella went up to the helo deck and looked shoreward from where the *New Jersey* was quietly lying to. "You could see the Marines," he recalled. "They were probably shooting the rounds off just for the joy of it, because the whole sky was lighting up over there." For once, the *New Jersey* remained silent.

During that middle part of the deployment, Warrant Officer Ed Flamboe—newly promoted to that status and new on board as well—received on-the-job training on what a warrant officer was supposed to do. As an enlisted electronics technician, he had long found both pleasure and satisfaction in troubleshooting a piece of equipment, finding the problem, and repairing it. He loved to get his hands into the gear, and so he indulged himself after reporting to the *New Jersey*. Then one day, Electronics Technician First Class Ron Sousa came to Flamboe's stateroom and diplomatically gave him the best advice he ever got on how to be a warrant officer. Flamboe remembered Sousa telling him, "I realize you like to get your hands in, but you kind of destroy the confidence of the technicians when you do. Stand back and let them at it." It was a great leadership and management lesson—that people have to be allowed to try things themselves and learn through their mistakes rather than having the boss do the job for them.

A different sort of problem in officer-enlisted relations involved Bill Partain, the ship's warrant carpenter. From time to time, Ensign Chris Reed of the FA division would go to the carpenter shop, approach one of Partain's men, and ask him to do a certain job in the weapons department office if he had time. The jobs were done, but after a while Partain came to Reed to complain that he was jumping the chain of command. Reed explained that he'd just been trying to save time for Partain by not getting him involved. The warrant officer finally had to yell at the ensign to get him to understand: "When you ask an enlisted man something, no matter how you phrase it, it's an order. And you can't order my men around." Reed got the message—that he should make his requests through Partain.

Warrant officer country was on the port side of the second deck, beneath the barrels of turret two's guns when they fired overhead. The turret's firing sometimes made sleeping difficult, and it caused Ed Flamboe a different sort of problem. The repeated jarring imparted by the big guns damaged the bevel gears that turned the antenna for the SPS-6 air search radar. Some of his electronics technicians went up the foremast and retrieved the two gears that were supposed to mesh at a 45° angle with their stems perpendicular to each other. Ordering replacement gears through the supply system would take some time, and the radar would be useless in the meantime.

Thus Flamboe sought to have replacements made in the *New Jersey*'s machine shop.

Machinery Repairman Third Class Ken Kersch responded to the challenge with particular dedication. First he worked up computations and then stayed up all night making new gears from scratch. Unfortunately, the shank on one gear was too long, so Kersch put it in a vise to cut it down. When he did, the gear popped out, slid across the steel deck, and was smashed. Since there was no use crying over spilled milk, he immediately spent four more hours making another one. Then Flamboe and a couple of his technicians went up the foremast and installed the new gears, ducking behind the foremast for protection whenever turret two's guns were going to fire.

During the first thirteen days of 1969, the *New Jersey* supported troops in South Vietnam. From 11 to 13 January, she provided direct support for Operation Bold Mariner, an amphibious landing on Batangan Peninsula by two Marine Corps battalion landing teams. On the thirteenth, the ship was released to proceed to Subic Bay. On 14 January, men in turret three had to move some 16-inch projectiles on the shell deck. The gunner's mate who was supposed to be supervising was elsewhere, and the consequences were nearly fatal.

During the course of fastening in one of the projectiles, Seaman Andy Tobias didn't hear the alarm that warned the movable deck was being rotated. The man at the controls was not in position to see Tobias from his station. As the deck moved, Tobias' body was caught between a projectile hoist and a clump of projectiles. Slowly he was crushed into an ever more narrow space. When the movement was finally stopped, Tobias had suffered traumatic injuries, including compound fractures of both upper and lower legs, a crushed pelvis, and severe damage to many blood vessels. Feigley and others immediately began parbuckling projectiles away from Tobias. They were afraid that pulling away the last one might do still more damage, so husky Gunner's Mate striker Wayne Johnson—no doubt fueled by a supply of adrenaline—knocked it out of the way. Tobias was put on a stretcher and transported up through "Broadway," the long third-deck passageway that runs between the forward and after turrets. Sick bay and the operating room were in the forward part of the ship, so it was essential that he be moved.

Tobias, in shock and weak from the loss of five pints of blood, nearly died during the course of the surgical repair performed by Lieutenant Commander John Denby. The ship had what Denby described as a "walking blood bank" in the form of the hundreds of men on board; volunteers responded quickly and donated blood that matched Tobias' type. Denby's skillful work saved both the young man's life and his legs. It was a masterful, perhaps even miraculous, job. After a night in sick bay, Tobias left the ship as soon as she reached Subic Bay the next day. As the *New Jersey*'s surgeon, Denby was a holdover from the time when the smaller ships of the fleet looked to battleships for types of underway medical treatment they themselves could not provide. Providence was kind to Seaman Andy Tobias in putting a skilled surgeon on board the *New Jersey* on 14 January 1969.

The battleship's stay in the Philippines lasted until 20 January. She steamed to Yokosuka, Japan, where she arrived on the twenty-fifth for upkeep and liberty. Dress blues and peacoats were definitely called for on liberty—much in contrast to the liberty uniforms in the Philippines. Personnelman Third Class Hank Strub rode one of Japan's efficient electric trains to Kamakura to see the great Daibutsu, a giant statue of Buddha.

Fire Controlmen Tom Mumpower and Rick Crawford rented a taxi and had the driver take them on a sightseeing tour. One of the places they visited in Yokosuka was *Mikasa*, the battleship that was Admiral Heihachiro Togo's flagship at the Battle of Tsushima Strait in 1905, during the Russo-Japanese War. Now encased in concrete, it is a memorial and museum. While the Americans were visiting the Japanese battleship, hundreds of Japanese were visiting the American battleship.

The *New Jersey* was under way again on 5 February, and within a few hours of leaving port she ran into gale-force winds with gusts up to sixty-five knots. Topside, the heavy seas damaged exterior fittings. The ship arrived off Danang on the morning of 10 February and immediately began gunfire support of Korean troops fighting there. On 14 February, she fired a mission into the demilitarized zone when a U.S. observation aircraft came under fire from the ground. The next day, the men on board the ship received information that the communists were setting up a rocket site for night firing from the southern half of the DMZ, about eleven miles northeast of the U.S. Marines' post at Con Thien. Opening up about dusk with her main battery, the ship fired until well after dark. A ground observer reported twenty-five secondary explosions and seven fireballs that rose five hundred feet.

On the afternoon of the fifteenth, Chief Lew Moore was manning a 5-inch mount, because he had been a gunner's mate before converting to ship's serviceman.

In February 1969 the *New Jersey* takes water over the bow while involved in Seventh Fleet operations. *Courtesy Howard Serig*

His ears and mind had become so accustomed to the routine of the ship that a break in the pattern was disturbing. He heard the first two buzzes of the salvo alarm but then didn't hear the customary roar of a 16-inch projectile being sent on its way. The center gun of turret two had a misfire. After repeated attempts to fire the gun were unsuccessful, a two-and-a-half hour cooling-off period ensued to see if the round would be fired by a residual spark in the breech.

When it wasn't, the crew went to general quarters, and two men went into the center gun room: Lieutenant Roger Glaes, the turret officer, and Chief Gunner's Mate Harold Sykes, the turret captain. Outside in the turret booth, peering through a circular window into the gun room, was Lieutenant Commander Albrecht. The main battery officer recalled that he was describing "in excruciating detail exactly what was going on" for the benefit of Captain Snyder and Lieutenant Commander Roy Short, who had replaced Commander Pete Roane as weapons officer.

Glaes and Sykes risked their lives as they went in to clear the unfired round. First they took out the firing lock and pumped in water with a hand pump. Then, cautiously, they opened the mushroom-shaped plug that sealed the breech of the gun. Fortunately, nothing happened. When the two men looked in, they saw the problem. The powder bags were reduced charges and thus smaller in diameter than the full service charges. The last bag had tilted to a cockeyed position when the gun was raised to firing position after loading. When the primer was fired at the askew bag, it missed the red ignition pad and black powder at the rear end of the bag. Instead, it burned a hole into the silk portion of the bag. Sykes and Glaes, much relieved, pulled the bag out of the breech, and the emergency was over. The ever-curious Captain Snyder came to the turret and insisted on seeing the bag before Lieutenant Glaes energetically heaved it into the South China Sea. New powder was put into the gun, the breech closed, and the projectile was cleared from the barrel. Snyder prohibited the use of reduced powder charges after that incident.

The "mushroom" cap is shown atop the breech block of a 16-inch gun. In the lower left corner is a handle used to swing the device into position after projectile and powder bags have been rammed into the barrel. The ridges then rotate to interlock with ridges inside the barrel and thus produce a gas-tight seal. *Courtesy Howard Serig*

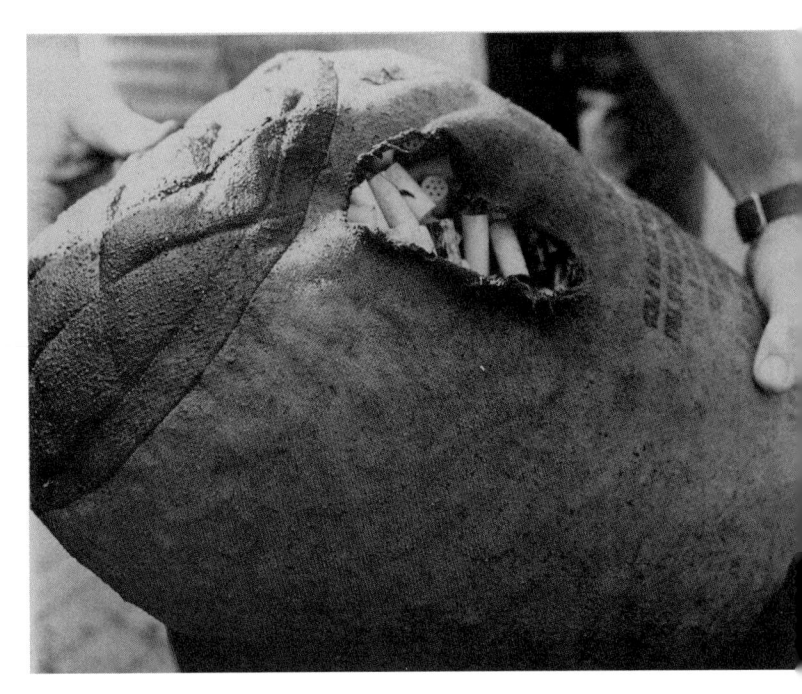

Grains of powder are visible through the ripped covering of a 16-inch reduced powder charge that did not explode during a firing attempt in February 1969. The quilted area at left is the red-colored ignition pad, covering the black powder into which the primer is fired. *Courtesy Howard Serig*

The *New Jersey*'s most noteworthy exploit of the Vietnam War occurred in the early morning hours of Saturday, 22 February. At 1:06, while she was firing an unobserved mission, the ship's combat information center received an urgent radio call for help. A large number of enemy troops was attacking a Marine outpost about one thousand meters south of the demilitarized zone. The *New Jersey* promptly began firing salvos of 5-inch projectiles, first with two mounts and then with four. The 16-inch guns joined in as the action intensified. The *New Jersey*'s guns were augmented by those of the Coast Guard cutter *Owasco* nearby.

The calls for fire from both ships came from one spotter on the ground, Marine Lance Corporal Roger Clouse. Radarman Third Class Bob Fulks marveled as he listened to the crackling of the radiotelephone net in the ship's combat information center. Speaking of the spotter, Fulks said, "He was very calm, very cool, as I recall, very skilled in what he was doing, even though he was facing immense odds. . . . He did a heck of a job, and he was on it all night."

Warrant Officer Ed Flamboe was also fascinated by what he heard over the radio that night, because the spotter's transmissions were punctuated by the staccato bursts of machine guns firing close by. The initial rounds from the two ships offshore were directed at positions practically on top of the Marines' outpost. As the ships fired on and on through the night, their projectiles moved the enemy forces back and away from the Marines. Fire Controlman Rick Crawford stayed in the *New Jersey*'s plotting room that night, even though he was no longer on watch, because he was captivated by the unfolding drama. He looked at grid coordinates where the spotter was calling for fire and noticed that, after a while, the spots formed a circle. The Marines were surrounded by the enemy.

Down below, Lieutenant Dick Harris was busy, even though his 5-inch guns on the starboard side were not involved. Following usual practice, the ship was heading northward at slow speed, and so the port side guns were engaged. Harris sent his men in relays to relieve tiring gun crews on the port side,

A salvo of 5-inch projectiles is in the air at left after firing from the secondary battery. *Courtesy USS New Jersey public affairs office*

One of the 40-mm gun tubs serves as a repository for empty 5-inch powder cans after the charges have been used for firing. *Courtesy John Hayes*

because the business of loading 5-inch projectiles and powder cases into the breeches as fast as they could was physically demanding. Harris also had his men transfer 5-inch ammunition from starboard to port to replenish supplies steadily being exhausted. That meant carrying the powder and projectiles across "Broadway" and thence to the handling rooms on the other side.

By 5 a.m., the firing by the two ships had forced the enemy troops to diminish the intensity of their attack. They began withdrawing. Finally, at 6:33, the attack had been completely repulsed, and the firing ceased. When the crewmen went out on deck that morning, they found the area of the port side mounts knee-deep in empty powder casings. After the cases had been ejected from the mounts, there hadn't been time to stop and clear them out of the way. The demand for fire was so heavy that the shooting went uninterrupted, and the brass casings piled higher and higher. The battleship fired 1,710 5-inch rounds that night.

Memories of that night were recorded in the ship's cruise book, *Dreadnought 68–69*. Gunner's Mate Second Class Mike Lucas, one of the mount captains, observed, "We kept up a barrage of four-, six-, and eight-gun salvos until dawn. The guns became so hot that the grease on the recoil slides was bubbling, and an hour after we finished firing the barrels were still hot to the touch." The grateful Major Ron Smaldone, who had been on shore and in command of the outpost that was nearly overrun, expressed his evaluation in one sentence: "If it hadn't been for the *New Jersey*, they would have zapped our ass."

The intense firing that night had started from Condition III and was quickly upgraded to Condition I for the people of the 5-inch mounts. It demonstrated the flexibility of the partial battle manning that allowed most of the crew to relax when not required for duty. Gunner's Mate Larry Pousson remembered that men in Condition III watches could lie on deck and sleep in turrets if they weren't being called upon to fire at a given time. When completely off duty, the gunner's mates enjoyed watching closed-circuit TV, chatting, and playing poker.

Poker games took place in the chief petty officers' quarters as well. Andy Lavella, the chief personnelman, remembered that Captain Snyder used to visit fairly frequently and josh with the chiefs. One greeting was "How's the game going tonight?" Chief Ship's Serviceman Lew Moore said that Snyder used to kid the chiefs during the daytime as well, once remarking, "What's going on? The lights are on in here." It was the responsibility of the chief petty officers to make sure the work was done, not to do it themselves unless it was beyond the capability of the enlisted men working for them. Thus, recalled Moore, chiefs' quarters was often dark during the day, a sort of sleepy hollow.

Despite their propensity for entertainment, the *New Jersey*'s chiefs had a vital role in the running of the ship. Chief Moore recalled that Captain Snyder's frequent visits were a way of reinforcing his support and confidence in the chiefs. He depended on them in matters large and small, and they, in turn called on knowledge gained during long years of service to see that their divisions performed well in their particular specialties. In the ship's laundry, for instance, it was Moore who was summoned to the captain's cabin when Snyder's shirt collar and cuffs weren't done properly the first time. Moore remembered that Snyder "relied on his chief petty officers, and he told them so. If you were a chief and you screwed up, he was the first one to greet you. But he backed his chiefs up all the way, and I've got to give him credit for that. Like he said, 'You guys have got the experience.'"

Between 14 February and 9 March, the *New Jersey* spent twenty-four consecutive days in support of the Third Marine Division. Most of that time she was keeping station in the relatively small area just south of the demilitarized zone. As the deployment wound down, the heavy cruiser *Newport News* came alongside the battleship on 13 March to receive turnover material for her scheduled relief of the *New Jersey* on the gun line. Army General Creighton Abrams Jr. was commander, U.S. Military Assistance Command Vietnam. He had previously told Captain Snyder of his efforts to get the battleship extended in her Vietnam deployment because of the valuable contribution she was making to the war effort. His

In March 1969 the *New Jersey* fires a nine-gun salvo toward targets in South Vietnam, the first full salvo since recommissioning.
USN photo 1137972 by Kenneth Barrett in U.S. Naval Institute photo archive

request was not approved, and the ship was scheduled to go back to Long Beach and then return to Southeast Asia in the fall when she could do the most good—during the season of monsoon rains.

The battleship made a five-day stop at Subic Bay in mid-March before returning to the coast of Vietnam for one final line period before heading home. She was back on station from 21 March to 1 April. The last spotter-observed mission was fired on the evening of 31 March at a bunker complex three and a half miles northeast of Con Thien. The aerial observer reported seven bunkers destroyed. After midnight, the ship fired unobserved missions, which qualified the crew for combat pay for the month of April. As she concluded her Vietnam efforts, the battleship had amassed 120 days on the gun line. In that time she fired nearly 12 million pounds of ordnance—5,866 16-inch rounds, and 14,891 of 5-inch.

The next stop after Vietnam was Subic Bay, where the ship stayed 2 and 3 April, and then to Yokosuka from 6 until 9 April. The crew had hoped to wind up the Far East cruise with an even more exotic port visit, which was the basis for one of Captain Snyder's more whimsical tricks. While in a crew's berthing compartment toward the end of the Vietnam stint, the skipper picked up a telephone, acted as if he were calling the bridge, and pretended to tell the navigator to break out charts for Australia. Rumors raced through the length of the huge ship, and before long it was accepted as gospel that the *New Jersey* would visit Australia and New Zealand before going back to the States. The single men were delighted. The married men reported in letters home that the cruise was going to be extended. Some of the men's wives began lodging protests with Navy officials and members of Congress. Since the ship did not go to Australia—which she had not been scheduled to visit in the first place—the wives smugly congratulated themselves for what they viewed as a successful protest campaign.

Unlike the *New Jersey*'s visit to Japan in January, the one in April was low key. Then the battleship set her course for Long Beach, leaving Yokosuka on 9 April as part of Task Group 77.7, which included the aircraft carrier *Coral Sea* and three destroyers. On the morning of 15 April, the *New Jersey* was only four days and eighteen hundred miles away. Lieutenant Dick Harris was looking forward to the homecoming with his family. He recalled, "We were all listening to the San Diego or Long Beach radios. . . . We were that close. I remember them passing the word, 'Stand by to list to starboard.'"

The ship heeled over as she made a long turn to port. Petty Officer Bill Sosnowski and Lieutenant (junior grade) Walt Migrala were two of many crew members up on deck as the battleship was headed east toward the rising sun. Soon, however, the sun was behind them, and they were pulling away from the *Coral Sea*. A voice radio message had come in, ordering the battleship to turn west. Surprise and disappointment filled the vast dreadnought. Captain Snyder briefed the officers, and then the word began to filter down. Fire Controlman First Class Rick Crawford received an inkling when the FM division officer, Lieutenant (junior grade) Larry Whitman, came down to main battery plot and asked if the ship had any shore bombardment charts of Korea; she hadn't.

As the crew eventually learned, a U.S. Navy EC-121 electronic intelligence plane had been shot down by North Korean aircraft, killing all thirty-one crew members. Back in Washington, recalled Admiral Thomas Moorer, then the Chief of Naval Operations, the Joint Chiefs of Staff were urging retaliation to prevent still further attacks. The Nixon administration, newly in office, was hesitant to start a round of hostilities with North Korea when it was already bogged down in a war against North Vietnam.

Reaction throughout the ship was mixed. As had been the case when the bombing halt was ordered at the beginning of November, some men were disbelieving, but international politics had again forced a change in the ship's mission and schedule. At the same time, said Carl Albrecht, there was a sense of excitement. Maybe the ship would be getting into the kind of action she had been denied in North Vietnam. As a result, he said, many people were thinking, "Boy, let's get over there."

The unexpected diversion from original plans spawned a host of difficulties back in the United States. By midweek, officers at the Long Beach naval base knew that the ship would not be coming in on Saturday morning, the scheduled arrival time, but they were forbidden by Washington to say anything for security reasons. Thus, many relatives of crew members did not learn of the schedule change until too late and showed up in Long Beach. Mrs. Sally Elfelt, wife of the ship's executive officer, took charge. Nearly two hundred families in the area provided temporary lodging for relatives of *New Jersey* men, but even that wasn't sufficient, and so the base movie theater became a dormitory.

Far to the west, the *New Jersey* arrived at Yokosuka on 22 April. In the thirteen days since she had last been in that port, she had steamed 7,042 miles at an average speed of 22.4 knots. Her crew wasn't permitted liberty; instead, the men spent seven hours in port taking on provisions. Then the ship headed out to get lost in an operating area that was centered about 175 miles southeast of Yokosuka. The ship's orders were to stay out of sight. Even while a force of four aircraft carriers, three cruisers, and twenty-two destroyers was parading ostentatiously in the Sea of Japan near Korea, the *New Jersey* was kept hidden in the background. Obediently, she steamed around in her holding area at eight knots to conserve fuel. Shortly after noon on 26 April, the ship received a most welcome message, directing her to head for the United States. At 12:35, her conning officer, Lieutenant (junior grade) Randy Ghilarducci, ordered "Right full rudder, all engines ahead full, indicate turns for twenty-two knots, steer course 090." The trip back to the Far East had proved an empty gesture. Fortunately, the *New Jersey* hadn't joined the other ships off Korea itself, or her long trip would have been even longer.

As the ship reached Long Beach on the morning of 5 May, Captain Snyder was interviewed by radiotelephone for the benefit of the news media. If the level of hostilities continued as it was in Vietnam, Snyder told the listening newsmen, "Only an idiot would not send the *New Jersey* back." A crowd of more than one thousand people gathered on Pier Echo of the shipyard to welcome the battleship. Her first mooring line hit the pier at 9:43, and as soon as the brows were over to the pier, there were conspicuously happy reunions between crew members and those who had waited behind for so long. For some wives, the wait had been too long. Looking shoreward from the deck of the *New Jersey*, Personnelman Hank Strub saw a group of men dressed much more formally than the casually clad Southern California crowd. The men in coats and ties carried briefcases, and in the briefcases were divorce papers to be served on returning crewmen. Welcome home from the war!

During the next month, the ship settled in for a refit period, and crew members were given early liberty on days when they weren't in the duty section. Into this atmosphere, the author reported to the *New Jersey* on 20 May to join the crew and to begin a period of training and indoctrination for the planned deployment to Vietnam in the autumn.

The *New Jersey* had done a splendid job during her first deployment to Southeast Asia, despite the change in role soon after she arrived on the scene. Credit for a ship's performance was ascribed principally to her commanding officer, so there were expectations that Captain Snyder would be on the selection list for flag rank. Lieutenant Commander Carl Albrecht was the *New Jersey*'s command duty officer one evening when Captain Snyder called him from a dinner party he was hosting in the captain's cabin. He told Albrecht that he had been receiving congratulations on being chosen for rear admiral. He wanted Albrecht to track down the official selection list as quickly as he could. There was a Captain Ed Snyder on the selection list, but it was Edwin K. Snyder, skipper of the *Newport News*, not J. Edward Snyder of the *New Jersey*. The *New Jersey* Snyder was selected for rear admiral two years later.

On 2 June, Rear Admiral Lloyd Vasey, commander, Cruiser-Destroyer Flotilla Seven, moved on board with his staff so that he could command that summer's Pacific midshipman training squadron. The training period began on 9 June when the *New Jersey* got under way for a two-week period in the Southern California area. On board were 104 midshipmen from the Naval Academy and NROTC units. It was a far cry from the seven hundred midshipmen the *New Jersey* routinely took on board each year during her cruises in the 1950s. By the late 1960s, midshipmen were dispersed much more widely throughout the fleet.

After the offshore training, which included shore bombardment requalification at San Clemente Island and observation of missile-firing exercises, the crew had one last liberty weekend in the Long Beach / Los Angeles area. On Monday morning, 23 June, the battleship was under way as flagship of Task Group 10.1. In her wake as she began her journey northward were the fourteen destroyers that composed the remainder of the training squadron. The *New Jersey*'s austere reactivation package had specified that she was not being equipped to serve as a flagship, and so

The *New Jersey* steams under the Golden Gate Bridge upon her arrival at San Francisco on 24 June 1969. *Courtesy Lloyd Vasey*

her communications gear was limited accordingly. The battleship's radio spaces were swamped while trying to handle the communications for fifteen ships, not just one. Two officers who got very little sleep during the early part of the midshipman cruise were Lieutenant Tom Thornton, the ship's communication officer, and Ed Flamboe, warrant electronics technician.

The arrival at San Francisco on 24 June was an impressive one, with so many ships stretched out astern of the *New Jersey* in column. The battleship passed under the Golden Gate Bridge and moored at the naval air station at Alameda.

By mid-1969, the nation's mood had swung considerably in the direction of opposition to the Vietnam War. On the night of the ship's arrival, Admiral

Rear Admiral Lloyd Vasey, *center*, commanded the summer 1969 midshipman training squadron with the *New Jersey* as his flagship. Here he holds a news conference at Alameda, California, on 24 June 1969. *Courtesy Lloyd Vasey*

Lined up are some of the more than 12,000 people who visited the *New Jersey* at Alameda, California, on 25 June 1969. *Courtesy Paul Stillwell*

Vasey's official car was surrounded by unfriendly people who used him as a symbol upon which to vent their frustration. The next day, however, the appeal of the *New Jersey* herself was demonstrated when 12,730 people came to see the ship during general visiting. Vasey recalled, "Throngs of visitors stood quietly and almost in reverence to visit Admiral 'Bull' Halsey's Flagship."

A few days later, the battleship was under way once again, steaming farther up the Pacific Coast and arriving on 30 June at Tacoma, Washington, to help that city celebrate its one hundredth anniversary. More visitors came on board, although this time their numbers were curtailed. Because the ship was anchored instead of moored to a pier, visitors had to stand in line to catch boat rides to the ship. I particularly recall one evening when I stood beach guard watch during the general visiting. I had a radio link with the *New Jersey* and was expected to maintain a semblance of order over the shore end of the boating expeditions.

One young woman in a miniskirt rode out to the ship early in the evening, accompanied by a *New Jersey* crew member whom she had evidently met while he was on liberty. At taps I called out to the ship by radio and was assured that all the tourists had gone ashore. But an hour or so later, a boat heading in toward the landing contained Miss Miniskirt, and this time she was with a sailor other than the one who had taken her to the battleship. She looked considerably rumpled at this point, and I overheard a few snickers from *New Jersey* men about her experiences in the "lower handling room"—a term I now realized could apply to more spaces than just those adjacent to the powder magazines.

As the clock edged toward midnight, I had to preside over the loading of the drunk and tired into boats returning to the ship. One pot-bellied petty officer first class resisted suggestions to get him into the liberty boat. From a position overlooking the boat, I told a couple of shore patrolmen to get the obviously intoxicated man on board and keep him as quiet as possible. He reluctantly acquiesced, but once in the boat, he pointed a finger up at me and admonished, "Hey, you in the Navy suit, if you're lucky you might grow up to be a battleship sailor someday."

On the morning of 5 July, the *New Jersey* prepared to go to sea once more. As some of the crewmen were coming on board at the end of their liberty, they brought with them a young woman wearing a Navy uniform. Her hair was tucked under a sailor's white hat. She managed to make it and was put into hiding. The woman's cohorts from the crew began taking her food, and she was having sex with them in return for her expected passage to Hawaii. Alas, the secret was too good to keep, and the men with her took to bragging. Machinery Repairman Third Class Bill Sosnowski heard the rumors that were spreading through the mess deck, and the rumors reached topside as well. Since she wasn't discovered until the ship was at sea, she had to be removed by a Coast Guard helicopter.

At about noon on Saturday, 12 July, the great gray dreadnought and her brood of destroyers swept past Diamond Head and through the narrow channel into Pearl Harbor. During the ten days the ship was in Hawaii, many crew members took tours, and many more went to Waikiki Beach. Near the end of the time in Hawaii, on Sunday, 20 July, astronaut Neil Armstrong made history by becoming the first man to walk on the moon.

From Pearl Harbor, the training squadron ships moved under way once again and steamed to San Diego, arriving on 28 July. The battleship moored at the North Island Naval Air Station in Coronado. Two days later, the *New Jersey* left for Long Beach, and on the morning of 30 July the main battery used the decommissioned fleet minesweeper *Raven* as a target. As Edgar Allan Poe might have written if he had seen the shooting, it took twenty-six rounds of 16-inch fire to spell "nevermore" for the *Raven*.

On the last day of July, the *New Jersey* arrived once again at her home port, disembarked her midshipmen and admiral, and got ready for one final month

Ensign Robert C Peniston and his bride, Fran, pose in front of turret one in January 1947. *Courtesy Robert C Peniston*

The same couple in front of the same turret during the ship's family day cruise on 25 August 1969. *Courtesy Robert C Peniston*

of preparations before the scheduled fall deployment to Vietnam. Three weeks later, Captain Robert C Peniston reported to begin turnover conferences with Captain Snyder. This was a homecoming for the prospective commanding officer, because the *New Jersey* was the first ship Peniston had been on board as a Naval Academy midshipman in 1943 and his first as an ensign in 1946.

On the morning of 21 August, the day after he arrived from duty in the Bureau of Naval Personnel, Captain Peniston was in the office of Commander Jim Elfelt, the executive officer. A telephone call from Washington reported that the secretary of defense was just about to announce that dozens of Navy ships were to be decommissioned. The name at the top of the list was the USS *New Jersey*. Peniston was stunned, because his dream assignment had fallen apart after one day. The rest of the crew got its shock later in the morning when Captain Snyder passed the word over the general announcing system that the ship was to join the mothball fleet instead of the Seventh Fleet.

Lieutenant Dick Harris observed that it was "a pretty low day for everybody, a very low day. I don't think anybody thought it should happen." Personnelman Third Class Hank Strub considered it a great mistake, but recognized that those in the ship had no control over their own destiny. He said, upon reflection, "I guess the *New Jersey* was a pawn and got involved in that particular chess game, and we lost."

As historian Malcolm Muir reported in his book *The Iowa Class Battleships*, politics at an even higher level than before led to the *New Jersey*'s departure from active duty and the war. The Under Secretary of the Navy was John W. Warner, who had served as a Navy enlisted man during World War II and a Marine Corps officer in the Korean War. Even though Secretary of the Navy John Chafee claimed that the ship was ineffective in her Vietnam mission, Warner was not willing to accept that assessment. In a Senate debate after the fact, Warner said that the decommissioning decision was against

Hot dogs, hamburgers, and other goodies were on the serving line during a dependents and friends cruise that meandered toward Catalina Island on 25 August 1969. It was a bittersweet day for prospective skipper Robert C Peniston, who was on board. He had already learned that the ship was due for imminent inactivation. *Courtesy Robert C Peniston*

Dress whites are the uniform of the day as the ship changes command from Captain J. Edward Snyder Jr. to Captain Robert C Peniston on 27 August 1969. *Courtesy Robert C Peniston*

his recommendations. He added, "I went down and personally saw the Secretary of Defense and was ordered from the White House that the ship should be deactivated because it was impeding the peace negotiations." To use petty officer Strub's metaphor, the ship was only a temporary pawn in the game. The U.S. combat mission in Vietnam did not end until March 1973.

During the remaining two weeks in Long Beach, the crew members were able to bring their families on board for a one-day cruise. On 27 August, Captain Peniston took command, and Captain Snyder made his valedictory speech. During the course of his prepared address, he said, "War is hell, and it is also expensive, and the American people have tired of the expense of defending freedom. And so this year when the winter monsoon comes to Vietnam . . .

the American boys who looked to the 'Big J' for their very lives must look elsewhere."

As officer of the deck at Long Beach that evening, a few hours after Captain Snyder's departure, my curiosity got to me. I walked from the quarterdeck to one of the old gun tubs that Snyder had used as a swimming pool. It was already painted haze gray inside instead of light blue. Captain Peniston was setting a different tone immediately—one of dignity and formality. Even though he was to be in command only long enough for the *New Jersey* to be inactivated and decommissioned, he was going to be a traditional battleship captain.

The *New Jersey* had been scheduled to depart for Vietnam on Friday, 5 September, one year to the day after she started her war cruise in 1968. Instead, on 2 September 1969, she moved out to an anchorage

Captain Robert C Peniston commanded the *New Jersey* from 27 August 1969 to decommissioning on 17 December that year. *U.S. Navy*

In early September 1969 the crew offloads 16-inch projectiles into a barge alongside while at the Seal Beach Naval Weapons Station near Long Beach. *John Cary image in U.S. Naval Institute photo archive*

off Seal Beach, California, to spend three days offloading the tons of ammunition she carried. Soon, she would be off for the Puget Sound Naval Shipyard at Bremerton, Washington. On the morning of Saturday, 6 September, a subdued pier-side farewell ceremony took place in Long Beach. Captain Peniston sat on the speakers' platform ashore, dabbing a handkerchief to his eyes, for the hurt touched him deeply. Then he returned to the ship and climbed to the 08 level bridge for what seemed then the last time a battleship would be under way on her own power. At 9 a.m., to the strains of the Navy hymn, "Eternal Father, Strong to Save," the *New Jersey* edged slowly away from the pier. Peniston emphasized smartness and tradition.

As the *New Jersey* made her way to the harbor breakwater and headed for sea, the day was hazy. Coming from the other direction was a squadron of minesweepers returning to Long Beach after a deployment to the Western Pacific. On the bridge of the USS *Esteem* was Lieutenant (junior grade) John Lewis. Because of the haze, the four small ships were using radar navigation to find their way into the Long Beach harbor channel. Suddenly Lewis saw the silhouette of a huge ship emerging from the gloom, and he knew she must be the *New Jersey*. He climbed as high in the *Esteem*'s superstructure as he could. Then, he said, "As we rendered honors she glided past like some great alp moving silently out to sea."

As the steel-gray Pacific lapped at the battleship's sides during the journey northward, Captain Peniston stuck to the bridge. That's where he considered a battleship's captain should be when she was under way. On Monday, 8 September, the *New Jersey* made her way through the tree-lined waters of Puget Sound. She arrived at Bremerton in the late afternoon and moored. On the other side of the pier were three long since decommissioned cruisers, the *Pittsburgh*,

Quincy, and *Pasadena*. Their faded gray paint was mottled by the droppings of hundreds of passing seagulls. To every appearance, the cruisers had died but had never been given a decent burial. Lieutenant (junior grade) Chris Reed looked over at the sickly old ships and felt, with a considerable sense of sadness, that he was seeing the future of the *New Jersey*.

Once the ship's officers had had a chance to sort things out with shipyard officials at Bremerton, recalled Jim Elfelt, the executive officer, it became more obvious than ever how precipitous the inactivation order had been. He felt that the ship had been hustled out of sight as quickly as possible to minimize the chance that supporters could organize and overturn the decision. Back in the 1950s, the *New Jersey*'s crew had known months ahead of time when she was going to be mothballed. In this instance, however, there had been only two weeks between the order and its execution.

Captain Peniston was in an awkward position. His personal feelings were completely against the decommissioning order. As a naval officer, however, he was compelled to follow orders and keep a lid on the whole thing. The Navy was deliberately downplaying all publicity in an attempt to avoid discussions about what some would obviously see as the folly of reactivating a ship for one deployment and then putting her back into mothballs.

For the crew at large there was much to be accomplished. Complicating the task were the steady Pacific Northwest rains that drummed upon the ship day after day. For a while, food was served on board, and then the crew moved off and occupied barracks ships. They afforded the men a far lower standard of living than they had known in the *New Jersey*. Personnelman Hank Strub and others moved into a house trailer just to get away. They had a huge job, because everybody in the ship had to be transferred. That meant paperwork to be typed from early in the morning until late at night. After coping with service records and transfer orders for hours at a time, a stop at Bill's Tavern was obligatory before heading for the trailer.

The battleship completes the final under way lap of her third period in commission as she steams toward the Puget Sound Naval Shipyard on 8 September 1969. *Courtesy Robert C Peniston*

The *New Jersey* approaches Puget Sound Naval Shipyard on 8 September 1969 at the end of the last voyage of her Vietnam War period of service. On the fantail are crew members' cars that have been ferried north from the home port of Long Beach. *Courtesy Bremerton Sun*

Senior Chief Storekeeper Al Scarselletta was one of a number of *New Jersey* men who made a trip to the mothballed *Missouri*, already berthed at Bremerton, so they could get an idea of what the *New Jersey* would be like at the conclusion of the process. Back on board their own ship, one of the storekeepers' chores was to check air vents. Scarselletta's men found one of the vents that hadn't been cleaned for an especially long time. The evidence was a sailor's hat dyed dark blue. It had evidently been there since World War II, when white hats were turned into blue hats to reduce their visibility topside at night.

Chief Ship's Serviceman Lew Moore found a definite morale problem during the inactivation, and there was no real cure for it. The crewmen had lost the collective sense of purpose that had sustained them since the days in Philadelphia. As Moore remembered, "Nobody wanted to do anything." There were some chances to get away on liberty. Personnelman Andy Lavella and some of the other chiefs enjoyed spending weekends with a fellow they met in the chiefs' club at Bremerton. He was retired Chief Machinist's Mate Orville Greenwood, who had served in the old *Pennsylvania*. His home on Bainbridge Island was a haven for visits by the *New Jersey* men, and they reciprocated by inviting him to visit their ship. When Greenwood got down into the *New Jersey*'s engineering spaces, he was, remembered Lavella, "like a kid in a candy store."

Finally, on 17 December, it was time to close out the log and end the third chapter in the *New Jersey*'s life story. The day was cool, rainy, and overcast—much in contrast to the beautiful spring weather in Philadelphia just twenty months earlier. Rare are the times when men serve in a ship from commissioning to decommissioning, but that was the case for a number of the *New Jersey*'s officers and men in the late 1960s. Two who did were Radarman Bob Fulks and Machinery Repairman Bill Sosnowski. As they stood in ranks that day in Bremerton, their peacoats gave them some protection against the cold, but no protection whatsoever against the chilling sense of sadness and loss they felt.

Andy Lavella, the chief petty officer who had served on board longest, lowered the national ensign at the fantail. Senior Chief Al Scarselletta, as the *New Jersey*'s senior enlisted man, lowered the commissioning pennant and presented it to Captain Peniston. The captain was especially sad, because this grim day in Bremerton was in such contrast to what he had expected the ship to be doing in December of 1969. As he remembered, "I think all the crew were betting that I would break down, but I didn't." Many in the crowd that day did resort to tears, because this was commonly believed to be the end of the battleship era.

Peniston's legacy from his brief command tenure was to preserve the *New Jersey*'s sense of honor and to oversee the inactivation so that she would be well preserved in a material sense as well. As he neared the end of his formal remarks, he said, "The hour cometh and now is to say farewell. But, before doing so, my last order to you—battleship *New Jersey*—is rest well, yet sleep lightly, and hear the call, if again sounded, to provide 'firepower for freedom.' She will hear the call, and thanks to her magnificent crew, she is ready."

During his decommissioning speech on 17 December 1969 the commanding officer, Captain Robert C Peniston, exhorts the ship to be ready in the event of yet another potential call to active service.
Courtesy Paul Stillwell

CHAPTER VII
FROM MOTHBALLS TO LEBANON
July 1981–May 1984

With each passing year of the 1970s, the World War II–built ships in the mothball fleet at Bremerton, Washington, became older and older—or else they ceased to age further. The end of the line came for a number of them that were sent to be scrapped. Two battleships remained, however, as their dehumidification machines hummed steadily. In June 1979, the *New Jersey* was moved from amid the other decommissioned vessels to a spot on public display—across a pier from her sister *Missouri*.

As the decade drew to a close, the *New Jersey*'s gray paint had faded, but it was apparent that she had not faded from the consciousness of those concerned with U.S. interests in an unfriendly world. The autumn of 1979 was not a happy one. Iranian militants seized the U.S. embassy in Tehran, and Soviets invaded nearby Afghanistan. It was a time when the United States was perceived in some parts of the world as weak and unable to exert its accustomed influence.

The atmosphere was made to order for Charles E. Myers Jr., a former Pentagon official who had become a part-time defense consultant and part-time unofficial lobbyist. Myers made the case for battleship reactivation in the November 1979 issue of the magazine U.S. Naval Institute *Proceedings*. To describe the intended role of the *New Jersey* and her sisters, he used the term "interdiction/assault ships," because it was less fraught with controversy and emotion than the word "battleship." Myers was tireless; he put together a detailed paper and talked, whenever he could, to members of Congress, congressional staffers, uniformed military officers, and civilian officials in the Department of Defense. The Chief of Naval Operations, Admiral Thomas B. Hayward, actively supported the idea.

In mothballs at Bremerton, Washington, the *Missouri* is at left, flanked by the *New Jersey* across the pier. Other ships include two guided missile cruisers and three *Essex*-class aircraft carriers. *David Frazier*

The administration of President Jimmy Carter exerted considerable pressure in 1980 to defeat the reactivation measure in Congress and finally succeeded. The victory was only temporary, though, coming as it did at a time when Carter himself was solidly trounced by Ronald Reagan in that year's presidential election. The new president brought with him a Secretary of the Navy, John Lehman, who had a vision of a much-enlarged U.S. fleet. Recommissioned *Iowa*-class battleships would serve two purposes. They would symbolize the nation's intent to rearm itself in the wake of the setbacks of the late 1970s, and the ships would have a substantive role as well with their 16-inch guns and new missile batteries. What's more, they would be relative bargains. The cost of bringing the *New Jersey* back from mothballs and modernizing her would be roughly comparable to that of a new guided missile frigate, a ship with only a fraction of the battleship's combat capability.

When battleship proponents received support rather than active opposition from the civilian officials in the Defense Department, congressional approval was relatively easy. Without such support, the margin of defeat in 1980 had been close. Part of the reason for the success in 1981 was that Secretary Lehman made the battleship program almost a personal crusade. He pledged that the modernization would be accomplished on time and within budget.

President Reagan's signature was still fresh on the defense legislation that summer when things began stirring in Bremerton. The Navy made plans to tow the *New Jersey* to the Long Beach Naval Shipyard for reactivation and modernization. The tow began on 27 July, in the middle of the highest tide period of the season. At 5:30 a.m., after the last mooring lines had been cast off, the commercial tug *Shelley Foss* pushed the *New Jersey* away from her pier.

Two fleet tugs were placed at the stern so their screws and rudders could substitute for the battleship's. The USS *Moctobi* was made up on the *New Jersey*'s starboard quarter, and the USS *Takelma* was

With the tree-lined banks of Puget Sound as a backdrop, tugboats tow the *New Jersey* on 27 July 1981 as she begins her journey to reactivation hundreds of miles south at Long Beach. *Puget Sound Naval Shipyard*

in a similar position to port. Both tugs were listed outboard three degrees to tilt their superstructures away from the battleship and minimize the likelihood of damage. The *Shelley Foss* then sent up a tow wire through the port hawsepipe, which had been cleared by putting one of the *New Jersey*'s huge anchors in a newly created notch in the spray shield on her forecastle. The push-pull tow progressed, although the *Moctobi* had to be replaced by the USS *Quapaw* because of engine difficulties.

Once the group of vessels was clear of restricted waters, the *Shelley Foss* was released, and the *Quapaw* and *Takelma* took up positions ahead of the battleship and began pulling. Late in the morning of 28 July, the *New Jersey* passed through the Strait of Juan de Fuca for the first time since September 1969, and then she moved southward in the Pacific.

Aided by the Humboldt Current, the cluster of vessels proceeded at speeds averaging slightly more than seven knots. Outside the Long Beach breakwater, six harbor tugs met the *New Jersey* on 6 August and took over the job. They guided her in alongside the shipyard's giant Pier Echo that had been her home during the Vietnam War.

Chief Personnelman Andy Lavella had lowered the American flag when the *New Jersey* was decommissioned in December 1969. By the summer of 1981, he had retired from active duty and was working in northern Virginia. Such was his enthusiasm that he traveled across the country to welcome the *New Jersey*. She was soon to begin the reawakening process that would transform a nearly forty-year-old inert hull into one of the most modern warships in the fleet.

The program laid down for her return to service was ambitious. Within a year and a half, she was to be reactivated and undergo major surgery. The modernization would include the removal of four of her ten 5-inch gun mounts and the installation of launchers for thirty-two Tomahawk missiles and sixteen Harpoon missiles. This would not be an "austere" reactivation of the type that had cost $23 million back in 1967–68. This time the price tag would be $326 million.

The Navy chose Captain William M. Fogarty to command the *New Jersey*. He had previously served as chief engineer of the antisubmarine carrier *Wasp* and then put the destroyer escort *Jesse L. Brown* into commission as first skipper in 1973. The shipyard experience thus acquired would prove invaluable in coping with the tightly scheduled milestones that lay ahead. In addition, Fogarty had demonstrated that he was an articulate spokesman for the Navy. The latter ability was especially important because of the unusual nature of the job for this prospective commanding officer. Not only would he have to fulfill Secretary Lehman's promises that the *New Jersey* would come in on time and on budget, Fogarty would have to try to convince thousands of people that reactivation of the other three *Iowa*-class ships would also be worthwhile. Fogarty performed this public role superbly in the months ahead; he made dozens of appearances and was interviewed by members of the media.

The decision to bring back the battleship struck a resounding chord in many Americans. Thousands visited the *New Jersey* in Long Beach soon after her arrival, and other thousands volunteered to serve in the crew. Many Naval Reservists wanted to be recalled to active duty. Men were willing to come out

A long line of potential visitors attests to the popularity of the newly arrived *New Jersey* in August 1981. Only 15,000 of the estimated 50,000 people who showed up were able to go on board. Long Beach Independent Press-Telegram

of retirement, and many who were still in the Navy yearned for a taste of battleship life. When it came to selecting the crew, Captain Fogarty was pleased with the names submitted by the Naval Military Personnel Command (formerly the Bureau of Naval Personnel) to fill key officer and enlisted billets on board the *New Jersey*.

Some of the crew members were selected from among the thousands of volunteers, but for the most part they came through standard channels, in part because crew members were needed sooner than the volunteers could be screened and in part because a substantial portion of the *New Jersey*'s crew at any time is made up of nonrated men fresh from boot camp or Navy schools. Some reservists and retired personnel were recalled because their experience with 16-inch guns and fire control equipment was sorely needed. A high percentage of the volunteers had to be disappointed.

The size of the Marine detachment was settled at two officers and forty-two enlisted men. They would be sufficient to man one 5-inch gun mount and to have some left over for other duties. The Marine Corps sent some of its finest. The battleship was a prestige assignment, and the reputation of the Corps would be judged by the actions of these few good men. As it turned out, a harmonious relationship developed between Navy men and Marines. The latter were accepted as exactly what they were—members of the crew—and not treated as outsiders. Even so, there was a Marine Corps pride that could not be quelled. Once the ship went into commission, the eagle, globe, and anchor insignia was painted on the outside of the Marines' 5-inch gun mount all the way aft on the starboard side.

The *New Jersey*'s crew as a whole was to comprise about fifty fewer men than it had for Vietnam, when there were 70 officers and 1,556 enlisted men. This time, in addition to the 44 Marines, there were to be 70 officers and 1,460 enlisted men. Some of the first crew members began showing up in the late summer and early autumn of 1981, not long after the ship herself arrived. They were struck by the immaculate condition of the ship's interior. The decommissioning crew had done its job well.

One man in both groups was Senior Chief Gunner's Mate Don Davis, who served in the *New Jersey* in 1956 and again in 1968–69. After having retired in 1975, he was recalled to duty because his turret experience was a rare commodity. After Davis arrived in September and had a chance to look around, he told a reporter for *All Hands* magazine, "Nothing has changed. The first thing I did when I went aboard this time was go back to the chiefs' quarters. My name was still on the old locker. . . . On the bulkhead in the second gun turret, there's a brass plate with the names of the last turret crew to serve aboard. My name's on top as turret captain."

Lieutenant Commander Chris Johnson came in October 1981 as the prospective navigator. There was not much navigating to be done in a ship that would shortly go into dry dock, so initially he spent his time going through the vessel to become familiar with her many compartments. He saw how solidly she was built, and he poked through the files that had been left behind by his predecessors. All that he learned reinforced the sense he felt that this vessel represented a tangible link with the Navy's past. He explained, "It's always very special to bring a ship back to life. I've been on a commissioning crew of a new ship, and it's not the same. The ship doesn't seem to have a spirit yet."

Another of the early arrivals was Storekeeper Second Class Richard Wolpin. His first task was to commute some twenty miles north each day to a government warehouse near the town of Florence. He and the storekeepers working with him matched up the shipboard allowance lists with stocks of parts coming in from the Naval Supply Center in Oakland, California. Some of the parts were needed for the reactivation itself, while others would equip the battleship's many storerooms. The quantities of various items allocated were based on usage rates compiled during the ship's active service in the late 1960s. In other cases, the allowance lists were educated guesses, based on the experiences of other ships, because some equipment and weapons, such as the Vulcan/Phalanx close-in weapon system, weren't around in 1969. The storekeepers also had to see that supplies of consumables were laid in, both for the shipyard period and beyond. Two items sure to be called for often were toilet paper and paint.

Gunner's Mate First Class Carl Farmer encountered a number of supply problems, which was certainly not unexpected in putting such an old ship back together. It wasn't always easy to convert a part number to the federal stock number needed to order it. And even when ordered, some items were no longer available because there hadn't been any demand for them in a long time. Thus it might be necessary for the shipyard to manufacture items such as gaskets that were needed in a turret. Then a contract could be let to enter new gaskets into the supply system. It was a time-consuming process to go through all the systems in a turret and untie the knots that had developed with age. Hydraulic lines were a perpetual problem. Because of the special attention paid to finishing the reactivation on time, the schedule was a demanding one for the shipyard workers and the future crew members working with them. Farmer remembered that after mustering at quarters in the morning, the Navy men sometimes had to work until 8 or 9 p.m. before being able to knock off.

Fortunately, many of them didn't have far to go when the day's work came to an end. Moored near the ship were the living quarters. These were three berthing barges—two YRBMs (Yard Repair Berthing and Messing) and one APL (Auxiliary Personnel Lighter)—and one messing barge. Captain Fogarty and his prospective executive officer, Captain Richard McKenna, moved early to make the routine on board the barges parallel as closely as possible to that the crew members would experience once they moved on board the battleship. There were watches to stand, quarters for muster, compartment cleaners,

The cluttered topside includes scaffolding and a fantail trailer during the ship's dry dock period in early 1982. *U.S. Naval Institute photo archive*

and even a closed-circuit television system that was later transferred to the ship.

For the most part, the men who would form the crew of the *New Jersey* were involved more with training for their jobs than with the modernization and reactivation work. Schools were set up at the naval weapons station at Seal Beach, California, for the men who would be in gunnery and fire control. Experienced crew members such as Senior Chief Fire Controlman Rick Crawford and Chief Gunner's Mate Larry Pousson constituted what Captain Fogarty called the "truth squad." If the school's instructors failed to mention something, or if what the instructors said wasn't quite the way things had been in the *New Jersey* during the Vietnam War period, the veteran battleship men gave their future shipmates the correct information. In part, that was necessitated by the age of the equipment. In an era of digital computers and microchips, Crawford had to teach such things as vacuum tubes and mechanical computers that weren't covered in the normal Navy training programs.

For the men who would be working with the 16-inch guns, remembered Pousson, the turret crews were sent one at a time for four weeks of classroom training at Seal Beach, where there were no equipment mockups. "When we got back to the ship," he explained, "we started a training program to make sure what we learned in school was applied to the equipment and everybody got qualified." The reactivation schedule for one of the turrets had been sped up so it could serve as a hands-on training device for the crews of all three turrets. Men destined for the 5-inch/38 gun mounts were sent north to Seattle to practice on board an aging Naval Reserve Force destroyer equipped with such mounts.

In March 1982, the battleship came out of dry dock and was moored to a pier in the shipyard as work continued. The living barges were across the pier. Nearby was a sign that proclaimed the area was "Battleship Country." As new men came into this country, they were introduced to Senior Chief Fire Controlman Al Gambetta and the I division. The division's purpose was to indoctrinate those just reporting for duty, and it would remain in operation after commissioning as well. Gambetta had developed a strong affection for the *New Jersey* when he served in her main battery plotting room during the Vietnam War. Now he was back again as the command master chief, the principal "sea daddy" for the enlisted men in the crew.

When new people reported, Gambetta and those working for him told the men about the ship and her policies and helped solve their problems. New men also met their division officers, department heads, the exec, and the skipper. One thing that Captain Fogarty and Chief Gambetta made a particular issue was Admiral Hayward's "Pride and Professionalism" program. This meant wearing smart, squared-away uniforms, obeying the rules, and—above all—avoiding the use of drugs. When the men had been thus warned, Fogarty was stern and almost invariably unforgiving at captain's mast on the subject of drugs. Of the drug users delivered before him, he estimated that he threw more than 95 percent of them out of the Navy.

Hard-hatted shipyard workmen cheer as the *New Jersey* is pulled from dry dock at the Long Beach Naval Shipyard on 13 March 1982. *U.S. Navy: DN-SN-82-05371*

Barges line the ship's side as the reactivation proceeds on 7 April 1982. Notice the office trailer on the fantail. *Mel Fredeen image in U.S. Naval Institute photo archive*

As the year 1982 progressed, Captain Fogarty was pulled in many directions. He made speeches on behalf of the battleship in Southern California and elsewhere in the country. He visited the state of New Jersey to meet Governor Thomas Kean and others. He went to Washington for a "charm school" gathering of commodore selectees, for he had already been chosen for promotion to flag rank. He even attended a reunion in Dallas, Texas, of former crew members of the battleship *Tennessee*. When he was back in Long Beach, Fogarty had frequent conferences with shipyard officials. He explained that the shipyard commander made a wise move in putting a widely respected supervisor in charge of the battleship project, because it ensured cooperation on the part of the union organization.

On 9 July, a "mast stepping" ceremony occurred to mark the installation of the battleship's new tripod foremast. On 6 August, the men of the crew began moving on board from the barges. The furnishing of the living compartments was substantially changed from the Vietnam period. For one thing, all the old racks and lockers had been moved out and replaced. Instead of the four-tier pipe frame bunks, there was now a new type known to Navy men as "coffin racks." They were of much more substantial construction than their predecessors and had an arrangement whereby the mattress and frame lifted up like a lid to permit access to a horizontal locker underneath. The old square-front silver-colored lockers were gone, and in their place were standup vertical lockers less than a foot wide. The new racks were only three high, but they were still confining. Storekeeper Second Class Richard Wolpin had to squeeze to get his 73-inch frame into a 72-inch rack. One advantage that the new arrangement offered was greater privacy than before. Each bunk had its own reading light and a curtain that could be drawn.

The mess deck and galley area were renovated as well. In addition to the new equipment installed, a new philosophy went in as well—catering to a greater extent than before to individual tastes. The program, which was based on tests previously conducted in other Navy ships, was run by Master Chief Mess Management Specialist Donald Smith, and it was a hit with *New Jersey* men. Given an allocation of $3.40 per man per day for food, Smith and his crew turned out meal after meal that had men saying the chow in the *New Jersey* was the best of their naval service. Part of the key to such success was variety. On the starboard side was a standard mess line with full-course meals. The port serving line was modeled on the fast-food establishments that had become a national phenomenon in the lifespan of the junior crew members. A new generation of Navy men had grown up on such fare and went for it eagerly. Among the selections available on the port side were hamburgers, cheeseburgers, hot dogs, sloppy joes, po'boy sandwiches, and French fries.

The McDonald's chain was the obvious inspiration for some of the menu items. The "Jersey Burger" was patterned after the Big Mac and featured "secret Jersey sauce." For breakfast there were Jersey McMuffins. For the *New Jersey* man who wasn't tempted by either the fast food or the slow food, there was a salad bar. The crew also had special dinners, such as steak night, seafood night, and soul night. For the benefit of dieters in the crew, the calorie count of each item was listed on the serving line.

During the course of the time pierside, the *New Jersey*'s engineering plant was gradually brought back to life. On 6 May, for instance, boiler number seven was given a ceremonial light off by Captain Joseph Gildea, the shipyard commander. After that, the various other boilers were tested, as were the main engines, generators, reduction gears, pumps, and so forth. The underway watch organization was set up, and finally all seemed in readiness for the first sea trials, beginning on Saturday, 25 September. Not quite all, it turned out. With Captain Fogarty on the 08 level conning station and prepared to begin the ship's movement away from the pier, he learned that the ship's whistle wasn't working. He refused to go to sea until he had a whistle, so departure was delayed until it was fixed.

Crewmen stand at the hawsepipe to wash down the anchor chain as it is pulled on board the battleship prior to her departure on sea trials in October 1982. *U.S. Navy: DN-SN-83-00900*

For Lieutenant Commander Chris Johnson, under way for the first time as a ship's navigator, he had an equipment malfunction to deal with. As the battleship headed away from the pier at the shipyard and out toward the harbor breakwater, Johnson's quartermasters were taking visual bearings with the gyrocompass peloruses on the bridge wings. They called them in to the chief quartermaster, who was plotting the lines of bearing on a chart. All was going well, remembered Johnson, until "my port pelorus died." When the chief announced that the visual bearings were no longer producing position fixes, all eyes on the 08 level turned to Johnson. The shipyard's gyro man went below, and fifteen minutes later the gyro was working again. By that time, the ship was out of the harbor and headed to sea. The harbor pilot was experienced enough to handle the situation without incident, but it was another demonstration that sea trials could indeed be trying.

The trials lasted several days, taking the battleship toward San Clemente Island near San Diego. A fairly high sea was running, and so a guided missile frigate was along to serve as lifeguard for the *New Jersey*, which did not yet have her boats on board. The battleship nearly reached full power, and the frigate, trying doggedly to keep up the pace, took green water over her bow, white water over her bridge, and lost her helo nets to the sea. Meanwhile, the *New Jersey* plowed steadily onward, throwing off waves with scarcely an effort. Men who had never been to sea in a battleship before came to the bridge and were awed by what they saw.

Once the first trials were ended, the battleship returned to the shipyard to fix some of the things that had gone wrong. The ship then prepared for the second trials, beginning on 18 October. Two days later came an event long anticipated, the first firing of the 16-inch and 5-inch guns and the Vulcan/Phalanx system. Secretary of the Navy John Lehman, the ship's principal cheerleader, was on board. He wore a jacket that proclaimed, "The Battleship Is Back."

The *New Jersey* has just passed through the Long Beach breakwater on the occasion of her sea trials in the autumn of 1982. *U.S. Naval Institute photo archive*

On 18 October 1982 crew members pass 5-inch ammunition down the line in preparation for the ship's second set of sea trials. On the twentieth, the ship test-fired 16-inch, 5-inch, and the close-in weapon system. *U.S. Navy: DN-SN-83-00896*

This close-up of the Vulcan/Phalanx close-in weapon system (CIWS) was taken during its initial firing by the ship on 20 October 1982. *U.S. Navy: DN-SN-83-00902*

When the first 16-inch round went out, members of the crew who were topside began screaming and cheering for what was obviously a substantial mark of progress in the ship's return to service. Storekeeper Second Class Richard Wolpin was on the 05 level, not far from turret two. He was wearing protective "Mickey Mouse ears" headgear but still wasn't prepared for the concussion. He had a camera along to take pictures of the firings and found that there was nothing to it. He just held his finger on the shutter release button, and the explosive force of the guns going off made picture-taking essentially an involuntary reflex action.

In mid-November, the *New Jersey* went out and passed her third and final set of tests, the InSurv (inspection and survey) trials. The next major event was her fourth commissioning. Originally scheduled for 15 January 1983, the date was moved to 28 December 1982 to accommodate President Reagan's desire to participate during a year-end vacation trip to his California ranch. The schedule, which had been tight to begin with, became even tighter. Invitations were sent, the crew rehearsed, and security precautions were gone over in great detail.

Bob Fulks, who had been a radarman in the *New Jersey*'s crew in 1968 and 1969, flew from Florida to California for the ceremony. He found that he couldn't get into the shipyard for a preview look on 27 December because the Secret Service had already buttoned up the place. On the day itself, Fulks and his wife showed up early and were glad they did because of the need to go through a security check. It included passing through a metal detector and having agents conduct a thorough search through Mrs. Fulks' jammed purse. They made their way to bleachers set up on Pier Echo, facing the starboard side of the ship.

After Reagan arrived by helicopter and inspected the *New Jersey*'s Marine detachment, he went on board and spoke of the ship's role in his administration's rearmament program. In describing the *New Jersey*, Reagan said, "She's gray, she's had her face lifted, but

The crew stands mustered at quarters during the recommissioning of the *New Jersey* at Long Beach Naval Shipyard on 28 December 1982. *U.S. Navy: DN-SN-83-00896*

President Ronald Reagan stands with the *New Jersey*'s commanding officer, Captain William M. Fogarty, during the ship's recommissioning at Long Beach on 28 December 1982. *U.S. Navy: DN-SN-83-03790*

she's still in the prime of life—the gallant lady *New Jersey*." At the conclusion of his fifteen-minute speech, the president, acting as commander in chief of the armed forces, said, "I hereby place the United States Ship *New Jersey* in commission. God bless and Godspeed." With that, the national anthem enlivened the scene, and Senior Chief Don Davis, in his third tour of duty on board the ship, raised the American flag.

When Captain Richard McKenna, the executive officer, ordered the first watch set, Lieutenant Commander Johnson, as navigator, had the honor of being the first officer of the deck. Captain Fogarty instructed Johnson beforehand to count the individual rounds of the twenty-one gun salute honoring President Reagan and to bring his salute down smartly after the twenty-first gun so Fogarty would

know it was completed. Johnson never got that far. When the first gun was fired, he raised his right hand to the visor of his cap. As he did so, a gold button popped off the jacket of his blue uniform and rolled across the deck. He was so distracted that he lost track of the guns and didn't know when to lower his salute. Johnson wondered afterward what Captain Fogarty thought of a navigator who couldn't count to twenty-one.

During the early stages of the ceremony, the crew members were in ranks on the pier. Finally, they were called to man the ship. They hurried on board and took up positions along the rail on the main deck and up into the superstructure. The last man to board, Gunner's Mate First Class Carl Farmer, was one of the shortest in the crew, because the ranks had been lined up by height. Along with the men running to their positions, a colorful array of signal flags ran up from bow to stern, the ship's deep-throated foghorn sounded, gun barrels and Tomahawk launchers rose to attention, the 5-inch mounts rotated, and the Vulcan/Phalanx mounts began spinning and bobbing. It was a spectacular show for the guests.

Once the formal ceremonies were over, Captain Fogarty conducted a tour of the ship for the president and found Reagan to be genuinely enthusiastic, taking an almost boyish pleasure in visiting the bridge, a turret, and other spaces. At the end of the tour, Fogarty and Reagan ended up in the captain's cabin. While dignitaries such as the Secretary of the Navy, Chief of Naval Operations, and the commandant of the Marine Corps stood around waiting, Reagan exchanged pleasantries with Fogarty's mother. She recalled to him how she had listened to him when he was a radio announcer in Des Moines, Iowa, years earlier. He asked her if she remembered a certain speakeasy from that time, and indeed she did.

Captain William M. Fogarty commanded the *New Jersey* from recommissioning on 28 December 1982 to 15 September 1983. *U.S. Navy*

Once Reagan left, the huge crowd ashore was able to clamber aboard for refreshments. Putting some 10,000 people on board the ship soon made for a free-for-all. Despite the crowd, Gunner's Mate Farmer was delighted that his wife had been able to come out from Indiana to see that day's impressive ceremony. Until then, the battleship had been largely an abstraction to her, but here were her husband, the Navy's only battleship, and the president all together. Said Farmer, "That day of the ceremony helped make up for all the hard work."

The next major milestone was the structural firing of the 16-inch guns to see how newly installed equipment would stand up. The ship went under way on 7 March 1983 and was in the Southern California operating area much of the month. When the big guns were trained around close to the superstructure and fired, Captain Fogarty was pleasantly surprised that there was no effect on new systems such as the Vulcan/Phalanx and the antennas for the SLQ-32 electronic warfare system that he had been concerned about.

On the other hand, more mundane things were suffering. Chris Johnson said of the tests, "We told the captain we were destroying the bridge, and we were. I mean, speakers were blown apart. Things were just leaping off the bulkheads. And most of all, it was like you were getting punched." Lieutenant Commander Johnson was serving as officer of the deck, and he observed that the junior officer who was conning the ship was briefly disoriented by the blasts and had a bit of difficulty making a connection. Johnson told him to bring the *New Jersey* around to head north, and the officer temporarily forgot the compass course, 000°, to steam in that direction.

During the weapons tests in March, the *New Jersey* fired her 16-inch and 5-inch guns at a target sled. The Vulcan/Phalanx system was also put through its paces, splashing two drones. On 23 March, she became the first battleship to fire a Harpoon missile. It erupted from a canister launcher aft on the superstructure amid a blast of fire and smoke. Much of the crew had to be below decks for the missile firing, so Quartermaster John Trail was thrilled to have the opportunity to be topside and watch. He was struck by the way the stubby wings unfolded after the missile left the canister and began the trajectory that would take it more than forty miles to score a direct hit on an old LCU (landing craft utility) used as a target.

After spending the latter part of March at Long Beach, the ship was under way on 1 April for a two-week period of refresher training. It included practice for the bridge and deck crews in going alongside other ships for underway replenishment. Captain Fogarty faced a situation that previous conning officers of the *New Jersey* hadn't encountered. The ship had matched up well with the low-freeboard, relatively short fleet oilers of yesteryear. On the other hand, when going alongside a new, long, high-sided replenishment oiler such as the USS *Wichita*, different hydrodynamic forces took effect. Rather than smoothly gliding along on parallel courses, a push-pull effect sometimes occurred because of the way the underwater hull contours of the two large ships matched up. He found that there was a tendency for a venturi effect to build between ships and thus the need for special vigilance on the part of conning officers. He found as well that the position of the replenishment ship's hose rigs at a higher level than the *New Jersey*'s imposed a greater likelihood of strain than with the older oilers.

Upon completion of the refresher training and a short stay in Long Beach, the battleship proceeded north to San Francisco for a weekend visit that began on 22 April. Many of the crew members headed off to enjoy the club atmosphere in north San Francisco. Included among the many visitors to the ship were Mayor Dianne Feinstein and members of the local news media. On the way out of San Francisco harbor, navigator Johnson had his gyrocompasses working this time, but he still felt uncomfortable with the quality of the visual fixes he and his quartermaster team were coming up with. So he asked the captain to slow down, and the ship proceeded out very carefully. It was then, said Johnson, that he came to the realization that his position plotting wasn't always going to work out so neatly as it did in textbooks, so he and his men would have to rely on radar, fathometer, navigator's eye, and other tricks of the trade. Still new as a navigator, he was finding out what many others had before him—that navigation is an art as well as a science.

After San Francisco, the *New Jersey* returned to her home port for a few more days and then set out for San Clemente and her first shore bombardment requalification since the spring of 1969. It was time for the fire control organization to demonstrate its capability and to put into practice all those things that Senior Chief Crawford had been so patiently explaining to a new generation of fire controlmen. It was a test not only of the equipment but of following the procedures for putting projectiles on specified targets and making the necessary corrections when supplied by spotters. The shore bombardment qualification also supplied further training and practice for the crews of the turrets. For Chief Gunner's Mate Larry Pousson, one of the crew in 1968–69, he experienced both the pleasure and the responsibility of being the top enlisted man in turret three.

The replenishment oiler *Wichita* refuels the battleship in the spring of 1983. *Photo by G. A. Whiteside Jr.*

FROM MOTHBALLS TO LEBANON 195

Turret one fires off a round on 2 May 1983 as part of the *New Jersey*'s pre-deployment training period. *Courtesy Paul Stillwell*

The newly installed refueling rig on the starboard side is used for the benefit of the guided missile destroyer *Callaghan* in May 1983. *Courtesy Paul Stillwell*

Following the successful gunfire qualifications, the *New Jersey* joined up with other Third Fleet ships for ReadiEx 1–83, a mini war game off the West Coast. Surveillance forces flew overhead as they tried to spot the *New Jersey* and her escorting destroyers for simulated launch of weapons. From time to time, ships such as the guided missile destroyer *Callaghan* and the guided missile frigate *John A. Moore* came alongside to starboard to take a drink from the battleship's newly installed refueling rig.

The *Callaghan*, new to the fleet after having been intended originally for service in the Iranian navy, was nearly forty years younger than the battleship, but both were frontline combatant ships of the U.S. fleet. Another reminder of the *New Jersey*'s longevity came in the form of a visit by helicopter from commander, Third Fleet, Vice Admiral William P. Lawrence. In speaking to the battleship's officers in the wardroom, he told them that this was the first time a Third Fleet commander had been on board the *New Jersey* since Admiral Halsey left in early 1945.

Shortly after Lawrence's departure, the *New Jersey* set out to do something that was beyond the realm of possibility in Halsey's day. One of the arguments that helped sell Congress on the reactivation of the battleship was the idea that she would be equipped with long-range missiles. Although the *New Jersey* was designed in the late 1930s to have an offensive role in ship-to-ship combat, she played that part only incidentally during her career. For the most part, her years of active service were consumed in providing antiaircraft protection for carriers, gunfire support for ground troops, and showing the flag. While all these roles were important, none had the glamour of wielding the big stick, going on offense. Long-range Tomahawk missiles enabled her to do that. The spring of 1983 was a time for testing.

On board for the test was a host of civilian technicians and Navy experts. The test was delayed several times to provide the *New Jersey* and the Tomahawk with the best chance. Even then, the conditions on Tuesday, 10 May, were not ideal; the day was sunny but windy. Crew members gathered with their cameras on the fantail to observe and photograph the test. In the early afternoon, the ship ran along parallel to

On 10 May 1983 the *New Jersey* fires the first battleship-launched Tomahawk cruise missile. Here the booster kicks in to send the missile to a target five hundred miles away in Nevada. At left, angled upward, is the armored box launcher that initiated the event. *U.S. Navy: DN-SC-83-08075*

San Nicolas Island and then turned to starboard to head out to sea. On the fantail, the crew had to scurry to and fro at times because the wind-whipped sea was producing waves so high that they leaped over the side of the ship and tossed showers of spray onto the deck.

Up in the combat engagement center on the 02 deck in the superstructure, Lieutenant Commander Gene Bernard, the ship's missile systems officer, was watching consoles linked to the Tomahawk system and discussing the situation with visiting technicians. In the amidships area of the superstructure, where a missile deck had been inserted after the removal of four 5-inch gun mounts between the stacks, one of the armored box launchers on the starboard side elevated to firing position. The installation was designed so that the missile would go across the ship, and most of its fiery exhaust would be absorbed by a heavy metal blast shield.

At last, the waiting period was over. On the fantail, this author and hundreds of others watched as flame and smoke accompanied the exit of the missile body from the launcher. Then it hung in the air for just an instant. Was something wrong? No, the pause was the time for the Tomahawk's booster engine to kick on, and then the missile was on its way. It soared off into the bright blue sky, leaving a trail of smoke and picking up a convoy of escort planes to go inland with it. Excited cheers erupted on the fantail. The missile grew ever smaller in the distance as it sped off to its target, some five hundred miles away in Tonopah, Nevada. Eventually, a report came back to the ship. The Tomahawk test vehicle, which was not armed with a warhead, had scored a direct hit on its target. The *New Jersey* thus became the first surface warship to conduct a successful firing of the land-attack Tomahawk. (The Tomahawk also has an antiship version.)

After returning to port two days later, the *New Jersey* was in Long Beach for much of the next four weeks to prepare for her first deployment since commissioning. Again, the scheduling was brought about for political reasons—to demonstrate how quickly the ship could be ready for overseas duty. Her departure from Long Beach on 9 June was a time of triumph and expectation. True, the married members of the *New Jersey*'s crew would be away from their families for three and a half months, but the overseas schedule—ten ports in seven countries—would provide

An aerial view of the first Tomahawk launch *U.S. Navy: DN-SN-83-08074*

Tourists on the USS Arizona Memorial gawk out of viewing ports as the *New Jersey* steams by and renders honors with her crew manning the rails. This was taken shortly after the ship began what became an extraordinarily long deployment. *USS* New Jersey *public affairs office*

plenty of interesting things to see and do. The idea of being feted in one port after another carried with it a sense of adventure. The enjoyment ahead would be a payback for the months of hard work and preparation that had brought the *New Jersey* to this point. At least that's the way it seemed at the time.

When the *New Jersey* arrived at Pearl Harbor on 17 June, the moment that made the deepest impression on the crew came while steaming past the USS Arizona Memorial. A bugler played taps, and *New Jersey* men cast a wreath on the water near the memorial in honor of the battleship sailors entombed below. Lieutenant Commander Chris Johnson was especially moved, because he had a long association with the scene. Having spent part of his childhood in Hawaii as the son of a naval officer, he had observed the old *Arizona* seeping oil and remembered her from a time even before the striking white memorial was built over her hull. He felt a kinship between battleship sailors of different generations. That was literally true. His father, then an ensign, had been at Pearl Harbor as a member of the staff of Admiral Husband Kimmel on the December morning in 1941 when the *Arizona* exploded.

Liberty in Hawaii was as appealing as it had been for members of previous *New Jersey* crews, and the tie with the *Arizona* enhanced the experience. Quartermaster John Trail and two of his buddies from the navigation gang donned summer white uniforms with blue *New Jersey* patches on their right shoulders and headed for a tour of the *Arizona* memorial. While the three sat in the front row during a lecture, the guide said, "We have an extra-special treat here. We have three live battleship sailors from the *New Jersey*." With that, applause erupted from the entire crowd. On the boat run between the memorial and the landing ashore, the three men did little besides pose for pictures. As it turned out, the day had an even happier ending. The *New Jersey* trio was picked up by a group of three women who evidently sensed the special allure of battleship men.

The *New Jersey* and her escort, the USS *Callaghan*, left on 20 June and headed westward toward the Philippines. Upon arrival in Manila on 3 July, the battleship had to anchor a mile and a half out in the roadstead because of the shallowness of water closer in. The U.S. Independence Day on 4 July was also Philippine-American Friendship Day, so Quartermaster Trail was somewhat surprised by what he learned when he pursued his interest in history during his time ashore. He went to an old fort and saw a display telling of the guerrilla war fought

The *New Jersey* steams as part of the carrier *Midway*'s battle group in the Western Pacific in July 1983. Soon afterward, her planned post-reactivation cruise was extended, and she was ordered to Central America as head of her own surface action group. *USS* New Jersey *public affairs office*

at the beginning of the century between U.S. forces and a Filipino insurrectionist named Emilio Aguinaldo. Besides the sightseeing, other pleasures were available. They included shopping for relatives back home, dancing with Filipino women in bars, and a nighttime activity he described as "hell-raising with the guys."

Once at sea again, from 6 until 11 July, the *New Jersey* joined other Seventh Fleet warships in an exercise known as Battle Week 2-83. The ship steamed for a while in the battle group of the carrier *Midway*. One of the roles envisioned in the planning for battleships in the 1980s was that their missile batteries could add to carrier battle groups a punch to reinforce that provided by the air wings. To demonstrate that capability, the *New Jersey* fired one of her Harpoon missiles on 9 July and scored a direct hit on a target hulk.

Once the fleet exercise was concluded, the *New Jersey* pulled in on 12 July to the port that had been a paradise for her sailors during the Vietnam War—Subic Bay in the Philippines. Chief Gunner's Mate Larry Pousson was surprised by how civilized Olongapo City had become since his last visit there on board the battleship in 1969. He said, "I couldn't believe all the changes they had in '83 when I went back. Back then [1968–69], there were a lot of dirt streets and stuff like that, and now I went back—street lights, paved streets, sidewalks. It really had been cleaned up a lot." Alas, the rough weather that plagued the ship a week earlier at Manila was after her again, only it was worse this time. The crewmen had only one day of liberty ashore before an approaching typhoon forced their recall from liberty and the ship's hurried departure on the thirteenth. So urgent was the need to leave port in the face of the coming storm that some men were left behind and had to rejoin the ship later.

As it happened, the leave-taking from Subic was only a day earlier than planned, so the *New Jersey* did not return, but headed south toward the equator and Singapore. The line-crossing ceremony this time was much the same as it had been for the previous crew in 1968. One feature was a "beauty show" beforehand with men in drag. But there was one significant difference. This time the ship was commanded by a pollywog, so Captain Fogarty had the dubious privilege of leading the parade of the uninitiated. He was outfitted in khaki trousers, T-shirt, a loosely tied necktie, and the khaki cover from his scrambled-egg combination cap. In addition to getting his bottom paddled, the captain had to stick his face into a garbage-filled toilet bowl and blow bubbles.

Storekeeper Richard Wolpin, also a pollywog when 17 July began, considered the ceremony "degrading and fun at the same time." As he explained, "It degraded the person, but it was a Navy tradition, so I had to take it in stride." Initially, one of the officers in the supply department wasn't going to permit Wolpin and other storekeepers to take part, telling them that they had too much work to do. Instead of feeling relieved, they considered themselves cheated because they did not want to be the only remaining pollywogs in a ship full of shellbacks. Through the intercession of their leading enlisted man, Senior Chief Storekeeper Robert Johnson, they appealed against the ruling and got it reversed. Wolpin was sore afterward but pleased to be so, especially after he had a good shower.

One shellback who enjoyed himself during the initiation of more than one thousand pollywogs was Quartermaster Third Class John Trail, the history buff. He wore a dress white jumper of the type that dated back to the pre–World War II era. The leader of the affair, playing the part of King Neptune, was Gunner's Mate First Class Curtis McAdams, a veteran of the old battleship *Nevada*. His not-so-regal crown proclaimed his feat of crossing the line in November 1943, nearly forty years before. While McAdams sat next to the pollywog princess from the beauty contest, the uninitiated came by to kiss his feet.

The next item on the schedule was a port visit in Singapore from 19 until 21 July. *New Jersey* men were struck by the cleanliness of the city, enforced through statutes against such things as spitting on sidewalks. Just as Chief Pousson had noticed changes in the past fifteen years at Subic Bay, he saw them also in Singapore. In place of people selling goods out of little shacks and roadside stands, he now saw high-rise buildings everywhere. But some things remained reassuringly the same: "All the vices were still there—the cars, the girls, the booze. Different faces, different names."

After a one-day transit, the *New Jersey* arrived in the resort community of Pattaya Beach, Thailand. It was probably the crew's favorite liberty port of the Western Pacific cruise. The beach gradient was a shallow one, so again the *New Jersey* had to anchor out, as she had done in Manila and Singapore, and small boats hauled men in on liberty. When they got to the beach, it was literally that. Since there were no piers, the boats ran right up onto the beach itself; men took off their shoes and socks and rolled up their trouser legs to wade ashore. Returning to the *New Jersey* after liberty was even more difficult, and some of the more unsteady among the men fell in the water in the process of trying to get on board.

The men of the battleship were especially taken by the friendliness of Pattaya Beach residents, which resulted in part from the fact that visits there by Navy ships were rare occurrences. As a consequence, local merchants welcomed the free-spending ways of the visitors. What's more, the people of Pattaya Beach hadn't experienced some of the less-than-pleasant aspects of sailors on liberty and so hadn't developed anti-Navy attitudes. Because the small town served as a resort for civilian foreign visitors also, it was set up to cater to the wishes of visiting sailors. Like Singapore, it was clean, and it featured a number of colorful attractions such as Hindu merchants peddling their wares, motorcycles available for rent, and low-priced tours to Bangkok.

In Thailand, as elsewhere during the course of the swing through foreign ports, Captain Fogarty was playing the public relations role at which he was so smooth. After thirty-seven reporters arrived aboard in helicopters, the skipper held a press conference to augment the tour of the ship supplied by Lieutenant Commander Eric Willenbrock and his public affairs staff. Fogarty had been through so many press interviews that the questions by now had considerable sameness to them, and his answers were down pat. In 1968, Captain Snyder had had to answer many questions about the possible threat posed by Styx missiles because they had been used to sink an Israeli destroyer the year before. Coincidentally, Fogarty was also asked about a missile threat because Exocet missiles fired by the Argentine Navy had sunk the British destroyer *Sheffield* in the 1982 Falklands War. Fogarty told a reporter from the *Bangkok Post* of the *New Jersey*'s heavy armor and said of the effect an Exocet would have: "It would be like a bee sting to me."

On 24 July, two days after her arrival in Thailand, the ship was ordered to cancel the remainder of her planned Western Pacific cruise, including visits scheduled for Hong Kong, Korea, Japan, and Guam. Instead, she was to steam to a position off the coast of Central America to reinforce the nation's naval presence there. The interest of the U.S. government was especially piqued by an increasing number of Soviet and communist-bloc merchant ships steaming toward Nicaragua, presumably carrying vehicles and arms destined for the Sandinista regime there. The aircraft carrier *Ranger* and her battle group had been on their way to the Western Pacific on 19 July when they were diverted to augment the naval forces on the Pacific side of Central America. Now the *New Jersey* would head there.

Once the *New Jersey* was at sea on 24 July, she steamed toward Subic Bay to begin resupplying for the long voyage to Central America. Fire Controlman Second Class Dan Clairmont was among the many listening when Captain Fogarty came on the general announcing system an hour or so out of port and told the crew where they were going. A lot of people were depressed, Clairmont said, because of the sudden change in plans. Those who had prudently saved their money to spend in Hong Kong, Korea, and Japan now wished they had spent it in the ports already visited. Along with the disappointment, though, Chris Johnson observed the reaction of a number of officers who were used to the carrier escort duties they had known while serving in destroyers. He recalled their feeling was, "We're finally on a surface ship that counts. We, the surface Navy, finally have a ship that is really in the focus, that can go places and do things and isn't just escorting somebody else."

Lieutenant Frank Brown, who had been in Thailand during a temporary duty assignment in the cruiser *Sterett*, was transferred on board the *New Jersey* by helo to ride part of the way to Subic after the cruiser was also diverted from her schedule. The Medical Service Corps officer had a chance to help out in the battleship's sick bay and was struck by the number of older men in the crew, certainly more than he was used to seeing in the average Navy ship. This came about from the recall to active duty of retired men and reservists. Gunner's Mate McAdams, for instance, the King Neptune of the equator ceremony, was one of several who had been in the Navy in World War II. As a consequence of having a sprinkling of such veterans in the crew, Brown found himself seeing sick call visitors with other than the normal problems. Some came, for example, with complaints of lower back pains, while others were in sick bay to have their blood pressure checked to make sure their hypertension medicine was having the desired effect.

After two days in Subic Bay, the *New Jersey* left for Hawaii on 29 July. While at sea, she was joined by other ships destined for Pearl Harbor and thence Central America. They were the cruiser *Leahy*, guided missile destroyers *Robison* and *Buchanan*, destroyer *Ingersoll*, and frigate *Roark*. In essence, the *New Jersey* and those with her constituted a surface action group.

While the *New Jersey* was in Pearl Harbor from 11 until 14 August, there was more Waikiki Beach sunbathing and swimming, and Fire Controlman Dan Clairmont had a joyous first wedding anniversary with his wife, Gail. She and other wives of *New Jersey* men had caught super-saver flights from the West Coast for the ship's brief stay in Hawaii. All too soon, there were more goodbyes of the sort when the battleship left Long Beach in early June.

During the trip eastward from Hawaii, the *New Jersey* and the other five members of her task group conducted tactical exercises. On 17 and 18 August, the exercises also involved the USS *Ranger* and her battle group, which had completed duty off Central America. The commander of the battleship surface combatant task group was Rear Admiral Peter Hekman. By tradition, he should have been embarked in the *New Jersey* as the biggest ship, but the reactivation at Long Beach had wiped out her flag quarters and flag mess, so he was in the cruiser *Leahy* instead. The newer *Leahy* boasted more extensive command and control facilities than the *New Jersey* and also the Navy tactical data system (NTDS), which the battleship did not. During the 1981–82 reactivation, Admiral Halsey's old flag spaces were gutted to make room for Tomahawk missile control equipment and computers. Part of the former flag space on the 02 level was designated the combat engagement center and took over the functions previously performed by the combat information center down on the fourth deck. In the *New Jersey*'s final incarnation, the CIC was manned by a skeleton crew that was a backup for the people topside in the CEC.

The *New Jersey* and the five ships with her arrived off the west coast of Central America on 26 August. Their mission was officially indicated as training and surveillance. More to the point, the battleship and her consorts were providing naval presence, ready to exert themselves on behalf of U.S. national interests if the situation warranted. For the men on board the battleship, it was a time of watchful waiting. It certainly was a good deal less enjoyable than the port visit routine that was so recently interrupted.

The *New Jersey* and the destroyer *Robison* left the patrol station to make a port visit in Balboa, Panama, from 2 until 5 September. As usual, dignitaries came on board, including an officer who had been on board the *New Jersey* as part of Rear Admiral Edward Parker's cruiser division staff in 1955. He was Vice Admiral Joseph Metcalf, who was now commander, Second Fleet. On 7 September, while back off the Central American coast, the *New Jersey* received a visit from Secretary of Defense Caspar Weinberger and the president of El Salvador, Alvaro Magana. The two men and their retinues were posted at various stations in the superstructure to witness a firepower demonstration. In this case, it was an eight-gun broadside, which would have been nine except for the fact that the barrel liner was cracked and worn in the center gun of turret two so that it wasn't fired at any time during the deployment.

The *New Jersey* generally operated out of sight of land when off the coast, and it would have been tough to see the shore even if closer, because the weather was frequently overcast and rainy. Navigator Chris Johnson said, "I have never seen thundershowers erupt so quickly in my life as down there." Heavy rain was drenching the ship on 9 September when the *New Jersey*'s SH-2 Sea Sprite helicopter brought on board Captain Richard D. Milligan after a harrowing trip over from the frigate *Roark*, which had transported him out from Panama. Captain Fogarty met him on the fantail, and then the two ran for shelter in the after part of the superstructure. It was a wet welcome for the man who had been ordered in to relieve Captain Fogarty as commanding officer. The *New Jersey* was scheduled to return to Long Beach on 17 September and hold a change of command there on 1 October. Rather than wait for the ship to come in, Milligan thought it would be wise to go on board and spend some time under way with Captain Fogarty before taking command. There was, however, to be no opportunity for a leisurely turnover period and ride back to Long Beach. On the very day of Captain Milligan's arrival, the *New Jersey* was ordered to leave the surface task group and steam south to a position off the Panama Canal. The day after that, she was ordered to anchor off Balboa, Panama, and to prepare to go through the canal into the Atlantic Ocean.

Information as to plans for the ship leaked out to the crew in the form of rumors. When the ship reached Balboa, crew members were allowed to go ashore for a few hours to telephone their relatives and tell them that they would be going to an undisclosed location for an unknown period of time. Fire Controlman Second Class Dan Clairmont telephoned Santa Ana, California. He remembered, "I called my wife, and she was already in tears, because it had . . . been on the news that we were heading for Beirut, Lebanon. . . . I was really upset because we weren't told." Soon both Clairmonts were crying at long-distance rates. The scheduled happy homecoming had been only seven days away. They now had no idea when they would see each other again.

The day of 12 September was spent going through the canal. Crew members who didn't have other duties were able to go topside and take pictures. John Trail and another quartermaster were trading off two-hour stints at the helm on the way through. When Trail was off duty, he could observe the sights but at the same time was supposed to maintain a sense of decorum. Thus, he was apprehensive when Captain Milligan came over and asked what he was doing when he was, in fact, using a pair of binoculars to check out a bikini-clad woman ashore. Milligan was so new on board that the crew didn't yet know how he would react to things. The concern was soon allayed when Milligan borrowed Trail's binoculars, took a look, said "She's not bad-looking," and walked away. This new guy was going to be all right, Trail decided.

For both Milligan and Fogarty, the change of plans forced some adjustments. With the likelihood that the *New Jersey* would be going into combat in the Middle East, Captain Fogarty had an understandable desire to stay. Milligan, who had commanded the cruiser *Wainwright* in the Mediterranean within the past year, was eager to command the battleship there. He thus felt a sense of satisfaction when ordered to relieve Fogarty forthwith and take the ship eastward. In a line that he probably polished in after-dinner speeches, Milligan said of Fogarty, "When the ship was redirected, there was a little bit of reluctance, I

Captain Richard D. Milligan commanded the *New Jersey* from 15 September 1983 to 7 September 1985. *U.S. Navy*

think, in his mind to leave the ship. We're about the same size, so it would have been a hell of a fight to see who could throw who overboard."

On 13 September, the day after clearing the canal, the *New Jersey* was under way from Panama and soon chewing up the miles at twenty-five knots. The two captains went through an amiable but rushed turnover. Instead of having two or three weeks to finish fitness reports on the *New Jersey*'s nearly seventy officers, Fogarty had only two or three days. On 15 September, the ship slowed down briefly while north of Puerto Rico for a change of command ceremony on the forecastle. She was still moving along at such a clip that the relative wind made it difficult for crew members on deck to hear the words spoken by the principals.

For Fogarty, it was a bittersweet leave-taking. As soon as he was relieved, he was frocked in the rank of commodore, and his one-star flag was broken at the top of the ship. On the other hand, the brief ceremony did not permit the sort of public acclaim that would have been his in Long Beach. More importantly, he was forced to withdraw prematurely from this ship he loved so much that he got feelings of exhilaration when he thought about being in command of her. Sunglasses masked from most the moistness in the new commodore's eyes as he moved aft to the helicopter that would take him away.

Once the ceremony was over, the *New Jersey*'s speed climbed back to twenty-five knots for the trip across the Atlantic. One result was that the customary vibration in the chief petty officers' quarters near the propellers became considerably worse than usual. Senior Chief Rick Crawford remembered that the chiefs couldn't set their coffee cups down because the mess tables were shaking so much. They had to hold onto their plates while they ate. Chief Gunner's Mate Larry Pousson sometimes woke up at 2 or 3 a.m. and found twenty or thirty chiefs sitting up because they couldn't sleep. A number of them chose to bed down in their work spaces or elsewhere in the ship.

When the *New Jersey* reached Rota, Spain, on 21 September, she slowed down for the first time since Puerto Rico so helos could ferry aboard mail, cargo, and new crew members who had initially reported to Long Beach. She soon went through the Strait of Gibraltar into the Mediterranean. The speed run finally came to an end twelve days after it started. The battleship arrived off Lebanon, and Vice Admiral Edward Martin, commander, Sixth Fleet, came on board. In a four-month period, from June to September, the battleship had been in all four of the U.S. Navy's numbered fleets—Third, Seventh, Second, and Sixth—and the commanders of all four had visited her.

The *New Jersey*'s mission off troubled Beirut would be to try to stabilize a situation that had gone from bad to worse. Initially, U.S. Marines had gone into Lebanon in the summer of 1982 as part of a multinational peacekeeping force designed to maintain order among the nation's warring factions. The situation was further snarled by the presence of Israelis, Syrians, and the Palestine Liberation Organization.

On 28 September 1983, while in the Mediterranean, crewmen stand by as an SH-3 helicopter prepares to land on the stern for refueling. *U.S. Navy: DN-SC-87-01518*

The PLO had been evacuated successfully, but things blew up soon afterward when Palestinian refugees were massacred and President-elect Bashir Gemayel of Lebanon was assassinated.

The Marines were transformed from peacekeepers to targets as they hunkered down in a compound at the Beirut International Airport. If tactical considerations had prevailed, they would have taken the high ground—the mountains overlooking the city. But this was a war of political rather than tactical maneuvering. The mountains were thus left to the Syrians, who regularly used the elevated vantage point to fire on the Marines. On 8 September, the day before the *New Jersey* was ordered to Panama, the frigate *Bowen* became the first American warship to provide shore bombardment in support of Lebanese military forces. Given the steadily rising pressure in the area and the addition of naval gunfire to the explosive mixture, it is little wonder that the Joint Chiefs of Staff decided to order in the biggest and most powerful gunfire ship of all.

Within hours of the *New Jersey*'s arrival, a ceasefire was arranged ashore. It appeared that the battleship had achieved her purpose without firing a shot, the essence of gunboat diplomacy. In this instance, though, with the complex web of relationships and antagonisms, a ceasefire was as easily broken as it was established, and the situation soon degenerated to the status quo prior to the *New Jersey*'s arrival.

In lieu of orders for her to shoot, the *New Jersey*'s mission was again naval presence, and that was initially quite an anticlimax after the expectations that had developed during the furious steaming from Central America. From the ship's bridge, Captain Milligan could look toward the city of Beirut and see sunbathers on the beach, motorboat races, and—the most irritating of all—a merry-go-round that rotated steadily day and night as if it weren't in the middle of an urban battleground. That battleground was at its most bizarre during darkness. To Lieutenant Commander Chris Johnson, it seemed as if the Lebanese and others went to work during the daytime, then went home afterward, got out their guns, and started shooting. First came the small arms, then the machine guns, later the rocket launchers, and even tanks.

Amid this madness, it appeared at times as if the *New Jersey* would be called upon to join the fray. On a number of occasions, recalled Gunner's Mate Larry Pousson, the orders did come through to man the turrets for possible firing missions. Men went to their stations, powder tanks were opened in the magazines, and powder bags sent up the hoists to the gun rooms. Projectiles were sent up to the turret cradles, ready to be rammed into gun breeches. The permission to fire didn't come, and the ammunition was sent back down and put away. Said Pousson, "This was really the frustrating part about it—the Marines getting pounded on, but you can't do anything about it."

The training of the *New Jersey*'s crew members had prepared them for this new existence in a military sense—they knew how to operate their equipment and fight the ship—but not a psychological one.

One factor that helped enormously in their ability to cope was the presence of their new commanding officer. Captain Milligan quickly demonstrated that he had brought a seabag full of leadership qualities with him. He was as much as possible—given the demands of the situation—a peripatetic skipper. He moved about the ship to talk to the men of the *New Jersey*, to learn of their concerns, and to do what he could to alleviate those concerns.

The time off the coast of Beirut quickly settled into a stultifying routine. Men got up, went to their spaces, trained at their jobs, cleaned up, watched television, read, ate their meals, and cursed their collective fate. The early part of October was frustrating. Not only was the ship not able to go home, but she wasn't doing anything else either—at least nothing overt. By her very presence, however, perhaps she was preventing something far worse from happening ashore. But then, in the early hours of Sunday, 23 October 1983, something far worse did happen ashore. The near-daily firing at the Marines' compound by rockets, artillery, and snipers had been bad enough, but now a suicidal terrorist drove a truck full of explosives into the compound and detonated it under the Marine barracks.

A shroud of fog blocked off the battleship's view of the beach. As the morning progressed, word began filtering to the crew that something had happened ashore—something bad. Then Captain Milligan came on the loudspeaker to report of the tragedy, and the ship went to general quarters. More than anything, the crew had a desire to retaliate for the hurt that had been done to so many of their fellow Americans. But, as Captain Milligan knew well, it was not at all clear whom such retaliation could be aimed at, and the men were eventually released from their battle stations.

Quartermaster John Trail was in the battleship's armored conning tower that morning, and from time to time he looked at an electronic ticker aft of the helmsman's station. It was bringing in the grim news, and with each report the number of deaths and injuries climbed higher and higher. Ultimately, the death toll mounted to 241 American servicemen. Included was the *New Jersey*'s Chief Electronics Technician Michael Gorchinski, who had gone ashore to help the Marines with their radars.

The battleship sent one of her doctors ashore, about three-fourths of her Marines for security duty, and a working party of Navy men to help in the efforts to rescue still-living men from the rubble of the building that had housed hundreds of healthy young Marines such a short time before. There was no hesitation in volunteering, said Milligan, despite the tenuous nature of the situation ashore. He said, "If they had taken sixteen hundred, they probably could have gotten sixteen hundred." The immediate reaction was a response to assist.

Finally, the ship received a respite from the pattern of steaming and waiting for the unknown. On 4 November, the *New Jersey* was permitted to travel to Alexandria, Egypt. She arrived there that morning and anchored outside the breakwater for a planned four-day port visit. Captain Milligan went ashore to make calls on local officials. Some men went on liberty, while others stayed on board in the duty section. Soon after the captain returned, the battleship received orders to get under way as soon as possible. The terrorists had struck again, this time blowing up a suicide truck at the Israeli military governor's headquarters in the village of Tyre and killing forty-six. The situation was too volatile for the *New Jersey* to stay away. The word went out to recall men from liberty. By midnight, the ship again was under way with all her men and boats on board. Then, as Milligan phrased it, he and the rest of the crew returned to "our home port off Beirut."

Back in Washington during that month of November, people in the councils of government raised questions about what to do with the *New Jersey*. Navy officials advocated a return to Long Beach, because the deployment was nearing the six-month mark, and the crew was already well past the scheduled time for return. Members of the Marine Corps, whose compatriots had died in faraway Beirut and were continuing to be shot at, argued that there was a more compelling need than the welfare of the crew. The lives of the Marines were at stake, and so the *New*

Marine Captain Michael K. Hicks and Navy Captain Richard Milligan preside as the ship celebrates the Marine Corps birthday in November 1983.

Courtesy Paul Stillwell

Jersey should stay. She was valuable as a deterrent and as a potential fire support ship. The Marine viewpoint prevailed, and the Joint Chiefs of Staff ordered the *New Jersey*'s stay off Lebanon extended indefinitely. Her sister ship *Iowa* was then in a shipyard in Pascagoula, Mississippi, while undergoing reactivation. Money was soon approved to step up the pace and hasten her recommissioning. But even at the most optimistic, she wouldn't be able to replace the *New Jersey* until the late spring or early summer of 1984. It was now beyond question that the *New Jersey* would not be home for Christmas in 1983.

Almost immediately, a team of officers flew out from the Naval Military Personnel Command in Washington to confer with Captain Milligan about possible measures by which to provide relief for the men of the ship's crew. Back in World War II, those who sailed away in the *New Jersey* were in "for the duration." But that was a different era and a different kind of war. Now the deployment patterns and resulting expectations were different. In late 1983, the situation in the Navy's only battleship was clearly extraordinary, and so extraordinary measures would be instituted.

The most attractive proposal was to send members of the crew home on leave in relays. Reservists from the States would come out to take their places. New fathers could go home to see their babies for the first time. Crew members who had planned to be married could try to work out new arrangements after scheduled wedding dates had come and gone. Some men were already facing divorces, but perhaps there were some shaky marriages that could be saved if the husbands came home soon rather than half a year later.

Even before the leave program could be put into effect, there was more frustration. Part of the U.S. response to the shelling of the Marines ashore was to institute reconnaissance flights by photo-equipped F-14 fighter planes from the Task Force 60 aircraft carriers some sixty to eighty miles offshore. Under the rules of engagement then in effect, U.S. forces could fire only if fired upon, and the F-14s were being shot at as they flew their missions over Syrian-controlled areas of Lebanon. On 4 December, the carriers *Independence* and *John F. Kennedy* launched an air strike against Syrian antiaircraft batteries. Two U.S. planes were lost; one flier was killed and one taken prisoner.

When it came time for the first group of lucky *New Jersey* men to head home on leave, Captain Milligan set aside one block of seats for what he considered humanitarian cases. The rest of the 104 seats on the plane were distributed by lottery. The journey took twenty-eight hours. There would have been 104 men on board the Naval Reserve C-9 transport, but one of the men showed up for the flight obviously unprepared for a long journey, and so he was held back. During the remaining six flights in subsequent months, the 104 seats were filled every time. The crew members began with a helicopter ride to the tank landing ship *Manitowoc*, and she took them into Larnaca, Cyprus. From there, the plane hit a series of refueling stops—in Sigonella, Sicily; Lajes in the Azores; St. John's, Newfoundland; and Norfolk, Virginia.

While the happy *New Jersey* crew members were heading home, the first group of activated reservists arrived at the ship, having made the long, circuitous journey in the opposite direction. They had been flown from Cyprus to an amphibious assault ship and then rode the last lap in an LCM-8 landing craft. They climbed up the *New Jersey*'s side by Jacob's ladder. Accompanying the approximately seventy-five reservists who would fill slots in the ship's organization—though not on a one-for-one basis—was Journalist Second Class Lance Johnson. He was on active duty at Naval Reserve headquarters in New Orleans and was sent along to provide public affairs coverage of the substitute crew members. Johnson recalled the considerable feeling of pleasure he experienced when he stepped on board the deck of the battleship and was greeted by a *New Jersey* sailor who said, "Welcome aboard, shipmate."

In December 1983 a contingent of Naval Reservists from the state of New Jersey reported to the battleship to permit members of the crew to go home on leave during the long Mediterranean deployment. Here they climb on board via Jacob's ladders. *U.S. Naval Institute photo archive*

The new men got into action almost immediately. They arrived on 13 December, and on the fourteenth the *New Jersey* was finally ordered to fire her big guns. Syrians were firing on U.S. reconnaissance planes, so the operational commander unleashed the *New Jersey*. Captain Milligan was even told specifically how many rounds the ship should fire—eleven. The number was limited mainly because the firing was intended as a signal. Milligan explained, "I think it was primarily an attempt to send a pretty strong message that, 'When we send the F-14 aircraft in for reconnaissance missions over Lebanon, we don't expect them to get shot at. This is going to be the price.'" A good deal of anger and frustration were dissipated that day, because crew members finally had the feeling that they were contributing.

Despite the happy mood, all was not well on board the battleship *New Jersey*. Though her projectiles had traveled some sixteen to eighteen miles beyond Beirut and scarred the landscape with craters as large as tennis courts, there was never any indication that they had hit the antiaircraft batteries or any information on how close they came. The Syrians sent back a signal of their own; they were contemptuous of the shooting. The lack of airborne observers frustrated members of the ship's fire control team. They were not able to benefit from normal practice in naval gunfire support, which calls for spotters to observe the fall of shot in relation to a target and then provide appropriate corrections to the fire controlmen on board ship.

More solutions to the morale problem were at hand. The firing of 14 December had already done a great deal, as had the idea that more and more crewmen would be going home on leave as the R&R flights continued. Now USO shows arrived to entertain the crew. On 15 December, Las Vegas singer Wayne Newton visited and performed his routine for the crew on the fantail helo platform. That evening the *New Jersey* responded to a call for fire from ashore and shot forty rounds of 5-inch, which silenced the guns firing on the Marines.

On 24 December, the ship was one stop on a tour of the area by Bob Hope. He had been on board the *New Jersey* on Christmas Day of 1968; here he was again, fifteen years later, almost to the day. With him were actresses Brooke Shields, Cathy Lee Crosby, Ann Jillian, Miss USA Julie Hayek, singer Vic Damone, and comedian George Kirby. More than three hundred Marines from the Beirut compound were on board to help the crewmen enjoy the show. Ann Jillian made probably the strongest impression on the men of the battleship because of the sense of genuineness and concern she brought. She was truly touched by the plight of the sailors and Marines who were so far from home.

On Christmas Eve 1983 Bob Hope and a group of women entertained a new generation of *New Jersey* men. New executive officer Richard Genet reported for duty soon after. When a crew member showed him to his cabin while he waited to take over, the escort said to Genet, "We like to think of this as the bed Brooke Shields slept in."
USS New Jersey *public affairs office*

On Christmas Day itself, the celebrations were far different from the ones that would have been enjoyed back home and thus even more touching. Wives and children in the United States had made and sent videotapes in which they talked about events at home and expressed their love and concern for the *New Jersey* men who weren't there in person to celebrate.

The *New Jersey* pulled into nearby Haifa, Israel, on 29 December for a five-day port visit. Because the November stop in Alexandria, Egypt, had been aborted abruptly, this trip to Haifa marked the battleship's first full day in port in 111 days. Lance Johnson took a two-day trip to religious sites—Bethlehem, Jerusalem, and the Church of the Nativity. The guide in his tour bus was a man of perhaps seventy-five years. While pointing out the various historical landmarks, he also provided full particulars and capabilities on Israeli tanks and other pieces of military equipment that passed the bus.

Religion was more important in the life of Jewish Storekeeper Second Class Richard Wolpin than for many in the *New Jersey*'s crew during that period. He had received special leave when the ship was in Panama in September so that he could fly home and celebrate the holidays of Rosh Hashanah and Yom Kippur with his parents. A trip to Israel thus meant much to him, especially since he was able to visit a friend from high school who was a student at the University of Haifa. For the New Year's holiday to begin 1984, Wolpin visited some relatives on his father's side, and accepted invitations as well from friendly Israeli citizens who asked him to come to their homes for dinner. He also went to Bethlehem and Jerusalem, and during the course of his travels was so attracted by the beauty of the Israeli female soldiers that he was sure it would take little effort for him to fall in love.

Before there could be an opportunity for that, however, the *New Jersey* weighed anchor on 3 January and returned to her station off the coast of Beirut.

Seaman Thomas Martin buffs the deck in a crew living compartment. The privacy curtains and "coffin racks" are a far cry from accommodations in the ship's berthing compartments in years past. *U.S. Naval Institute photo archive*

Naval Reserve seaman Clarence Christie, *center*, serves as a phone talker in forward secondary plot on 9 December 1983. With him are two of the ship's fire controlmen. Christie was part of the augmentation force that freed crew members to go on leave during the Mediterranean deployment. *U.S. Navy: DN-ST-84-05338*

Lieutenant Commander John Baker, *center*, led the detachment of reservists from the state of New Jersey. Here he stands officer of the deck watch on the ship's bridge. *Courtesy John Baker*

Soon the second group of reservists came in, and this time there were 104 *New Jersey* men ready to occupy the seats of the C-9 headed for the States. When the first group of crew members was returning to the ship, the first contingent of reservists was leaving about the same time.

Captain Milligan reflected on what a treat the whole experience had been for that initial group of reservists. His description of their time on board became a staple in the after-dinner routine he was called upon to deliver when the ship later returned home. In his tale, he recounted what the reservists had experienced: the 14 December main battery mission, the Wayne Newton show, the show with Bob Hope and the women, the secondary battery mission, and the port visit to Haifa. Then he delivered the punchline: "And we paid them, too."

A new contingent of reservists arrived at Haifa in early January. Lieutenant Commander John Baker, a banker in civilian life, led a group of twenty-five men to free still more crew members. A Naval Reserve unit he commanded had been assigned to support the cruiser *California*. In the autumn of 1983, with the battleship's return to the fleet, detachment 6204, based in West Trenton, New Jersey, was reassigned to the namesake warship. Soon after their arrival on board, the detachment's members developed a harmonious relationship with the regular crew. In his first meeting with Captain Milligan after reporting, Baker said he wanted to qualify as officer of the deck under way. So, in addition to serving as a liaison between his detachment and the regular crew, Baker began standing bridge watches with an experienced officer as a coach. After a time, he qualified for the top watch, even conning the ship during an underway replenishment.

Also among the men who came to the *New Jersey* in January 1984 were some prospective crew members from the *Iowa*. The *New Jersey* people were glad to have them on board, not only to fill in for crew members on leave, but also because the training might speed the *Iowa*'s arrival to relieve the *New Jersey* off Beirut. Included in the *Iowa* group were three ensigns who had been undergoing training in Norfolk—John Donovan, Barry McDonough, and Greg Miller. One thing that impressed the newcomers was the great strain upon the officers of the *New Jersey*. They had been under pressure for months because

Secretary of the Navy John Lehman speaks on the mess deck to Naval Reservists who relieved members of the *New Jersey*'s crew during the deployment off Lebanon. Lehman had a key role in pushing for reactivation of the four *Iowa*-class battleships in the 1980s. USS New Jersey *public affairs office*

of the operations off Beirut, and they faced the prospect of several more such months. It would be well to describe the ship's patrol routine for the winter of 1983–84 in some detail to appreciate the sources of that strain.

To be most effective in her presence role, the *New Jersey* had to operate in close to the beach and to remain ready to shoot at any time. That called for constant alertness. Generally, the battleship ran her patrol legs about two to three miles off the coast, and the destroyers with her picked patrol legs that were relatively close but out of her way. Even as she cruised back and forth, her fire controlmen down in the plotting room kept the Mark 13 radar constantly on a reference point ashore and had the computers set to provide solutions on short notice.

One of the destroyers was the USS *Tattnall*, whose skipper was Commander Pete Deutermann. Since the battleship's old fire control system took longer to generate solutions than his modern Mark 86 type, the practice was that the *New Jersey* would settle on a course and stay on it for a while, and Deutermann would pick a course of his own to keep clear of the battleship. The *New Jersey*'s speed was generally in the five-to-ten knot range, and it was varied so that it would be more difficult for gunners ashore to obtain their own fire control solutions. The *Tattnall* generally steamed faster, because she was a more vulnerable target and because the more frequent U-turns necessitated by higher speed had less effect on her fire control setup. When the battleship ran her figure eight patterns, Ensign Donovan observed that at the end of each run parallel to the shore, the *New Jersey* habitually turned toward the beach in coming around. Turret one was the ready turret, and the crews of the other turrets rotated through it. By turning as she did, the battleship could have the guns of turret one always ready to bear on potential targets.

The whole purpose of the sea patrols by the ships, of course, was to protect the Marines in their vulnerable positions ashore. The destroyers were there to protect the Marines with their rapid call-for-fire response capability, and the battleship was there to augment the fire of the destroyers and to protect those destroyers as well. Commander Deutermann of the *Tattnall* said that such a role called for the *New Jersey* to be clearly visible from the shore: "The presence mission—it was important to be big and ugly out there, and the closer you got, the bigger and uglier you were." Deutermann was convinced that it was the presence of the *New Jersey* that kept the Syrian gunners on the beach from shooting at the destroyers. While the Syrians did fire on the F-14 reconnaissance planes, he surmised that they recognized that it would be an obvious step of escalation to shoot at the ships and could well bring 16-inch projectiles thundering down on their heads.

The threats to the ships ranged from the plausible to the outlandish. The Beirut International Airport, where the Marines were holed up, continued in operation throughout the period that the *New Jersey* was offshore. It was all too conceivable that terrorists could hijack one of the planes headed to or from the airport and crash it onto a ship. Intelligence messages bombarded the ships, warning of all manner of potential evils—hang gliders powered by lawn mower engines and possibly carrying men and satchel charges; speedboats filled with explosives; terrorist merchant ships, submarines, mines, rockets fired from trucks, and so forth.

Even some of the really bizarre things seemed somehow possible, given the terrorists' willingness to kill themselves to achieve their aims. The situation was so filled with possibilities that the *New Jersey* was required to be able to respond on very short notice. After the bombing of the Marine compound on 23 October, Captain Milligan never ventured far from the bridge because he had to be close to communications and ready to direct protective measures. He was thus inhibited in his ability to get out for the personal contact that had meant so much to him and the crew.

In this demanding atmosphere, several of the *New Jersey*'s routines were adjusted. Down inside the ship, mealtimes turned out to be whenever men could get to the wardroom or mess deck. The food was served cafeteria-style, and men just went in and filled up plates or trays when they felt the need. Ensign Donovan observed that there were few people watching movies in the wardroom, because most of the officers were either standing watches or sleeping in order to be ready for the next watch. Because a smaller proportion of the enlisted men had to stand watches than officers, there was more of a social life in the mess deck. Greg Miller said, "The morale was remarkably high, particularly among the enlisted personnel. They had a lot of activities going aboard the ship that were very enjoyable. Every night, in addition to the standard movies, they played games. They had bingo . . . certain nights of the week and other [nights they had] raffles. I felt like the chaplain [Commander Benny Hornsby] and a lot of the junior officers had key roles in keeping morale up."

Another thing that helped the morale of the crew was the outpouring of concern from the United States. Sometimes an entire grade school class wrote to the ship. Crew members could drop down to the post office and pick up handfuls of letters to read and answer. The Long Beach *Press-Telegram*, the newspaper in the ship's home port, sent to the *New Jersey* fifteen hundred copies of a special edition jammed with messages of support. For Valentine's Day, the ship received a giant heart, filled with 450 pounds of chocolates. The candies were in fifteen hundred individual boxes for distribution to the crew members.

From time to time, the patrol routine was broken when the ship had to haul out from station and conduct an underway replenishment so that the hundreds of *New Jersey* men could keep eating and the engines could keep running. And the ammunition supply had to be taken care of, especially with the need to replace deteriorated powder bags that caused range inconsistencies during the initial firing in December.

Because of the obvious value of minimizing the time spent off station, such replenishments were a matter of necessity rather than convenience. Otherwise, the battleship was kept on a fairly short leash. Early in the new year, a reporter and photographer from *Life* magazine visited the ship. Their article, which appeared in the March 1984 issue, said of her, "Having her close to shore is considered so important that when her skipper asks for permission to sail 50 miles out to sea to dump garbage, he is frequently turned down." The article also talked about the crew members' obvious desire to go home and their parody of Rolaids television commercials. In the TV spots, the question was, "How do you spell relief?" The answer was "R-O-L-A-I-D-S." When the men of

In January 1984, during operations in the Mediterranean, the crew gathered for a group portrait. The two gentlemen front row center are Captain Richard McKenna, executive officer, and Captain Richard Milligan, commanding officer. A photo virtually identical to this one appeared with the *Life* magazine article. *USS New Jersey public affairs office*

the *New Jersey* were asked how they spelled relief, the answer was "I-O-W-A."

The situation for the peacekeeping force changed dramatically on 7 February 1984 when President Reagan announced in Washington that the United States was going to withdraw the bulk of the Marines from their position on shore and redeploy them to the ships of the amphibious force off the coast of Lebanon. A residual force would remain behind to protect the U.S. embassy and other American interests. As a consequence of the reduced force, there would be greater reliance in the future on air strikes and naval gunfire. Since the beginning of 1984, the *New Jersey* had had two call-for-fire missions with her 5-inch battery, shooting thirty-two rounds on 15 January and seven rounds on 7 February, the day of the president's announcement. Those paled into insignificance when compared with the events of 8 February.

Early on the afternoon of the eighth, the *New Jersey* was authorized to shoot at Druze and Syrian gun positions that were shelling Beirut. John Donovan recalled that Captain Milligan spoke to the crew on the general announcing system and said, "The *New Jersey* has a fire mission. Man your gunnery stations." The reaction in the ship was instantaneous. Recalled Donovan, "You could hear the crew cheering. They finally had something to do instead of just driving back and forth. You could hear them banging on the bulkheads and just running around."

Most of that day's targets were in mountains east of the town of Hammana, about fifteen miles east of Beirut. They included artillery, antitank artillery, antiaircraft emplacements, and command bunkers. Because the day was a cloudy one with low overcast, and because some of the sites were antiaircraft batteries, aerial spotting was not feasible. Instead, the ship counted on volume of fire to blanket the targets. At long ranges, the 16-inch projectiles have patterns of dispersion. So, explained Milligan, "If you want to really get on target, you might have to move that dispersion pattern around a little bit." As a result of the firing of a number of missions that day and the expenditure of a total of 288 rounds, the *New Jersey* achieved what she set out to—the silencing of the gun batteries ashore.

Throughout much of the long day, which called for the ship to move from place to place between missions, Captain Milligan was in the combat engagement center on the 02 level. With him were the ship's weapons officer and a tactical action officer. Although Milligan was clearly in overall charge of the operation, he ran it by the principle of negation—interfering only if something needed to be corrected. His role was that of overseer and decision-maker. As Milligan explained afterward, "I had awfully capable people, and if everything was going exactly the way it should go, then, of course, I wasn't going to step into anything. But, of course, I took all the reports. I knew exactly what was going on." Even so, observed Ensign John Donovan, the captain did a lot of pacing back and forth that day. He had an understandable desire to do something, and the system meant that subordinates were, in nearly all cases, doing things before they reached the captain's level.

With the commanding officer in the combat engagement center and viewing the situation by electronic means, the executive officer, Captain Richard McKenna, was on the bridge as the skipper's alter ego. McKenna had a supervisory function, which included keeping an eye on the gun target line as safety observer and monitoring the ship-handling functions, as a captain did in days of old. As always, though, the exec had to keep up with paperwork, so he had a little table next to the captain's chair and handled administrative chores there. When he heard the salvo alarm for each projectile, he ducked down to avoid the blast but kept his hands on the table so his papers wouldn't be blown away. Once a round was gone, he stood up again and resumed writing.

Ensign Greg Miller concluded that the officers and men of the *New Jersey* spent that day doing something that was at the same time satisfying and very demanding. Handling nearly three hundred heavy projectiles and six times as many powder bags was exhausting physically, so there was a special concern to observe all the proper safety procedures in the turrets, the magazines, projectile decks, and so forth. Otherwise, fatigue could lead to carelessness or inattentiveness, and problems could result. The bombardment was carried off without a hitch. Remembered Miller, "It was an incredible strain on the crew, particularly the officers. The turret officers [and] the plotting room officers . . . were basically

The *New Jersey* fires a broadside to starboard as part of her 288-round bombardment on 8 February 1984. USS New Jersey *public affairs office*

Bow view of the 8 February bombardment USS New Jersey *public affairs office*

going in port-and-starboard shifts. But yet, we were so excited it really didn't matter. The adrenaline was really pumping."

Late in the afternoon, the firing was still in progress. Fire Controlman Dan Clairmont was off duty for a while in the port-and-starboard routine in the plotting room. He had taken his life jacket to his bunk in case the massive bombardment provoked retaliation. As he lay in his rack, an urgent message came through the general announcing system, delivered in a shaking, frightened voice, "Now man all Harpoon stations." On the bridge, the junior officer of the deck looked at Ensign John Donovan and said, "My God, we're actually at war."

Ensign Barry McDonough saw a chief petty officer running down a passageway with the engagement keys for the Harpoon missile console in the combat engagement center. All sorts of thoughts went through McDonough's mind, including the notion that the Soviets might have decided to retaliate on behalf of the Syrians. McDonough's general quarters station was in the wardroom, which was to be set up as a battle dressing station. Even though general quarters hadn't been set, McDonough concluded it soon would be, so he went running forward to the wardroom, frantically whipped open the door from the starboard passageway, and ran right into the senior officers' table, where dinner was in progress. The executive officer, Captain McKenna, looked up calmly from his meal in response to McDonough's dramatic entrance, and the ensign realized things weren't so bad as he thought. So, he said, "I figured I'd sit down and eat dinner."

Ensign John Donovan had come down from the bridge and begun eating also. Then another frantic message came through over the loudspeaker, because Commander Task Force 60 had ordered all Navy ships in the eastern Mediterranean to go to general quarters immediately. The general alarm went through its strident bong-bong-bong, and the man passing the word called the crew to battle stations. Donovan said of the word-passer: "He was terrified—you could tell.

Everyone just looked at each other for a split second and said, 'Oh my God, this is it.'"

Donovan decided that if he was going to war, he didn't know when he would next be able to eat, so he determined to finish his lasagna. He was sufficiently unnerved that it took him five tries to get the last bite into his mouth, because it fell off the fork on the first four attempts. Even as he was finishing his meal, he observed that the mess specialists on duty weren't bothering to clear the wardroom tables in customary fashion. Instead, they just bundled up the tablecloths, plates, glasses, silverware, lasagna, and all—and tossed the whole pile into a corner. Before Donovan left the wardroom, two battle dressing stations had been set up.

Down in the mess deck, the menu that evening also had an Italian flavor. Storekeeper Second Class Richard Wolpin was in charge of a mess line, clicking off the numbers to show how many men were eating the spaghetti dinner. Then came the word over the loudspeaker. He remembered, "Everybody froze for a split second, then everybody scattered like ants when you pour water on them." Some people sent their trays clattering to the deck as they departed, leaving piles of spaghetti in their wakes.

The threat did not materialize and the ship's crew relaxed from general quarters, although the firing of the big guns went on until the final 16-inch mission was finished about 11 p.m. that night. In explaining the manning of the antiship missile battery that day, Milligan offered, "We did, in fact, man the Harpoon stations, based on a potential threat, and I'll say no more. And then I would also tell you that we were prepared the next morning for any potential retaliation against us."

The men of the *New Jersey* never did find out exactly what they had accomplished by their heavy gunfire on 8 February. Greg Miller recalled, "There was a big question mark over everyone's head on February the ninth. We wanted to know what had been done. Outwardly, what we observed was that everything quieted up in Beirut. . . . There was no small arms fire for maybe the entire week after that, that I was aware of." According to the "mess decks intelligence," the ship had taken out several Syrian gun emplacements, some rocket launchers, and a Syrian command post. The latter suggestion was heightened by a rumor that the *New Jersey*'s fire had killed a Syrian general and his staff. The concussions from the many salvos did produce internal damage in the ship, including bursting a water pipe in the captain's sea cabin. Milligan discovered that his bunk was soaked when he was about to lie down and rest in the early morning hours of 9 February.

As it happened, there was no retaliation for the big day of shooting, and so the *New Jersey* resumed her pattern of patrolling off the beach, ready to respond if necessary. On 21 February, the Marines began their redeployment from the airport compound to the Sixth Fleet amphibious warfare ships offshore. On the twenty-sixth, the redeployment of the 22nd Marine Amphibious Unit was completed, and only a small force of Marines remained behind. Also on 26 February, the *New Jersey* fired thirteen rounds of 16-inch after U.S. reconnaissance planes were again fired upon by hostile forces ashore.

Throughout the early months of the new year, the R&R flights back to the States were continuing—amounting to seven eventually for a total of 727 men who managed to get home. The crew as a whole got a break on 2 March when the ship pulled in and anchored at Haifa, Israel, for a seven-day port visit. This was the first chance the crew had for liberty since last leaving Haifa on 3 January. After the second visit, the ship once again returned to her patrol station off Beirut. Though the bulk of the Marines had gone, the ship's presence was still considered necessary.

On 2 April, Captain Milligan spoke to the crew on the closed-circuit television system to tell them that as far as he knew, the mission was going to continue until the ship was relieved by the *Iowa*. About an hour and a half later, he was called to the combat engagement center where he received a radio message directing the ship to leave Beirut right away. Three days later, the *New Jersey* was in Naples, Italy, and the six-month ordeal off the coast of Lebanon was over. With the Marine force having gone and the United States reluctantly concluding that its presence in the multinational force was not keeping peace after all, it was no longer necessary to wait for the arrival of the *Iowa*. She wasn't coming.

The *New Jersey* stayed in the Italian city until 11 April and then went to the picturesque port of Villefranche, France, for a visit from 12 until 15 April. France, Italy, and the United States had all been partners in the effort off Beirut, so it was a nice touch for those Mediterranean nations to put out the welcome mats on the ship's way home. After all the time off Lebanon without liberty, the situation had reversed itself. Now there were port visits back to back, and so the deployment was ending as it had begun, with stops in foreign ports. For Storekeeper Richard Wolpin, Villefranche was a delight. The French government had requested that the battleship's crew members wear civilian clothes ashore, and so they went from place to place as American tourists. While in Monaco, Wolpin visited the ritzy section of Monte Carlo and concluded that the prices there were even worse than the ones he'd been put off by in Singapore. At Nice he saw lawn bowling and a beach set aside for nude sunbathing. And in Villefranche itself, he was invited home for dinner by a French man and his wife who came originally from Michigan.

On 15 April, the *New Jersey* was again under way, heading this time for the Strait of Gibraltar, which she passed through two days later. On 27 April, she went through the Panama Canal after a transatlantic crossing that wasn't so rapid as the one in September but still faster than normal for a peacetime passage.

A solemn event occurred on 4 May. The cremated remains of Chief Electronics Technician Michael Gorchinski were committed to the deep. He had been killed in the bombing of the Marine barracks at Beirut the previous October. The chief's

The ship received a joyous reception when she returned to Long Beach on 5 May 1984 after an eleven-month deployment that took her to the Far East, Central America, and the Middle East. *U.S. Navy: DN-SN-84-09720*

In 1984 the Wendy's fast-food chain ran a commercial that mocked competitors that had too little beef in their hamburgers. Three little old ladies looked quizzically at a tiny patty on a big bun, and one of them demanded, "Where's the beef?" Over the head of the Marine Corps captain in this photo is a homecoming sign that proclaims that the *New Jersey* has the beef. *U.S. Navy: DN-SN-84-09695*

Crew members stream joyously off the ship to meet with members of the waiting crowd. *U.S. Navy: DN-SN-84-09697*

widow observed the ceremony after being flown to the ship by helicopter. Captain Milligan served as her escort.

The *New Jersey* finally approached her home port on 5 May with the crew in dress whites and paraded at every available space topside. It was fifteen years to the day from the time of the *New Jersey*'s return to Long Beach from the Vietnam War. In both cases, the return had been delayed, but this time the wait was far, far longer. The ship was surrounded by small boats, and streams of water spouted skyward from fireboats.

Some five thousand people were waiting to welcome the returning battleship that bright May day.

Fire Controlman Dan Clairmont's eyes were filled with tears of happiness; he was also so eager to be ashore that it was hard to maintain the discipline that kept him standing at his spot on deck. On land, Clairmont's wife Gail and his father Ray, an ex-Navy man, held the two ends of a five-foot hand-painted sign that welcomed their man in red, white, and blue. As tugboats moved the mighty gray warship in toward the pier, Gail Clairmont spotted her returning husband and began jumping up and down with excitement, screaming, "There he is."

For long minutes, which seemed even longer to those both on ship and on shore while the giant dreadnought was being moored to the pier, people on both sides waited anxiously for the brows to be put into place. At last—at long last—the waiting was over. The two groups swarmed toward each other and joined in hundreds of happy embraces. The USS *New Jersey* was home from her fourth war after a deployment that lasted 331 days.

A girl makes no secret of her happiness as she greets a smiling *New Jersey* man newly ashore. *U.S. Navy: DN-SN-84-09717*

CHAPTER VIII
BATTLESHIP BATTLE GROUP
May 1984–November 1988

As soon as she returned to Long Beach in early May 1984, the *New Jersey* was transformed from a combat-ready warship to a barracks vessel for those few who had to be on board at a given time. The next year would be spent in reversing the process and preparing her to assume her operational duties once again. The year after that would be devoted to getting her ready for a challenging new role as the centerpiece of the Navy's first battleship battle group.

The shipyard period in 1981–82 had not been a full overhaul. It was a modernization superimposed on a reactivation. Items of shipyard work that were nice to have but not essential were deferred for the post-shakedown availability period scheduled for the autumn of 1983. If a piece of gear worked at reactivation time, shipyard attention went to other things. Equipment that was supposed to hold up for a three-month deployment to the Western Pacific had instead been subjected to nearly eleven months of use, day in and day out. Wear and tear had taken their toll on both men and equipment. Remedies were at hand for both.

For the ship herself, the Long Beach Naval Shipyard set to work fixing the many things that needed attention. For the crew, there had to be a duty section on board each day, but for the first month the rest of the men could go on liberty shortly after quarters each morning. During the second month back home, men were working only half days as they spent time with their families or otherwise enjoyed the pleasures of being ashore. Signalman Third Class Dave Hammond enjoyed resuming activities that are normally taken for granted but just weren't possible during the long months at sea. "It was kind of strange being on land again after being out of circulation for so long," he remembered.

Disneyland was a popular attraction for *New Jersey* men and their families. Crew members could bring in their ticket stubs for recreational events—except for movies—and be reimbursed from the ship's welfare and recreation fund. The money had accumulated from the profits generated in the ship's store during the long deployment, so it was their own money they were using for their outings in Southern California.

Lieutenant Eric Massa of the *New Jersey* established a program for inter-ship athletics, setting up teams in softball and bowling. Men formed a scuba-diving club, and there was even a rodeo club whose members rode Brahman bulls while wearing wide-brimmed Western hats with the ship's name on the front.

Symbolic of the *New Jersey*'s status that summer as a noncombatant was the offloading of ammunition at Seal Beach, California, from 4 to 7 June in preparation for her shipyard period. She returned to the Long Beach Naval Station on the seventh, but this stay was brief. On 9 June, little more than a month after her return to home port, the battleship was under way for a leisurely seven-hour family day cruise toward Santa Catalina Island and back. Fire Controlman Dan Clairmont especially enjoyed the opportunity to bring his wife and other relatives on board. After months of having him gone, they could now see the spaces in which he lived and worked instead of having to try to imagine what they were like. He and others had a chance to demonstrate their technical proficiency with the ship's gear.

All told, 2,266 family members and guests were on board that day as the ship ran through a series of pre-overhaul trials of her equipment. The guests enjoyed an open-air meal on the fantail. The *New Jersey*, with no ammunition, was escorted by the guided missile cruiser *Fox* during the day.

On 15 June, the *New Jersey* shifted to pier one at the Long Beach Naval Shipyard and began her availability period. One example of the work that had been deferred during the reactivation was the replacement of the center 16-inch barrel of turret two. In the 1981–82 shipyard period, excessive wear was discovered in the barrel's liner, and so it was not to be used during the short summer deployment in 1983. Eventually, of course, a much longer delay intervened before it could be used again. In August 1984, the barrel was replaced by one that had been in storage for many years. Robert Weston, a technical adviser from the naval ordnance station in Louisville, Kentucky, was quoted in *Surface Warfare* magazine concerning the complexity of the undertaking: "We're talking about a barrel 68' long weighing 239,156 lb. You can't work fast with something like that." It was the *New Jersey*'s first 16-inch barrel replacement since 1954.

Elsewhere in the ship, habitability was improved in areas that hadn't received the full treatment during the reactivation. In the heads new deck coverings were put down and new partitions and privacy screens installed. The ancient interior communication system underwent a substantial upgrading. Chief Interior Communications Electrician Arturo Mota explained that the 1MC, the ship-wide general announcing system, was of an outmoded tube type that overheated during prolonged use. Once a new system was installed during the yard period, troubles were a thing of the past. Mota was also involved in the modernization of the ship's telephone system. The old switchboard, down near the after main battery plotting room, was manned in port by enlisted men as operators. Thanks to a new digital, computer-controlled system, the phones could now be programmed automatically to hook up to outside lines when in port and thus no longer needed human operators.

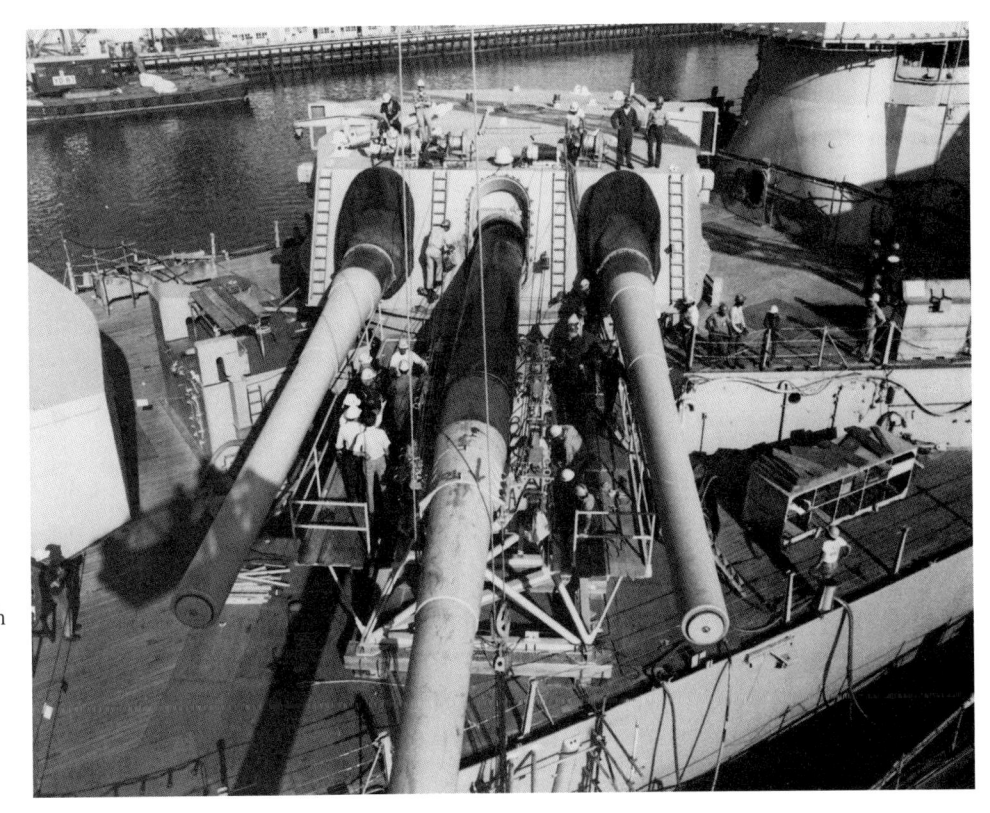

In August 1984 the Long Beach Naval Shipyard replaces the center barrel of turret two. It was the first barrel change for the ship since the 1950s.
USS New Jersey *public affairs office*

Equipment was also installed and improved in the engineering spaces, including upgrades to the lube oil service pumps in the engine rooms. In October, the ship passed her light-off exam, administered by the Propulsion Examining Board. She was thus certified to fire up her propulsion plant in early November. Then it was out to the Southern California operating area on 14–15 November for two days of sea trials to certify work done in the shipyard. Captain Richard P. Genet, the new executive officer, was accustomed to post-overhaul sea details that involved collective confusion as a ship prepared for sea after a long break. He was pleasantly surprised by how smoothly the *New Jersey*'s crew moved her out of port and headed for sea. The yard period ended officially on 21 November when the battleship moved from the shipyard to the Long Beach Naval Station.

The move facilitated access for the members of crewmen's families as they came on board the following day, 22 November, to celebrate Thanksgiving. It was a welcome contrast to the setting of 1983 when the holiday fell during the battleship's ceaseless patrolling off Lebanon. For the 1984 version, Ensign Jim French, the *New Jersey*'s food service officer, had his staff of fifty cooks working for hours to prepare the feast to be served to eight hundred people. The dinner consisted of forty-four roasted turkeys, ten steamship rounds of beef, three hundred pounds of baked ham, four hundred pounds of mashed potatoes, forty gallons of gravy, and three hundred pies—apple, cherry, and pumpkin—for dessert.

All too soon, it was back to sea again, on 3 December. First was a partial reloading of ammunition at Seal Beach and then a trip to the operating area offshore to conduct further engineering trials and to test-fire the 16-inch guns, 5-inch, and the Vulcan/Phalanx close-in weapon system. Included was the first firing of the center gun of turret two since 1969. In mid-January of 1985, the ship passed her inspection and survey (InSurv) trials and demonstrated that her material condition was satisfactory for fleet service.

Along with the rebuilding of the ship in a material sense, there also had to be a rebuilding in crew readiness. With the coming of the new year of 1985, the crew had experienced much turnover in the nearly eight months since the return to Long Beach. During the long in-port period, experienced petty officers such as Fire Controlman Dan Clairmont passed on acquired knowledge to new men. Clairmont, who had learned much under the tutelage of Senior Chief Rick Crawford in 1983, was now a senior man himself.

In mid-January, the ship passed final contract trials conducted by Rear Admiral John D. Bulkeley and the Board of Inspection and Survey. The trials had been postponed a year because of the extended deployment. Then the lectures and lessons by people such as Clairmont had to be applied during a period of refresher training that would exercise the crew as a whole. Refresher training was advanced two months for the ship, recalled Captain Genet, the exec, and it was also shortened from six weeks to three because of the possibility that the *New Jersey* would be called for an out-of-area contingency operation. The situation that might have called back the *New Jersey* in a fashion similar to that of 1983 did not eventuate in 1985. On 4 February, the *New Jersey* left Long Beach and steamed south for San Diego and exercises conducted by the fleet training group based there. The training, interrupted by weekends in port, went on for much of the month.

One feature that provided some respite for the crew between the training periods was the opportunity to use two new shipboard gymnasiums. The forward area had a piece of equipment known as a universal gym and was primarily for weightlifting and strength development. The after gym was created in the area that had previously served as the brig. It was set up for aerobic training with equipment such as stationary bicycles and rowing machines. This was a far cry from the old days.

After the refresher training wrapped up on 28 February, the ship anchored off the Seal Beach Naval

Weapons Station that evening and completed the loading of ammunition on 1 March. She arrived at Long Beach that day and soon began a twenty-day period in port for upkeep. During one of the battleship's returns to home port, Captain Rich Milligan saw evidence that confirmed the value of the sewage collection, holding, and transfer systems installed in the *New Jersey* and the rest of the Navy's ships. As the ship approached her assigned pier, a sea otter was catching fish in the *New Jersey*'s berth. "I don't think you would have seen that fifteen years ago," said Milligan. "I think that's a good indication of what that program's done for us, ecology-wise."

One highlight of the in-port period was a day of running sponsored by the ship and two local businesses on Sunday, 10 March. Included were a one-mile run and a 6.2-miler. Officially, the latter was ten kilometers, but 6.2 miles had more of a ring to it because of the similarity to the *New Jersey*'s hull number. The event was also opened to the first one thousand members of the public who were willing to pay an entry fee of $9.00. Along with the chance to run, the civilians received a *New Jersey* T-shirt, refreshments, and a visit to the ship herself at the conclusion of the race.

In late March, the ship was under way once more as part of the long, long process of preparing her for her next overseas deployment; included was more and more training. In mid-April, she requalified her main and secondary battery guns at the shore bombardment range on San Clemente Island. Then it was back to port for another engineering test beginning on 6 May, the Operational Propulsion Plant Examination. The notorious OPPE became the bane of many a warship's existence when introduced in the 1970s, because it set higher standards for conventional steam propulsion plants than many ships were used to maintaining. For years, the Navy's

The battleship sports a newly earned battle efficiency 'E' ribbon on 30 March 1985 as crew members line the superstructure. Aft of the ship's ribbons are painted letters signifying excellence in individual shipboard departments. *USS* New Jersey *public affairs office*

A fireman stands burner watch in one of the *New Jersey*'s boiler rooms during at-sea operations in March 1985. *U.S. Navy photo by Al Diaz*

nuclear-powered ships had been forced to meet high standards, and now the standards were upgraded for the other ships as well. The *New Jersey* failed her first attempt at the OPPE. The test was terminated as incomplete on 9 May and later passed when conducted from 26 to 28 June.

Executive Officer Genet offered an explanation for the first test, "Perhaps we were a little bit too overconfident and perhaps also there were problems which surfaced in the bringing up of 1945 systems to 1985 standards which were not trivial in their resolution." Part of the difficulty was in the documentation of training done on the old systems. Also, for instance, the OPPE requirements on such things as steam leaks and water leaks were much more stringent than when the *New Jersey*'s equipment was manufactured. It wasn't that the ship was unsafe, because she had been steaming for years, but her men had to do even better. Still another factor was that the *New Jersey* no longer burned the heavy black Navy special fuel oil of yore. During the early 1980s modernization the ship began burning a different fuel. Now going into the boilers was the lighter DFM, a blend of diesel fuel essentially the same as kerosene. It was much more likely to find piping leaks than its predecessor.

The ship was in and out of port the next several months, including a visit to San Diego in early June. On 9 June she received the Spokane Trophy. It had been donated by the citizens of that Washington city in 1908 and was presented for years thereafter to the Navy ship with the best gun turret marksmanship. After being in limbo since the beginning of World War II, the trophy was reinstated in 1985 to honor excellence in surface ship combat systems readiness. On 15 June, while the *New Jersey* was at the Long Beach Naval Shipyard, Captain L. M. Hardt relieved Captain Genet as executive officer.

On 28 June, after passing the OPPE retest on her propulsion plant, the *New Jersey* arrived at Long Beach for a brief stay. She left for the Central Pacific on 10 July in company with the cruisers *Jouett*, *Halsey*, and *England*; the destroyers *Chandler*, *O'Brien*, and

Postal clerks John Irwin, *foreground*, and Robert McKee sort mail in the battleship's post office. *U.S. Navy photo by Barry Orell*

Working on the starboard side of the *New Jersey*'s 04-level bridge, members of the navigation team plot the ship's track on a harbor chart. *U.S. Navy photo by Al Diaz*

In the ship's bakery, dozens of fresh doughnuts await hungry *New Jersey* men. *U.S. Navy photo by Al Diaz*

Members of the deck department prepare to lower the ship's utility boat from the port davit. *U.S. Navy photo by Barry Orell*

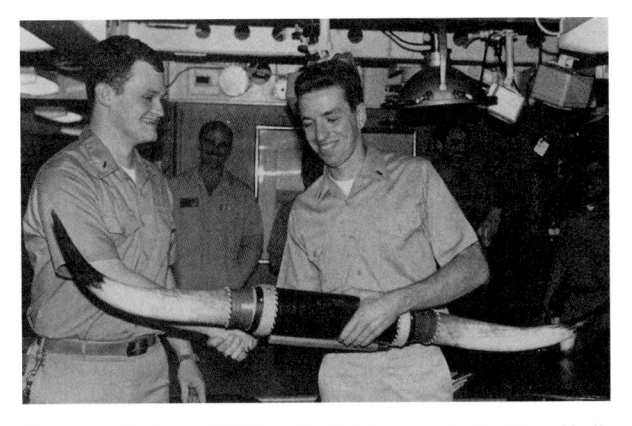

Lieutenant (junior grade) Glenn Cook, *left*, passes the traditional bull horns to Ensign Robert Evans. On board ship the title "Bull Ensign" goes to the senior-most officer in that rank. *U.S. Navy photo by Rick Sforza*

Ingersoll; and the frigate *Reasoner*. The battleship arrived in Pearl Harbor on 18 July and rendered honors to the *Arizona*, as she had during her visit in 1983. The effect on the *New Jersey*'s crew was much the same. Photographer's Mate Third Class Barry Orell observed, "The atmosphere got almost churchlike. It was almost like a cold chill when you passed, then a festive occasion again." The festive occasions in Hawaii included the many liberty attractions usually available and highlighted this time by a luau for the crew. Following a local custom, Hawaiian women lined up to greet a line of *New Jersey* men with kisses, something that Petty Officer Orell found to be a most agreeable practice.

The ship went under way on 22 July for an exercise in the Hawaiian operating area. Embarked for the day was actor Tom Selleck, who played a former naval officer in the popular *Magnum P.I.* television series. The ship was back to Pearl on 29 August and then again under way on 1 August for a voyage to San Francisco. On 3 August, the *New Jersey* fired a nine-gun broadside with the main battery. Because of the previous problems with the center gun in turret two, this was the first time she fired a nine-gun salvo since recommissioning.

The ship arrived at San Francisco on 8 August to enjoy a visit to the port and to participate in a celebration commemorating the fortieth anniversary of VJ Day, the victory over Japan. Because of modern sensitivities, however, the occasion was billed as the "Fortieth Anniversary of Peace in the Pacific." Mayor Dianne Feinstein of San Francisco made the men of the *New Jersey* feel especially welcome. For crew members who had too much to drink, the San Francisco police joined the hospitable spirit. The

On 3 August 1985 the *New Jersey* fires a nine-gun broadside for the first time since recommissioning. *U.S. Navy photo by Rick Sforza*

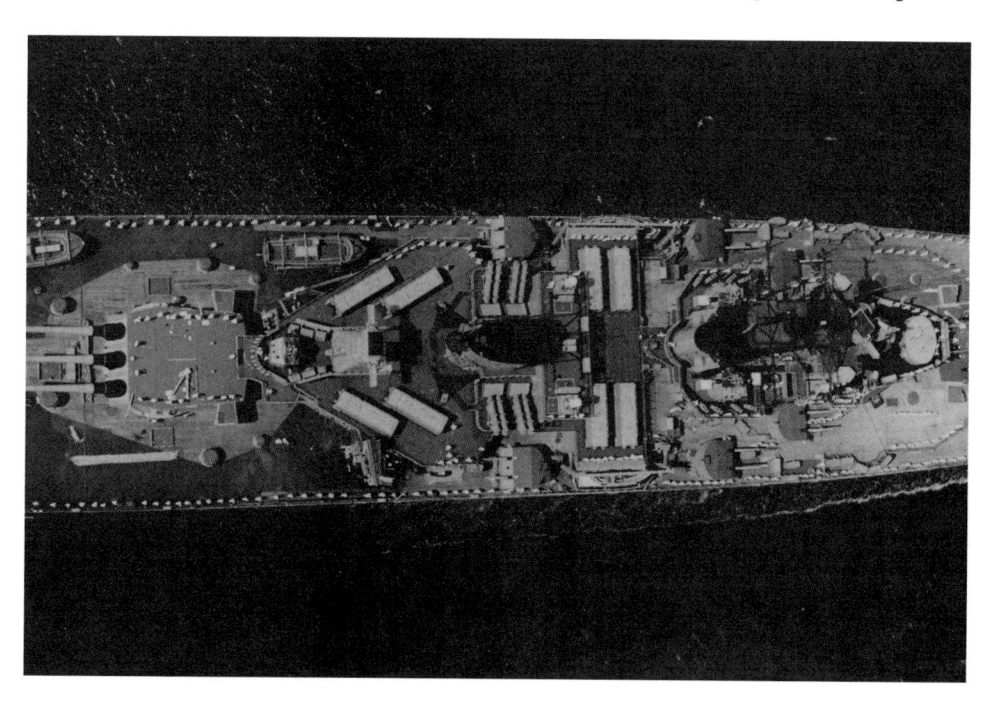

This aerial view amidships was taken when the ship visited San Francisco in August 1985. It depicts the eight armored box launchers for Tomahawk missiles and quadruple canisters for Harpoon. *Giorgio Arra photo courtesy of Norman Polmar*

police gave such men "courtesy rides" back to the ship rather than taking them to a police station and writing up official reports.

On 14 August, the day of the cease-fire anniversary, the battleship joined other ships in making a circuit past the anchored aircraft carrier *Enterprise* with Vice President George H. W. Bush embarked. The *New Jersey* and *Enterprise* exchanged gun salutes as the battleship passed. Forty years earlier, the *New Jersey* and an earlier USS *Enterprise* were part of the victorious fleet at the end of World War II. The battleship left for Long Beach on 15 August with more than seventy male relatives of crew members on board for a three-day "tiger cruise."

On 7 September, during the course of a long in-port period at Long Beach, the battleship underwent a change of command. Captain Milligan had taken over on 15 September 1983, during the hurried transit toward the Mediterranean. Milligan received the acclaim due him for the long, arduous service off Lebanon and was frocked in the rank of commodore, for he had been chosen for flag rank by the previous year's selection board.

Now he was relieved by Captain W. Lewis Glenn Jr. in a traditional in-port format. On this occasion, the new man—tall, thin, and polished—reported

Captain W. Lewis Glenn Jr. commanded the *New Jersey* from 7 September 1985 to 8 August 1987. USS New Jersey *public affairs office*

from a tour in Washington, DC. The easygoing, friendly new skipper brought a background combining postgraduate education, staff duty, and service in surface combatants. Born in 1940, Glenn took over on his forty-fifth birthday; he was the ship's youngest commanding officer to date in the rank of captain. (Commander J. William Leverton Jr., then thirty-nine, had moved up from serving as executive officer to take temporary command for a few months prior to the ship's 1948 decommissioning. Most skippers had been in their late forties when they took over.)

During the latter part of his command, Captain Milligan was no longer so accessible as he had been in the months soon after reporting aboard. Part of his isolation was inevitable because of the demands of staying in close reach of communication circuits while off Lebanon. Later, like many in the crew, he was doubtless tired after the month-in, month-out strains of watchful waiting near Beirut. The early Glenn much resembled the early Milligan—frequently walking around the ship, striking up conversations with the sailors, eating in the various messes, and making himself accessible to anyone who wanted to speak personally.

The new man's approach was fueled by an infectious enthusiasm and a desire to share his feeling for the ship with those serving in her. The closed-circuit television station was a sometime medium for this approach, but far more frequent was Glenn's use of the general announcing system. *New Jersey* men grew accustomed to hearing from him on an almost daily basis and even more frequently when the ship was at sea and operating.

Mess Management Specialist Charles Frakes recalled that another of Glenn's attributes was the desire for team-building—literally. He initiated a number of sports teams to participate in games ashore during in-port periods. That had not been a real option during the long, long deployment, much of which was at sea. The sports events built both morale and camaraderie. Frakes said that the skipper wanted to get as many crew members as possible involved in off-ship activities. Men joined in volunteer activities to benefit various groups.

In late October 1985, the *New Jersey* went under way for training off Southern California, including naval gunfire support qualification on the thirtieth and thirty-first at San Clemente Island. On 3 and 4 November, she took on more ammunition at Seal Beach, and then participated in a fleet readiness exercise. The workout provided a test of the usefulness of the missile-armed battleship in a combat environment.

Part of the time was spent with a nuclear-powered aircraft carrier working up to prepare for a deployment to the Western Pacific. On one occasion the carrier and the battleship were separated by several hundred miles, recalled Captain Glenn, when the carrier's planes located some surface targets. Using targeting information provided by the aircraft, the *New Jersey* simulated firing at them with her missiles. The exercise ended with the battleship making a high-speed run at night and coming in for a simulated main battery shore bombardment mission at first light the next morning, as if supporting an amphibious assault. After that, the *New Jersey* returned to her home port on 22 November.

She was back at sea again on 3 December and was soon trailed by a Soviet intelligence collection vessel. The *New Jersey* steamed south during the night with her electronic equipment turned off in order to be difficult to detect. Not long after midnight, the battleship turned north, having evaded the Soviets, and didn't turn on her electronic gear until shortly before her Tomahawk firing mission that day. In May 1983, the battleship fired a land-attack version of the missile. This time, she used the antiship type.

As had the Tomahawk in 1983, this one hesitated momentarily after leaving the launcher until the booster caught hold, and then it roared away. This time, however, there was a lower trajectory than for the much longer range of the land-attack version, which went several hundred miles. As the missile flew away, it left behind a plume of white smoke. The missile scored a direct hit on a target hull, making the first battleship test of an antiship Tomahawk a successful one. The *New Jersey* returned to Long

The battleship is festooned with lights during the holiday season at Long Beach in 1985. On 16 December Santa presented gifts to the children of crew members during a Christmas party on the fantail. *USS* New Jersey *public affairs office*

Beach the following day and closed out the year with a leave period for the crew and a visit by Santa Claus for the children of crew members.

In December 1985 Lieutenant Michael Murphy, a Supply Corps officer, joined the crew. He took over the S-2 division, food service. Feeding a crew of some sixteen hundred crew members three regular meals a day plus midnight rations ("midrats") for watch standers was a tall chore. All told, the S-2 division comprised five chief petty officers and more junior enlisted men in the rating of mess management specialist. (The rating was changed to culinary specialist in 2004, years after the ship was decommissioned.)

A real challenge in keeping the ship adequately provisioned was that she was built with no elevators—except, of course, those that hoisted ammunition to the guns. That resulted in working parties that sometimes contained as many as 250 men. They had to manhandle and strike down the food as it came on board. Quipped Murphy, "OSHA would have a nightmare." The quantities were massive: many, many frozen chickens, for example, and hundreds of dozens of eggs. Given the capacity of the storerooms, the ship could probably have gone sixty days between

Crew members on the fantail watch on 4 December 1985 as the *New Jersey* fires the antiship version of the Tomahawk cruise missile for the first time. *U.S. Navy photo by Lon Cabot* reloads, but at sea the interval was often about ten days. The system used almost exclusively was vertical replenishment by supply ship helicopters that landed pallets of goods on the fantail.

Said Murphy, of the time when the ship was built, "They decided 'We'll use the backs of the crew.'" There was an added cost to that procedure. Following the example of *New Jersey* men years earlier, crewmen put pilfering on the agenda. For instance, when strawberries were arriving, numbers of them disappeared on their way to the storeroom. Naturally, those doing the hauling—including sending food down ladders—had to keep up their strength. The rationale was that the fruit was for the crew anyway, and a bit of sidetracking made the men happy.

One of the rated men who worked in the galley was Mess Management Specialist Charles Frakes. One thing he observed was the upgrading of the facilities in the mess deck as time passed. When he first joined the crew, he explained, the food service equipment was essentially unchanged from the Vietnam period. He welcomed the changes. The addition of juice machines, ice machines, and more soda machines improved access and shortened lines. Other amenities included salad bars and condiment bars. Some of the galley's food-preparation equipment from the late 1960s deployment was replaced. He compared the receipt of the modern gear to receiving Christmas presents.

The mess deck crew included a group long known as mess cooks. (In an era of upgraded job titles, they became known as "food service attendants.") These were generally nonrated newcomers who did the chores that the rated cooks did not. They had to clean the galley and mess deck, serve the food to those passing by with trays, and man the scullery in which eating utensils and trays were washed.

The Long Beach routine was interrupted for a while in mid-January 1986 as the ship again enjoyed the delights of San Francisco and once more opened up for general visiting. From mid-February to early March, the *New Jersey* was involved in yet another new role during her latest manifestation—preparation for deployment at the heart of a battleship battle group. Since World War II, the striking power of the U.S. Navy has been built around aircraft carriers. Combined with the escorts of their battle groups, they have conducted hundreds of overseas deployments on behalf of national interests. Because of the carriers' strenuous operating schedules, Navy planners sought ways to provide relief for their crews.

The tentative solution—for peacetime, at least—was to build some of the battle groups around battleships as substitutes for carriers in the deployment rotation. During her at-sea period in early 1986, as part of Battle Group Romeo, the *New Jersey* worked with the cruiser *Long Beach*, destroyers *Merrill* and *Fletcher*, frigates *Bronstein*, *Copeland*, *Stein*, and *Thach*, and the replenishment oiler *Wabash*. Despite

New Jersey crewmen enjoy a "steel beach picnic" as part of Sunday holiday routine on 23 February 1986. Above them is the refueling rig added during the 1982 modernization. *U.S. Navy photo by Lon Cabot*

The *New Jersey* steams as the centerpiece of the first battleship battle group in early 1986. To starboard of her is the nuclear-powered cruiser *Long Beach*, which served as Rear Admiral R. A. K. Taylor's flagship. USS New Jersey *public affairs office*

being the biggest ship in the group, the *New Jersey* was not the flagship because her previous flag quarters had been replaced by the combat engagement center. As a result, the battle group commander, Rear Admiral Raynor A. K. Taylor, was embarked in the *Long Beach*, which did have flag accommodations.

Together the ships worked out tactics and procedures to be used during a deployment to the Western Pacific, beginning in mid-May. Captain Glenn explained that since the *New Jersey*, *Long Beach*, and *Merrill* were equipped with Tomahawk missiles, they were able to demonstrate the concept of distributed offense. Several ships firing together could send missiles toward a target from different points on the compass. With all the combatants in the battle group equipped with Harpoon missiles, the ships were able to demonstrate a distributed capability in that area as well. The finale to the workup came with simultaneous firing of Harpoons from an aircraft, submarine, and surface ship. Glenn said,

"We were able to accomplish this mission with three hits within minutes of each other, and . . . when they went to search for the target, there was nothing but debris."

As the *New Jersey* was returning to Long Beach following the workup, she encountered a long-lost sister. The *Missouri*, not yet in commission, was out on sea trials. It was the first time since 1954 that the two ships had operated within sight of each other. With her return to home port on 8 March, the at-sea preparations were complete. Now the last items of upkeep and maintenance were attended to during the two remaining months before deployment. Several hundred *New Jersey* men and their guests gathered on the deck of the battleship for a striking Easter sunrise service on 30 March.

Nearly two weeks later, on 14 April, a new man reported for duty as the ship prepared for a cruise that would involve a good deal of contact with foreign nationals. He was Lieutenant Commander Steven

Chesser, a former line officer who had graduated from journalism school before beginning active duty. He qualified as a surface warfare officer, designator 1110, before converting to public affairs specialist, 1650. He concluded that the SWO pin would give him enhanced credibility as he told the Navy's story. When he turned in his orders at the ship's office, he received a round sticker the size of a quarter to attach to his identification card. The color of the sticker was haze gray, and in black it contained the ship's name, hull number, and silhouette. That small circle brought with it an instant sense of belonging.

In preparation for deployment, the *New Jersey* added a surgeon to her crew. Since there would not be a carrier along to provide support for the small boys, the escorts would look to the battleship, as their predecessors had so often in times past, to keep the group self-sufficient. The deployment offered the prospect of tactical exercises, port visits, and demonstrations of the newly constituted battle group's combat capabilities. The deployment began on 13 May 1986, ten days before the forty-third anniversary of her first commissioning.

The battle group was bound for Pearl Harbor. En route its ships exercised in the Hawaiian operating area before the *New Jersey* entered port on 24 May. The ship's youngest and oldest crewmen participated in a wreath-laying ceremony at the USS Arizona Memorial. The battleship's men also fanned out for community-relations projects. Crewmen who had formed a clown troupe were a real hit when they entertained patients at the Tripler Army Hospital. Once under way again, the ship took part in Seventh Fleet exercises before a port call at Inchon, South Korea, 14–18 June. She followed that with a naval gunfire support demonstration at Chik-do Island. The next port of call was Hong Kong, where the ship arrived on 30 June to provide the crew with several days of rest and recreation opportunities.

On 5 July the ship began a transit from Hong Kong to Subic Bay. Two days later, unconscious Seaman James Walter Fox was discovered at the bottom

On 24 May 1986 the *New Jersey* nears the *Arizona* memorial. *U.S. Navy: DN-SC-86-08698*

The *New Jersey*'s clown troupe was a hit wherever it went; it entertained many grateful audiences. *U.S. Navy photo by Robert Taylor*

of a dumb-waiter shaft that ran from the previous flag quarters down to the wardroom galley on the second deck. Fox died without regaining consciousness. To quote the ship's official history for 1986: "Death was due to massive head injuries, and was later ruled a homicide. His remains were flown ashore that evening." (After the incident, that dumb waiter was not

During the 1986 cruise to the Western Pacific, the ship's officers gather on the forecastle for a group portrait. The two four-stripers front and center are Captain L. M. Hardt, executive officer, and Captain Lew Glenn, commanding officer. *Courtesy S. R. Foley III*

used again.) The crew held a memorial service on the fantail on 9 July.

Resolution of a sort came the following year. An investigation concluded that Fireman Recruit Damion Bessard was a likely suspect in the premeditated murder. The ship convened a general court-martial, but the prosecution was unable to produce sufficient evidence, so the charge was dropped before a potential trial could begin. As the result of Bessard's conviction in an unrelated previous court-martial case, the Navy dropped him with a bad conduct discharge.

After a period of upkeep at the Subic Bay ship repair facility, the battleship hosted a VIP cruise to Manila Bay for distinguished visitors. Next on the docket after a port visit in Manila Bay were more exercises, some of which involved the Australian navy. Then followed another port visit, this time to Pattaya Beach, Thailand. As in other stops, the ship hosted distinguished visitors, and the clown troupe provided entertainment. From 5 to 14 August, the ship participated in Exercise Cobra Gold '86 in conjunction with the Royal Thai Navy.

On 21 August the *New Jersey* participated in an attack on the ex–USS *Grayback*, which had been a missile-armed diesel submarine. She was painted bright orange to stand out prior to her demise. Her fellow attackers included a U.S. nuclear submarine, an Air Force B-52 bomber, Navy P-3 patrol plane, and a Harpoon missile fired by the battleship. The old diesel boat succumbed to the multi-prong attack and sank.

In preparation for arrival in Sasebo, Japan, on 24 August, the ship embarked Rear Admiral R. A. K. Taylor, the battle group commander, and a pool of news media representatives. Dozens of boats escorted the *New Jersey* into the port. Some of the boat crews were in favor of the visit and some against. Still more reporters came on board. The cameras of the media people focused mostly on the protesters and their signs, a continuing degree of sensitivity based on the U.S. use of nuclear weapons against the nation in 1945. The ship's public affairs officer, Lieutenant Commander Chesser, briefed Captain Glenn and Admiral Taylor about media interest on whether the

Crew members man the rail as the battleship enters port at Sasebo, Japan, on 24 August 1986. She is escorted by Japanese patrol boats to protect against protesters. *U.S. Navy: DN-ST-87-04544*

ship was armed with nuclear weapons. He told them the standard Defense Department guidance—neither confirm nor deny their presence on board.

The NBC network had requested an interview with the admiral once the *New Jersey* was moored in the port. The correspondent's first question was, "Do you have nuclear weapons aboard?" Taylor said he had been in touch with the Japanese Foreign Ministry. The correspondent quickly interjected: "Do you mean you told them whether or not you had nuclear weapons aboard?"

Chesser jumped in and said: "No, it was just to assure the Foreign Minister that the visit was in accordance with our treaty obligations." The correspondent was satisfied with that and continued the interview. As far as liberty opportunities for the crew, security was excellent on the base, but crewmen who ventured into the town itself were pretty much on their own. As a result, most of the men stayed nearby to avoid the protesters. The plan had been for the *New Jersey* to proceed to another Japanese port, Yokosuka, but that was scrubbed because of the atmosphere in Sasebo.

In September, the battleship visited Pusan and Inchon, South Korea. On the nineteenth, at the latter port, Admiral Taylor and Captain Glenn hosted a dinner on board the *New Jersey* for the top military leadership of the nation. Also in attendance were the U.S. ambassador and the commander of the United Nations Command in Korea. Still another dignitary visited. Governor Thomas H. Kean of New Jersey came on 21 September. He was in Seoul, the nation's capital city, on a Far East trade mission. Lieutenant Commander Chesser briefed the governor as a car took them to Inchon. The governor presented a proclamation honoring the ship's long service to the nation. Kean gave Captain Glenn a state flag, and later Kean posed in a plotting room with his hand on a firing key for 16-inch guns. PAO Chesser suggested a useful venue for a meal was the mess deck, and that proved to be the case. There the governor ate with thirty-four crew members from New Jersey. Kean's emphatic evaluation of the overall experience: "That is some ship!"

In late September the *New Jersey*, accompanied by the cruisers *Long Beach* and *Vincennes*, made a visit to the Far North, operating in the Sea of Okhotsk. The ship was there a few days before exiting through the Kurile Islands. This was a freedom-of-navigation operation in the vicinity of the Soviet Union, a first

Rear Admiral Raynor A. K. Taylor, commander of the U.S. Navy's first battleship battle group, welcomes one of the many South Korean guests during a VIP dinner held on board on 19 September 1986 at Inchon, Republic of Korea. *USS New Jersey public affairs office*

On 21 September 1986 an obviously enthusiastic Governor Thomas Kean, accompanied by Captain Glenn, poses with a trigger for the 16-inch guns in a main battery plotting room. USS New Jersey *public affairs office*

for the battleship. Recalled Petty Officer Charles Frakes, "The big thing about that was going about as close to Russia as you could get without actually being there. It was cold, I'll tell you." He remembered Captain Glenn saying to the crew, "We're going to give them a wakeup call tomorrow morning." That led to a high-speed transit at darken ship, emitting no radiation, to reach a position close to the Soviet Union without encroaching on it territorial waters.

The Asian landmass was visible in the distance. On 28 September the ship reached the northernmost point of approach at 56° north latitude. For those who had to be outside, warmth came in the form of watch caps and parkas with fur-lined hoods.

The battleship was there a day or two before the Soviets responded. A "Bear" bomber flew over the ship, and soon afterward appeared Soviet ships and still more aircraft to take closer looks at the visitor. As the ship's cruise book depicted in photos, Glenn heaved a piece of teakwood over the side as a symbolic gesture of the *New Jersey*'s close approach. Senior Chief Intelligence Specialist Joseph Kalman reported in the ship's 1986 cruise book *Surface Strike at Sea*, "We did gain some new intelligence data and we were able to get some very good photographs." Navy crew members prize certificates that attest to specific achievements. A prime example is that for an equator crossing. The ship in this case gave each man a certificate titled "The Order of the Bear's Lair" for his close encounter with the Soviet navy.

Afterward the ship began heading for the United States. En route the *New Jersey* conducted battle force operations with the aircraft carriers *Ranger*

In September 1986 the *New Jersey* steams with the aircraft carrier *Constellation* during an exercise in the Gulf of Alaska. Soviet aircraft overflew the U.S. warships as they invaded the "lair of the bear."
U.S. Navy: DN-ST-87-04541

This signalman is well bundled while sending a semaphore message during operations in the frigid North Pacific in September 1986.
U.S. Navy: DN-ST-87-04540

The ship's public affairs officer, Lieutenant Commander Steven Chesser, took this spectacular shot in mid-October 1986 when the ship was two days out of Seattle. The weapons officer, Commander K. C. Nicolin, had the idea, and Captain Lew Glenn enthusiastically approved. Chesser was on the bow and clicked the camera shutter at the third klaxon of the salvo alarm, the moment of firing. The image depicts a fiery twenty-one-gun salute as the *New Jersey* fires her nine 16-inch guns and twelve 5-inchers at split-second intervals.
USS New Jersey *public affairs office*

and *Constellation*. She detached from Battle Group Romeo on 7 October, and a few days later public affairs officer Steve Chesser took a photograph that came to be known as the "twenty-one gun salute." The *New Jersey*, of course, had nine 16-inch guns, and in the remaining six 5-inch dual mounts she had twelve—a total of twenty-one. The weapons department came up with the idea of firing them all at once, and the captain approved. Chesser and one of the photographer's mates went up to the forecastle. He was coached not to react to the gun but to the warning signals that precede the firing. He pressed the shutter release on the third sound, which was overwhelmed by the sound of the blasts. The guns didn't fire completely simultaneously; there were very brief intervals to keep projectiles from colliding in flight. The result was spectacular.

When she arrived back in the States, the *New Jersey* visited Seattle, Washington, 12–15 October. There she hosted more than 16,000 visitors. The ship rounded out the deployment with a return to Long Beach on 20 October. Later, she spent more time at sea to fire her weapons, hosted a visit by Secretary of the Navy John Lehman, and was in her home port to celebrate Christmas with a party for children of crewmen. On the twenty-first the ship's command choir and Marine color guard performed before the 60,000 fans in the stands and a national television audience at the final home game of the season for the Los Angeles Raiders football team.

Throughout much of her 1982–91 period in commission, the *New Jersey* had on board an instructor who taught courses through the Navy's Program for Afloat College Education (PACE). Ervin Cooper joined the ship for her first deployment in 1983 and became essentially a civilian member of the crew. He had been a Navy shipboard supply officer during World War II and the Korean War. He later taught in the San Diego school system and retired before joining PACE. He brought with him a master's degree in school administration and supervision. The appeal for him was the opportunity to travel at government expense.

Cooper taught crew members who were high school graduates. For those who had not made it that far or whose aptitude test scores were low, he taught three-week courses in functional skills. With the assent of division officers, men attended the basic skills course during working hours. Class sizes varied from ten to fifteen. Cooper's professional subjects included introduction to business management, personnel management, human relations, and economics. The education amounted to forty-eight hours of instruction per course. Some men came to him to seek counseling on personal issues; he provided an avenue outside the regular chain of command.

The college-level instruction took place after working hours ended at 4 p.m. Men heard lectures, did homework, and did research in the ship's library. Attendance was good, because the courses enabled men to improve their knowledge and better prepare them to fulfill their life goals. The ship benefited from having a better-educated crew. Because some men left and others came, Cooper had a continuing supply of new students. Some were commissioned officers, but most of the pupils were petty officers. Successful completion included a transcript with college credits that could be transferred to an accredited institution and provide a head start toward a degree.

Other forms of life-skills improvement were available. Near the end of the ship's active service, personal computers became more and more prevalent. They changed the lives of Americans in many ways. Plenty of space was available on board the huge ship, so a computer training center was established. Another service was financial counseling. Lieutenant Chuck Jennings, whose primary billet was boilers officer, provided that for the benefit of enlisted crewmen with little experience in budgeting. For many of the young men it was the first time they had been on their own financially.

In prior eras of the ship's history, many men in the lower pay grades were single and lived on board ship because they could not afford to do otherwise. Now wives and cars were factors, so Jennings showed them how to calculate monthly income and encouraged them to adjust expenses accordingly. While the ship was deployed, food and berthing were provided. Time back in the home port raised the challenges. Jennings observed that the pressure of accumulated, compounding debt diminished work performance, but it was not a rampant problem. Financial knowledge served as an incentive for men to advance in rate, both to increase salaries and to qualify for sea pay as petty officers.

During the early parts of 1987, the *New Jersey* was mostly in and around her home port. At times she was across the pier from her sister *Missouri* at the Long Beach Naval Station. An exception came between 9 and 20 January when the ship was moored at the North Island Naval Air Station in Coronado, California. When between deployments, the opportunity existed for crew members to attend Navy schools in San Diego. To preclude transportation and lodging costs, the ship brought the men to the schools so they could stay in their regular berths at night after attending daytime classes. After her stay, the ship was under way for two days of 16-inch and 5-inch shore bombardment qualifications at San Clemente Island off Southern California. She returned to Long Beach on 23 January.

On 29 January, the *New Jersey* had a temporary change of identity when she masqueraded as the

In mid-January 1987 the author, *left*, met with the ship's operations officer, Commander Kraig Kennedy. The two had stood combat information center watches together in 1969 when the former was a lieutenant and the latter an ensign. *USS* New Jersey *public affairs office*

The three principals of the August 1944 conference meet in the captain's in-port cabin to plan strategy. Left, complete with wheelchair and cigarette holder, is Ralph Bellamy as President Franklin D. Roosevelt; center is Walker Edmiston as General Douglas MacArthur; at right is William Prince as Admiral Chester Nimitz. *Courtesy Steven Chesser*

heavy cruiser *Baltimore*. The occasion was the filming of an episode of the television mini-series *War and Remembrance*, based on Herman Wouk's sprawling World War II novel. In late July 1944, President Franklin D. Roosevelt met with the major Pacific theater commanders, Admiral Chester Nimitz and General Douglas MacArthur, on board the cruiser. The purpose was to plan strategy for coming months of the war. Nimitz favored a path through Formosa, while MacArthur pushed for a return to the Philippines, from which he had been evacuated in 1942. The president opted for MacArthur's approach.

For the reenactment, the *New Jersey*'s brow curtain was changed to read "USS *Baltimore* (CA-68)." Filming took place on the main deck, forward of the turrets, and in the captain's in-port cabin. More than one hundred of the *New Jersey*'s crew members and dependents were extras. Captain Glenn, wearing the uniform of a vice admiral, portrayed an officer from years earlier as he welcomed Roosevelt on board. Actor Ralph Bellamy played President Roosevelt. One scene involved the ship's public affairs officer, Lieutenant Commander Chesser. He was disguised in an Army enlisted uniform, including khaki necktie tucked into his shirt front. He drove a vintage 1936 Cadillac convertible that delivered the MacArthur character down the pier to the ship. Walker Edmiston played MacArthur. During the actual event in 1944, wrote historian Alfred L. Castle, the general rode in an open touring car provided by "a well-known Honolulu brothel madam."

The CO's in-port cabin was also used for another sequence in which the *New Jersey* became still another ship. This time she was HMS *Duke of York*, the British battleship that transported Prime Minister Winston Churchill to the United States to meet with Roosevelt in

On 29 January 1987 the *New Jersey* was artificially renamed USS *Baltimore* for the filming of scenes for the television miniseries *War and Remembrance*. Here the *New Jersey*'s public affairs officer Steve Chesser appears as the Army enlisted chauffeur for General MacArthur's character. *Courtesy Steven Chesser*

"General MacArthur" waves to the assembled crowd as he moves along the brow to go on board the "USS Baltimore." *Courtesy Steven Chesser*

The *New Jersey* is shown in dry dock in Long Beach Naval Shipyard on 1 April 1987. She remained there for a number of months because of extensive hull pitting. Long Beach Independent Press-Telegram *photo by Bruce Chambers*

the aftermath of the attack on Pearl Harbor. The scene on board the *New Jersey* depicted the prime minister's meeting with his war cabinet and telling them the objective was to convince Roosevelt to concentrate first on defeating Germany. British character actor Robert Hardy portrayed Churchill in the TV series.

The *New Jersey* spent a good-sized chunk of 1987 in the Long Beach Naval Shipyard to upgrade and repair the ship after four years of substantial operating. She entered dry dock on 9 February. Included in the work package were replacement of number-three shaft and screw, curing the vibration in number-three main engine, installation of SPS-67 surface search radar, better communications, addition of decontamination stations, replacement of asbestos lagging in machinery spaces, resurfacing of the flight deck on the fantail, air-conditioning and other habitability upgrades, and a laundry list of other improvements. The initial period in dry dock began on 9 February.

Commander Dennis Ryan reported in the spring of 1987 to serve as chief engineer. When he arrived, the ship was in dry dock. The original plan after the previous deployment had been a quick dry dock period to scrape barnacles off the hull, repaint, and then resume operational duties. When the water was pumped out, a wet-hull inspection revealed heavy marine growth. After the water evaporated, a further examination revealed, as recalled later by Ryan, "It looked like the ship had a bad case of acne." Moreover, water was coming out from inside of the hull—not a good sign. The bottom was pockmarked, and a number of the holes went all the way through the hull. As a result, the dry dock period was extended until late August to make necessary repairs.

One factor in the deterioration was that the paint originally applied in the 1982 reactivation was supposed to provide protection for two or three years. The dry dock inspection did not occur until more than four years later. What Ryan described as "the really egregious thing that happened" was the improper installation of pieces of zinc on the underwater hull. The rectangular pieces of metal were intended to be sacrificial anodes. In their cathodic protection role, the zincs' role was to absorb electrolytic erosion rather than it acting on the steel hull. An inspection revealed that previously installed zincs were in great shape; the lettering on them was still readable. They had been put on backward, with the result that the deterioration was to the steel hull, not the zincs. (Ryan's relief as chief engineer was Commander Joseph Herger. He recalled later that new zincs were installed by divers, a project that lasted throughout much of the 1988 deployment.)

Ryan recalled that the shipyard had hundreds of welders working for months to eliminate the problems. A further challenge came from damaged rivets that had loosened, thus permitting water to leak around them. The shipyard had to put out a call to bring back retired workers who still had the skills to tighten and replace rivets. The rivets were heated on deck and then went down a chute, there to be caught in a bucket and pounded into position. Naval Sea Systems Command, which oversees the construction and repair of Navy ships, granted a waiver that permitted building up the damaged areas to a thickness of only half an inch instead of the normal full inch. Still another problem concerned water leakage from deteriorated tanks inside the ship.

The *New Jersey* was sitting atop substantial wooden keel blocks on the floor of the dock. At times the ship had to be "bounced" to permit access to the damaged areas over the blocks. That meant refloating the ship, moving, and setting down in a different position. Rotted interior piping was another problem. Among the many tasks accomplished during the dry dock period was the removal from the forefoot, that is, the bottom of the bulbous bow, a paravane guide that looked like a large circle welded to the hull. When the ship was built, the intent was that paravanes could be streamed aft of the opening and thus push away moored mines to prevent contacting the hull and exploding. By 1987, the technique was long since a thing of the past for a large combatant.

In the midst of the shipyard stint, fate was cruel to Captain Glenn on Sunday, 21 June. He was double-parked while his thirteen-year-old son Russell was delivering a newspaper in Huntington Beach, California. A truck rammed into Glenn's car from behind. The truck's driver had reached down to pick up some papers and momentarily took his eyes off the road. The damage to the skipper's car was so severe that he was trapped inside. Firefighters rescued him and delivered him to a hospital, where he remained for a few days. Glenn lost consciousness in the accident and was ruled to be in serious condition. The collision's impact unfortunately had lasting effects. Glenn, by then a retired rear admiral, died in 2011 after several years of a debilitating cognitive condition.

The executive officer was Captain L. M. Hardt, who was described by Lieutenant Commander Steve Chesser as "the classic enforcer . . . [who] kicked ass when people needed it." This is a frequent shipboard pattern; the skipper is the gentleman, and the exec is the individual who sees to discipline and the internal running of the ship. It's not exactly a good-cop/bad-cop routine, but it bears at least a resemblance. Following the devastating injuries to Captain Glenn, Hardt took over briefly as acting commanding officer, but he was detached soon afterward. The new exec/acting CO was Captain Daniel Salinas II.

Because of the injuries he incurred, Captain Glenn was not in position to resume command. That led to the need to find a relief for him several months earlier than expected. Captain Douglas J. Katz was then head of the Naval Academy's professional development department. Vice Admiral Joseph Metcalf III was the deputy chief of naval operations for surface warfare, so the issue fell squarely in his bailiwick. One day he called Sharon Katz and said that he and his wife, Ruth, wanted to take her to lunch. She replied, "Well, Doug's not available."

In a gruff voice, Metcalf said, "Doug's not invited." So she joined them, and they asked "numerous, numerous questions" for more than an hour. Their purpose was to decide whether she would be suitable as the wife of a battleship commanding officer. Years later she quipped, "I guess I did okay in my interview," because two days later her husband received orders to the *New Jersey*. She said it was something they didn't expect, but they were totally honored by the decision. She said, "It was probably the highlight, for me, of Doug's entire career." (The cherry on top was that their son Robert, who was in the NROTC program, later made a summer midshipman cruise on board while his father was in command. The stipulation was that the executive officer would write the son's fitness report. Robert eventually retired as a one-star flag officer.)

Captain Glenn relinquished command when Captain Katz relieved him as skipper on 8 August 1987. Katz broke Glenn's record as a youngest four-stripe skipper of the ship. Glenn, Naval Academy class of 1962, had taken command on his forty-fifth birthday. Katz, from the class of 1965, was forty-three years and eight months old when he became CO. Glenn, who had already been selected for rear admiral, returned to the ship for the change of command, made a departure speech, and was frocked in his new rank as part of the ceremony.

In a rare dry dock change of command, Captain Douglas Katz relieves Captain W. Lewis Glenn Jr. on 8 August 1987 in Long Beach Naval Shipyard. *Courtesy Sharon Katz*

Captain Douglas J. Katz commanded the *New Jersey* from 8 August 1987 to 19 May 1989. *Courtesy Sharon Katz*

The day after the change of command was a Sunday. Captain Katz took his wife to tour the ship and let her see this marvelous entity that was now his domain. She saw the sophisticated electronic gear in the combat engagement center and was impressed. Then the skipper reached into his pocket and drew out a key. He told her that this was the key to Admiral Halsey's bedroom and asked if she would like to see it. She replied, "Of course, I want to see everything." Her husband smiled at her as he turned the key and opened the door. The next thing she saw remained vivid memory years afterward, "There was a young couple having fun on Halsey's bed." The captain reacted by screaming for the executive officer so loudly that Mrs. Katz had to put her hands over her ears. The XO arrived quickly thereafter, and the young man went to captain's mast a few days later.

When it was time for the nonjudicial punishment, recalled Sharon, all the chief petty officers wanted to attend in order to see what this new captain was going to do. Because of the crowd, mast was held in the wardroom. Katz began the event by warning the audience members: "If any of you even laugh, so help me, you'll regret it." The particulars of the miscreant's adventure were discussed as part of the case, and the chiefs were tight-lipped as they exerted maximum effort to keep from bursting out. As expected, the skipper reduced the petty officer's pay grade but then added, "However, if we ever go to war, I want you beside me, because you've got some balls." At that point, the dam broke, and the chiefs—unable to control themselves any longer—burst into uproarious laughter. The skipper gave the petty officer an opportunity to redeem himself during their remaining time on board. He often stayed close to the captain on the bridge, reclaimed his previous pay grade, and advanced beyond. Katz capped him when the man eventually became a chief petty officer.

As soon as the Katzes settled into their new roles, Sharon began contacting the wives of the crew members. When new men reported aboard, she called them and their wives to offer welcome, tell them about ombudsman services, and see if they had any needs for which she could provide help. Some of the young women were surprised, albeit a bit skeptical initially. To build rapport, she encouraged them to call her Sharon rather than Mrs. Katz.

A number of the wives were due to deliver babies while the ship was later deployed overseas. Six times Sharon accompanied the new mothers in delivery rooms of hospitals when their husbands were unavailable. The new fathers received discreet photos of the deliveries. Communication went the other way as well. The ship made videos of crewmen speaking to their wives and then sent them to Sharon. She assembled the wives and played the videos for them.

The months of August and September were spent getting the ship ready to return to sea. On 29 August the ship left dry dock, and tugs delivered her to Pier Echo of the naval shipyard so the repair work could be concluded. Chief Warrant Officer Jim Palladino had reported for duty in late August and was taken aback by the condition of the propulsion plant after the long period in dry dock. He thought the *New Jersey* faced insurmountable odds in view of the tight timeline, the age of the ship, and what he observed. In a number of cases the companies that manufactured parts long ago had since gone out of business.

On 9 October 1987 Secretary of the Navy James R. Webb visits the battleship near the end of her long shipyard period in Long Beach. At right is Captain S. R. Foley III, commanding officer of the *New Jersey*'s Marine detachment. Webb, a fellow Marine, received the Navy Cross for his service in Vietnam and later became a prolific author. *Courtesy S. R. Foley III*

The ship failed the initial light-off exam (LOE), which Palladino took as a slap, because it was the first time in his career that he had not passed one. One of his shipmates, Machinist's Mate Second Class Don Lowery, had a discomfiting experience during an inspection visit. The ship's cruiser-destroyer group commander, Rear Admiral David K. U. Kihune, was in an upper main engine space when Lowery collided with him physically. Lowery was initially apprehensive, because he did not know the penalty for running into an admiral. No repercussions ensued.

On 28–29 September, the ship did succeed on the exam and thus ensured the engineering plant was ready to be fired up. On 19 October the ship took on ammunition at Seal Beach and then went through sea trials. On the twenty-first the *New Jersey* fired her 5-inch and 16-inch guns for the first time since January. On 29 October, she performed a full-power run during sea trials off Southern California. The *New Jersey* reached the speed of thirty-two knots, the fastest she had steamed since the 1982 recommissioning.

The high-speed run required bringing in all the crewmen from the main engine and boiler divisions to be able to operate all eight boilers. During normal underway watches, the ship ran only four boilers, which were sufficient to produce twenty-seven knots. The whole process, including preparation, took about six hours. At high speeds the plant produced considerable vibration and noise. Standard procedure called for engineering personnel to wear at least single hearing protection and sometimes double if necessary. What's more, there was a visible manifestation as well. A ship's wake at high speed is known as a "rooster tail," and in this case it rose more than twenty feet high above the sea. Another challenge in the firerooms was heat. When the ship operated in hot climates, the temperature could rise above 100°, an unkind environment for boiler technicians. The remedies were rotating personnel and drinking lots of fluids. (The Navy disestablished the boiler technician rating in 1996 to reflect the fact that the majority of shipboard propulsion plants by then employed gas turbines rather than steam.)

Trying to cope with all the problems involved in operating an engineering plant that was forty-five years old gave chief engineer Dennis Ryan considerable frustration, because so many things went wrong. Corroded fuel-oil piping was one example. One day, he recalled years later, he essentially gave up. While the battleship was anchored, he went to his stateroom and prayed, "That's it, God. I quit. I'm going up and tell the captain, 'I can't take any more. Get somebody else.' Well, the Good Lord has such a sense of humor."

Just as he finished with his entreaty, the general announcing system called away the oil-spill team. That posed still another challenge, because pollution control is a big item. Commander Ryan ran topside and saw that there was a leak aft on the port side, explaining later, "I never did have time to quit." As the ship headed to port, Ryan could see that she left a slight sheen on the water as more fuel leaked out. In port, divers went down and discovered a hole in a fuel tank near the number-two propeller shaft. The solution came in the form of draining the tank and applying quick-setting putty, both inside and outside.

The ship rounded out the month with a dependents' cruise. Many of the crew members who brought family and friends were new to the ship. The long shipyard period resulted in a great deal of personnel turnover. A considerable amount of training lay ahead to bring the crew up to speed figuratively, just as the engineering plant had been brought up to speed literally. For example, chief engineer Ryan recalled that all the officers in his department, including himself, had joined the ship after she was last deployed.

One man who had recently arrived on board was Gunner's Mate First Class Leon Tucker. He joined the ship in September 1987 after having been through a number of specialized Navy schools ashore. He explained that the schools had prepared him so well that he felt right at home when he reached the ship. In

Captain Douglas Katz, *left*, welcomes a visit from Admiral Carlisle A. H. Trost, Chief of Naval Operations. *Courtesy Sharon Katz*

assessing the hands-on work as captain of turret one, he said, "It seemed like I'd already been here."

A few years later, he recalled of Captain Katz's tenure: "He loved to shoot these guns. We shot going out; we'd shoot coming back in." That observation of the skipper's enthusiasm for gunnery was shared by many of the shipmates. Said Tucker of Katz, "He was missed when he left. He took care of his crew." Chief Warrant Officer Jim Palladino described Katz as "a high-energy individual [and] that's an understatement." College instructor Ervin Cooper touted Katz for his enthusiasm and sense of humor. He recalled that when the skipper addressed the crew on the general announcing system, he frequently said, "It just doesn't get any better than this."

A sign in the mess deck displays Captain Douglas Katz's oft-expressed description of service in the *New Jersey*. *Courtesy Sharon Katz*

The crew of the *New Jersey* was primarily Christian. For those who were not, Fire Controlman Len Jablon served as the Jewish lay reader. He held services every Friday night in the ship's chapel on the starboard side of the second deck. A couple of men in his division asked if they could attend, primarily so they could have a cup of the kiddush wine that was part of the service. Actually, though, the cup was tiny; the "worshippers" expected it would be much bigger.

Normally, Jablon explained, a Jewish service is about an hour or hour and a half, but he held his to a half hour because he knew his shipmates had other things to do. He skipped the basics and concentrated on the more important parts of prayer. The ship's on-board television station filmed an interview with him about Jewish holidays. For the production he wore a prayer shawl and a yarmulke skull cap. That attracted more men who inquired about the wine. His response, "You want to learn about Judaism, fine, I'm happy to teach you. But just coming for the wine, that doesn't cut it." Once, when the ship was in Long Beach, he held a Passover Seder meal in conjunction with a visiting rabbi. It was not feasible for Jablon to maintain a kosher diet during shipboard operations, but for the Seder meal, local Jewish war veterans provided funds for kosher food.

The year wound down with an ecumenical Thanksgiving service on 26 November. Crew members and their families enjoyed holiday meals in the wardroom and mess deck. Shortly afterward the *New Jersey* loaded Harpoon and Tomahawk missiles while alongside her pier in Long Beach.

On the subject of crew turnover, Lieutenant (junior grade) William Shipley, who had reported in the summer of 1986, observed that at one point the wardroom's occupants included more than thirty ensigns. Traditionally, the process of preparing for operations is known as refresher training. For ensigns who arrived as blank slates, there was no previous experience to refresh. Shipley recalled a few years later that restoring operational capability was a difficult process, "It was rough going all through there, all those exercises and inspections we had to do."

On 7 December, in preparation for the deployment to come, the ship was under way to begin eleven days of interim refresher training. The organization that administrated the format was the fleet training group, which was known for having high standards. The training included drills at battle stations almost every day. Among the many areas covered were damage control and warfare capability. On 14–15 December, the ship fired her 16-inch and 5-inch guns at San Clemente Island and aced the test with a score of 100 percent.

Among the other firepower available on board ship were four Vulcan/Phalanx close-in weapon systems (CIWS), though the full formal title was rarely used. The shorthand version was the much more pronounceable "SEE-wiz." Fire Controlman Len Jablon was in charge of one of the four and explained their capabilities. The self-contained device stood about fifteen feet high, did its own fire control, and included a six-barrel Gatling-type rotating 20-mm gun that could spit out three thousand rounds a minute. The bullets were coated with depleted uranium designed to penetrate armor. The equipment was topped by a white-domed cylinder that contained the radar systems. (One might think of the *Star Wars* character R2D2, though it was a different color.)

As the name suggests, the weapon was designed as a last-ditch defense measure against antiship missiles or aircraft attacking the ship. Firing drills against drones were conducted, recalled Jablon, "every once in a blue moon." One occasion stood out in his memory. Explaining that the gun would continue to fire as long as it had a radar target, he recalled that the capability could be a problem. A drone aircraft was towing a shape that resembled a missile. The rotating barrels quickly dispatched the fake missile, and then began climbing along the towline toward the drone. Jablon had to intervene and shut off the gun before it could take out the drone as well. Alas, free of the missile, the drone dropped into the sea and was lost. The CIWS was the 1980s equivalent of the 20-mm and 40-mm antiaircraft guns that festooned the *New Jersey*'s topside spaces during World War II. After the refresher training concluded, the battleship returned to Long Beach to celebrate the holidays.

Twenty-year-old gunner's mate striker (that is, trainee) John Dugas reported to the ship in January 1988 as a self-described rookie. When the billet was offered, he leaped at the opportunity, because he considered the *New Jersey* to be the ultimate gunnery ship. He served in G-2 division that operated turret two. Years later, Dugas still had warm memories of the camaraderie with shipmates in his division's berthing compartment. It was equipped with tables that sported checkerboard patterns. The tables were useful for card games, checkers, and sometimes chess. In the turret, he worked with the center gun. His role was to be part of the backup firing crew in the event that the fire control setup was not able to shoot remotely from a plotting room below decks. As it happened, the gun never shot in local control during his time on board, but he still felt the concussion and jolt of firing. Dugas' experience was essentially on-the-job training by the turret's chief because the gunner's mate training manual was limited to smaller guns.

Activity in the new year began on 1 February, when the ship went back to sea for ten days of routine drills and operations off Southern California. On board during the period was Rear Admiral Robert K. U. Kihune, commander, Cruiser-Destroyer Group Five. By then, the ship had flag officer accommodations for the first time since 1969. In the interim, the old flag spaces on the 02 deck had been gutted and dramatically altered to make room for the combat engagement center when missiles were added during the 1981–82 modernization. No flag quarters were created during the modernization in order to defang critics who claimed the ship was being restored to the fleet as a fancy place in which to install an admiral.

Rear Admiral Robert K. U. Kihune, as Commander Cruiser-Destroyer Group Five, was instrumental in the installation of new flag quarters in the *New Jersey*. *Naval History and Heritage Command.*

With the ship scheduled to visit Australia in 1988, Admiral Kihune initiated a change. It involved the installation of new spaces for an admiral and his staff. Kihune expected to make the Western Pacific deployment and wanted the *New Jersey* as his battle group flagship. The project had started in early October 1987, at which time the space was used as a junior officer bunkroom. The work continued for months. In effect, the new flag quarters on the port side mirrored the captain's cabin on the starboard side of the 01 level.

The project involved adding more bunks in existing staterooms and adding command and control equipment and berthing for the staff. In describing the ongoing project, the ship's official history reported the changes as adding twenty-seven officer berths, flag wardroom and briefing room, and an intelligence evaluation space. (Lieutenant William Shipley said that adding two more berths to each two man stateroom produced crowding and hassles, especially when occupants were on different watch schedules. One sink served four officers, and storage space was often insufficient.) The renovation included connections between the new flag spaces and the CEC that operated in the previous flag quarters.

Approval for the project came from Vice Admiral George W. Davis Jr. He was the type commander, head of Naval Surface Force Pacific Fleet. Members of the ship's force accomplished the work under the leadership of the supply officer. Kihune recalled the work required as minimal, except for the evacuation of the junior officer bunks. The design work was a collaboration that involved both Kihune and people from the Long Beach Naval Shipyard. Included were a bunk for the admiral and a dining table comparable to the one in the captain's in-port cabin. A door connected the two cabins so that the overall space could accommodate shipboard receptions. A common galley provided meals for the admiral's mess and that of the commanding officer.

Davis told Kihune that the expectation for upcoming participation in Australia's bicentennial would be likely to involve Queen Elizabeth II being on board the *New Jersey*. Kihune said the flag space would be fine for her, except for the standard Navy head facilities. Kihune said he wanted the head to be modified so it would be "fit for a queen." That involved laying new tile on the deck and installing a commode and sink made of porcelain instead of the shipboard standard of stainless steel. Ryan Szimanski, historian and curator of the museum ship, described the head, "It is a large space for a toilet, shower, and sink. I bet the queen and her corgis could fit in there." Alas, there was no opportunity to find out, because the queen did not board the ship after all.

After that initial venture to sea on 1 February, the following day the ship stopped briefly in San Diego to embark Rear Admiral Kihune, so he became the first occupant of the new flag quarters. The only drawback was that he did not have a dedicated sea cabin; the skipper did. The admiral was able to operate from the new in-port cabin and to reach the flag bridge when appropriate. Kihune remained on board until

11 February while the ship went through training exercises. After being in port from mid-February to mid-March, the battleship spent ten more days at sea in March to continue the training process.

From 7 to 14 April, Admiral Kihune and his staff were again embarked, this time to participate in a series of war games dubbed ReadiEx 88. The *New Jersey* and other Third Fleet surface combatants were part of an adversarial exercise. The opposing force included an aircraft carrier that was working up for an overseas deployment, and the two groups were separated from each other. The objective was to inflict damage on the "enemy" while trying to remain undetected. Public affairs officer Steve Chesser observed that the battleship hit a guided missile ship with several simulated Harpoon missiles. The admiral remembered, "The carrier was looking for us. . . . We were trying to engage them and trying to do some kind of diversion so that they would go in the wrong direction looking for us while we sneaked in from the back door."

Among other things, the *New Jersey*'s force threw reflectors in the water to give the impression of a larger target than actually existed. The objective was to make her force appear to be random merchant ships. The deception also included lighting patterns at night. He concluded that the training was of more benefit to the carrier group than that of the battleship group. Kihune recalled that one of the features of the battleship battle group was that the escort ships operated at a distance from the flagship so that radar images would not make it clear that this was a naval formation. This, of course, was the opposite of the World War II task groups, in which the escorts steamed nearby to provide close-in antiaircraft gunnery.

In May and June the *New Jersey* continued training operations off the West Coast and made a Memorial Day weekend visit to San Francisco, where she played host to thousands of visitors. On 1 June, while en route from San Francisco to Long Beach, the ship fired a Tomahawk missile. She arrived in home port on 6 June and spent the following month in final preparations for the overseas deployment that lay ahead. As it happened, Admiral Kihune did not make the Australia trip for which he had prepared the ship. He remained behind in California to relieve Admiral Davis as commander, Naval Surface Force Pacific Fleet. Though he missed the deployment, he was promoted from rear admiral to vice admiral. Years later, he remarked with a laugh, "I couldn't complain."

Among the preparations for the multi-nation cruise ahead, Captain Katz began an initiative that went into effect during his tenure and remained a feature of the ship throughout her remaining service life. The skipper called in the commanding officer of the Marine detachment, Captain Sylvester R. "Bob" Foley III. Katz directed the young officer to form a silent drill team and have it ready to perform by the time the ship reached South Korea.

Initially he met resistance, because Foley explained that teams developed at the Marine Barracks in Washington, DC, had drill fields ashore on which to train and practice. Moreover, they had been screened to bring in men who were the best in the Marine Corps. Captain Katz told Foley to do it anyway, and Foley did. Commander Dennis Ryan observed the result at the first performance, which involved passing rifles among members of the team with no vocal orders involved. He said of the Marines: "They were spot on. They did everything exactly right." Sharon Katz said, with tongue slightly in cheek, "You could hear a pin drop," and she added, "They stole the show at every reception." Actually, there were sounds as hands slapped rifles and feet moved. One joke spawned was that "silent" drill team audio tapes were the worst sellers in the ship's store.

The *New Jersey* began her 1988 deployment when she pulled away from pier six at Long Beach on 7 July. By then, Captain Katz had gained experience in handling a behemoth that was far bigger than the destroyers in which he had served. Initially, he had sought to twist the ship away from piers by using rudders and

The Marine detachment's silent drill team goes through its paces.
Courtesy Ronald Tucker

propellers. Seniors, including Vice Admiral Davis, had advised him that too much torque could damage piers, so the skipper worked with tugboats. That knowledge came in handy when the ship reached her first overseas destination, Pusan, South Korea, on 24 July. The tug skippers spoke only Korean, but by this time Katz had learned how to communicate by other means.

Ensign Rob Rice was newly reported to the ship, shortly after being commissioned through Officer Candidate School. He was impressed by the number of attractive and aggressive women in Pusan. He talked with a mama-san, who told him that the locals knew as much about the ship's schedule as did the crew. As a matter of logistics, he recalled two years later, a large number of Korean women—perhaps thousands—had been imported from Seoul, South Korea's capital city, to meet U.S. Navy men while they were on liberty. Texas Street was particularly notable in that regard. Rice was struck by how Americanized and commercial Pusan had become in the thirty-five years since the Korean War.

After Pusan came a stop in Inchon from 31 July to 5 August. The tide range at Inchon was dramatic—as the U.S. Navy had dealt with during its September 1950 invasion in the area. That was a brilliant behind-the-lines operation led by General of the Army Douglas MacArthur. On this occasion in 1988, the battleship was able to moor at a coal pier that was about fifteen miles from the town. The range of tide there was twenty-two feet, which meant that the duty section had the added chore of frequently adjusting the mooring lines and the brow as the hull rose and descended. At low tide the brow was at a 45° angle, making it a real challenge to come on board for those who had imbibed heavily. Captain Katz was concerned that the ship's hull might have touched bottom after the tide went out.

During the Korea visit, Fire Controlman Len Jablon went sightseeing in an area near a university that the crew had been warned to avoid because students might riot in reaction to visiting American servicemen. Portraying himself as "a little bit of a rogue guy," Jablon went anyway to sightsee and take pictures while wearing civilian clothes. English-speaking college students asked if he was in the Navy, and he responded in the affirmative. The locals were friendly and invited him to a teahouse. They fed him tea and a delicious beef concoction; the upshot was a political conversation that lasted more than two hours. He offered his personal views on various topics. He told the Koreans that they perceived every Navy man as a caricature of some of the things that the United States does. He said: "We're not. We're just like you." He indicated that if they talked to men in the Korean army, they would find that the soldiers had to obey orders but were still free to have their own opinions. Years later, he recalled the visit as an enjoyable inter-cultural exchange.

During the 1988 deployment, as a morale booster, the crew engaged in a beard-growing contest. The awards were such as ugliest beard, nicest beard, weirdest beard, and so forth. One crew member included a waxed handlebar mustache as part of his hirsute entry. For Fire Controlman Len Jablon, who was twenty-nine, it was the first time in his life he had grown a beard. He recalled "having a couple of splotches here and there," so he won no awards, but it was a fun activity for the crew. At the end of the

In July 1988 members of the *New Jersey*'s crew engaged in a beard-growing contest at the beginning of the ship's Western Pacific deployment. They are shown here while the ship was en route to Pusan, South Korea. At lower left is Fire Controlman Len Jablon.
Courtesy Leonard Jablon

In preparation for a forthcoming voyage to Australia, the *New Jersey*, center, is moored at Subic Bay in the Philippines in August 1988. Astern of her is the British aircraft carrier *Ark Royal*.
U.S. Navy: DN-SC-92-08408

contest, crew members received two cans each of nonalcoholic "near beer," with masters-at-arms carefully checking to see that no one got more than two. As Jablon put it, "You couldn't get drunk if you drank a case of those."

From 5 to 11 August, the ship steamed to Subic Bay, Philippines. There she took on more than three hundred 16-inch projectiles and the appropriate amount of powder bags. Later she had a maintenance and upkeep period. She was under way on 17 August in company with her battle group and the British aircraft carrier *Ark Royal*. The destination was Australia. Reaching that island nation required crossing the equator. In this case, the pollywogs far outnumbered the shellbacks, so there was a great deal of initiating. For Lieutenant (junior grade) William Shipley, a pollywog, it was an hours-long experience during which he was unable to stand up until the ceremony was over. The alternatives for pollywogs were on their knees or on their stomachs. Reveille was at 4 a.m., and "breakfast" was perhaps some sort of pasta that had

been dyed a disgusting color. Many of his shipmates elected to skip that meal. Pollywogs crawled from stern to bow, which was highly congested because so many "wogs" were stacked there. Shipley compared it to a Los Angeles traffic jam.

Water hoses from fire stations sprayed the bunch with cold water even before the sun rose. Then the pollywogs sort of swam/crawled down the starboard side, which was covered with a layer of water. Some while later, Shipley looked back and deemed that the occasion had been fun, though it did not seem so at the time. Ensign Rob Rice came in for special attention; he was thumped by a senior chief with a shillelagh (a three-foot section of fire hose) as the young officer crawled his way through a chute filled with leftover food from the galley.

Rice, who is Black, was the ship's equal opportunity officer. He observed that the crew included a large group of minority personnel. He felt that these men needed someone with whom they could feel comfortable talking. Part of the rapport stemmed from the fact that he was in his early twenties and thus close in age to many of the enlisted men. He played with them on the ship's basketball and softball teams and was often visible to minority individuals. As a result, men would bring to him issues that they were apprehensive about raising with their chiefs or officers. These would often involve a perception of discrimination on board.

After he had investigated a problem himself, the command structure permitted him to forward the men's concerns to the legal officer, executive officer, and sometimes the captain. Overall, the racial situation was good, he explained, but some problems are inevitable in society, perhaps more so in an enclosed community. The typical occasion came when someone got drunk or angry and uttered a racial slur. Said Rice, "The Navy, of course, has a zero-tolerance policy on this."

The resolution usually came at mast, during which the offender's record and history would have a bearing on the outcome. Rice said he often went to a crewman who used offensive racial language and said, "My feeling is I can't change your attitude. If this is really you, then it's you. If it was a slip, and it's not the way you normally are, then I hope you're going to keep that in mind from now on." He did tell the slur-hurlers that if racial animus really was their attitude, they had to keep it to themselves. Otherwise, it would be detrimental to good order and discipline. Sometimes the shoe was on the other foot, so to speak. Minority members were taken to mast if they used unacceptable racial terms. Expressing the expectations without favoring either side gave Rice credibility.

Rice added that sometimes a situation would arise, and the captain would occasionally call and ask whether something was considered normal or abnormal. In that sense, the junior officer became something of a sounding board on racial matters. One of the topics was haircuts. Chief petty officers would sometimes prevent men from going ashore, even though they had what Rice considered "normal haircuts." On the other hand, Rice sometimes met men whose hair was too long by Navy standards or drew too much attention and encouraged them to have it cut shorter.

While en route to Australia as part of the naval formation, the *New Jersey* was practicing for a firepower demonstration to be conducted later for the Aussies. A commercial tanker was approaching on the port side of the battleship. The radar picture revealed CBDR—constant bearing, decreasing range, which is the formula for collision or a near miss—passing through the naval column. Attempts to raise the tanker by radio received no response, as did attempts by signal light. Captain Katz, on the bridge, was understandably concerned. He ordered the sounding of the ship's internal collision alarm and five short blasts on the ship's whistle in an attempt to get the attention of the tanker's crew. Lieutenant William Shipley heard later that the skipper ordered emergency ahead full to speed up and get the *New Jersey* out of danger. While the incident was in progress, Shipley was topside and saw the action himself as the tanker came within a few dozen feet of the battleship's stern.

Gunner's Mate John Dugas enjoyed the attention-getting role in going from one liberty port to another once the ship was "down under." Another gunner's mate, Leon Tucker, expressed the reaction of the locals, "They couldn't wait for us to get out there." The *New Jersey* began the visits by anchoring off the western port of Fremantle/Perth on 26 August. More than five thousand visitors made the round-trip boat voyages to and from the ship for tours. Captain Katz hosted a reception for 250 guests.

Ensign Rob Rice observed that Katz was a great host in dealing with the many visitors who attended receptions during the Australia sojourn. Rice described him as "friendly, always making the right move at the right time" in observing preparations and execution. Rice, who was adept on a keyboard, pulled together a seven member jazz band at the captain's suggestion to provide entertainment during the gatherings.

Lieutenant Brian Gleason credited Captain Katz with keeping the big picture in mind during the cruise. That meant creating toward the media and visitors a best-foot-forward approach. Pulling that off involved plenty of extra work for the crew to boost the image of the ship and of the Navy as a whole. After such effort by the crew members, Katz passed along to them, via the general announcing system, the positive feedback they had garnered for the ship. Among the accolades, for example, was that the *New Jersey* was "the best-looking ship I've ever seen." Messages such as that made their way to Washington and elsewhere in the Navy.

Subsequent stops included Albany, Brisbane, and Sydney. In Brisbane crew members took part in a march through the city, and two hundred local children gathered on the flight deck aft for a bicentennial birthday party. Media coverage included television and front-page newspaper stories throughout her nine-day visit. A planned Brisbane media event, however, was foiled. One night a deck sentry looked over the side and saw some men in a boat that was just moving away. The boat occupants were protesters who had painted "No Nukes" and a giant peace symbol on the side of the hull. A group of crew members received haze gray from the paint locker. Then, without showing any lights, they descended on a stage and covered up the new decorations. The following morning, observers on board the *New Jersey* looked across to the opposite bank. They saw a news camera pointed at the ship, prepared to film sunrise on the protesters' artwork. Instead, all the camera could photograph was newly applied gray paint.

On 26 September the ship conducted an offshore firepower demonstration before arriving at Sydney the following day. Ensign Brian Gleason considered that shooting the guns was part of the entire political process of showing the flag and making a good impression on a valued ally. Earlier in the cruise, because of operating with the British carrier *Ark Royal*, Katz had established a relationship with

Sailors in blue line the rails of the battleship as she arrives in Sydney, Australia, on 27 September 1988. On the forecastle a gaggle of news media representatives observes the scene. *U.S. Navy: DN-SC-89-02126*

Captain Michael Harris, her commanding officer. On 27 September *Ark Royal* led the parade of ships from several nations into Sydney Harbor. The harbor was filled with protesters in kayaks and other boats. Prior to the arrival, Vice Admiral Paul David Miller,

A massive hammerhead crane looms above the *New Jersey*, which moored at Garden Island Australian naval base in Sydney on 27 September 1988. *USS* New Jersey *NavSource: Tom Strasser photos via Yu Chu*

commander, Seventh Fleet, had called Katz and said: "You will not take on these kayakers, and you'd better not hit one. Don't take any chances. Don't get in trouble."

Katz relayed the gist of his conversation to Captain Harris, who replied, "I have no such orders." The crew of the *Ark Royal* had charged fire hoses and used them to spray the kayakers with water and knocked them over. The crewmen of the *New Jersey* watched the spectacle and cheered for their British counterparts.

On the evening of 30 September, fireworks lit up the night sky. An international naval fleet moored in the harbor, despite encountering protesters. Present were more than fifty warships that represented sixteen nations. On 1 October, the Duke and Duchess of York (Prince Andrew and his wife Fergie) boarded HMAS *Cook*, an oceanographic research ship. As more than two million people watched, they proceeded to conduct a mobile review of the multinational ships. Lieutenant (junior grade) William Shipley recalled later that those on board the *New Jersey* had practiced for two weeks beforehand so they could render the customary salute called "cheer ship." They removed their hats and shouted, "Hip, hip, hooray" to the passing royals. On one occasion, Captain Katz provided a guided tour of the *New Jersey* for Prince Andrew and Fergie. Andrew reciprocated by hosting a guided tour of the *Ark Royal*.

During the Sydney visit, the *New Jersey* brought on board more than 40,000 visitors; included were eighty-four media people. Eleven hundred people were guests at a reception on the pier. The Seventh Fleet band provided the music. John Dugas enjoyed liberty in the various Australian ports; he fondly remembered "the food, the atmosphere, the people." Specifically he had happy experiences with women who liked Navy men. Sometimes they invited crew members to their homes to meet their families and provided dinner. Lieutenant (junior grade) William Shipley recalled later that some of the encounters between U.S. Navy men and Australian women led to marriages and new lives in the United States for the women.

Boatswain's mates moor the *New Jersey* to a harbor buoy during the ship's visit to Sydney, Australia, in October 1988. *U.S. Navy: DN-SC-89-02120 and DN-SC-89-02121*

The entertainment load was heavy because the ship hosted so many visitors for special receptions and other events. Lieutenant (j.g.) Brian Gleason recalled that the big receptions were known generically as "sweat-exes" because so much extra effort was involved. Said Mess Management Specialist Charles Frakes of the Australia visits, "That was just one party after another." During that time he was assigned to the officers' mess. The requirements for feeding so many outsiders produced quite a workload in the food-service area. He recalled that over the four-month cruise he and his cohorts in the wardroom had only nine days off, "If we were in port, we were throwing a party somewhere." In Sydney, said Frakes, the ship expected six hundred to eight hundred hungry mouths, and the final head count was more than twenty-two hundred.

The remedy for the onslaught, said Frakes, was to use shortcuts and "throw some things together." He remembered that the Australians were especially energetic guests: "We had several of them, we'd start them about 5:30–6 o'clock in the evening, and it'd be 2:30 or 3 o'clock in the morning before we could finally push them off." Among the guests at a

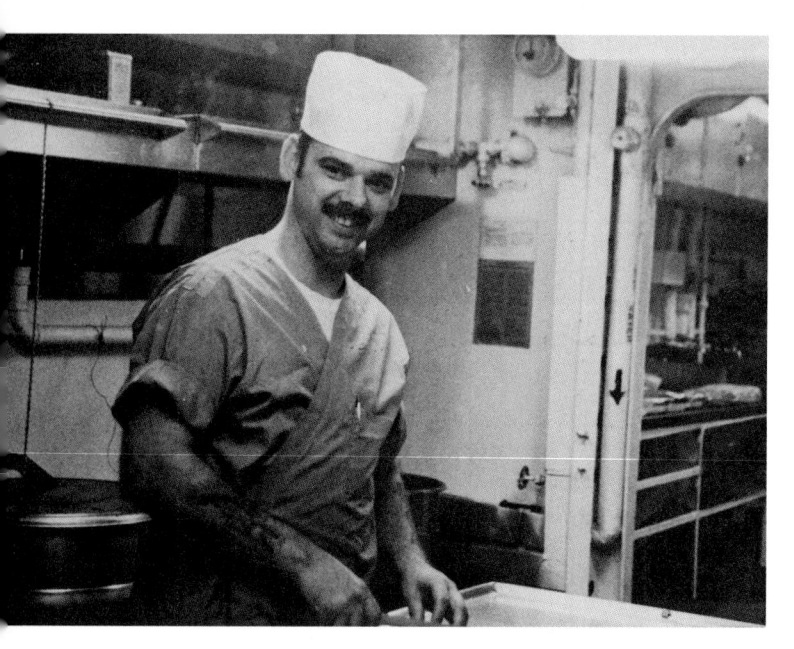

Mess Management Specialist Charles Frakes, assigned to the wardroom galley, prepares meals for the ship's officers.
USS New Jersey *public affairs office*

reception in Sydney were Admiral William J. Crowe Jr. and his wife Shirley. Crowe was then chairman of the Joint Chiefs of Staff, the highest-ranking officer in the U.S. armed services.

One element added to receptions during the 1980s was alcohol. That was the result of an initiative on the part of Secretary of the Navy John Lehman. From 1914 onward, at the direction of then-Secretary of the Navy Josephus Daniels, wine messes were prohibited. Navy ships were dry for decades. Now at official receptions, light wine and beer could join food on the menu, especially in foreign ports. In the United States it tended to be champagne more often. Hard liquor was reserved for events ashore. For those who visited the ship in Australia, beer was the number-one choice.

Next stop for the *New Jersey* was Hobart, Tasmania, luring more thousands of visitors and continuing as a media darling. She finally got under way for Pearl Harbor after a ten-day visit. The total number of visitors during the Australia flag-showing venture amounted to 77,750, reported the ship's annual history. Lieutenant Commander Chesser, the public affairs officer, recalled years afterward, "I never worked so hard in my life as I did on that cruise." In addition to dealing with many news media representatives, he had to make a lot of arrangements for upcoming events, making him the de facto event planner. He said his typical workday at sea began at reveille and ended about 10 p.m. That involved sending invitations to various functions and responding to the many incoming invitations.

Even when the *New Jersey* wasn't junketing, Chesser was frequently busy. The public affairs office put out a daily newspaper at sea and a newscast on the ship's closed-circuit television every evening. As Katz recalled the cruise years later, he said he really depended on Chesser to respond to the intense interest in the ship and thus take pressure off the captain. Back in home port, the public affairs officer interacted with community leaders and such organizations as the civilian Navy League. He fielded speaking invitations when in various ports and evaluated their usefulness in terms of which to accept. The media coverage of the battleship was largely positive.

Gunner's Mate Dugas recalled the Australian people being "very friendly" in port after port. He was coach of the ship's softball team and enjoyed playing against local Australian teams. In his recollection the battleship's team won at least 75 percent of the games. Interestingly, Coach Dugas, who is Black, was the authority figure but experienced no resentment at all from members of the team. The team comprised men from a variety of shipboard departments, so it was a means of forming friendships that might not otherwise have developed. On the way back north, the crossing of the equator was even more special than on the outbound trip. This time the ship passed from one hemisphere to the other at the 180th meridian, the international date line. That conferred a special designation on those who made it; they became "golden shellbacks."

To wind up the 1988 deployment, the ship made a "tiger cruise" for 256 male guests of crew members. The format called for individuals to meet the ship in Hawaii and then remain on board for the final leg of the trip, from Pearl Harbor to Long Beach. The captain permitted a number of crew members to go on leave to free up bunks for the visitors.

One such tiger was fifty-nine-year-old Stanley Jablon, whose son Len had been on board throughout the trip to the Far East. He flew to Hawaii and spent a couple of days on Oahu with Len before the ship got under way on 1 November from Pearl. Stan took over his son's regular bunk, and Len slept in his CIWS office on the 04 level in the superstructure. He took a pillow and blanket along to sleep on a desk, adding: "No big deal." The next morning, his dad ate chow in the mess deck, found Len, and said of his accommodation: "Ah, this is like a hotel."

Len responded with a chuckle, "Maybe for you it is, Dad, but it's not a hotel for me." When his duties permitted, Len showed his father around the ship, and the command had also set up special tours of places such as the engineering spaces at times when the fire controlman was not available. Stan went into a turret and watched with amazement as crewmen, who were slimmer, crawled through the 16-inch barrels and came out of the muzzle ends. When Len had been growing up, he didn't spend a lot of time with his father, who was a traveling salesman. Now, years later, the time together proved a wonderful bonding experience. Both father and son enjoyed the cruise. As Len put it, "We got close, closer than we ever were."

Another tiger on the cruise was a distant uncle of a ship's officer. The relative was a carpenter who ran a cabinet shop in California. He was rooming with Chief Warrant Officer Jim Palladino, who termed the visitor, a man in his early sixties, as "a real, real likable guy." After dinner one evening, Palladino and the uncle ate ice cream together while watching a wardroom movie. The visitor said he was tired and left for their room. When Palladino returned to the stateroom around midnight, he discovered that the lights and radio were still on.

He looked in the bottom bunk and saw that the uncle had an ashen color. He found the man was cold to the touch and had no pulse. A *New Jersey* physician ascertained that the visitor had died of a heart attack. Palladino was unable to sleep that night. He moved to another room for the remaining two or three days of the cruise. The corpse was wrapped in plastic and stored in a ship's refrigerator until the *New Jersey* reached Long Beach on 9 November. Perhaps the excitement of the experience was a factor. Earlier in the cruise, Palladino had asked the visitor whether he was enjoying himself. His ironic reply was, "I'm having the time of my life."

CHAPTER IX
GOING OUT IN STYLE
November 1988–February 1991

The remainder of 1988 was essentially anticlimactic as the *New Jersey* spent the balance of the year in her home port. During the last month and a half, she had a repair and maintenance period. Her crew enjoyed a Christmas party at the Long Beach Hyatt Regency Hotel. From January through March of 1989 she was periodically under way off the coast to participate in exercises. Interspersed were in-port periods and an ammunition onload at the Seal Beach Naval Weapons Station.

Senior Chief Damage Controlman Bill Romer reported to the ship that March after serving as a company chief at the Navy's boot camp in San Diego. He had requested duty in the battleship because she had recently returned from Australia and Tasmania. He concluded that such a showboat would probably be returning to that area, and he wanted to be along. As it happened, she did not return again, and a visit to that area remained on his bucket list.

Romer's work included serving as the supervisor of the ship's damage control program—DC central, repair parties, and preventive maintenance of firefighting systems. Each shipboard division had an assigned damage control petty officer to make sure fire extinguishers and hoses were maintained. That included unrolling and rerolling hoses to prevent dry rot. The ship did have fires during his time on board. One, interestingly, was in the burn room that was used to destroy outdated classified material. This time the burn took four or five hours and produced a foot-high pile of ashes in the oven. The pile prevented a draft of air needed to burn further bags of material. The men operating the facility decided to scrape ashes out to restore the draft; some ashes set fire to bags waiting outside the oven to be burned. The crewmen quickly reacted by dogging down the outside door of the room and called for help. A repair party arrived, waited for the space to cool, opened the door, and discovered the fire was out. The heat had activated a fire extinguisher inside the oven; it sprayed CO_2 and put out the flames. That night the damage control crew created a set of burn-room instructions to prevent a recurrence of the mishap.

In the spring the ship operated off Southern California, qualified in naval gunfire support, and participated in a practice InSurv inspection. A big change

Captain Douglas Katz receives a congratulatory kiss from his wife, Sharon, as he is relieved of command of the *New Jersey* on 19 May 1989 at Long Beach. He had already been selected for rear admiral and would soon don the insignia of his new rank. *Courtesy Sharon Katz*

Captain Ronald D. Tucker commanded the *New Jersey* from 19 May 1989 until the ship's decommissioning on 8 February 1991. *Courtesy Ronald Tucker*

to the routine occurred when Captain Ronald Tucker relieved Captain Katz as commanding officer on 19 May. The new skipper's background included three separate tours of duty in the guided missile destroyer *Cochrane*; he served as the ship's executive officer and later as commanding officer. Ashore he was a member of the DDG-51 study group and commanded the Pearl Harbor Naval Station.

About five thousand guests provided an audience for the ceremony. When it was time for the Katzes to leave the ship, Sharon remembered later that she was very emotional, "a mess," because she and her husband had become so attached to the crew. As they departed, they were greeted at the end of the line by the petty officer who had consummated Admiral Halsey's bed the day after Katz took command. On the occasion of the couple's departure nearly two years later, he said, "Captain, I can shake your hand, but I'm going to hug your wife. You have changed my life forever."

Unlike the situation during the *New Jersey*'s three previous periods in commission, the executive officers in the 1980s also held the rank of captain, rather than commander. In 1989 the exec was Captain William H. Smith. Observed Lieutenant (junior grade) Brian Gleason, "It's always difficult to think of the captain without thinking of the XO. So when I talk about it, I have to talk about the team of Captain Tucker and Captain Smith, and they were a perfect combination."

One example he cited was improvement in the cleanliness of the ship. The two of them moved about the ship a great deal to make inspections. Gleason said of Smith, who went around the interior of the dreadnought almost daily in coveralls, "Here's a man with a master's in physics degree, looking at urinals . . . with a flashlight." Gleason deemed Smith's close inspection procedures an improvement over those of his predecessor, who was more inclined to delegate. Chief Warrant Officer Jim Palladino agreed with that assessment and described the results of Smith's messing and berthing inspections as "you get what you inspect, not what you expect."

Commanding officer Tucker, *left*, and executive officer Smith share a laugh. *USS* New Jersey *Public affairs office*

Commander James P. Nickols reported to the ship as senior chaplain in the spring of 1989, about the same time Captain Tucker took command. His program included weekly worship services in the ship's twenty-two-seat chapel. Enhancements included a choir and crewmen who played various musical instruments. Attendance was normally skimpy in port. It increased dramatically, up to sixty men, when the ship was under way. As a result, the services moved to larger accommodations, first on the mess deck, later in the wardroom. During his tenure, Nickols confirmed three crew members in the Christian faith. He also held prayer sessions and Bible study groups. One of his challenges was coming up with a topic for each night's evening prayer, delivered before taps.

Nickols recalled that he particularly enjoyed the at-sea periods because they provided plenty of opportunity for dealing with his flock. As he put it while on board the ship in 1990, "The crew isn't going to go anywhere. You get around and talk to the sailors, eat on the mess deck, and have a good deal of personal interaction. . . . I tell my counterparts, civilian clergy, that I get to live, move, and breathe among ship's company." The men with whom he conversed included any number who might not otherwise have had any connection with church and religion.

Nickols also dealt with the men's personal problems. When an individual approached him with issues, he listened and perhaps discussed the situation with the man's division officer. As he explained, "One thing I do is assist people in helping [with] their problems. I don't solve their problems for them." Sometimes he was able to help by offering a sympathetic ear when individuals felt they received unfair treatment. In one instance, several men from one division complained that the top enlisted man they worked for was "a pretty hard-nosed old-salt Navy type." Without revealing the names of those who had come to him, Nickols talked to the man to make him aware of what was going on. As a result, the chief did make some changes in his style of leadership.

The chaplain observed that many of the enlisted men in the late 1980s–early 1990s were not from nuclear families. They were often from blended families. Many of those who got into trouble had low self-esteem and had not been loved while growing up. A drawback from such backgrounds was that problems arose in how to fit in with the ways society functions. One path toward improving the situation is through positive feedback, but that is not necessarily available in the Navy environment, where seniors are more likely to point out what a man was doing wrong than what he was doing well. Nickols credited Captain Tucker with holding meritorious mast sessions to deliver positive reinforcement.

A more specific difficulty came during the 1989–90 deployment when crew members arranged for allotments from their pay to be sent to family members back home. The money did not always reach the intended recipients, so intervention was needed in the effort to open the pay spigots. The problem was often that the allotment requests were submitted in timely fashion but were somehow garbled, which led to hardships back home. Nearly half the crew was

Commander James Nickols, *left*, the ship's senior chaplain, eats with the crew. He considered it his mission to make himself available for private conversations with shipmates. *USS* New Jersey *public affairs office*

married, a far cry from the early part of the ship's career when the percentage was small. In a number of cases, crew members were married to Navy women. In the lower pay grades, the couples could not afford a place in which to live together, so the husband lived on board the ship and his wife in barracks ashore. The chaplain observed that a number of crewmen, whether married to civilians or service women, often married too young and after short courtships. The result was that they had not yet established solid relationships before the ship headed for distant lands.

Another challenge was dealing with alcoholic crew members. The Long Beach Naval Hospital had a six-week in-patient rehabilitation program, which meant that an individual would be lost to the ship during the recovery. For those who really worked at finding a solution, it was effective. Abuse of narcotics was something of a problem, as detected by random urine tests. Even so, remembered Nickols, the problem in the Navy had diminished considerably after the Chief of Naval Operations, Admiral Thomas Hayward, had taken a strong stand against illegal drugs during his tenure from 1978 to 1982.

In 1989, the ship's top enlisted man, Master Chief Gunner's Mate Wally Denman, was about to transfer to shore duty. Master Chief Operations Specialist Marvin Williams sought to replace Denman as command master chief. He was interviewed by Captain Ron Tucker and gained the job when the ship was in Long Beach. An interesting background had brought him to the billet. He had been a high school dropout and served in the Navy during the Vietnam War. After his service, he spent only three months at the University of Maryland before concluding that he didn't fit in. He realized that he missed the Navy and so reenlisted. He had been in the crew on board the *New Jersey* soon after her early 1980s reincarnation.

As command master chief, Williams served as the senior enlisted advisor to the skipper and the executive officer, Captain Smith. He remembered them as "two of the easiest people to work with." The exec was "probably the most even-keeled individual that I've ever met." Williams was the liaison man between the officers and enlisted crew members. He made it a practice to check in daily with the CO and XO, and on occasion they would summon him for visits. The master chief had an open-door policy that made him approachable for men who wished to voice their concerns. He also walked around the ship daily to make himself available.

Williams encouraged his fellow chief petty officers to get out and around the ship, including divisional work and berthing spaces. At one point Williams kicked all of them out of the mess for a week, except to eat and sleep. The impetus came when the exec mentioned to the master chief that the crew's

Command master chief Marvin Williams, *right*, poses with crew members who have received awards. The commanding officer, Captain Ron Tucker, is at left.

USS New Jersey *public affairs office*

sleeping quarters were a mess. After their expulsion, the other chiefs saw to it that the crew members ameliorated the situation. One of Williams' practices was to post notices concerning various topics on the bulletin board in the chiefs' mess. He often added, "Just remember, only God loves you more than I do." His subordinates responded by having a flag made in the Philippines to hang in his office. It proclaimed, "Pope Willie I."

Another practice was to have division chiefs invite their division officers and, at other times, department heads to join them for lunch in the chiefs' mess. The purpose, of course, was team-building through communication. The interactions were more relaxed than in the customary working environments. The meals enabled the chiefs to understand the officers' viewpoints. It was also a way for chiefs to raise understanding on the part of young ensigns, for example, by training them in the ways of the ship. It was a way of encouraging mentorship on the part of the visitors. Another venue for discussion was the mess deck. Reflecting on the beauty of the ship, Williams enjoyed going out onto the fantail with a cup of coffee to watch the sun come up. He recalled, "It was so peaceful and quiet and serene."

The racial climate on board was fine, with one notable exception that gave some pause to Master Chief Williams. A Black petty officer first class put a junior crew member on report for disrespect. The junior man claimed that the first class was lying. Williams asked the leading petty officer of the man on report whom he believed, and that first class supported his own man. Williams challenged him, asking, "You take his word over a fellow first class petty officer? You think a first class petty officer lies?" The kid finally admitted he had said what was alleged. Williams took the miscreant to executive officer's mast, where he was recommended for two weeks' restriction rather than captain's mast. That was how it played out. Subsequently the leading petty officer apologized to Williams. The master chief told him it was a one-time event, a lesson taught and learned.

On 19 April 1989, while operating in the Atlantic, sister ship *Iowa* suffered a turret explosion that killed forty-seven crew members. Gunner's mate John Dugas of the *New Jersey*'s turret two recalled that his ship was doing a lot of firing in the vicinity of San Clemente Island during that period. He said that the turret was "locked and loaded" for firing when the news of the *Iowa* tragedy reached the *New Jersey*. A message soon arrived to order a suspension of 16-inch firing by all four ships of the class while the Navy investigated the problem. Gunner's Mate Leon Tucker of the *New Jersey*'s turret one raised the obvious question, "How did this happen?" He wondered what preceding events had led to the disaster.

Rear Admiral Richard Milligan, former commanding officer of the *New Jersey*, conducted the first investigation. It concluded that Gunner's Mate Clayton Hertwig in the *Iowa*'s turret two had sabotaged it, perhaps by inserting an explosive device into the loaded barrel, thus killing himself and shipmates. It fell to former *New Jersey* skipper Doug Katz to inform Hertwig's family of the finding.

Subsequent tests by the Department of Energy's Sandia Laboratory, independent of the Navy, came to a different conclusion. It ascertained that a probable cause of the explosion was an over-ramming of the powder. It did not conclude that the cause was the insertion of a detonator, chemical or electronic device, as the Navy's investigation claimed. It then fell to Katz to inform the Hertwig family that the petty officer was not the culprit. In June the moratorium was partially lifted to permit 16-inch gunfire in a limited number of circumstances. The ships were then able to fire the 16-inch guns in wartime, self-defense, and to send political messages if necessary.

During the interim, when the *New Jersey* was not able to shoot the main battery, the turret crews still had to maintain the equipment. For Gunner's Mate John Dugas, that meant repairing leaks in hydraulic lines and cleaning up pools of fluid that had collected. Preventive maintenance system procedures also continued. Dugas recalled the claustrophobic feeling he encountered when he had to grease the wire ropes that were used in the ammunition hoists.

Gunner's Mate Leon Tucker recalled that the crew of his turret one continued to train in the procedures involved in normal operations so that the turret remained in the condition of maximum readiness while awaiting the end of the moratorium. Even though the crew couldn't load the barrels with projectiles and powder, the men continued to go through the motions, literally. They brought up dummy bags of powder and dummy projectiles on the hoists and then sent them back down. When the order eventually came to resume firing, Petty Officer Tucker felt no sense of apprehension, and he radiated that sense of confidence to the others in the turret crew, with whom he had established solid rapport. He recalled telling his men: "The place where we work is the place where we can die if we don't look out for each other. If you're not safe, you can't work with us."

On 2 June, at San Diego, the ship embarked Rear Admiral J. Paul Reason, commander, Cruiser-Destroyer Group One. Soon afterward, the battleship and other ships of the Third Fleet participated in a readiness exercise, ReadiEx 89-3A, off Southern California. Afterward the *New Jersey* visited Seattle. Since 1949, the annual Seattle Seafair has been—except for Covid years—a summer festival to honor the Navy and other maritime organizations. Among the events are parades, shows, dinners, and boat racing. The Blue Angels flight demonstration team often adds a show to complement the Navy ships moored to piers. The *New Jersey* made her port visit to Elliott Bay, 1–8 August. For Admiral Reason it was a homecoming. His first flag assignment had been as commander, Naval Base Seattle. It was the initial *New Jersey* port visit for Captain Tucker. All told, the mini fleet comprised a dozen warships, including the USS *Blueback*. She was the Navy's last diesel-electric combatant submarine. Her decommissioning in October 1990 marked the end of an era.

Naval Reserve Captain Joe Valenta was recalled to seventeen days of active duty to act as the ship's visit

During the 1989–90 deployment, the embarked group commander, Rear Admiral J. Paul Reason, kept his flag quarters well stocked with paperback books. Here he reads one on the 03-level flag bridge. *Battleship* New Jersey *Museum and Memorial*

officer for the Seafair. His duties included delivering the mooring plan to the ship when she arrived. That meant boarding a pilot boat to ride out to the *New Jersey* before docking. Then he would communicate with a base chief to coordinate with line handlers ashore to moor the ship when she arrived at her assigned Pier 66. On 1 August, the day of the battleship's arrival, he donned his summer white uniform and met the pilot boat at 6 a.m. He rode out to the ship through choppy water and then faced the challenge of climbing a vertical Jacob's ladder to reach the main deck.

Years later he recalled that he managed to retain both his cap and the envelope containing the mooring plan while dealing with the ladder. He went to the bridge where he was introduced to the skipper and intoned, "Welcome to Seattle, Captain, and my [reserve readiness commander] sends his regards."

Once the ship was safely at the pier, Valenta hustled down to the quarterdeck as guests were arriving. In an account he wrote some years later, he said he "observed a smiling Skipper saluting a happy mayor as he came aboard."

It was a period of happy celebration that involved the citizens of the Pacific Northwest accepting the invitation to visit the ships, especially the battleship. In nearly all cases, the response was one of enjoyment. Not so pleasant during that stay in port, said Ensign Jon Lundquist, was the agenda of some antinuke protesters who came on board during a visiting period. They spewed red fluid on turrets and on one or more Marines. The incident upset the tour, because the crew had to carry off the protesters and clean up the mess. That forced the line of waiting visitors to remain on the pier in the interim.

Fire Controlman Len Jablon was Captain Tucker's duty driver when the skipper went to various places in the area as part of the public relations venture. One evening he dropped off the captain at a dinner Jablon called "some big shindig" and then waited outside with the other duty drivers while it was in progress. His recollection warmed as he said, "Captain Tucker actually came out with a plate of food for me. I've never, ever seen a captain do that before. He cared about his men." It was a small gesture that made a big impression. Jablon applied a Yiddish term to describe the captain: "A mensch."

Tucker often emulated his predecessors by touring throughout the ship. It is a technique known as "management by walking around." In his visits with crew members, the skipper radiated enthusiasm. Often he was on the general announcing system to keep the crew up to date, and he hosted captain's calls on the ship's closed-circuit television system. Tucker had a slogan, of which the short version was "WETSU." In polite language it meant, "We eat this stuff up." The crew was inclined to substitute a less decorous word for "stuff." It was useful in achieving Navy priorities—readiness, safety, and quality of life, which he described as buzzwords. The skipper

A sailor armed with a line-throwing gun awaits a call to action. The purpose is to fire a shot line across to another ship alongside in order to facilitate hookup for underway replenishment.
USS New Jersey *public affairs office*

himself called WETSU a "gimmick" that was useful in translating the buzzwords into something useful for the crew. He also said the idea was not original with him. As a junior officer, more than twenty years earlier, he saw a "WETSU" banner on board the destroyer *Richard B. Anderson*, inquired of the other ship about its meaning, and stored the answer in his mental file for later use.

One of Captain Tucker's practices was to talk in person with every new man who reported to the ship. He told the listeners how he expected the buzzwords to be translated into action. In the area of quality of life, he wanted an environment in which people could grow. He especially emphasized the need to know what to do in an emergency. Another motivational tool was to have recognition programs so that excellent work produced positive feedback. One example was a superstar program that went to the top 10 percent of the crew, as evaluated by their supervisors. It came with extra benefits, such as self-approval of special request chits and blue-and-gold star badges to be worn on uniforms. He summed it up in a sentence: "Guys love to be recognized."

During an interview while the ship was still in commission, Gunner's Mate Leon Tucker provided a further testimonial about the skipper: "He feels what we feel, and that's a rarity in an officer." The gunner's mate had also liked Katz's leadership and whimsically suggested that perhaps the best qualities of both Captain Katz and Captain Tucker could be combined in one person. Lieutenant Chuck Jennings recalled that a factor in Tucker's popularity with the crew was that he made crew members feel at ease when he talked with them. They could relax rather than feeling in awe.

On 11 August the Navy lifted the firing ban that had followed the *Iowa*'s turret explosion. Captain Tucker recalled that the *New Jersey* was under way on the day the 16-inch guns were deemed safe to fire. As a result, she was the first of the battleships to shoot as soon as the ban expired. Tucker went into one of the turrets for that first firing as a demonstration to the crew members that he had complete confidence in them and their equipment. In succeeding months, she fired more often and never had a problem. The ship put on firepower demonstrations for various groups.

When the time came for the ship to head overseas, Rear Admiral Reason was assigned to lead the *New Jersey*'s Battle Group Romeo to the Western Pacific. The deployment began with a departure from Long Beach on 15 September. The group also comprised the Aegis cruisers *Lake Champlain* and *Antietam*, destroyer *Lynde McCormick*, and frigates *Stein* and *Lockwood*. During the outbound voyage, the ship ran into two instances of heavy weather. The admiral's barge was in a deck cradle, not in one of the ship's regular davits. A large wave lifted the boat out of the cradle and onto a stanchion that ripped it from bottom to top. It was repaired and then replaced. In the meantime, the captain's gig was painted black so that it could serve as the admiral's barge.

Ensign Jon Lundquist recalled that the extreme weather in the North Pacific was what did the damage. The *New Jersey*, with her deep draft, could smash through the seas and take rolls of only about 5°. The frigate *Stein*, on the other hand, reported by radio that she was taking 25° and 30° rolls. So much spray wound up on the 03 missile deck that the crew went out in the morning and swept up piles of dried salt that were three or four inches deep. Exterior light fixtures filled with water. A wave ripped off a port side "watertight" door that led from the main deck into officers' country. It wound up on the fantail. A repair party attached a plywood frame over the opening where the door had been.

The initial mission for the deployment was to participate in Pacific Exercise 1989 (PacEx 89). Conducted in October, it was a multinational event that included ships from the U.S. Navy, Canadian navy, Japanese Maritime Self-Defense Force, and the Republic of Korea Navy. Writer Tyler Rogoway described it as "the largest combined allied armada since the end of World War II." All told, it involved fifty-four surface ships and what Rogoway described

Battleship recycling station *USS* New Jersey *public affairs office*

In PacEx 89, held in October of that year, the ships steamed at three-hundred-yard intervals. *Left to right*: aircraft carrier *Nimitz*, battleship *New Jersey*, and cruiser *Lake Champlain* Courtesy Ronald D. Tucker

as "a number of submarines that were never disclosed." Along with the two battleship battle groups, *New Jersey* and *Missouri*, were at various times four carrier battle groups, *Carl Vinson*, *Enterprise*, *Constellation*, and *Midway*. Other U.S. missile-armed ships took part as well.

During one phase of the exercise, at the beginning of October, Battle Group Romeo went into the Bering Sea. Then the ships looped around the top of the Aleutians for an attack on the island of Shemya. Captain Tucker described the area as "a hell of a place to fight a war. It's ugly: cold, wet, nasty seas." The *New Jersey* was flagship for Orange forces during battle problems. The *New Jersey* followed closely behind the cruiser *Lake Champlain*. The cruiser was at darken ship except for a light at the bow; the *New Jersey* showed only a stern light. The *Lynde McCormick* had proceeded ahead as a decoy, pretending to be the battleship. The battleship did not send any electronic emissions and thus disguised the fact that she was masquerading as a merchant ship. As Senior Chief Bill Romer observed, "To anybody looking through binoculars, they see this big, huge space between the two lights, they figure 'super tanker.'" At dawn the Orange ships steamed up near the carrier *Carl Vinson*'s battle group, which apparently concluded that the battleship was the *Missouri*, part of her group. The *New Jersey* flashed lights that said, "Guns, guns, guns, you're dead." The *New Jersey* then proceeded to steam through the other ships in the *Carl Vinson*'s battle group and "shot" at them as well. Her next target was the *Enterprise*, which apparently had not been warned by the crew of the *Carl Vinson*, so she, too, became a victim.

For Lieutenant (junior grade) William Shipley, rough seas were an unavoidable ingredient during operations in the North Pacific. A particular challenge was underway replenishment. Part of the evolution was to find a course that was relatively smooth for both delivering and receiving ships. During one replenishment, he was on deck with other crew members, and a wave came up and caught them, "It was incredible the force of the water when it hits you." In

In this photo, taken from the aircraft carrier *Enterprise*, the *New Jersey* leads a battle line. Following are the battleship *Missouri*, cruiser *Long Beach*, and destroyers. NavSource: U.S. Navy photo N-0000X-042

The Pioneer unmanned aerial vehicle (drone) served in the scouting and spotting missions performed in World War II by catapult planes. The difference was that the World War II planes had pilots on board. This drone was piloted by a joysticking crew member from a compartment in the ship's superstructure. *USS* New Jersey *public affairs office*

A rocket booster sends the Pioneer aloft from the fantail. *USS* New Jersey *public affairs office*

The drone's flight ends as it is captured by a "volleyball" net at the ship's stern. *USS* New Jersey *public affairs office*

one instance, it came up to his mid-thigh and immediately knocked him off his feet and onto the deck. Then it was a matter of scrambling to grab whatever he could. The result for Shipley was a sprained ankle.

One of the newest assets on board the *New Jersey* was the Pioneer unmanned aerial vehicle. It was a drone that Admiral Reason described as being "like a huge model airplane with a 6-foot wing span." Rockets launched the propeller-driven craft off the battleship's fantail, and then it could fly for hours. It was equipped with a black-and-white television line-of-sight link to the ship. Crewmen controlled the plane with a joystick on a console in an on-board compartment. The ability to see remotely was valuable for the scouting of targets and could direct gunfire if necessary. At the end of a drone's mission, the joystickers directed it back to the fantail, where it was captured in a contraption that resembled a volleyball net. The net caught the propeller and stopped the engine.

In preparation for an amphibious landing on Shemya, the *New Jersey*'s Pioneer flew along the beach and then inland, where the "enemy" forces were, and sent back video. Reason called the amphibious group commander and asked if he wanted to see what the beach looked like. The response was, "No, thank you, sir. We've got good maps, and we have some photo-reconnaissance from a couple of weeks ago."

Reason said, "No, I mean I can show you exactly where the gun placements are. I can show you where the trucks are. I can show you where people are living."

"Our maps show most of that."

"Listen, send a helicopter over here."

The helo arrived and then carried the Pioneer's videotape to the amphibious commander's flagship, where it was copied. Within ten minutes, as Reason recalled it, came the reply, "You got any others? When are you going to fly again? Jesus, this is great."

Reason described the experience as "an eye-opener" on the new capability. Soon the other ships in the exercise received downlink antennas so all could view the drone video at the same time. That eliminated the need for transferring videotapes. In 1991 the Pioneer system was used to great effect by the battleships *Missouri* and *Wisconsin* in the Desert Storm Gulf War.

A highlight of the PacEx was a massive firepower demonstration on 14 October off the coast of Japan. The *Missouri* and *New Jersey* unleashed their big guns. Moreover, aircraft flew over the huge multinational formation of ships to take pictures for posterity. A later aspect of the month's exercises combined a simulated amphibious landing on the coast of Korea with naval gunfire support.

Once the huge war game concluded, the *New Jersey* visited Pusan, Korea, Subic Bay in the Philippines, Hong Kong, and Singapore. By coincidence, Admiral Reason's wife, Dianne, and Captain Tucker's wife, Christie, shared the same birthday, 16 November, as did the owner of the Hong Kong company where both women bought fur coats. Since the visit to the port was close to the birthdays, the five in the group celebrated Chinese style. As the admiral recalled it later, "I ate things during that meal that I doubt I should ever eat again: jellyfish and eel and every variety of raw fish." A crew member who enjoyed that same port was Gunner's Mate John Dugas, by then a petty officer third class. Part of the attraction was walking the streets to see exotic Asian sights. Explaining that he was not a womanizer, Dugas saw women posing in windows to advertise their availability. His approach, recalled with a chuckle, was strictly "Look, but don't touch."

Later that month, Reason established a connection with astronaut Frederick Gregory, with whom he had been a childhood friend in Washington, DC. On 22 November, the space shuttle *Discovery* blasted off from Cape Kennedy in Florida. On that mission Gregory became the first Black person to command a NASA space flight. The *New Jersey* had the capability to track space missions. Reason sent a message to his friend: "We're down here in the middle of the [Indian] Ocean. You will see a battleship with six ships behind it, and we're all looking up at you." Reason added that it was a thrill for both of them. After seventy-nine orbits, the five-day mission ended when the shuttle landed at Edwards Air Force Base on 27 November.

Later, on 9 December, the ship entered the Persian

This shipboard wrestling encounter features, *left to right*, Seaman Apprentice Charles Mason, Seaman Eric Jones, and Gunner's Mate Paul Seitz, the referee. (Jones won the match) USS New Jersey *public affairs office*

Damage control Olympics promote professional development through inter-division competition. USS New Jersey *public affairs office*

Fantail cookouts are always popular. *USS* New Jersey *public affairs office*

Gulf, which was then a hot spot because of ongoing hostilities between Iran and Iraq. The United States had transferred Kuwaiti tankers to U.S. registry so the U.S. Navy could protect oil convoys as they steamed down the gulf and out through the Strait of Hormuz. Up to then, U.S. battleships remained in readiness in the Gulf of Oman, ready to retaliate in the event of attacks on the tankers. The *New Jersey* was the first battleship to enter the gulf itself. She went through the strait at night and at general quarters because she was in range of Iranian Silkworm missile sites. Once inside, the ship anchored off the island nation of Bahrain.

For Gunner's Mate Leon Tucker, taking the ship through the strait was a way of making a statement—that the U.S. Navy would go where necessary to fulfill its mission. The purpose of the visit was to set a precedent—that the gulf was now "battleship country." Admiral Reason sensed tension in the atmosphere. His take was that the event was something imposed by the Defense Department on a reluctant State Department.

Though there was potential for harm, Petty Officer Tucker had confidence that there would not be a problem the ship couldn't handle. He quoted the old saying that provided generations of battleships with a nickname: "Fear God and dread nought."

Not everyone shared Tucker's sense of bravado. Of the days immediately before entering the gulf, Petty Officer Charles Frakes observed, "There were quite a few walking around. You could tell a little bit of nervousness going around, because it had gotten serious by then." He recalled that the captain had told the crew it was going to be "almost an at-war situation."

Lieutenant (j.g.) Brian Gleason was one of many who had to adjust to a new set of rules of engagement. While the ship was operating in the Middle East, the rules were different than they had been while steaming as part of the Seventh Fleet in the Pacific. In the Pacific, overflights by Soviet aircraft were routine and not a matter of concern, because procedures had been established for such situations. The Persian Gulf demanded a different level of awareness and communication. In May 1987 Iraqi aircraft mistakenly attacked the frigate *Stark* with Exocet missiles and inflicted considerable damage to the ship and killed about three dozen of her crew. In July 1988 the cruiser *Vincennes* shot down an Iranian civilian airliner; it resulted in heavy loss of life. Thus the *New Jersey*'s crew was in a potentially lethal environment and had to be both ready for it and cautious. The ship had to avoid any actions that could be perceived as provocative. Comparing the Persian Gulf venture with operations in the Pacific, Gleason explained: "I guess the key difference there was [that] you were always walking on pins and needles."

The commander of the U.S. Joint Task Force Middle East was Rear Admiral William M. Fogarty, who previously served as the *New Jersey*'s recommissioning skipper in 1982–83. His headquarters were on the island of Bahrain. He invited Admiral Reason to join him ashore to watch the annual Army-Navy football game. It was played on 9 December in East Rutherford, New Jersey, and started at 2 a.m. the next day in Bahrain. The two of them saw the telecast in Fogarty's office. Reason recalled it as a delightful time because Navy managed a fourth-quarter field goal to win 17–14. Reason took special pleasure because his son Joe was in his final year as a Naval Academy midshipman.

During her operations in the Persian Gulf, remembered Fire Controlman Len Jablon, one day Captain Tucker decided to have some fun. While the *New Jersey* was at general quarters, he permitted three Iranian gunboats to move within a mile or two of the ship. On the general announcing system, the skipper said, "Fellows, listen to this." He played the theme music from a Clint Eastwood movie. Then he got on the radio to have the words translated so the Iranians could hear. He ordered turret one to train on the boats—far more firepower than would be needed for the job—and said to the boat crews: "Make my day!" As soon as a Farsi translation reached them, the gunboats executed three U-turns and left the premises in a hurry. Jablon admired the sense of humor involved in the escapade. As he remembered, laughter enveloped the battleship.

A positive aspect of the Bahrain visit was that crew members were able to go ashore by barge and shop in the local souks and bazaars. Senior Chief Bill Romer was amazed by the variety of luxury goods, including foreign cars, available for sale. The crew was required to wear uniforms on liberty. In that port, far from home, he found himself cautiously looking over his shoulder at times for potential danger. He did treat himself to a couple of beers; alcohol was not permitted in nearby Saudi Arabia.

The ship had embarked a few news media representatives. One asked how the ship would react if hit by an Exocet missile. Captain Tucker replied: "We'll just send out a sweeping party and clean it up." His reaction was virtually identical to that of Captain Snyder during the Vietnam War when he was asked about the possible threat posed by Soviet-made Styx missiles.

Even though the Persian Gulf mission had been potentially hazardous, Chaplain James Nickols recalled soon afterward that attendance at worship services had remained relatively stable, no sudden concern about mortality. He added, though, "I think everybody was relieved to be out of there." The gulf venture had been brief: through the Strait of Hormuz on 9 December, in port Bahrain 9–10 December, in port Dubai, United Arab Emirates, 11–12 December. Ensign Jon Lundquist recalled hearing jibes in which Iranians claimed that the ship was trapped inside the gulf. But, he added, "We steamed out, and they didn't even come out and take a look." Captain Tucker recalled no hostile indications during trips in and out of the gulf. He said of potential enemies, "They'd have been nuts to take us on. I've never been on a ship that was more ready in my life. . . . We'd have given them a lot to chew on."

From the Persian Gulf, the ship headed to Singapore for Christmas and to Pattaya Beach, Thailand, for New Year. K. T. Touzin served in the rating of journalist, part of the ship's public affairs program. (The rating was subsequently merged into the new rating of mass communications specialist in 2006.) While ashore on liberty, he was warned that ice cubes might be contaminated. He asked for a fresh drink without cubes. What he got instead was probably the same drink with the ice cubes removed, and he paid the price in the form of severe gastric distress.

One of Touzin's duties on board the *New Jersey* was as petty officer in charge of the ship's shipboard information, training, and entertainment (SITE) television channel. For the following week, as he recounted years later, he was "bright green" while reading the daily news after the Thailand beverage experience. The channel could operate only when the ship was in international waters. When in port, the ship received news from local stations via aerials. Most of the news put out on the SITE channel during each day's thirty-minute presentation arrived via teletype from such agencies as the Associated Press and Reuters. Another of Touzin's roles in the crew was with the "Snoopy" intelligence team that took photos of ships and aircraft and collected sound signatures of the craft as well.

On 10 January 1990, the dreadnought began a nine-day maintenance period at Subic Bay in the Philippines. One evening Captain Tucker joined several of the wardroom officers for dinner at the Cubi Point officers' club. Someone suggested that it would be useful to stage an event that would rebuild esprit for the tail end of the cruise. A new operations officer, Commander Chris Martin, was due to report for duty.

A wit among the group offered a suggestion, "Why don't we have someone impersonate the CO, because he doesn't know what the CO looks like?" Then the question centered on which officer could pretend to be Tucker. Someone nominated Chief Warrant Officer Jim Palladino. Captain Tucker concurred, suggesting that if anyone could pull off the joke, it was Palladino. Shipmates egged on the warrant officer until he agreed to do it.

Newcomer Martin and his wife had had lunch with Tucker's wife and learned that the skipper was somewhat of a prankster. Martin showed up at the ship later in the day, and Palladino made sure to stay out of his way to avoid giving away his identity. The next morning, Palladino donned his dress khaki uniform and went to the captain's cabin to borrow Tucker's campaign ribbons, the eagles denoting captain's rank, and his command at sea button. He also assured the skipper that he would make the prank work. Many crew members had been tipped off on the gag and went along with it.

Palladino set himself up in the captain's in-port cabin, and the ship's secretary brought in Martin to be introduced. The warrant officer took off his glasses, stood up from the captain's desk, and said, "Welcome aboard, Chris." He observed that Martin was nervous. In such a situation, the new man didn't have the opportunity to ask questions, merely to respond. Palladino said, "I understand you lost your uniforms," because Martin's luggage had been late in arriving.

The imposter said, "Yeah, leave it to the Air Force to lose uniforms." He then invited the newly arrived officer to sit down. Palladino asked a series of questions and received long, detailed answers. After about ten minutes or so of this interrogation, Martin was really on the defensive, because he wanted to be sure to give the right answers. Then the executive officer came in and addressed Palladino as "Captain." By this time, the real Captain Tucker had to enter the cabin to prepare for the Pacific Fleet change of command, and Martin was shuffled out.

After a time, Palladino went to the ship's office, where he talked to the ship's secretary, Ensign John Jones. Jones, who had heard the first part of the dialogue with Martin, complimented the fake skipper on his performance: "That was great, Jim. I couldn't believe how you were pulling it off. That was fantastic." So Jones arranged for a ship's photographer to take pictures of Jones and Palladino, the latter in his disguise.

Just then, Commander Martin walked into the office. He resumed his conversation with the fake skipper. The latter suggested they have a picture taken together in the wardroom. A meeting involving fifteen or twenty people was in progress, and someone yelled, "Attention on deck," the traditional honor when the skipper enters. Palladino said, "Carry on," and everybody sat down. The two were photographed standing near a model of the *New Jersey*. The whole charade went on for the rest of the morning. Martin went into the captain's cabin, saw the real skipper, Tucker, and turned around because he thought he was in the wrong place. Tucker invited him in, and the new man said, "There must be some mistake." Tucker told him that he was the actual commanding officer, and Martin responded, "What the hell is going on here?" Palladino walked in after having changed into coveralls, and the chagrined Martin said, "I can't believe you guys screwed me like this. I thought you looked too young to be the CO, but who the hell am I to ask?"

The whole thing went down without a hitch, and the stunt led to a good bond between Martin and Palladino. Sometime later, recalled chief engineer Joe Herger, Martin got his revenge. Members of the ship's crew went out for a special day of golfing. Palladino borrowed a set of clubs from the welfare and recreation locker and played them. After the round, Martin arranged for the clubs to be swiped, put in the trunk of a car, and returned them to the ship without Palladino's knowledge. Back on board, shipmates who were in on the gag told Palladino that he would have to pay a few hundred dollars to replace the clubs that were lost. After about three days, the clubs were returned to Palladino, and he returned them to the welfare and rec locker. Tit for tat.

The schedule had called for the Subic stop to be followed by a visit to Hokkaido, Japan. Instead, the crew spent part of the time in Subic preparing for the upcoming change of command in which Admiral Charles Larson would relieve Admiral David Jeremiah as commander in chief, Pacific Fleet, in Pearl Harbor. Command Master Chief Marvin Williams was disgruntled by the change of plans, because the crew had to repaint the ship quickly so she would provide a swanky platform for the ceremony on 15 February. Ensign Jon Lundquist was dismayed by all of the extra effort involved in sprucing up the ship. It was helpful, though, because the ship had encountered rough weather and took some topside damage during the Alaska portion of the cruise earlier.

The ceremony was held on a gorgeous day, and the ship was immaculate. The event was successfully pulled off with the appropriate pomp and circumstance and loads of dignitaries, including the Secretary of the Navy. Lundquist said that "there were more admirals than you could shake a stick at." Admiral Reason left the ship after the event. The *New Jersey* then went under way for Long Beach on 19 February for the last leg of the deployment. It was the occasion for another tiger cruise, similar to the one at the end of the 1988 deployment. This time 213 male relatives of crewmen were on board for the voyage.

On the night of 24 February, the ship observed a coming-home tradition. The chief petty officers made dozens of pizzas to be consumed during movies in the mess deck. Master Chief Marvin Williams joked afterward that "we put Pizza Hut and them out of business." The occasion emphasized the camaraderie among the crew. As Williams described the treat, it was a big hit, a way of giving back to men who had given so much to the ship during the deployment.

Ensign Rob Rice had to deal with the results after the port boat davit was badly damaged by a storm during the transit between Subic and Pearl. The water had slammed a boat into the davit and separated it. Once the *New Jersey* was back in Long Beach, Rice worked with the ship's superintendent, a naval officer who was a liaison to the shipyard, as the repair work

A basketball goal temporarily attached to turret two offers a form of recreation. The game has drawn a considerable audience.
USS New Jersey *public affairs office*

progressed and was completed. He remembered that the weather was turbulent during a good deal of the ship's final overseas deployment, the one exception being her time in the Indian Ocean.

In April 1990, the *New Jersey* went under way for local operations off Southern California. Included, on 18 April, was what proved to be the final firing of the dreadnought's 16-inch guns, almost exactly one year after the *Iowa*'s mishap. Soon afterward another moratorium descended. Sandia Laboratory tests determined that a likely contributor to the *Iowa*'s explosion was an insufficient number of pellets in the trim layers of powder bags. As a result, the *New Jersey*, which had gone into commission nearly forty-seven years earlier, had fired major-caliber projectiles for the last time.

When the directive reached the ship that she would be mothballed and decommissioned, Gunner's Mate Leon Tucker spoke for many of his shipmates when he said, "We don't want to go; this is our home. . . . It's hard to say 'goodbye'; it really is." Tucker conceded that members of the *New Jersey* ship's crew invariably had gripes about this, that, and the other. But criticism by men from other ships was not tolerated. He quipped, "We can talk about our ship amongst ourselves, but don't let [anybody] else say the *New Jersey* is nothing." He noted in particular

Dr. Frank Blair served as a *New Jersey* dentist in World War II. During the ship's final incarnation, he often visited the ship and played his clarinet along with musical crew members. Years later, Admiral Tucker said of Blair, "He was a star and awesome shipmate." *USS* New Jersey *public affairs office*

Judging by the cases stacked at left, spreadable tuna salad is a popular item in the ship's store gedunk. *USS* New Jersey *public affairs office*

the rivalry between his ship and the other battleship homeported in Long Beach, the *Missouri*. The gunner's mate compared it to a homecoming showdown game between crosstown high schools in the same city. He said the *Missouri* people thought they were better, but they were wrong.

That relationship took on a humorous turn in the spring of 1990. A group of the *New Jersey*'s junior officers concocted a stunt aimed at the *Missouri*. They bought a classified advertisement in the local newspaper, the *Long Beach Press-Telegram*. The language was along these lines: "For sale. National Monument. Built in 1944, very low mileage." The ad included the telephone number for the *Missouri*'s executive officer, Captain Joe Lee Frank. It did produce a few calls, and Frank was not amused. Captain Tucker learned

The ship was a popular tourist attraction at Long Beach on 19 April 1990. Long Beach Independent Press-Telegram *photo by Christina Salvador*

of the audacity of the ringleader, Lieutenant (junior grade) Hoot Gibson, and his cronies. Nevertheless, he directed them to report to the sister ship and apologize in person to Captain Frank. The *Missouri*'s exec conceded some years later that he got a laugh out of the prank—sort of.

Lieutenant William Shipley said that the skippers essentially played up the relationship with the *Missouri* as a friendly rivalry. Even so, he explained, the *New Jersey*'s men said they served in "*the* battleship," while the vessel across the pier was "the *other* battleship." Ensign Jon Lundquist recalled two other sobriquets: "Building 63 [the *Missouri*'s hull number]" or "The National Park." Cleanliness was one way of comparing the two ships. In days of yore, holystoning was a frequent exercise to keep the teak decks looking sharp. However, during his time on board Shipley observed that it had become essentially an annual event. Instead, the crew now used industrial chemical teak cleaners. The chemical was mixed with water, swabbed on the decks, and the sun performed a role by bleaching the wood.

In June 1990 the ship left Long Beach on the outbound leg of the last voyage of her decades-long career of service. The specific mission was to serve as the showpiece of the annual Rose Festival in Portland, Oregon. Her presence came about because Admiral David Jeremiah was a native of that city. After being relieved as commander in chief, Pacific Fleet, on board the *New Jersey* in February, he was now vice chairman of the Joint Chiefs of Staff. He had been selected as grand marshal of the Portland festival and arranged for the battleship to be there as the main attraction.

Reaching Portland from the Pacific Ocean was no easy task, especially for a ship so large. Chief engineer Joe Herger observed that a lot of advance planning went into the trip, which involved a long, arduous sea detail from ocean to city. Included in the preparation was a prior observation trip, guided by river pilots, on board a large tanker.

As the New Jersey approached the mouth of the Columbia River on 6 June, her crew received warnings that protesters might attempt to interfere with the voyage upriver. Captain Tucker delayed the entrance to the river, but the Greenpeace contingent was persistent. The environmental activists were determined to prevent the ship from bringing nuclear weapons into the area—not that she had any actually on board. Eight protesters came equipped with ropes, harnesses, and banners that proclaimed "Nuclear Free Seas." They lowered themselves from the bridge span, which is two hundred feet above the river, in what proved a futile attempt to impede the New Jersey's passage.

Captain Tucker had planned to have the crew manning the rail during the trip but then decided to have the men move inside the skin of the ship to protect them from possible flying objects. He was on the 08-level bridge, high above the water, as the ship neared the high Astoria-Megler Bridge that spanned the river. He directed the conning officer to slow the ship to bare steerageway, which just maintained forward momentum. Once the New Jersey neared the bridge, she slowly steamed between the two closest protesters suspended from the bridge. It was a careful maneuver to avoid them, because the top of the foremast reached nearly to the structure's roadway. All were safe, and the battleship continued the upriver transit while driving through a strong downriver current.

On board for the transit were the cruiser-destroyer group commander, Rear Admiral Reason, and his staff. Lieutenant Chris Bott was assistant intelligence officer on the staff and later described the scene on the 03-level flag bridge. He recalled that Admiral Reason told staff members around him that Greenpeace was not the enemy. Its members were entitled to free speech in expressing their opinions. It was the job of the Navy to ensure that right. Bott wrote years later, "His decency came from a place of strength and confidence in what was right, fair, and just in the American experiment, and he counseled us with a smile that won us over." It is worth mentioning that J. Paul Reason later became the first Black four-star admiral in the history of the U.S. Navy.

Thoroughbreds at twilight—the Missouri and New Jersey moored at pier six of the Long Beach Naval Station in the summer of 1990. The crews of the two ships had a friendly rivalry. *Courtesy Terry Cosgrove*

Joseph Paul Reason was the first Black four-star admiral in the history of the U.S. Navy. *Battleship* New Jersey *Museum and Memorial*

The ship's reception, both along the riverbanks and in Portland itself, was friendly, enthusiastic, and flag-waving. Lieutenant Chuck Jennings described the experience as "heartwarming." Once in Portland, the *New Jersey* was a big draw for visitors. Master Chief Bill Romer, who had recently been promoted, volunteered to take a group of crew members to the Oregon Lottery TV program. The men sat in the audience in white uniforms. At the end of the program, the director approached Romer and asked, "How does one get on the ship for a tour? We stood in line for three hours yesterday and got turned away."

The master chief told him to show up at nine o'clock the next morning, which was a Saturday. The following day, Romer met the director and his group at a gate and took them on a tour. They walked through the entire ship, from magazines to superstructure. They wound up seeing much more than did the people who had stood in line for three hours on Friday. They had lunch in the chiefs' mess and then bought some souvenirs on the fantail. The director was thoroughly impressed and said, "This has been a fantastic day. What can I do for you?"

"You work for the lottery show. Send me a million dollars," quipped Romer. A while later, when the ship was back in Long Beach, the master chief was summoned to his department head's office. While witnessed by shore patrol and other authority figures, Romer opened a package. It was a brick from the U.S. mint; it contained shredded U.S. currency in a clear cellophane package. It was essentially green-and-white confetti. On the side of the brick was an explanation: "A million dollars, more or less."

The ship then stopped in San Francisco for a three-day port visit, 16–18 June, en route to Long Beach. That was essentially the last voyage of the *New Jersey* as a warship. Rumors had been swirling for a while that she was on the chopping block, and then the rumors became reality. In the summer of 1990 began the process of preparing the ship for inactivation. From 9 to 11 July she offloaded her missiles. They had returned her to an offensive role when installed in the early 1980s. Now the economics of the situation had caught up with her. The Cold War was over, the ship cost $37 million a year to operate, she had a large crew, and smaller ships with smaller crews were equipped with those same types of missiles.

From 16 to 20 July, the ship was at the Seal Beach Naval Weapons Station, not far from Long Beach. There her crew offloaded a shipload of ammunition; included was the manhandling of 16-inch projectiles and powder. Subsequently, the crew observed the irony that this inactivation was happening even though Iraq had invaded Kuwait on 2 August. The United States soon deployed military and naval forces to the area in what was termed Desert Shield. It was a temporary buildup to attempt to compel Iraq to withdraw.

On 20 July, shortly before the Iraqi invasion, the *New Jersey* returned to Long Beach, her final voyage under her own power. It was truly the end of an era for the great leviathan. Commander Joe Herger, the chief engineer, opined that the nearly fifty-year-old cake. Generally, though, the mood throughout the ship was one of sadness; crewmen were about to leave their no-longer-seagoing home. To prepare the men for their next Navy jobs, detailers from the Bureau of Naval Personnel came on board and sat down with each man to discuss potential assignments and the impact they would have as they progressed through the service. It was a matter of convenience for both sides to have face-to-face discussions. Master Chief Marvin Williams observed that most of the men received new duties that they wanted. As it happened, a number of the *New Jersey*'s crew members reported afterward to the *Missouri*, which was then engaged in the Persian Gulf War.

For Gunner's Mate Leon Tucker and his crew in turret one, the inactivation process involved draining all the systems that contained fluids; included were hydraulics and the sprinkling systems designed to fight fires. They placed moisture-absorbing desiccant in the receiver-regulators and in other places applied substances to prevent rust on metal surfaces. The ship as a whole was outfitted with dehumidification systems. Once a project was completed by the crew, that area passed to the shipyard's responsibility. Obviously other inactivation procedures were taking place throughout the ship. It was a huge chore in the engineering plant because so much equipment was involved: pumps, valves, boilers, engines, reduction gears, and piping.

The process of turning an operating ship into an inert collection of thousands of physical components was a collaboration that involved the ship's crew, shipyard workers, and technical advisers from various equipment manufacturers. During that summer of 1990, members of the crew moved from their customary bunks to a berthing barge when not doing their jobs. For Chaplain James Nickols, it was a frustrating period because crew members were split up. That was especially so when they ceased living on board the ship and were away on weekends, the prime time for a preacher. There was no longer the sense of continuity that the at-sea routine imposed.

In July 1990, at Long Beach, near the beginning of the ship's inactivation, a floating crane removes a Tomahawk missile to be taken away by barge. *Courtesy Paul Stillwell*

propulsion plant had performed remarkably well, although there were problems with fuel oil piping. The piping had been replaced with new material, a few sections at a time in what he called an incremental program.

One brightener during the inactivation period was that a boatswain's mate and his bride were married on the bow. Then they descended to the general mess for the reception. Included was a multi-tier wedding

As the inactivation process steadily made the *New Jersey* less than she was before, the command added to WETSU with another slogan: "Going out in style." Captain Tucker attracted goodwill for the ship by encouraging crew members to perform volunteer services in the community. That included running senior citizen olympics, painting community centers, manning telephones during fund-raising telethons, and donating to Navy Relief and the Combined Federal Campaign.

When it came time to put the *New Jersey* out of service for the final time, the crew ran through rehearsals for the decommissioning ceremony. By that time, the crew had diminished in size to about eight hundred men—officers and enlisted—from the normal operating number of sixteen hundred or so. It was a time of sadness for those who had lived and worked on board, because there was little doubt that this was the end of the line for the battleship. Time and circumstance had passed her by; there would be no fifth period in commission.

On the final day, Friday, 8 February 1991, the weather was bright and sunny once the morning fog had burned off. More than three thousand spectators, including this author, were gathered on the Long Beach Naval Shipyard's Pier Echo, which had been the *New Jersey*'s home since 1982. We were there to observe the end of an era that stretched back more than fifty years from the time the ship's keel was laid. Sea stories abounded as past generations of *New Jersey* men shared recollections that were tinged with a great deal of nostalgia. The battleship was minus her antennas and missiles; the ends of her guns were sealed, and some sections of the teak deck on the fantail had been removed to reveal the joints of deck armor beneath. The ship gleamed with fresh haze gray paint. The Navy had funded a first-class inactivation.

The ship's enlisted men were outfitted in dress blue uniforms and lined the bunting-decorated rails. Officers, also in dress blues, were on the 01 promenade deck. The men of the last crew stood first at attention and then at parade rest as speeches reached out to the crowd. Many in the crew had hoped the ship could have participated in Desert Storm, then in progress. Now they were like firemen who had trained for years, only to see their firehouse closing as fire burned elsewhere. The principal speaker was Vice Admiral David M. Bennett, the type commander for Pacific Fleet surface ships. He remarked, "This ship has served us so faithfully for so many years, and now our task is to lay this great gray lady to rest. It is with some sadness, but great pride, that we must bid farewell to the *New Jersey*."

When it was Captain Tucker's turn to speak, he made the ceremony a celebration rather than a funeral. There was a bit of pomp and circumstance, but the event was remarkably low key. He recalled the ship's history and quoted from Herman Wouk's classic novel *The Caine Mutiny*, which mentioned the *New Jersey*. During his remarks, Tucker saluted a predecessor, Rear Admiral Lew Glenn, and observed that battleship captains belonged to a small group, even rarer than astronauts. What he didn't say was that every one of the five commanding officers of the *New Jersey* in her final period in commission was selected for flag rank. None of the ship's three sisters achieved that distinction.

Soon came the order to pull down the commissioning pennant. A bugler's sad melody accompanied the lowering of the union jack at the bow and the national ensign at the stern. The last watch was secured. Crew members departed in orderly fashion. Several crew members were headed toward the *Missouri* and *Wisconsin* in the Persian Gulf. Among them were Chaplain James Nickols, who gave the benediction at the ceremony, and Gunner's Mate Leon Tucker.

Captain Tucker had made clear to command master chief Marvin Williams that he wanted the final commissioning pennant for himself when it was hauled down for the last time. Williams spoke to the signalmen with special emphasis on that point. Tucker honored Williams by referring to him as his alter ego. As a band played "Auld Lang Syne," Williams and Captain Tucker went off, the last two members of the crew to leave the ship. Halfway down the brow, they turned and rendered a final salute to their ship. Once ashore, Williams shook hands with the last members of the chiefs' mess, and Tucker did likewise with the officers. It was finally over. The *New Jersey* did indeed go out in style.

Captain Tucker says goodbye to the ship's officers following the decommissioning. *Photo by Tom Dobyns, courtesy Ronald Tucker*

Captain Ronald Tucker, the last skipper of the *New Jersey*, speaks during the decommissioning ceremony. Hanging below the bridge is a banner with the ship's unofficial motto: WETSU. *Courtesy Paul Stillwell*

CHAPTER X
NEW ROLE FOR AN OLD SHIP
February 1991–Present

Following the decommissioning ceremony on 8 February, the Long Beach Naval Shipyard continued inactivation work. But the lifeless hulk did not remain there long. On 29 April tugboats shepherded the ship out of the harbor. Though her vitality had been drained, she still projected an air of stately dignity as she departed the port that had been her home for nearly ten years. A tugboat then took her to sea to proceed north to the Puget Sound Naval Shipyard, whence she had come in 1981 to begin her reactivation and modernization. No ceremony marked the departure, but news media covered the event.

This floating steel vessel had often steamed at more than thirty knots. Now there was no hurry on the way to the doldrums of the mothball fleet. She arrived at Bremerton, Washington, on 11 May, a transit of nearly two weeks. Once she was there, the inactivation process resumed. Of foremost concern was the installation of dehumidification systems so her innards would not rust. Men cleaned tank interiors and void spaces. In the subsequent years of inactivity, the topside spaces became the victims of weather and passing seagulls. The once-gleaming wooden decks were particularly vulnerable to degradation.

Two months after the final decommissioning, on 29 April 1991, the inert *New Jersey* on 29 April 1991 begins a tow from Long Beach to Bremerton, Washington. *Photo by Steven Chesser*

The *New Jersey* spent much of the 1990s as part of the mothball fleet at the Puget Sound Naval Shipyard in Bremerton, Washington. This aerial view depicts her with seven decommissioned *Knox*-class frigates. *U.S. Navy: DN-ST-95-01861*

On Veterans Day 1999, at the end of a long tow from Bremerton that included a trip through the Panama Canal, the *New Jersey* moves toward her intermediate destination, the former Philadelphia Naval Shipyard. *U.S. Navy: N-7676W-001*

The ship's mission as a potential candidate for reactivation changed with a congressional action in October 1998. It removed the *New Jersey* from the Naval Vessel Register to enable her transfer to a non-profit organization somewhere in the state for which the ship was named. The coast-to-coast voyage ahead was a long one. On the sunny morning of 11 September 1999, she departed Bremerton in the wake of the tugboat *Sea Victory*. The tugboat's skipper, Captain Kaare L. Ogaard Jr., plotted a course that took her 6,377 miles in sixty days to her interim destination, Philadelphia. En route the tug and tow encountered heavy winds before arriving in Balboa, Panama, on 16 October.

Governor Christine Todd Whitman of New Jersey was among those from the state who went to Panama in preparation for the ship being towed through the canal. Though the governor could not officially factor in the site decision, she was there to signify the state's interest in the preservation of the ship as a museum. Whitman hosted events in Panama and invited various interested parties to attend. She included in the invitation the opportunity for some people from the state to ride during the canal transit. At that point the ship's permanent destination was still undecided.

The tug and tow transited the isthmian canal on the eighteenth to pass into the Atlantic. They then proceeded up the East Coast and through Delaware

Bay. On 11 November, Veterans Day, the old ship was towed slowly up the Delaware River to the former Philadelphia Naval Shipyard. Swarms of onlookers observed from shore. In addition, a flotilla of watercraft served as an escort.

One who gained a vantage point from an accompanying tugboat was reporter Carol Comegno of the South Jersey *Courier-Post* newspaper. She covered the story of the *New Jersey*'s return to the East Coast and later activities with amazing thoroughness. Her articles in that era form a trove of information about the battleship. Comegno subsequently turned her material into a 2001 book, *The Battleship USS New Jersey: From Birth to Berth*, which is the best available source on the transformation of the ship into a museum and memorial.

On this occasion, Comegno invited a friend to join her on board the tug on a windy day that raised whitecaps. He was former Navy man Jeff Cary, who had served on active duty in the 1970s. He had been enamored of this gray behemoth since 1959, when he was in elementary school. He later saw the mothballed version in the nearby naval shipyard before her Vietnam War reactivation. He was now thrilled to view the object of his affection from the tugboat's deck. His emotional response was doubtless shared by many who watched from solid ground.

The destination decision rested with the Navy, which still owned the ship and could award it to a government entity or a private nonprofit. The Navy stipulated numerous criteria on which to make an impartial site selection. The decision factors included a financial plan, mooring plan, maintenance plan, towing plan, security plan, environmental plan, curatorial plan, potential for recruiting, and the extent of community involvement.

Patricia Jones had a key role in enabling the battleship to reside eventually in Camden. For a time she was a county political official, and later she was elected to the state legislature. Over the years, she had heard conversations about "the great battleship *New Jersey*." Moreover, her father-in-law had worked at the Philadelphia Navy Yard, and, as she put it, "his experiences and conversations were always ringing in the back of my head." Among other things, he taught her the difference between a ship and a boat.

Her interest developed further in the late 1990s when she learned the state already had a battleship commission; the legislature had created it in 1979. The commission's initial goal was to place the ship at Liberty State Park in Jersey City. The park provides a view that encompasses the Manhattan skyline, Ellis Island, and the Statue of Liberty. The placement seemed a done deal, but that location could not accommodate a ship with the *New Jersey*'s deep draft. Even without fuel and ammunition on board, she draws 34 feet at the stern and 23.5 feet at the bow. Making room for her would have involved blasting away bedrock. A fallback for the battleship commission was the port of Bayonne, New Jersey, a former Navy facility. At Bayonne the ship had been decommissioned in 1948 and recommissioned in 1950.

When Jones heard about the North Jersey situation, a thought began percolating in her head: "Why can't the commission look at Camden?" At an economic development meeting she talked with U.S. senator Robert Toricelli. When the subject of the ship came up, he told her that if the county would take a strong position, he could provide support. He believed the ship belonged in Camden, just across the river from where she was built at Philadelphia. As Jones explained years later, "He set my feet on the path." Then she sought support from the local government and from veterans in the area. She contacted the battleship commission and pointed out that Camden had a suitable location with sufficiently deep water. Another step was to bring together all the entities that had a stake in the Camden waterfront, including the city's mayor. Rear Admiral Thomas Seigenthaler, by this time retired, was a former commander of the Philadelphia Naval Shipyard; he still lived in the area and provided technical expertise.

The South Jersey group held meetings and invited commission members to tour the area, including the naval shipyard, which had closed as a U.S. government entity in 1995 and by 1999 was a commercial facility. The visitors also went to the prospective waterfront location to demonstrate the environment in which the ship could be berthed. But the commissioners remained unconvinced; Jones deemed the visit as a case of just being polite. The Camden group then created the Home Port Alliance, which was chaired by a retired naval officer, Captain David McGuigan. Jones gave great credit to McGuigan and Seigenthaler for their knowledge of ships and maritime matters as members of the nonprofit's board.

Future congressman Donald Norcross joined the board as a labor union representative because unions would undoubtedly have roles in the future of the ship. The Home Port Alliance sent the Navy a detailed seventeen hundred–page application for the ship to be in Camden. Pat Jones described McGuigan as the "spark plug" in developing that document. She also marveled at the way various waterfront organizations coalesced around the project, even though they frequently had their differences on other topics. Their collective support served as a unifying force. Navy representatives visited both prospective sites. They talked with members of the Homeport Alliance and the state battleship commission.

Pat Jones recalled being with Senator Toricelli when a report arrived on 20 January 2000 that the Navy had selected Camden. That day the South Jersey adherents, having been forewarned, were in the shipyard in Philadelphia. The jubilation was contagious. As she remembered, "We were doing high fives in the snow." Press photographers had also been alerted that the decision would be announced, so they were on hand. In response to their requests, the celebrants accommodated the media by doing some "instant replays" of their gestures of happiness.

Because the Navy has declined to provide a detailed explanation of the factors that resulted in the ship being established at Camden, some surmise is in order. Clearly, the towing plan would be more involved if the ship had to be delivered via the Atlantic Ocean to the port of New York. It was easier to bring her across the river from Philadelphia to Camden. Bayonne was essentially an industrial and port area, hardly the garden spot of the Garden State. Moreover, the group operating the carrier *Intrepid* memorial in the Hudson River, on the west side of Manhattan, did not welcome the competition.

A factor that favored the Camden site was that it was in a freshwater river rather than the seawater environment in North Jersey. Another plus for Camden was that the ship could join an existing aquarium as an attraction in the redevelopment of the waterfront area. An entertainment center was a further draw in summer months. The battleship could be an additional magnet to bring visitors to the once-rundown area. The clincher was probably the detailed application Captain McGuigan wrote for submission to the Navy. It was deemed a model of the genre and evidently blew away the competition.

A next step was to move the *New Jersey* to the nearby Broadway Terminal on the Delaware River. There the process began to transform the inert dreadnought into a museum capable of hosting thousands of visitors. Hundreds of women and men came forth and volunteered to be part of the process by donating many hours of labor. The volunteers were guided in their activities by McGuigan and Seigenthaler, whose professional knowledge determined what needed to be done. Part of the process called for throwing away items that were no longer needed. Pat Jones recalled with a chuckle: "I met a lot of . . . men standing in dumpsters, because something got in that shouldn't have. So they were in the dumpsters pulling things out."

Meanwhile, across the river in Philadelphia, on 19 May 2000 a pier supporting a new open-air bar collapsed and fell into the Delaware. Three people died as a result, and a few dozen were injured. A canvas tent over the bar went down also and landed on the survivors struggling in the water. Pat Jones recalled that the incident led to a reexamination of the plans for the *New Jersey*'s dock and a reason to make it stronger than in the original specifications. Subsequently, fore-and-aft elevators were added to the structure to facilitate access to the main deck by visitors in wheelchairs.

In the summer of 2000, the Republican National Convention was in Philadelphia. General Norman Schwarzkopf, hero of the victorious Desert Storm campaign in Kuwait in 1991, addressed the convention delegates remotely on 1 August. He was on the deck of the *New Jersey*, accompanied by a number of military veterans. He recalled the Middle East campaign and lamented the drawdowns that had taken place since then in the number of personnel in the armed forces. These cuts were justified as a "peace dividend" in the wake of the collapse of the Soviet Union. The decommissioning of the manpower-intensive *New Jersey* and her three sister ships was part of the cost savings that made up the dividend.

Disappointment shrouded the eventual move of the battleship northward up the Delaware River from her location at the Broadway Terminal. Tugboats took positions on either side of the ship in the early morning darkness of 23 September 2001. Under normal circumstances, the occasion would have been accompanied by a great deal of hoopla and well-wishing. Dignitaries and the volunteers who had worked so hard to improve the ship after years of mothball fleet neglect had expected to be on board for the move.

Alas, circumstances were far from normal less than two weeks after hijacked airliners had crashed into the World Trade Center and the Pentagon on 9/11. Security was understandably tight because of concern that the ship might also be a target for terrorism. Thus the move was accomplished in secrecy. Gradually, the rising sun provided a dramatic backdrop as the skies on the starboard side glowed in a palette of pink, orange, and purple. To port was the Philadelphia skyline. Finally, the tugs guided the towering dreadnought into the spot that was now her new home.

The formal dedication of the ship as a memorial was on 14 October 2001. A limited number of invited guests attended. The official opening to the public came the following day. The event was a day of celebration that honored armed services veterans and the many people who had done so much to make the *New Jersey* shipshape and gleaming. Naturally, the festivities included speeches and cake-cutting to celebrate the occasion. Once the official activities were

The ship's current role as a museum and memorial began in 2001. Seen from the air is her current berth at Camden, New Jersey, with the Philadelphia waterfront across the Delaware River. A built-for-the-purpose pier permits access by visitors. The awnings at the stern provide protection for special events. *Battleship New Jersey Museum and Memorial*

over, citizens swarmed to tour the ship. To do so, they stood in long lines after buying tickets at a recently constructed support building on the dock alongside.

Now, nearly a quarter century after the ship began her career as a tourist attraction and a source of learning by thousands of visitors, the management has settled into a continuing series of routines to fulfill the mission. The cost is not cheap. Maintaining the physical structure of a ship that is constantly at the mercy of weather is demanding. Battleship New Jersey, the nonprofit organization that operates the memorial/museum, embarked on an ambitious program of replacing the wooden deck planks that deteriorated during the inactive years in Bremerton. The results are noteworthy in upgrading the ship's aesthetic appeal. A wide variety of fundraising events brings in money to pay staff salaries, electricity bills, and the many other expenses involved.

A vocal part of the museum's outreach program is the work of its enthusiastic historian/curator Ryan Szimanski. He has steeped himself in the ship's equipment and operational achievements. He has created dozens of YouTube videos in which he explains the functions of various parts of the ship and conveys dreadnought lore in the process. Internet users across the globe can tour the ship vicariously; Szimanski's goal is to lure them to Camden to see and touch in person.

One of the museum's volunteer tour guides for a number of years has been Rich Meanor, a Naval Academy graduate who was on active duty for seven years before moving on to work for the defense industry. He stayed in the reserve until retirement. Included in his reserve active duty was a brief tour in the battleship *Wisconsin* in the late 1980s. He transmits his experience and knowledge to visitors as he shows them around. The official tour covers a mile and a half. Highlights include a fireroom and engine room; a lower shell deck and powder-handling rooms; gun houses for 16-inch and 5-inch; combat engagement center; cabins for the admiral and captain; enlisted berthing spaces; mess deck; laundry; television studio; and machine shop.

Meanor especially enjoys it when he is able to explain how the ship has evolved over the years. For example, modern bunks offer more privacy than those in earlier years when vertical chains supported tiers of racks three or four high. Though women, both officers and enlisted, are commonplace in today's active Navy ships, he explains that

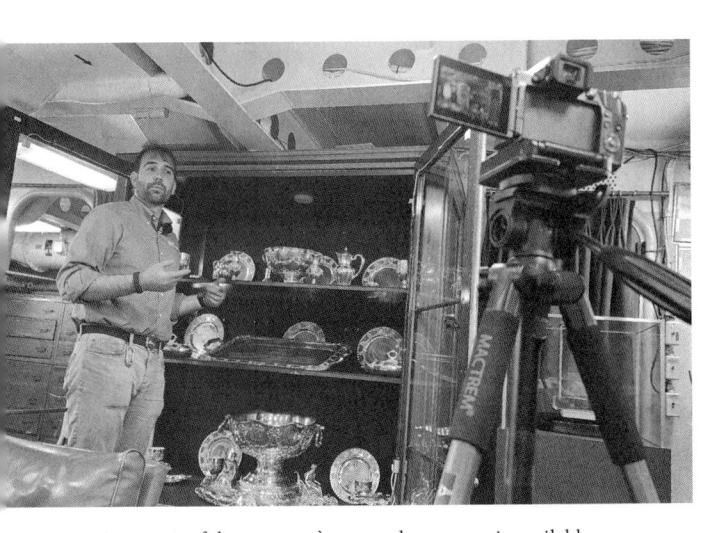

An aspect of the museum's outreach program is available through a website: youtube.com/c/battleshipnewjersey. Historian/curator Ryan Szimanski has created dozens of videos that depict and explain various spaces throughout the ship. Here he demonstrates the *New Jersey*'s silver service. *Battleship New Jersey Museum and Memorial*

A tour guide explains the role of a 40-mm gun mount that serves as a static display on the main deck. Mounts such as this were especially valuable for antiaircraft gunnery in World War II. The 40-mm mounts were removed from the ship during the 1967–68 reactivation because the ship's mission no longer included defense against planes. *Battleship New Jersey Museum and Memorial*

the *New Jersey*'s crew was all male throughout her career. Veterans of various services come on board to reminisce and recount their own experiences. And there is excitement among children who are awed by the immensity of the ship. School field trips afford those opportunities. A favorite part of tours is to take visitors to the forecastle and let them take pictures looking aft—toward the two forward turrets and the towering superstructure beyond them.

Ken Kersch, who served in the *New Jersey* during her 1968–69 Vietnam deployment, worked at several jobs in the state of New Jersey after his active tour ended. Once the ship reached her present location, he visited, along with his daughter Karen, a schoolteacher. She talked to him about preserving history, which inspired him to take and pass tests that qualified him to work as a volunteer tour guide. Years later, his role morphed into a position as part of the paid staff.

A tangible benefit of the museum's many fundraising programs over the years has been the restoration of the teak decks that were deteriorated considerably during the inactive years in Bremerton. *Photo by Walt Urban*

Smiling Cub Scouts in a *New Jersey* bunkroom *Battleship New Jersey Museum and Memorial*

A docent describes to young visitors the workings of the projectile deck deep inside a barbette. *Battleship New Jersey Museum and Memorial*

He now organizes and runs special events. For example, each year the ship hosts the initiation of newly selected chief petty officers. In years past, such initiations involved hazing, but times have changed for the better. Kersch calls this era's events part of a "team-building program" that involves mentoring by previously promoted chiefs. The selectees wear traditional Navy jumpers, accompanied by white hats and black neckerchiefs. As part of the team exercise, they run together in gym gear across the Ben Franklin Bridge to Philadelphia. This shared experience is part of the prelude for those about to don the combination hat with its fouled-anchor insignia and black chin strap. The annual program started small but has grown to such an extent that one year more than one hundred selectees—both active duty and reserve—were involved.

Another arrow in Kersch's quiver is serving as director of a weekend program that brings in needed revenue. Young people can pay to stay on board overnight. Watch officers arrive at 4 p.m. to set up and then put things away the following morning after the visitors leave. The original limit was thirty people a night; the maximum now is 292 to satisfy the fire marshal. Among those who participate are boy scouts, girl scouts, church groups, school groups, sea cadets, and families. Chaperones are necessary for the young people, but unaccompanied adults are not eligible. As Kersch puts it, "We're not a hotel; we're an educational experience."

The visitors eat dinner and breakfast in the mess deck. In between, they sleep in the former chief petty officer quarters on the second deck and enlisted berthing compartments on the third deck. Barriers and compartment locations separate the genders. For the occasional claustrophobes who are uncomfortable going down inside the ship, the staff makes other sleeping arrangements. Some groups come back every year, because the ship makes the experience fun, including tours, raffles, and custom-made dog tags. In other revenue-generating activities, the battleship *New Jersey* has been the site of numerous weddings, birthday parties, and other special events.

The *New Jersey* looms large in April 2024 while in dry dock at the former Philadelphia shipyard where she was built. *Photo by Walt Urban*

The ship's underbelly reveals her port rudder and two port-side propellers, one with four blades and one with five. *Photo by Jack Russell*

In this view looking aft, one sees the tunnel formed by the skegs that have the inboard propellers at the stern. Also visible are samples of the wooden keel blocks that support the ship's immense weight. *Photo by Jack Russell*

The man in the foreground provides perspective for the battleship's size. *Photo by Jack Russell*

On 21 March 2024, the umbilicals that had long tied the ship to the Jersey shore were unhooked. Then tugboats moved her down the Delaware River to another port, where she received preparatory work prior to dry docking. Further movement by tugs alongside came on 27 March, when she entered the former Philadelphia Naval Shipyard, now a private firm. The purpose was to put the ship in dry dock to investigate the underwater hull for the first time since August 1990. That she had remained so long between dry dockings is undoubtedly the result of the freshwater environment at her home in Camden. Once the shipyard work was completed, on 14 June, tugs towed the ship to nearby Paulsboro, New Jersey. Among those on board was Vice Admiral Douglas Katz, who had been retired from active duty for a number of years. He had the pleasure of sitting in the captain's chair on the bridge during the voyage; he had many times used the same chair when he commanded the ship in the 1980s. The Paulsboro stop was for the purpose of removing more than half a million gallons of ballast water that had been necessary for exiting the dry dock on an even keel. The *New Jersey* returned to her regular berth in Camden on 20 June, ready once again to host the approximately 80,000 annual visitors who want firsthand battleship experience.

At night the lighted battleship serves as a beacon on the Camden waterfront. *John S. Austin photo in U.S. Naval Institute photo archive*

APPENDIX I
USS *New Jersey* Commanding Officers

Captain Edward J. O'Donnell, *right*, shakes hands with his predecessor, Captain John C. Atkeson, on the day of their change of command, 18 March 1955. *Courtesy John C. Atkeson*

Captain Carl F. Holden, USN, 23 May 1943 to 26 January 1945.

Captain Edmund T. Wooldridge, USN, 26 January 1945 to 17 November 1945.

Captain Edward M. Thompson, USN, 17 November 1945 to 5 August 1946.

Captain Leon J. Huffman, USN, 5 August 1946 to 23 May 1947.

Captain George L. Menocal, USN, 23 May 1947 to 14 February 1948.

Commander Joseph W. Leverton Jr., USN, 14 February 1948 to 30 June 1948.

Captain David M. Tyree, USN, 21 November 1950 to 17 November 1951.

Captain Francis D. McCorkle, USN, 17 November 1951 to 20 October 1952.

Captain Charles L. Melson, USN, 20 October 1952 to 24 October 1953.

Captain John C. Atkeson, USN, 24 October 1953 to 18 March 1955.

Captain Edward J. O'Donnell, USN, 18 March 1955 to 31 May 1956.

Captain Charles B. Brooks Jr., USN, 31 May 1956 to 21 August 1957.

Captain J. Edward Snyder Jr., USN, 6 April 1968 to 27 August 1969.

Captain Robert C Peniston, USN, 27 August 1969 to 17 December 1969.

Captain William M. Fogarty, USN, 28 December 1982 to 15 September 1983.

Captain Richard D. Milligan, USN, 15 September 1983 to 7 September 1985.

Captain W. Lewis Glenn Jr., 7 September 1985 to 8 August 1987.

Captain Douglas J. Katz, USN, 8 August 1987 to 19 May 1989.

Captain Ronald D. Tucker, USN, 19 May 1989 to 8 February 1991.

APPENDIX II
USS *New Jersey* Ship's Data

GENERAL DIMENSIONS

Length overall: 887 feet, 6 ⅝ inches

Length at designed waterline: 859 feet, 10 ¼ inches

Extension beyond forward perpendicular: 20 feet, 0 inches (i.e., bow overhang)

Extension beyond aft perpendicular: 7 feet, 3 inches (stern overhang)

Beam to outside of plating, frames 121 to 129: 108 feet, 1 ⅜ inches

Freeboard at bow to design waterline: 35 feet, 8 ½ inches

Freeboard at stern to design waterline: 22 feet, 7 7/16 inches

Depth of inner bottom: 3 feet, 0 1/16 inches

Frame spacing: 4 feet, 0 inches

Number of frames: 215

Displacement, standard, designed: 45,000 tons

Displacement to design waterline: 54,889 tons

Design waterline: 34 feet, 9 ¼ inches above the keel, which corresponds to designed normal load and draft

Draft at full-load displacement: 38 feet, 0 inches

Distance between turrets one and two (axis to axis): 72 feet, 0 inches

Distance between turrets two and three (axis to axis): 346 feet, 0 inches

ENGINEERING PLANT

Boilers: Eight Babcock & Wilcox express type; designed working steam pressure, 634 pounds per square inch

Turbines: Four Westinghouse

Propellers: All four manufactured by Philadelphia Navy Yard
  Righthand inboard: five blades, 53,000 shaft horsepower
  Righthand outboard: four blades, 53,000 shaft horsepower
  Lefthand inboard: five blades, 53,000 shaft horsepower
  Lefthand outboard: four blades, 53,000 shaft horsepower

Total shaft horsepower: 212,000

Designed endurance: 15,000 nautical miles at 15 knots

Designed speed: 33 knots

ARMAMENT

Nine 16-inch/50-caliber guns in three triple turrets; maximum elevation of 45° and maximum depression of 2°; limit of train for the six forward guns to positive stops is 210° relative to port and 150° relative to starboard; the after guns have a limit of train of 330° relative to port and 030° relative to starboard. The turret barbettes contain the following decks, top to bottom: shelf plate, turret pan, electric deck, upper shell handling platform, lower shell handling platform, and powder loading platform. Turret two has one additional projectile platform. Projectile stowage: turret one, 405; turret two, 475; turret three, 385.

Twenty 5-inch/38-caliber dual-purpose guns in ten twin mounts. The guns of the second battery have a maximum elevation of 85° and a maximum depression of 15°. Four of the ten mounts, containing eight of the original twenty guns, were removed during the 1981–82 modernization to make room for a missile deck.

Sixty-four 40-mm antiaircraft guns in sixteen quadruple mounts. The number was increased to eighty guns in twenty mounts during the ship's yard period in the autumn of 1943. Subsequently, some mounts were removed and reinstalled; the ship still had all twenty mounts at the time of decommissioning in 1957. All were removed during the 1967–68 modernization.

Forty-nine 20-mm antiaircraft guns. This number was increased during World War II to fifty-seven—forty-one single mounts and eight twin mounts. All but a few of the 20-mm mounts were removed during the 1947–48 inactivation. All the remaining 20-mm mounts were removed during the yard period in 1952.

ARMOR

Citadel from 03 to 05 level: top, 7.25 inches; bottom, 4 inches; sides, 17.3 inches

Tube from second deck to 03 level: 16 inches all the way around

Turrets: front, 17 inches over 2.5-inch special treatment steel; sides, 9.5 inches; rear, 12 inches; top, 7.25 inches

Barbettes down to second deck: 11.6 inches forward and aft; 17.3 inches on sides

Second deck plating, frames 50–166: 4.75-inch class B armor

Third deck plating, frames 166–189: 5.6-inch class B armor

Third deck plating, frames 189–203: 6.2-inch class B armor

Frame 203 bulkhead between third deck and first platform: 11.3-inch class A armor

Frame 166 bulkhead between second and third decks: 11.3-inch class A armor

Frame 50 bulkhead between second deck and hold:
    tapered from 11.3 inches to 8.5 inches, class A armor

Upper side belt between second and third decks, frames 50–166:
12.1-inch class A armor

Side belt steering gear armor between third deck and second platform deck, frames 189–203: 13.5-inch class A armor

Lower side belt between third deck and hold: frames 166–189, tapered from 13.5 inches to 5.625 inches at frame 166; tapered from 13.5 inches to 7.125 inches at frame 189, class B armor

Lower side belt between third deck and hold, frames 50–166: tapered from 12.1 inches to 1.62 inches, class B armor

RUDDERS

There are two rudders located with the centers of their stocks 8 feet, 6 inches off the centerline of the ship at frame 201 ½. The area of each rudder is 340 square feet. The outside positive stops for each rudder limit the angle to 36.5°, port and starboard, from the zero helm position.

AIRCRAFT CRANE

The crane was manufactured by C. H. Wheeler Manufacturing Company. It had a rated capacity of 9,300 pounds and an outreach of 41 feet, 6 inches. (The crane was removed from the ship during the 1981–82 modernization to facilitate the helicopter operations on the fantail.)

ANCHORS

Each anchor is the stockless bower type, weighing 30,000 pounds; each chain is 187 fathoms long, including the outboard swivel shot.

EMBARKED AIRCRAFT

1943–45: Three Vought OS2U Kingfisher floatplanes

1945–47: Two Curtiss SC-1 Seahawk floatplanes

1951–53: One Sikorsky HO3S-1 helicopter

1983–90: One Kaman SH-2 Seasprite helicopter

SEARCH RADAR ANTENNAS

May 1943–May 1945: SK air search on foremast; SG surface search on mainmast and also on front of forward fire control tower

June 1945–February 1952: SK-2 air search and SG surface search on foremast

June 1945–August 1954: SP height-finder on mainmast

April 1952–90: SPS-10 surface search on foremast

April 1952–December 1969: SPS-6 air search on foremast

December 1954–inactivation in 1957: SPS-8A height-finder on mainmast

Summer 1982–90: SPS-49 air search on foremast

CHANGES AND ADDITIONS DURING 1981–82 MODERNIZATION

Eight armored box launchers for a total of thirty-two Tomahawk cruise missiles; potential loads included a land-attack conventional version with a range of 700 nautical miles and an antiship version with a range of 250 nautical miles

Four quadruple canister launchers for a total of sixteen Harpoon antiship missiles, each with a range of 60 nautical miles

Four Vulcan/Phalanx close-in weapon systems for defense against aircraft and missiles

Advanced communication systems

SPS-49 air-search radar substituted for the less capable SPS-6

Aviation facilities, including an enlarged helicopter landing pad on the fantail, parking area, helicopter control booth on the after end of the superstructure, and helicopter glide slope indicator

Conversion of the engineering plant to burn Navy distillate fuel in place of black oil

A sewage collection, holding, and transfer system to comply with upgraded environmental requirements

Improved habitability for the crew

Removal of the stern crane to avoid interference with helicopter operations on the fantail

Refueling rig on the starboard side to facilitate transfer of fuel to escorting ships

SLQ-32 electronic countermeasure suite

Satellite navigation and communication antennas

Mark 36 super rapid-blooming off-board chaff (SRBOC) launchers

New tripod foremast; removal of after mast

Removal of four of the original ten 5-inch/38-caliber twin mounts to make room for the installation of a missile deck between the smokestacks

APPENDIX III
Design Development of USS *New Jersey*

290 APPENDIX III

May 1943
As Commissioned

October 1943

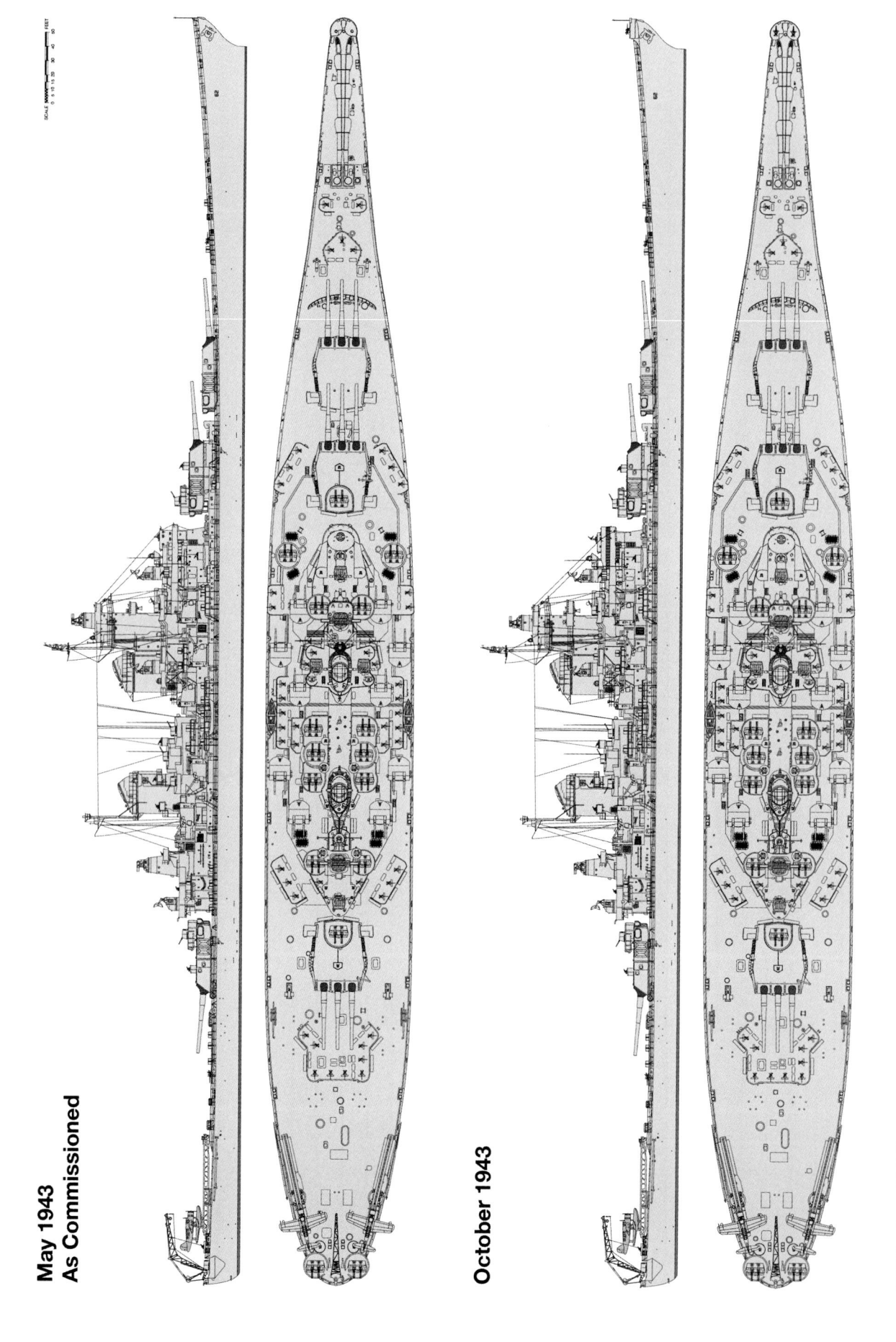

USS *New Jersey* 1943 Diagrams. *Redrawn by James M. Caiella*

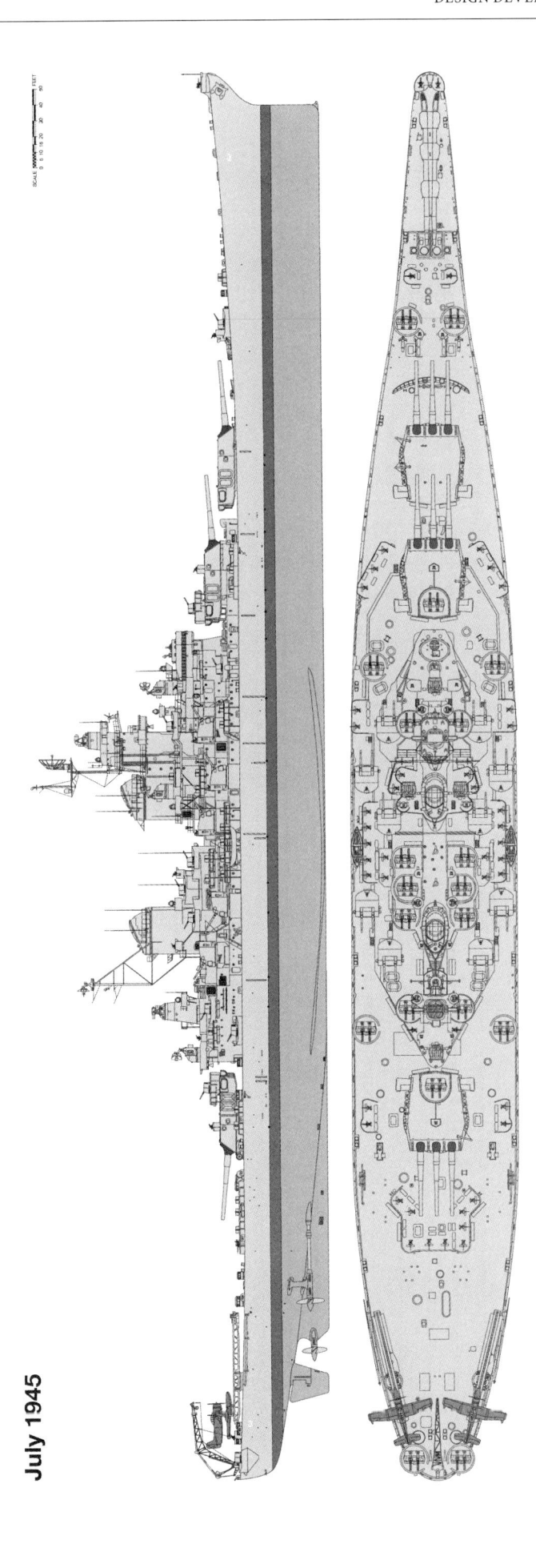

DESIGN DEVELOPMENT OF THE USS *NEW JERSEY* 291

July 1945

USS *New Jersey* 1945 Diagram. *Redrawn by James M. Caiella*

1953
Korea Deployment

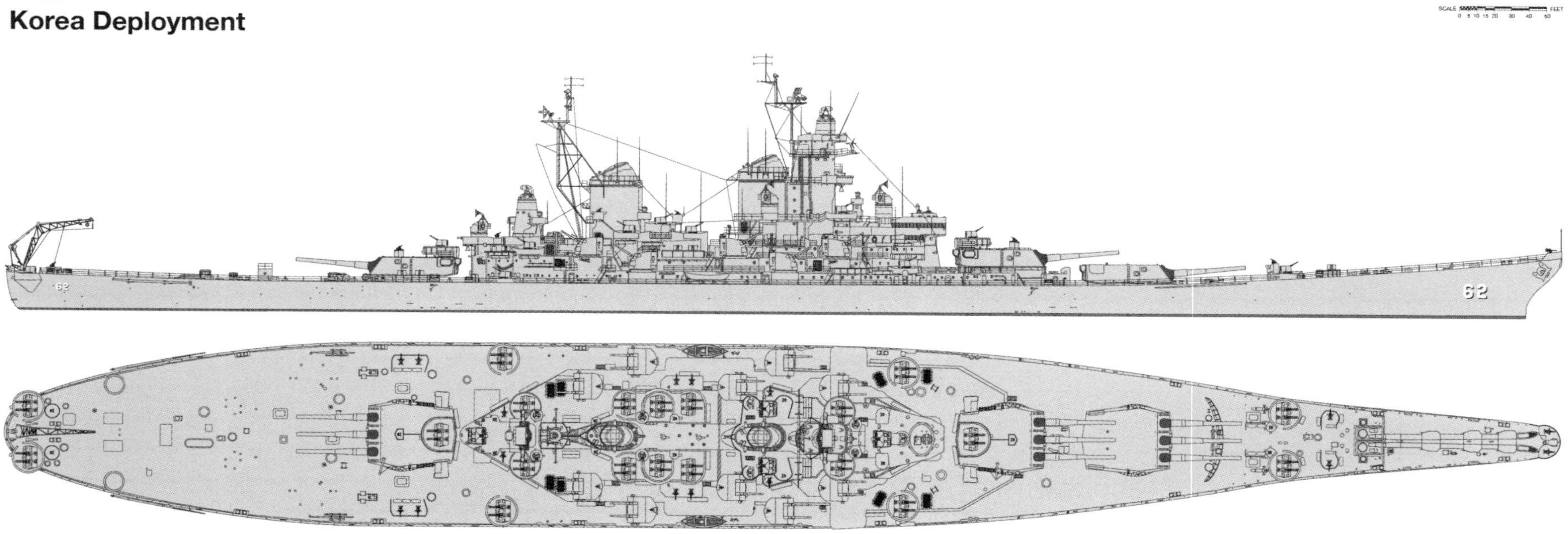

USS *New Jersey* 1953 Diagram. *Redrawn by James M. Caiella*

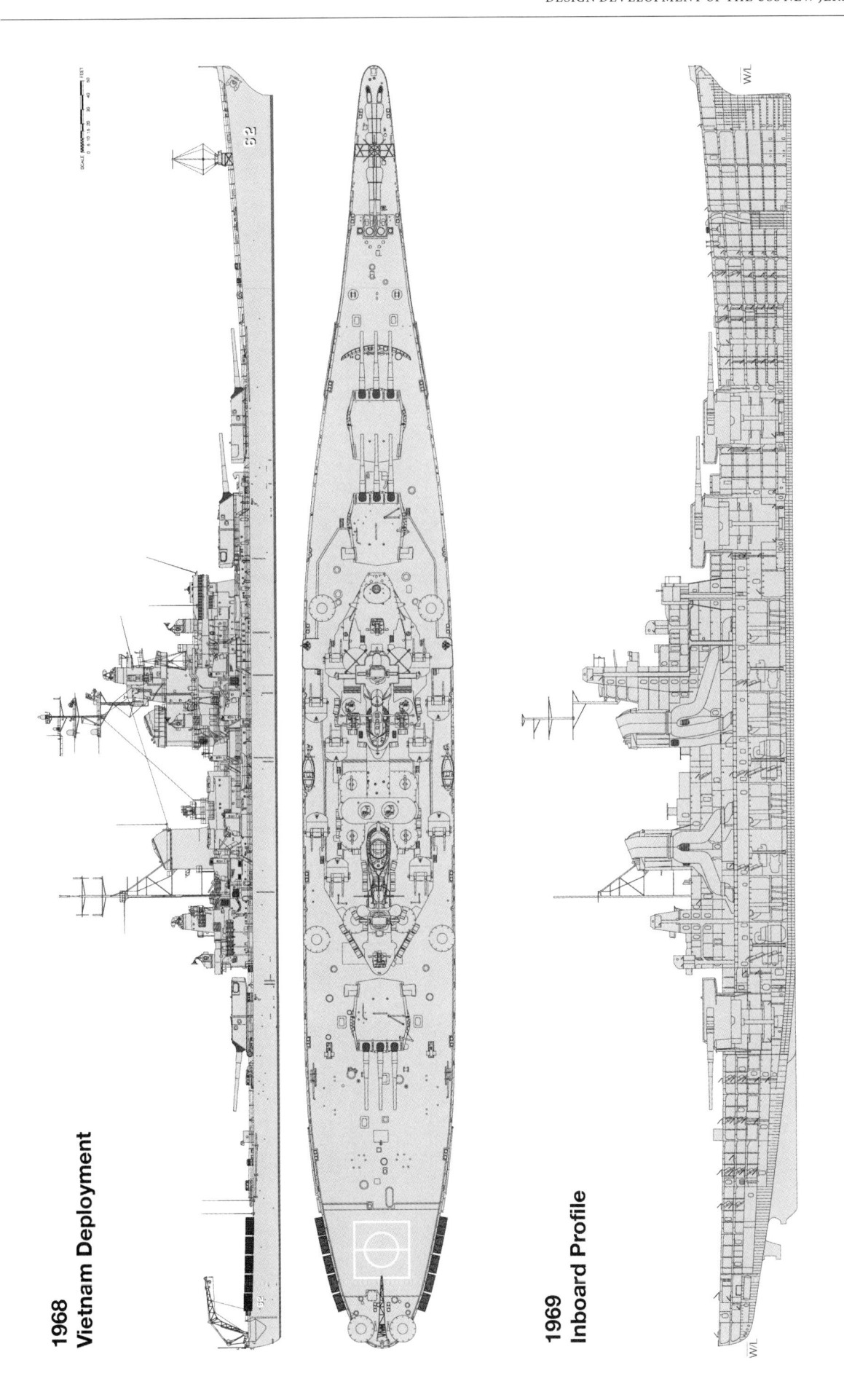

DESIGN DEVELOPMENT OF THE USS *NEW JERSEY* 293

1968
Vietnam Deployment

1969
Inboard Profile

USS *New Jersey* 1968 Diagram and Inboard Profile. *Redrawn by James M. Caiella*

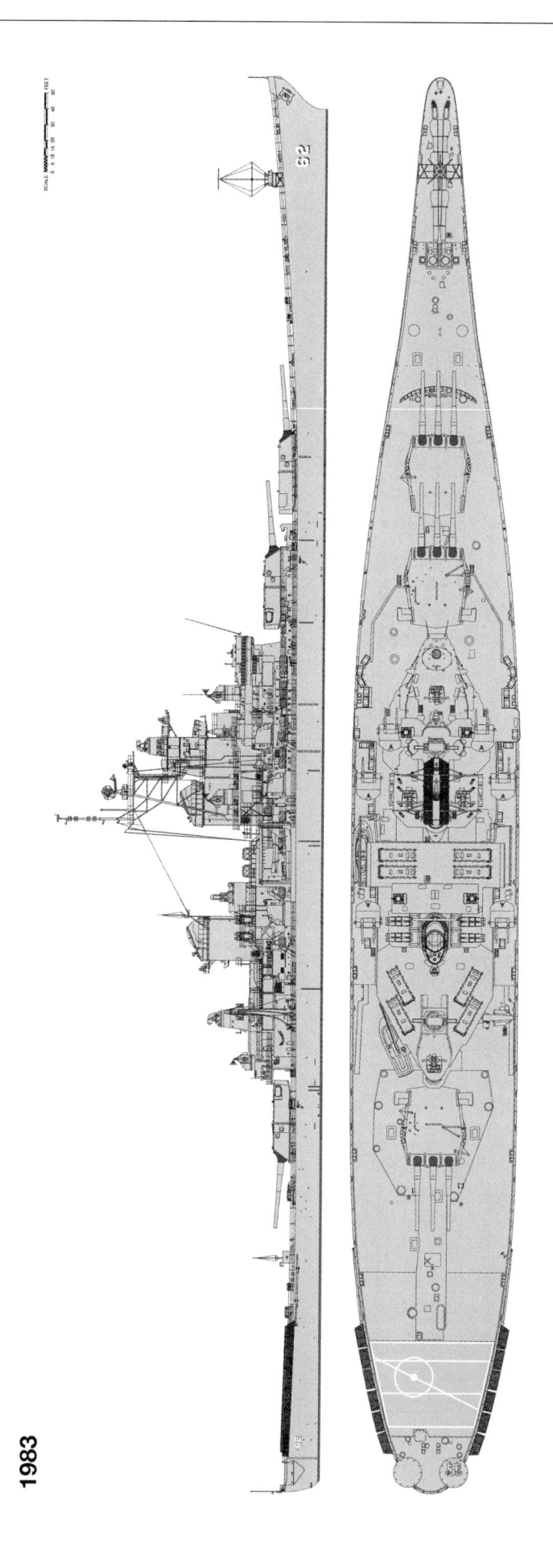

294 APPENDIX III

1983

USS *New Jersey* 1983 Diagram. *Redrawn by James M. Caiella*

BIBLIOGRAPHY

INTERVIEWS WITH AUTHOR

Abhau, William C., Rear Admiral, USN (Ret.), at Annapolis, MD, 14 June 1983.

Abrams, Richard, by telephone, 11 April 1984.

Addison, Edward S., Captain, USN (Ret.), at Annapolis, MD, 29 June 1983.

Albrecht, Carl J., Captain, USN, by telephone, 20 November 1985 and 1 December 1985.

Alexander, Richard G., Captain, USN (Ret.), at Washington, DC, 9 September 1970.

Amend, Wayne A., by telephone, 5 October 1985.

Anderson, Clyde B., Captain, USN (Ret.), at Virginia Beach, VA, 10 October 1983.

Atkeson, John C., Rear Admiral, USN (Ret.), at Norfolk, VA, 27 February 1983.

Bak, Michael, Jr., at Vienna, VA, 21 February 1984.

Baker, Captain John C., USN (Ret.), by telephone, 30 May 2023.

Ballou, Joseph F., Commander, USN (Ret.), at Washington, DC, 7 February 1986.

Bartusch, Willard, by telephone, 1 August 1985.

Begandy, Wayne, by telephone, 7 October 1985.

Bitting, Frederick E., Commander, USN (Ret.), by telephone, 2 October 1985.

Blanchette, Roland, by telephone, 6 September 1985.

Bowler, Roland T. E., Jr., Commander, USN (Ret.), at Annapolis, MD, 29 August 1984.

Brandt, King G., Commander, USNR (Ret.), by telephone, 11 February 1984.

Brattin, Sherman, by telephone, 23 July 1985.

Brega, Richard E., Captain, USN (Ret.), at Long Beach, CA, 15 May 1983.

Brooks, Clarence J., Jr., at Arlington, VA, 18 April 1983.

Brown, Frank C., Lieutenant, MSC, USN, by telephone, 27 December 1985.

Brown, Jacob, by telephone, 7 September 1985.

Brown, Russell, by telephone, 27 June 1985.

Cabot, Lon, Chief Journalist, USN, by telephone, 23 April 1986.

Cantacuzene, Rodion, Captain, USN (Ret.), at Washington, DC, 4 January 1983.

Cary, Jeffrey, at Runnemede, NJ, 12 May 2023.

Chesser, Steven B., Lieutenant Commander, USN (Ret.), by telephone, 7 March 2024.

Clairmont, Daniel R., by telephone, 15 August 1985.

Cooper, Ervin, on board USS *New Jersey* (BB-62) at Long Beach, CA, 13 July 1990.

Crawford, R. A., Senior Chief Fire Controlman, USN (Ret.), on board USS *Iowa* (BB-61) at Portsmouth, VA, 17 July 1985.

Cruppenink, John, by telephone, 14 October 1985.

De La Maza, Rafael, by telephone, 7 July 1985.

Denby, John L., Commander, MC, USNR, by telephone, 27 November 1985.

Deutermann, Peter T., Captain, USN, by telephone, 28 December 1985.

Donovan, John, Lieutenant (junior grade), USN, on board USS *Iowa* (BB-61) at Portsmouth, VA, 17 July 1985.

Duffy, Daniel J., at Baltimore, MD, 26 October 1983.

Dugan, William, by telephone, 2 August 1985.

Dugas, John, Gunner's Mate, at Charleston, SC, 21 September 2023.

Duncan, Eugene G., at York, PA, 1 November 1983.

Dunning, Allan L., Captain, USN (Ret.), by telephone, 18 December 1983, and at Stonington, CT, 19 September 1984.

Edelstein, Julius C. C., at New York City, 2 July 1983.

Elfelt, James S., Commander, USN, at Washington, DC, 21 August 1970.

Evans, John, by telephone, 6 October 1985.

Fagan, Harry P., Jr., by telephone, 7 January 1984.

Farmer, Carl V., Chief Gunner's Mate, USN, on board USS *Iowa* (BB-61) at Portsmouth, VA, 19 July 1985.

Faw, Roger A., at Accokeek, MD, 6 July 1985.

Feigley, Thomas, by telephone, 29 November 1985.

Fike, Irwin H., Captain, USN (Ret.), at Annapolis, MD, 30 April 1985.

Flamboe, Edward E., Lieutenant, USN (Ret.), at Annapolis, MD, 19 November 1985.

Fogarty, William M., Captain, USN, on board USS *New Jersey* (BB-62), at sea, 10 May 1983.

Frakes, Charles, Mess Management Specialist Second Class, USN, on board USS *New Jersey* (BB-62) at Long Beach, CA, 13 July 1990.

Frank, Allan, at Baltimore, MD, 19 June 1985.

Fulks, Robert P., by telephone, 17 November 1985.

Fuller, Philip J., at Reston, VA, 2 December 1983.

Genet, Richard P., Captain, USN, at Washington, DC, 13 February 1986.

Gleason, Brian, Lieutenant, USN, on board USS *New Jersey* (BB-62) at Long Beach, CA, 13 July 1990.

Glenn, W. Lewis, Jr., Captain, USN, by telephone, 17 March 1986.

Gray, Oscar E., Jr., Captain, USN (Ret.), at McLean, VA, 2 May 1985.

Grimes, Roff, Jr., by telephone, 8 September 1985.

Hamilton, Charles R., at Annapolis, MD, 19 June 1985.

Hammond, David, Signalman Second Class, USN, by telephone, 25 April 1986.

Harris, John R., Captain, USNR, by telephone, 21 November 1985.

Harris, Noble C., at Annapolis, MD, 28 November 1983.

Hartley, William, by telephone, 13 July 1985.

Hayward, Eugene F., at Annapolis, MD, 29 February 1984.

Heinl, Robert D., Jr., Colonel, USMC (Ret.), at Washington, DC, 7 September 1970.

Herger, Joseph F., USN, on board USS *New Jersey* (BB-62) at Long Beach, CA, 15 July 1990.

Hill, George, Jr., at Chester, MD, 6 August 1985.

Hood, Donald L., Seaman Apprentice, USN (Ret.), by telephone, 6 September 1985.

Hunt, William J., by telephone, 25 July 1985.

Huntington, Charles A., by telephone, 13 October 1985.

Ivey, Louis A., Commander, MC, USNR, at Silver Spring, MD, 6 October 1983.

Jablon, Leonard, Fire Controlman Second Class, at Charleston, SC, 18 and 21 September 2023.

Jacobus, Charles, Boatswain's Mate Second Class, at Moonachie, NJ, 30 July 1983.

Jennings, Charles, Lieutenant, USN, on board USS *New Jersey* (BB-62) at Long Beach, CA, 15 July 1990.

Johnson, Christopher H., Commander, USN, by telephone, 16 December 1985.

Johnson, Lance K., Journalist Second Class, USNR, by telephone, 30 December 1985.

Jones, Patricia, by telephone, 30 August 2023.

Jung, Leonard J., Chief Musician, USN (Ret.), at Hyattsville, MD, 23 November 1983.

Katz, Douglas J., Vice Admiral, USN (Ret.), at Annapolis, MD, 12 March 2024.

Katz, Sharon L., at Annapolis, MD, 12 March 2024.

Keithly, R. Myers, Captain, USN (Ret.), by telephone, 12 January 1984.

Kelly, Donald V., by telephone, 30 July 1985.

Kersch, Kenneth E., Machinery Repairman, USN, at Charleston, SC, 19 September 2023.

Kiehl, Elmer H., Captain, USN (Ret.), at Virginia Beach, VA, 10 October 1983.

Kihune, Robert K. U., USN (Ret.), by telephone, 5 March 2024.

Kirk, Neville T., Captain, USNR (Ret.), at Annapolis, MD, 2 September 1984.

Knoll, Robert G., by telephone, 1 August 1985.

Kosmela, Walter T., Captain, USN (Ret.), at McLean, VA, 13 October 1983.

Kubicki, Henry J., by telephone, 24 August 1984.

Lavella, Andrew, Chief Personnelman, USN (Ret.), at Annapolis, MD, 13 August 1983.

Leverton, J. Wilson, Jr., Rear Admiral, USN (Ret.), at Annapolis, MD, 1 June 1983.

Lillis, Mark A., at Washington, DC, 10 February 1984.

Loughan, J. P., by telephone, 28 July 1985.

Lowery, Donald D., Machinist's Mate, USN, at Charleston, SC, 19 September 2023.

Lundquist, Jon, Ensign, USN, on board USS *New Jersey* (BB-62) at Long Beach, CA, 12 July 1990.

Mamroth, Ellis, at Fraser, PA, 4 December 1983.

Mathias, Senator Charles M., at Washington, DC, 18 February 1983.

McCorkle, Francis D., Rear Admiral, USN (Ret.), at Providence, RI, 24 October 1982.

McDonough, Barry, Lieutenant (junior grade), USN, on board USS *Iowa* (BB-61) at Portsmouth, VA, 19 July 1985.

McDowell, Percival E., USN (Ret.), at Winchester, VA, 3 March 1977.

McDowell, Mrs. Percival E., at Annapolis, MD, 26 December 1983.

McDowell, Richard, by telephone, 5 October 1985.

McElwain, Harry W., Captain, USN (Ret.), at Falls Church, VA, 13 October 1983.

Meanor, Richard, Commander, USN (Ret.), by telephone, 5 June 2023.

Mehling, Ben, by telephone, 1 October 1985.

Meyer, Leo C., by telephone, 7 September 1985.

Migrala, Walter M., Jr., Commander, USN, at Washington, DC, 25 October 1983.

Miller, Gregory H., Lieutenant (junior grade), USN, on board USS *Iowa* (BB-61) at Portsmouth, VA, 16 July 1985.

Milligan, Richard D., Commodore, USN, at Arlington, VA, 1 November 1985.

Moore, Lewis, Chief Ship's Serviceman, USN (Ret.), by telephone, 22 November 1985.

Moore, Robert L., Commander, USN (Ret.), by telephone, 26 August 1984.

Moorer, Thomas H., Admiral, USN (Ret.), at Washington, DC, 2 May 1985.

Morse, Carl S., Lieutenant Commander, USN, at San Diego, CA, 11 August 1973.

Moto, Arturo, Chief Interior Communications Electrician, USN, by telephone, 23 April 1986.

Mrozinski, Roman V., at Chevy Chase, MD, 20 June 1983.

Mumford, Charles E., Lieutenant Commander, USN (Ret.), by telephone, 12 November 1985.

Mumpower, Thomas S., Lieutenant, USN, on board USS *Iowa* (BB-61) at Portsmouth, VA, 17 July 1985.

Murphy, Michael, Lieutenant, SC, USN (Ret.), at Charleston SC, 21 September 2023.

Nickols, James P., Commander, Chaplain Corps, USN, on board USS *New Jersey* (BB-62) at Long Beach, CA, 15 July 1990.

O'Bryen, Dale, by telephone, 1 August 1985.

O'Donnell, Edward J., Rear Admiral, USN (Ret.), at Monterey, CA, 12 May 1983.

Oliver, Frank, by telephone, 9 December 1983.

Orell, Barry, Photographer's Mate Second Class, USN, by telephone, 24 April 1986.

Palladino, James, CWO-2, USN, on board USS *New Jersey* (BB-62) at Long Beach, CA, 15 July 1990.

Parker, Edward N., Vice Admiral, USN (Ret.), by telephone, 7 October 1985.

Parmelee, Robert M., by telephone, 31 July 1985.

Peet, Raymond E., Vice Admiral, USN (Ret.), at Annapolis, MD, 17 May 1984.

Peniston, Robert C, Captain, USN (Ret.), at Annapolis, MD, 12 November 1982.

Poe, Donald T., Rear Admiral, USN (Ret.), by telephone, 10 August 1985.

Pousson, Larry, Senior Chief Gunner's Mate, USN, on board USS *Iowa* (BB-61) at Portsmouth, VA, 19 July 1985.

Pratt, Richard R., Rear Admiral, USN (Ret.), at Chevy Chase, MD, 16 October 1983.

Reason, J. Paul, Admiral, USN (Ret.), at Washington, DC, 29 March 2003.

Reed, Christopher, at East Douglas, MA, 20 September 1984.

Reynolds, Harry O., Commander, USN (Ret.), at Yucaipa, CA, 15 May 1983.

Rice, Robert, Lieutenant (junior grade), USNR, on board USS *New Jersey* (BB-62) at Long Beach, CA, 14 July 1990.

Rice, Robert H., Vice Admiral, USN (Ret.), at Winter Park, FL, 24 April 1984.

Robie, William A., Captain, MC, USN (Ret.), by telephone, 1 August 1985.

Romer, William, Master Chief Damage Controlman, USN (Ret.), at Charleston, SC, 18 September 2023.

Rossie, John P., at Annapolis, MD, 2 May 1984.

Rupp, David O., at York, PA, 1 November 1983.

Ryan, Dennis L., III, Captain, USN (Ret.), at Odenton, MD, 5 February 2024.

Scarselletta, Albert, Senior Chief Storekeeper, USN (Ret.), by telephone, 23 November 1985.

Shepherd, Lemuel C., III, Colonel, USMC (Ret.), at La Jolla, CA, 14 May 1983.

Shipley, William, Lieutenant, USN, on board USS *New Jersey* (BB-62) at Long Beach, CA, 12 July 1990.

Smith, Arthur H., Chief Electrician's Mate, USN (Ret.), at Allentown, PA, 29 October 1983.

Snyder, J. Edward, Jr., Rear Admiral USN (Ret.), at Newport, RI, 24 August 1970, and at McLean, VA, 26 November 1985.

Sosnowski, William, by telephone, 20 November 1983.

Soucek, Archie H., Captain, USN (Ret.), at Silver Spring, MD, 21 January 1983.

Storm, Robert J., at Leesport, PA, 29 October 1983.

Strub, Henry, by telephone, 21 November 1985.

Sullivan, John W., Captain, USN (Ret.), at Virginia Beach, VA, 10 October 1983.

Swayze, Frank B., Captain, JAGC, USN, by telephone, 27 November 1985.

Szimanski, Ryan, email to author, 7 March 2024.

Teller, George R., by telephone, 28 July 1985.

Thompson, William, Rear Admiral USN (Ret.), date unknown.

Thompson, Edward M., Rear Admiral, USN (Ret.), at Alexandria, VA, 21 January 1983.

Touzin, K. T., Journalist Second Class, USN, by telephone, 20 December 2023.

Trail, John, Quartermaster Second Class, USN, by telephone, 10 November 1985.

Trecartin, Allen, by telephone, 28 July 1985.

Triola, Salvatore, by telephone, 6 October 1985.
Tucker, Leon, Gunner's Mate First Class, USN, on board USS *New Jersey* (BB-62) at Long Beach, CA, 13 July 1990.
Tucker, Ronald D., Captain, USN, on board USS *New Jersey* (BB-62) at Long Beach, CA, 12 July 1990.
Tyree, David M., Rear Admiral, USN (Ret.), at Port Haywood, VA, 13 February 1983.
Vaught, Roy L., Lieutenant, USN (Ret.), by telephone, 10 June 1984.
Vining, Pierre G., Captain, USN (Ret.), by telephone, 9 October 1985.
Walker, Edward K., Jr., Rear Admiral, SC, USN, at Arlington, VA, 8 August 1984.
Walsh, John, by telephone, 5 October 1985.
Watts, Charles R., Commander, USN (Ret.), at Arlington, VA, 28 February 1983.
Westcott, Robert J., at Bridgeton, NJ, 16 June 1984.
Wilhite, Drewery R., Captain, USN (Ret.), at Fort Sumner, MD, 1 February 1983.
Williams, Marvin, Master Chief Operations Specialist, USN (Ret.), at Charleston, SC, 20 September 2023.
Winkelman, Val, Jr., by telephone, 10 August 1985.
Wolpin, Richard B., Storekeeper First Class, USN, by telephone, 23 December 1985.

LETTERS TO AUTHOR

Alexander, Richard G., Captain, USN (Ret.), 29 May 1986.
Amend, Wayne A., 13 September 1985.
Anderson, Clyde B., Captain, USN (Ret.), 2 October 1983.
Bierley, John R., Captain, MC, USN (Ret.), 10 November 1983.
Braybrook, William M., Captain, USN (Ret.), 28 January 1983.
Chesser, Steven B., Lieutenant Commander, USN (Ret.), 29 March 2024 and 4 June 2024 (emails).
Cheyne, Scott, Lieutenant, USNR, 5 February 1974 and 22 February 1974 (tape recordings).
Coley, Charles C., Captain, USN (Ret.), 29 August 1985 (tape recording).
Conroy, Benjamin J., Jr., 20 August 1985 and 6 September 1985 (tape recordings).
Coyne, William D., Captain, USN (Ret.), 11 August 1983.
Dale, Roland H., Captain, USN (Ret.), 21 August 1985.
Dobie, E. W., Rear Admiral, USN (Ret.), 8 February 1984 and 23 February 1984.
Douglas, Lee W., Lieutenant Commander, USNR (Ret.), 14 September 1983.
Dudley, Clayton R., Rear Admiral, USN (Ret.), 20 July 1985.

Dunning, Allan L., Captain, USN (Ret.), 12 August 1985.
Ekstrom, Clarence E., Vice Admiral, USN (Ret.), 10 June 1985.
Forest, Joseph A., 8 February 1985.
Fulks, Robert P., 9 May 1983.
Gill, Harold, 13 September 1985.
Goode, Leonard T., 29 August 1985.
Hastings, John S., 3 November 1985.
Hayes, John J., Commander, USNR, 22 April 1984.
Heselton, Leslie R., Captain, USN (Ret.), 9 August 1983 and 26 October 1983.
Holste, Peter N., 1 November 1972 (tape recording).
Huff, Robert L., 16 April 1984.
Keithly, R. Myers, Captain, USN (Ret.), 17 December 1983.
Kiehl, Elmer H., Captain, USN (Ret.), 3 August 1983.
Kierulff, Dudley J., Commander, SC, USN (Ret.), 22 January 1984.
Kosmela, Walter T., Captain, USN (Ret.), 17 August 1983.
Kretz, Walter T., Captain, SC, USN (Ret.), 4 September 1983 and 12 November 1983 (latter a tape recording).
Kuncevich, Sam, 17 April 1984.
Leverton, J. Wilson, Jr., Rear Admiral, USN (Ret.), 7 March 1983.
Lewis, John S., Commander, USNR, 17 November 1983.
McCormick, John W., Captain, USN (Ret.), 4 June 1983 and 10 August 1985.
Meilandt, Ralph L., Captain, SC, USN (Ret.), 19 August 1985.
Moore, Robert L., Commander, USN (Ret.), 7 June 1983.
Parsons, Joseph M., Commander, USN (Ret.), 21 November 1983 (tape recording) and 8 December 1983.
Peniston, Robert C, Captain, USN (Ret.), 9 December 1982.
Phelan, James F., Commander, USN (Ret.), 12 August 1985.
Pinney, Frank L., Rear Admiral, USN (Ret.), 4 November 1977.
Poe, Donald T., Rear Admiral, USN (Ret.), 8 August 1985 (tape recording).
Pratt, Richard R., Rear Admiral, USN (Ret.), 16 May 1983.
Pringle, James F., Commander, USN (Ret.), 23 October 1983.
Reed, Christopher, 21 February 1984.
Rose, Rufus E., Vice Admiral, USN (Ret.), 11 August 1985.
Rossie, John P., 13 August 1985.
Sadler, Stuart T., Captain, USN (Ret.), 30 May 1983 (tape recording).
Scott, Arthur, 22 December 1985.
Snyder, Philip W., Rear Admiral, USN (Ret.), 12 November 1983.
Taylor, Roger C., Commander, USNR (Ret.), 10 November 1983.

Terry, James H., Captain, USN (Ret.), 9 July 1985 and 22 July 1985.
Tiernan, William H., 2 August 1985.
Tyree, David M., Rear Admiral, USN (Ret.), 21 February 1983.
Vasey, Lloyd R., Rear Admiral, USN (Ret.), 21 August 1985.
Valenta, Joseph R., Captain, USN (Ret.), 17 January 2023.
Wellborn, Charles, Jr., Vice Admiral, USN (Ret.), 16 December 1983.
Winslow, Edward H., USN (Ret.), 10 November 1983.

PERSONAL LETTERS

Brooks, Charles B., Jr., Captain, USN, to Captain John O. Miner, USN, 13 May 1957. Copy supplied by Mrs. Elizabeth Brunelli.
McGowan, Joseph A., Radarman Third Class, USNR, to Mrs. Ray McDonough, 4 February 1944. Copy supplied by Colonel Joseph A. McGowan, USAR.
Wooldridge, E. Tyler, Captain, USN, to Mrs. Marion Wooldridge, 11 August 1945; 12 August 1945; 15 August 1945; 29 August 1945. All letters supplied by Mrs. Wooldridge.

ORAL HISTORIES

Atkeson, John C., Rear Admiral, USN (Ret.), East Carolina University Collection, Greenville, NC.
Duncan, Charles K., Admiral, USN (Ret.), U.S. Naval Institute Collection.
Hustvedt, Olaf M., Vice Admiral, USN (Ret.), U.S. Naval Institute Collection.
Kerr, Alex A., Captain, USN (Ret.), U.S. Naval Institute Collection.
Melson, Charles L., Vice Admiral, USN (Ret.), U.S. Naval Institute Collection.
Peet, Raymond E., Vice Admiral, USN (Ret.), U.S. Naval Institute Collection.

OFFICIAL LETTERS

Acting Secretary of the Navy to the Governor of New Jersey, 14 July 1939. Held by Ships Histories Section, Naval History and Heritage Command, Washington, DC.
Bureau of Ships, U.S. Navy, to Secretary of the Navy, 29 January 1941. Held by Operational Archives Branch, Naval History and Heritage Command, Washington, DC.
Commanding Officer, USS *New Jersey* (BB-62) to Commander in Chief, U.S. Naval Forces, Eastern Atlantic and Mediterranean, Serial 073, 2 July 1955; Serial 1142, 25 July 1955; Serial 1509, 1 October 1956; Serial 1575, 19 October 1956. Held by Operational Archives Branch, Naval History and Heritage Command, Washington, DC.
Commanding Officer, USS *New Jersey* (BB-62) to Commander Battleship-Cruiser Force, U.S. Atlantic Fleet, serial 1178, 28 July 1955. Held by Operational Archives Branch, Naval History and Heritage Command, Washington, DC.
Director, War Plans Division, U.S. Navy, to Chairman, General Board, U.S. Navy, 28 June 1939. Held by Operational Archives Branch, Naval History and Heritage Command, Washington, DC.
Director, War Plans Division, U.S. Navy, to Director, Fleet Maintenance Division, U.S. Navy, 10 February 1939. Held by Operational Archives Branch, Naval History and Heritage Command, Washington, DC.
Director, War Plans Division, U.S. Navy, to Director, Fleet Maintenance Division, U.S. Navy, 7 March 1941. Held by Operational Archives Branch, Naval History and Heritage Command, Washington, DC.

OFFICIAL RECORDS

Action reports of the USS *New Jersey* (BB-62) for World War II: Serial 015 of 25 February 1944; Serial 034 of 21 March 1944; Serial 037 of 6 April 1944; Serial 049 of 6 May 1944; Serial 078 of 12 July 1944; Serial 0101 of 27 October 1944; Serial 0102 of 3 November 1944; Serial 0105 of 9 November 1944; Serial 0113 of 25 November 1944; Serial 0118 of 24 December 1944; Serial 011 of 25 January 1945; Serial 023 of 5 March 1945; Serial 037 of 31 March 1945; Serial 044 of 16 April 1945; Serial 0129 of 11 August 1945. Held by Operational Archives Branch, Naval History and Heritage Command, Washington, DC.
Action Reports of the USS *New Jersey* (BB-62) for the Korean War: Serial 081 of 10 August 1951; Serial 0110 of 11 October 1951; Serial 0111 of 11 October 1951; Serial 0112 of 11 October 1951; Serial 0115 of 22 October 1951; Serial 0116 of 22 October 1951; Serial 0117 of 22 October 1951; Serial 0118 of 22 October 1951; Serial 0126 of 14 November 1951; Serial 0127 of 17 November 1951; Serial 06 of 11 January 1952; Serial 090 of 16 April 1953; Serial 091 of 17 April 1953; Serial 099 of 25 April 1953; Serial 0102 of 3 May 1953; Serial 0104 of 4 May 1953; Serial 0108 of 8 May 1953; Serial 0109 of 9 May 1953; Serial 0117 of 7 June 1953; Serial 0119 of 15 June 1953; Serial 0128 of 6 July 1953; Serial 0131 of 14 July 1953; Serial 0132 of 14 July 1953; Serial 0151 of 28 July 1953; Serial

0152 of 28 July 1953; Serial 0163 of 11 August 1953. Held by Operational Archives Branch, Naval History and Heritage Command, Washington, DC.

Command Histories, USS *New Jersey* (BB-62), 1968, 1969, 1982, 1983, 1984, 1985, 1986, 1987, 1988, 1989, 1990. Held by Ships Histories Section, Naval History and Heritage Command, Washington, DC.

Deck Logs of the USS *New Jersey* (BB-62), May 1943–December 1945. Held by National Archives and Records Service, Washington, DC.

Deck Logs of the USS *New Jersey* (BB-62), January 1946–June 1948, November 1950–August 1957. Held by Washington National Records Center, Suitland, MD.

Ship's name file of the USS *New Jersey* (BB-62). Held by Ships Histories Section, Naval History and Heritage Command, Washington, DC.

War Diaries of the USS *New Jersey* (BB-62), 1944–1945, 1950–1953. Held by Operational Archives Branch, Naval History and Heritage Command, Washington, DC.

SPEECHES

Holden, Carl F., Captain, USN, remarks at the commissioning ceremony, 23 May 1943. Copy supplied by Mrs. Percival E. McDowell.

Leverton, J. Wilson, Jr., Rear Admiral, USN (Ret.), remarks at the decommissioning ceremony, 30 June 1948. Copy supplied by Rear Admiral Leverton.

Peniston, Robert C, Captain, USN, remarks at the decommissioning ceremony, 17 December 1969. Copy supplied by USS *New Jersey* public affairs officer.

BOOKS

Adams, Hans Christian, Colonel, USAF (Ret.), and Captain George F. Kosco, USN (Ret.). *Halsey's Typhoons*. New York: Crown Publishers, Inc., 1967.

Buell, Thomas B., Commander, USN (Ret.). *The Quiet Warrior: A Biography of Admiral Raymond A. Spruance*. Boston: Little, Brown and Company, 1974.

Calhoun, C. Raymond, Captain, USN (Ret.). *Typhoon: The Other Enemy*. Annapolis: Naval Institute Press, 1981.

Clark, Joseph J., Admiral, USN (Ret.), with Clark G. Reynolds. *Carrier Admiral*. New York: David McKay Company, Inc., 1967.

Comegno, Carol. *The Battleship New Jersey: From Birth to Berth*. Orchards, WA: Pediment Publishing, 2001.

Dulin, Robert O., Jr., and William H. Garzke, Jr. *Battleships: United States Battleships in World War II*. Annapolis: Naval Institute Press, 1976 and subsequent editions.

Forrestal, E. P., Vice Admiral, USN (Ret.). *Admiral Raymond A. Spruance: A Study in Command*. Washington, DC: U.S. Government Printing Office, 1966.

Friedman, Norman. *Naval Radar*. Greenwich, England: Conway Maritime Press Ltd., 1981.

———. *U.S. Battleships: An Illustrated Design History*. Annapolis: Naval Institute Press, 1985.

Halsey, William F., Jr., Fleet Admiral, USN, and Lieutenant Commander Joseph Bryan, III, USNR. *Admiral Halsey's Story*. New York: Whittlesey House, 1947.

Karig, Walter, Captain, USNR, Lieutenant Commander Russell L. Harris, USNR, and Lieutenant Commander Frank A. Manson, USN. *Battle Report: The End of an Empire*. New York: Rinehart and Company, Inc., 1948.

———. *Battle Report: Victory in the Pacific*. New York: Rinehart and Company, Inc., 1949.

———. *Dreadnought Farewell*. Philadelphia: Kaye Publications, Inc., 1970.

Leifer, Neil. *Dreadnought Returns*. Philadelphia: Baum Printing House, 1969.

Morison, Samuel Eliot. *Aleutians, Gilberts and Marshalls*, Volume VII of *History of United States Naval Operations in World War II*. Boston: Little, Brown and Company, 1951.

———. *Leyte*, Volume XII. Boston: Little, Brown and Company, 1958.

———. *The Liberation of the Philippines: Luzon, Mindanao and the Visayas*, Volume XIII. Boston: Little, Brown and Company, 1959.

———. *New Guinea and the Marianas*, Volume VIII. Boston: Little, Brown and Company, 1953.

———. *Victory in the Pacific*, Volume XIV. Boston: Little, Brown and Company, 1960.

Muir, Malcolm. *The Iowa Class Battleships: Iowa, New Jersey & Wisconsin*. New York: Sterling Publishing Co., Inc., 1987.

Potter, E. B. *Bull Halsey*. Annapolis: Naval Institute Press, 1985.

———. *Nimitz*. Annapolis: Naval Institute Press, 1976.

Reynolds, Clark G. *The Fast Carriers: The Forging of an Air Navy*. New York: McGraw-Hill Book Company, 1968.

Sherman, Frederick C., Admiral, USN (Ret.). *Combat Command: The American Aircraft Carriers in the Pacific War*. New York: E. P. Dutton & Company, 1950.

Stillwell, Paul. *Battleship Missouri: An Illustrated History*. Annapolis: Naval Institute Press. 1996.

Taylor, Theodore. *The Magnificent Mitscher*. W. W. Norton & Company, 1954.

Terzibaschitsch, Stefan. *Battleships of the U.S. Navy in World War II*. New York: Bonanza Books, 1977.

NEW JERSEY CRUISE BOOKS

War Log (1943–45)

Salvo (1950–51)

A Half Year of History (1953)

U.S.S. New Jersey BB-62 (1955)

Dreadnought 68–69

Dreadnought 83–84

Surface Strike at Sea (1986)

Big Thunder Down Under (1988)

Modern Dreadnought (1990)

PAMPHLETS PUBLISHED BY THE NEW JERSEY

Decommissioning Program, 17 December 1969

Equator '68

European Cruise 1947

Familygram, various issues, 1966–69

The Log . . . of the U.S.S. New Jersey: 1943–1945

Midshipman Cruise 1956

Recommissioning Program, 6 April 1968

Recommissioning Program, 28 December 1982

ARTICLES

Aston, William J., Midshipman, USN, and Midshipman Alexander G. B. Grosvenor, USN. "Midshipmen's Cruise." *National Geographic*, June 1948.

Berger, Meyer. "U.S.S. New Jersey Being Reactivated." *New York Times*, 27 September 1950.

"Big Flagship 'In Mothballs.'" *New York Sun*, 22 May 1948.

Bott, Captain Christopher, USN (Ret.). "A Lesson in Tolerance from the Navy's First African American Four-Star Admiral." U.S. Naval Institute *Proceedings*, June 2020.

Brewer, Ralph Wright. "The Reds Are Firing Back at Us!" *Our Navy*, Mid-June 1952.

Castle, Alfred L., "President Roosevelt and General MacArthur at the Honolulu Conference of 1944," *The Hawaiian Journal of History* 40, 2004.

Chantry, Allan J., Rear Admiral, USN. "Launching of U.S.S. 'New Jersey' and U.S.S. 'Wisconsin.'" *Transactions* of the Society of Naval Architects and Marine Engineers, 1944.

Heinl, Robert D., Jr., Colonel, USMC (Ret.). "Welcome to the War." U.S. Naval Institute *Proceedings*, March 1969.

Hiatt, Fred. "U.S. Battleship to Stay in Mideast." *Washington Post*, 29 November 1983.

Jamieson, Robert D. "New Jersey Towed to LBSNY." *Deckplate*, November–December 1981.

"Jersey's Own Ship Leaves for Cruise after Ceremonies Here." *Newark Evening News*, 24 May 1947.

Jones, Franklin P. "20,000 See Launching of Mightiest Warship." *Philadelphia Record*, 8 December 1942.

Kennett, Warren H. "'Big J' Ready for Atom." *Newark Evening News*, 12 March 1951.

Lewis, Emanuel Raymond. "American Battleship Main Battery Armament: The Final Generation." *Warship International*, Number 4, 1976.

Morse, Carl S., Lieutenant, USN, and Lieutenant (junior grade) Charles C. Bream, USN. "The Activation of the U.S.S. *New Jersey* (BB-62) at Philadelphia Naval Shipyard." *Naval Engineers Journal*, December 1968.

Munro, Dana, "Long Career of Annapolis Resident Frederick Gregory Highlighted in New Book on Barrier-Breaking NASA Astronauts." *Annapolis Capital Gazette*, 21 March 2023.

Pineda, R. "Battleship Gunners Tackle Turrets." *Surface Warfare*, November–December 1984.

Rogoway, Tyler. "This Massive Naval Exercise in 1989 Was the Pinnacle of U.S. Cold War Maritime Might." The War Zone website: https://www.twz.com/24711/this-massive-naval-exercise-in-1989-was-the-pinnacle-of-u-s-cold-war-maritime-might.

Ruch, Walter M. "Dreadnought Tops 26 Ship Launchings." *New York Times*, 8 December 1942.

Schaefer, Crozier. "20,000 See Ship Floated." *Philadelphia Inquirer*, 8 December 1942, page 1.

Serig, Howard W. "The *Iowa* Class: Needed Once Again." U.S. Naval Institute *Proceedings*, May 1982.

Starr, Mark, and Kim Willenson. "Right Ship in the Wrong Place." *Newsweek*, 26 March 1984.

Stillwell, Paul. "The Battleship Battle, 1964–1967." *Marine Corps Gazette*, August 1981.

———. "Frustrated Crew Prepares New Jersey for Mothballs Not War." *Navy Times*, 11 March 1991.

Strassman, Neil. "Navy Bids Farewell to USS *New Jersey*." *Long Beach Press-Telegram*, 9 February 1991.

"USS *New Jersey*: New Chapter for Battleships." *All Hands*, March 1983.

Zeller, Bob. "When Smoke Cleared, 'Big Jay' Was in Service." *Long Beach Press-Telegram*, 29 December 1982.

NEWSPAPERS

Beacon (published by Philadelphia Navy Yard), 7 December 1942. The entire issue is devoted to the launching of the *New Jersey*.

Clean Sweep Down (published on board the *New Jersey*), various issues, 1943.

The Jerseyman (published on board the *New Jersey*), various issues, 1944–45, 1952–56.

UNPUBLISHED MANUSCRIPTS

Soucek, Archie H., Lieutenant Commander, USN. 1945 personal diary. Copy supplied by Captain A. H. Soucek, USN (Ret.).

Stillwell, Paul. "USS *New Jersey* Public Affairs/Media Coverage during the Vietnam War." Master's thesis, University of Missouri School of Journalism, Columbia, MO.

"United States Naval Administration in World War II: Commander in Chief Atlantic Fleet." Bound typescript on file at Navy Library, Naval History and Heritage Command, Washington Navy Yard, Washington, DC.

INDEX

A-7 Corsair II, U.S. attack plane, 161
Abhau, William C., 13, 25–29, 37–38, 41–42
Abrams, Creighton, 173
Abrams, Richard, 133
Addison, Edward S., 16
Admiralty Islands, 38
Airey, Henry J., 112
Air Force, U.S., 109, 124, 139, 230, 262, 265
Alabama, USS (BB-60), 29, 31
Alameda, California, 176
Albany, Australia, 248
Albany, USS (CA-123)
Albrecht, Carl, 154, 159–160, 162, 170, 174–175
Alcoholic Beverages, 1, 10, 12, 20, 25, 36, 39, 42–43, 53, 62, 73, 75, 85–86, 89, 91, 96, 111, 119, 123, 126, 133, 137, 139, 164, 168, 177, 199, 223, 241, 250, 254, 264
Aleutian Islands, 260–261, 266
Alexander, Richard G., 148–150
Alexandria, Egypt, 205
Allagash, USS (AO-97), 122
Almond, Edward M., 93
Amend, Wayne, 128
America (U.S. liner), 77
America, USS (CVA-66), 161
Amgok Peninsula, North Korea, 108
Ammon, William B., 126
ammunition, 17, 20–21, 31, 37, 54, 63, 66–67, 78–79, 84, 90, 97, 100, 107, 112, 114, 124–125, 143, 155–158, 162, 165, 180, 191, 204, 211, 218, 220–221, 225, 240, 246, 252, 270, 276
anchors/anchor chains in *New Jersey*, 4, 50, 55, 62, 69, 73, 75, 77–79, 87, 89, 118, 184, 189, 249
Anderson, Clyde B., 133, 138–140
Anderson, Walter S., 18
Andrew, Prince (Britain), 249
Angaur Island, 39
Annapolis, Maryland, 11–12, 68, 78, 122, 128, 130, 138, 140

Ann-Margret, 167–168
antiaircraft guns/firing, 6, 8, 13–14, 24–25, 29–30, 33–34, 40, 42–44, 46, 49, 60, 63, 67, 71, 84, 86, 158–160, 195, 206–207, 242
Antietam, USS (CG-54), 259
Arizona Memorial, 197, 223, 229
Ark Royal (British aircraft carrier), 246, 248–249
armor in *New Jersey*, 2–3, 5, 11, 17, 272
Army, U.S., 29, 56, 58, 77, 92–93, 96, 109, 122, 136, 161, 173, 229, 235
Army Air Forces, U.S., 28, 30, 32, 55
Arnheiter, Marcus A., 150, 158
Arnold J. Isbell, USS (DD-869)
Ashtabula, USS (AO-51), 90
Aston, William J., 68
Athens, Greece, 134–135
Atkeson, John C. (*New Jersey* CO, 1953-55), 117–119, 121–123, 125–127, 129–131
atomic bombs/projectiles, 55, 63, 85, 89, 124–125, 230–231, 269
Australia, 71, 174, 243–244, 246–250
Australian Navy, 230, 249

Badger, Oscar C., 41, 48–49, 51, 83
Bagley, USS (FF-1069)
Bahrain Island, 264
Bak, Michael, Jr., 50
Baker, John, 209
Ballou, Joseph F., 122
Baltimore, USS (CA-68), 234–236
Bangor, Washington, 63, 66–67, 78
Barcelona, Spain, 136–137
Barnes, James, 131–132, 135
Bartusch, Willard, 28, 42
baseball, 10, 39, 121, 144
Basilone, USS (DD-824)
Battle Group Romeo, 227–233, 259–266
Battleship *New Jersey* organization, Camden, 279–282

304 INDEX

Bayonne, New Jersey, 67, 78–84, 142–143, 145, 147, 276–277
Beadle, Robert, 89
Beagle, Ron, 130
Bear D, Soviet bomber, 158, 232
Beary, Donald B., 15, 17
Beirut, Lebanon, 203–204, 207, 209, 212, 214–215
Bennett, David M., 272
Bering Sea, 260
Bernard, Gene, 196
berthing compartments in *New Jersey*, 7, 12–13, 30, 40, 42–43, 68, 70–71, 82, 89, 92, 110, 116, 140, 148, 151–152, 173, 189, 208, 234, 242, 279–281
Bessard, Damion, 230
Betty, Japanese torpedo bomber, 33, 40
Beverly W. Reid, USS (APD-119)
Bierly, John, 137, 141, 144
Bikini Atoll, 25, 63
Biloxi, USS (CL-80), 54
Bismarck (German battleship), 17, 73
Bitting, Frederick, 132, 140, 143, 145
Blair, Frank, 267
Blanchette, Roland, 105, 108, 110
Blueback, USS (SS-581), 257
Bogan, Gerald, 39, 44
boilers, *see* Engineering Plant in *New Jersey*
Bonhomme Richard, USS (CV-31), 95
Borie, USS (DD-704), 48
Bornack, Frank, 3
Boston Navy Yard, 20
Bott, Chris, 269
Bowen, USS (FF-1079), 203
Bowler, Roland T. E., Jr., 37, 56
boxing, 55, 91, 129
Brandt, King G., 6, 19, 25
Brattin, Sherman, 36–37, 39
Braybrook, William, 104–105, 114, 116, 119
Brega, Richard, 120–121, 131
Bremerton, Washington, 51–53, 57, 63–65, 69, 180–184, 274–275 , 279
Brewerton, Peter, 93
bridge in *New Jersey*, 4, 10, 13, 15–16, 53, 56, 70–72, 75, 87–88, 92, 103–104, 108, 116, 122–123, 126, 128, 140, 163, 180, 193–194, 204–205, 209, 211, 213, 222, 239, 247, 257
brig in *New Jersey*, 39, 133
Brisbane, Australia, 248

"Broadway" (third deck passageway in *New Jersey*), 96, 169, 145, 169, 172
Bronstein, USS (FF-1037), 227
Brooks, Charles B., Jr. (*New Jersey* CO, 1956-57), 138–141, 144–146
Brooks, Clarence J., Jr., 81–82, 84, 86, 88–89, 91, 94–95
Brown, Frank, 200
Brown, Jacob, 104, 106, 115–116
Brown, Russell, 7, 18, 30, 45, 47, 50, 62
Brown, W. M., 109
Brown, Wilburt S., 98
Buchanan, USS (DDG-14), 200
buglers in *New Jersey*, 40, 57–58, 73–74, 92, 117, 133, 197, 272
Bulkeley, John D., 71, 75, 220
Bunker Hill, USS (CV-17), 24–25, 49
Bureau of Naval Personnel, U.S. Navy, 59, 82, 136, 139, 148–149, 178, 271
Bureau of Ships, U.S. Navy, 8, 10, 17, 65
Burke, Arleigh A., 91, 130
Bush, George H. W., 224
Butt, William A., 35

C-9 Skytrain, U.S. transport, 206, 209
Cabot, USS (CVL-28), 44
Caine Mutiny, The, 100, 272
Callaghan, USS (DDG-994), 195, 197
Camden, New Jersey, 276–282
Cannes, France, 133, 136
Cantacuzene, Rodion, 105, 108–109, 111–112, 117–118
Caperton, USS (DD-650), 35
Cap Lay, North Vietnam, 162
captain's cabin in *New Jersey*, 7, 235, 243, 279
Carl Vinson, USS (CVN-70), 260
Carney, Robert B., 37, 120–121, 165
Carney, Robert B., Jr., 165
Caroline Islands, 26, 29, 31, 39, 43–44, 46–49, 51
Cary, Jeff, 276
Casco Bay, Maine, 17–20
catapults in *New Jersey*, 35, 37, 63, 85–86
Chafee, John, 178
Chambers, William, 22
Chandler, USS (DD-996), 222
Changhang-ni, North Korea, 93
Chang_San_Got peninsula, North Korea, 97
chaplains in *New Jersey*, 32, 49, 74, 93–94, 132, 157, 211, 254–255
Charette, USS (DD-581), 12

Chauncey, USS (DD-667), 108
Chemung, USS (AO-30), 68, 70
Chenault, Frederick A., 117
Cherbourg, France, 102, 123
Chesapeake Bay, 11–12, 17, 78, 103, 138
Chesser, Steven, 228–231, 233, 235, 237, 244, 250
Cheyne, R. Scott, 152, 164–165
chief petty officers' quarters/mess in *New Jersey*, 110, 172–173, 186, 203, 255–256, 270, 280–281
Chinnampo, North Korea, 108
Chongjin, North Korea, 96, 107
Christmas celebrations in *New Jersey*, 20, 46, 98–99, 104, 119, 166–168, 207–208, 226, 233, 252
Clairmont, Dan, 200, 202, 214, 217–220
Clark, Joseph J., 50, 106–109, 111–113, 115
Clouse, Roger, 171
Clower, Robert, 46
clown troupe in *New Jersey*, 229–230
Coast Guard, U.S., 152, 171, 177
Colahan, USS (DD-658), 42
Coletti, Edward, 98
Coley, Charles C., 82, 87, 91, 93–94, 98, 100
Columbia River, 269
combat engagement center in *New Jersey*, 196, 201, 213, 215, 228, 239, 242–243, 279
combat information center in *New Jersey*, 65, 71, 90, 92, 101, 116, 159–160, 163, 171, 201
Comegno, Carol, 276
computer, Mark 48, in *New Jersey*, 162–163
Cone, USS (DD-866), 69
Congress, U.S., 100, 127, 147, 178–179, 183–184, 195, 265, 275
conning tower, in *New Jersey*, 15–17, 122, 204–205
Conolly, Richard L., 73–75, 77
Conroy, Benjamin, 82, 90, 92–93, 96–97
Constellation, USS (CV-64), 232–233
Con Thien, South Vietnam, 170, 173
Cook, August B., 25
Cook (Australian research ship), 249
Cooper, Ervin, 233–234, 241
Cooper, George R., 119, 122, 126
Copeland, USS (FFG-25), 227
Coral Sea, USS (CVA-43), 104, 137, 174
Cowpens, USS (CVL-25), 25
Coyne, William D., 6, 11, 14, 18, 20, 37, 41, 53
Crawford, Rick, 150–151, 157, 159, 167–169, 171, 174, 187, 189, 194, 203, 220
Crete, 133

Crommelin, Henry, 137
Crowe, William, 250
Cruppenink, John, 116, 121
Cuba, *see* Guantanamo Bay
Culebra Island, 77, 85, 101, 126
Cusumano, Sal, 98
Cyprus Island, 206

Dale, Roland H., 24
Dalrymple-Hamilton, Frederick, 73
damage control in *New Jersey*, 16, 242, 252, 262
Dam Neck, Virginia, 84
Danang, South Vietnam, 159, 162, 165, 170
Danese, Mike, 102, 111
Darroch, James, 103
DASH (drone ASW helo), 158–159
Davis, Donald, 186, 192
Davis, George W. Jr., 243–245
decontamination stations in *New Jersey*, 85, 236
De La Maza, Rafael, 9–10, 21, 23, 31, 34, 36, 40–41, 64, 80
Delaware Bay, 10, 276
Delaware River, 1, 4, 9–10, 15, 152, 154, 156, 276–278, 282
Delvecchio, Sam, 108
Demilitarized Zone, Vietnam, 159–161, 166
Denby, John, 169
Des Moines, USS (CA-134), 122, 130–131, 137–138
Deutermann, Peter T., 210
Dezekon, J. H., 88
directors in *New Jersey*, 6, 8, 30, 34, 77, 155, 160
disciplinary matters, 13, 52, 54, 60–61, 102, 133, 142, 164–165, 188, 230, 239, 247, 256
Divers, 4, 81, 237, 240
Dobie, E. William, 65–67, 71, 77
Dominican Republic, 126
Donovan, James, 121
Donovan, John, 209–214
Doremus, Irving S., 15
Draemel, Milo F., 7–8
drill team in *New Jersey*, 244–245
Driscoll, Alfred E., 67, 83
drones, 46, 71, 193, 242, 261–262
drugs-illegal, 188, 255
Dudley, Clayton R., 12, 15
Duffy, Daniel, 61, 63
Dugan, William, 36, 40
Dugas, John, 242, 247, 249–250, 256–257, 262
Duncan, Charles K., 73
Duncan, Eugene, 82

Dunning, Allan L., 2
Dyer, James, 79

EC-121 Warning Star, U.S. surveillance aircraft, 174
Eamigh, Charles Edwin, 32
Edelstein, Julius C. C., 7–8, 19
Edinburgh, Scotland, 72–73
Edison, Mrs. Carolyn, 1, 83
Edison, Charles, 1–2, 83
Edsall, Warner, 103, 106
Egypt, 205
Egyptian Navy, 157
Ekstrom, Clarence, 128
Elath (Israeli destroyer), 157
Elfelt, James S., 151, 161–162, 178, 181
Elfelt, Sally, 174
Elizabeth II, Queen (Britain), 76, 111, 242–243
El Salvador, 201
engineering plant in *New Jersey*, boilers/firerooms, 3, 6, 14, 22, 39, 45, 93, 96, 110, 120, 143, 153, 161, 189, 221, 240, 271, 279; condensers, 14–16, 143; evaporators, generators, main engines(turbines)/engine rooms, 3, 10, 15–16, 45, 88, 93, 96, 100, 109, 120, 132, 143, 189, 220, 236, 240, 271, 279; propellers/propeller shafts, 3, 11, 34, 93, 118, 153, 203, 236, 240, 281–282; reduction gears, 143, 271; smokestacks, 8, 22, 70, 153
England, 73 75–76, 123, 129, 139–140
England, USS (CG-22), 222
Engle, H. C., Jr., 95
English Channel, 101
Eniwetok Atoll, 25, 36, 55
Enterprise, USS (CVN-65), 224, 260
Esper, Ron, 123
Essex, USS (CV-9), 44, 49
Esteem, USS (MSO-438), 180
equator crossings, 23, 165–166, 198–200, 246, 250
Ethridge, W. A., 49
Evans, John, 133, 136, 142, 144
evaporators, *see* engineering plant

F4U Corsair, U.S. fighter, 112
F6F Hellcat, U.S. fighter, 34
F-14 Tomcat, U.S. fighter, 206–207, 210
Fagan, Harry, 58, 60, 62
Farmer, Carl, 187, 192–193
Faw, Roger, 20–22, 31, 52–54
Feigley, Thomas, 151, 163, 166, 169
Feinstein, Dianne, 194, 223

Fifth Fleet, U.S., 25–30, 33–34, 37–38, 40, 48, 51, 55–61, 140
fire control in *New Jersey*, 4, 16, 27, 29–30, 34, 65, 84–85, 88–89, 92, 107, 124, 156, 159, 162–163, 186, 188, 194, 207, 210, 213–214, 242
firerooms, *see* engineering plant
flag plot in *New Jersey*, 36, 101, 163
flag quarters in *New Jersey*, 31–32, 36, 98, 121, 134, 201, 228–229, 239, 242–243, 253, 257, 279
Flamboe, Edward, 164, 168–169, 171, 176
Fletcher, Frank Jack, 57
Fletcher, USS (DD-992), 227
Fluckey, Eugene B., 102
Fogarty, William M. (*New Jersey* CO, 1982-83), 185–189, 192–194, 198–203, 264
Foley, S. R. III, 239, 244
food, 9, 12–13, 19–20, 25, 35–36, 43, 45, 62, 70, 73, 76–77, 82, 90–91, 104, 110–111, 116, 119–120, 126, 128–129, 136, 158, 163, 165, 177, 179, 181, 189, 204, 211, 214, 220, 223, 226–227, 234, 241, 249, 262–263, 266
football, 130, 233, 264
Forest, Francis X., 2, 4, 124
Forest, Joseph A., 4, 123–124
Formosa, 40, 44, 47, 115
Forrestal, James V., 1, 10–11
Forrestal, USS (CVA-59), 137–138
Fort Mandan, USS (LSD-21), 69
Fowler, Arthur, 96
Fox, James W., 229–230
Fox, USS (CG-33), 219
Frakes, Charles, 225, 227, 232, 249–250, 263
France, 102, 123, 133, 136
Frank, Allan, 102, 110, 115, 118
Frank, Joe Lee, 267–268
Franklin, USS (CV-13), 49, 142
Franks, USS (DD-554), 50–51
Fremantle/Perth, Australia, 247
French, James, 220
fuel oil, 8, 22, 35, 66, 90–91, 138, 222, 240
Fulks, Robert, 158, 163–164, 171, 182, 191
Fuller, Philip, 21, 42–43
Funafuti Atoll, 23–25

Gaffney, James J., 32–33
galleys in *New Jersey*, 82, 110, 189, 227, 243
Gambetta, Al, 188
Gauthier, Robert, 162
Gedunk (soda fountain) in *New Jersey*, 42, 267

Gehring, Jack, 137
Gemayel, Bashir, 203
Genet, Richard, 208, 220, 222
Gentry, William, 134
George VI, King (Britain), 76
German Navy, 12, 17, 20–21
Ghilarducci, Randy, 175
Gibraltar, Strait of, 131, 137, 203, 215
Gildea, Joseph, 189
Gill, Harold, 65
Glaes, Roger, 170
Gleason, Brian, 248–249, 253, 263–264
Glenn, W. Lewis, Jr. (*New Jersey* CO, 1985-1987), 224–225, 228, 230–233, 235, 237–238, 272
Goode, Leonard, 49
Goodpasture, L. Harlan, 57
Gorchinski, Michael, 205, 215–216
Graffias, USS (AF-29), 90
Gray, Oscar E., 14, 16, 27–28, 31, 39
Grayback, USS (SS-208), 230
Great Britain, 69–77, 123, 129, 139–141
Greece, 134
Green, Clark L., 103–105, 119
Greenock, Scotland, 141
Gregory, Frederick, 262
Griffin, V. D., 33
Grimes, Roff, Jr., 88, 90, 106, 108, 118–119, 122–123
Grimm, James V., 21
Grosvenor, Alexander G. B., 68
Guam Island, 35, 55
Guantanamo Bay, Cuba, 67, 77, 84–85, 100, 102–104, 118, 124–125, 127, 130, 137, 140
guns in *New Jersey*, 20-mm, 11, 16, 21, 30, 33–34, 44, 84, 87, 99, 157, 242; 40-mm, 8, 11, 26, 30, 34, 44–46, 71, 78, 81, 84, 88, 144, 148–149, 157–158, 242, 279; 5-inch, 6, 11, 14, 23, 26, 29, 31, 33–34, 37–38, 49, 77, 84, 89, 93, 105, 107–108, 110, 133, 136, 151, 156, 160–161, 170–172, 185–186, 188, 190, 193, 196, 207, 212, 220–221, 233–234, 240, 242 , 279; 16-inch, 5, 8, 10–11, 15, 19, 24, 26–29, 31, 33, 41, 67, 77, 81, 84–85, 88–89, 97, 105, 118, 124–126, 128, 136, 139, 155–156 , 159–163, 165–166, 168–171, 173, 177, 184, 186–188, 190, 193, 201, 207, 212–215, 219–221, 223–224, 231–234, 240, 242, 251, 256, 259, 262, 267, 279; saluting battery, 72, 116, 135, 192, 224; Vulcan/Phalanx, 187, 190–191, 193, 220, 242, 251

HO3S, U.S. helicopter, 85–86, 90–92, 95, 112

Haakon VII, King (Norway), 74–75
Haifa, Israel, 208–209, 215
Haiphong, North Vietnam, 149
Haleakala, USS (AE-25), 160, 162
Halsey, William F., Jr., 36–37, 39–41, 43, 45–47, 55, 57, 83, 121, 165, 176, 195, 201, 239, 253
Halsey, USS (CG-23), 222
Hammana, Lebanon, 212
Hammond, David, 218
Hampton Roads, *see* Norfolk, Virginia
Hancock, USS (CV-19), 44, 46
handling rooms in *New Jersey*, 28, 155, 177, 279
Hamilton, Charles R., 125, 129, 131–132, 135–136
Hanscom, Clinton A., 19–20
Hardt, L. M., 222, 230, 237
Harris, F. Brayton, 152
Harris, Glenn, Jr., 57
Harris, John R., 149–150, 160, 171–172, 174, 178
Harris, Michael, 248–249
Harris, Noble C., 65, 71
Hartigan, Charles C., Jr., 131, 133, 136, 139
Hartley, William, 20, 23
Hastings, John S., 114, 124
Hayes, John J., 155
Hayward, Eugene F., 12, 31, 50–51
Hayward, Thomas B., 183, 188, 255
heads in *New Jersey*, 8, 46, 71, 102, 140, 219, 243
Heinl, Robert D., 159
Hekman, Peter, 201
Helena, USS (CA-75), 97
helicopters, 85–86, 90–92, 95–96, 109, 112, 158–159, 177, 191, 194, 200-203, 206, 216, 227, 261
Henderson, Don, 135
Herger, Joseph, 237, 266, 268, 270–271
Hertwig, Clayton, 256
Heselton, Leslie R., 18
Hicks, Captain Michael K., 205
Hill, George, 82, 89, 91, 94
Hiroshima, Japan, 55
Hokkaido, Japan, 57
Holden, Carl F. (*New Jersey* CO, 1943-45), 5–9, 11–13, 16–17, 19–20, 24–25, 28, 31, 33, 38–39, 47, 52, 56, 67, 83
Hollandia, New Guinea, 30
Holste, Pete, 164
Holystoning, 57, 71, 118
Home Port Alliance, 277
homosexuality, 54

Hong Kong, 47, 114–115, 229, 262
Hon Matt Island, North Vietnam, 161
Honolulu, Hawaii, 36–37, 86, 177, 200
Honshu, Japan, 56–57
Hood, Donald, 105, 107
Hope, Bob, 166–168, 207–209
Hornsby, Benny, 211
Hosta, Walt, 166
Huff, Robert, 50
Huffman, Leon J. (*New Jersey* CO, 1946-47), 64–65, 67
Hull, USS (DD-350), 46
Hults, Chester, 93
Humphrey, Hubert H., 162
Hungnam, North Korea, 95–96, 108
Hunt, William, 115, 128
Huntington, Charles, 121
Hustvedt, Olaf, M., 21, 24, 26, 28–29, 41
Hyuga (Japanese battleship), 40, 47

Ignatius, Paul, 150
Inchon, South Korea, 112, 229, 231, 245
Independence, USS (CV-62), 206
Independence, USS (CVL-22), 40
Indiana, USS (BB-58), 17, 31–32, 48, 138
Indianapolis, USS (CA-35), 30, 48
Ingersoll, Royal E., 17
Ingersoll, USS (DD-990), 200, 223
inspections, 13, 15, 17–18, 67, 99–100, 104, 120, 137, 154, 220–222, 240, 252–253
intelligence collection, 211, 226, 241, 232, 265
Intrepid, USS (CV-11), 44, 277
Iowa-class battleships (U.S), 2, 122, 128, 138, 147–148, 183–185
Iowa, USS BB-61), 17, 21–22, 24–26, 28–29, 31, 41, 44, 48, 51, 61, 63, 78, 105, 121, 130, 138, 147, 156, 206, 209, 211–212, 215, 256, 259, 267
Iran, 263–264
Iraq, 270
Ise (Japanese battleship), 40, 47
Israel, 203, 205, 208–209, 215
Israeli Army, 208
Israeli Navy, 157, 200
Istanbul, Turkey, 135
Italy, 136, 215
Ivey, Louis A., 119–120, 123, 127–128
Iwo Jima, 48

Jablon, Len, 241–242, 245–246, 251, 258, 264

Jacobus, Charles, 85, 87, 91–92, 95, 101
Japan, concern about nuclear weapons, 230–231; expansionist aims, 2; surrender and postwar occupation of, 55–58, 223; World War II attacks on home islands, 48–49, 55; Western Pacific stopover for *New Jersey* after World War II, 57–59, 61–62, 87, 91–93, 97, 106, 111, 116–117, 169, 173–174
Japanese Navy, 25–26, 29–31, 33–35, 40–41, 43
Jennings, Charles, 234, 259, 270
Jeremiah, David, 266, 268
Jersey City, New Jersey, 276
Jerseyman, The (ship's newspaper), 18–19, 116, 123–124, 136
Jill, Japanese fighter, 34
Joachim, Paul, 99, 105–106
John A. Moore, USS (FFG-19), 195
John F. Kennedy, USS (CV-67), 206
Johnson, Christopher, 186, 190, 192–194, 197, 200–201, 204
Johnson, Conrad, 123
Johnson, Lance, 206, 208
Johnson, Louis, 81
Johnson, Lyndon B., 153, 162
Johnson, Robert, 199
Johnson, Roy, 137–138
Johnson, Wayne, 167, 169
Joint Chiefs of Staff, U.S., 17, 27–28, 162, 174, 203, 206, 250, 268
Jones, John, 265
Jones, Patricia, 276–277
Jouett, USS (CG-29), 222
Joy, C. Turner, 90
Judy, Japanese dive-bomber, 49
Jung, Leonard J., 12, 18, 30, 32, 36, 39

Kaderli, Ron, 166
Kahoolawe Island, 86
Kalasinsky, Frank, 141
Kalma Gak, North Korea, 88–89
Kalman, Joseph, 232
Kamikazes, 43–44, 48, 58
Kansong, North Korea, 88, 92–93, 96
Katori (Japanese cruiser), 26
Katz, Douglas J. (*New Jersey* CO, 1987-1989), 237–239, 241, 244–245, 247–250, 252–253, 256, 259, 282
Katz, Robert, 238
Katz, Sharon, 238–239, 244, 252 - 253
Kean, Thomas, 189, 231–232

Kearsarge, USS (CV-33), 69, 74
Keithly, Myers, 55–56, 59, 61–62
Kelly, Donald, 39, 41, 44
Kennedy, Kraig, 234
Kerr, Alex A., 148
Kersch, Ken, 168, 280–281
Kiehl, Elmer, 65, 73–74
Kierulff, Dudley, 76
Kihune, Robert K. U., 240, 242–244
King, Ernest J., 5–6, 16–17
Kinkaid, Thomas C., 41
Kirk, Claude R, Jr., 91–92
Kirk, Neville T., 77, 129 –130
Klotz, D. E., 108
Knoll, Robert, 28
Knox, Frank, 2
Kojo, North Korea, 107–108
Korean War, activation of *New Jersey*, 81; armistice, 113 –114; bombardment of North Korea, 81, 85–90, 93, 95–97; support of friendly troops, 92, 162, 171, 207, 212 -214
Kosmela, Walter T., 70–71, 75
Kosong, North Korea, 88
Kretz, Henry C., 63, 65–66
Krstich, Wesley, 32
Krueger, Walter, 56, 61–62
Kubicki, Henry, 57–58
Kuncevich, Sam, 2
Kurita, Takeo, 40–41
Kwajalein Atoll, 25, 27, 39
Kyushu, Japan, 49, 51, 56

Lake Champlain, USS (CG-57), 259–260
Lake Champlain, USS (CVA-39), 136
Larnaca, Cyprus, 206
Larson, Charles, 266
Larson, Gunner's Mate J. A.
laundry in *New Jersey*, 99, 102, 168, 173, 279
Lavella, Andrew, 164, 168, 172, 182, 185
Lawrence, William P., 195
Laws, USS (DD-558), 107
Leahy, USS (CG-16), 200–201
Lebanon, *New Jersey* fire support, 207, 212 -214; Marines at Beirut airport, 203–206, 210–212, 215; presence of *New Jersey* off coast, 203–215, 224–225; terrorism, 204 205, 211
Lee, Willis A., Jr., 28–29, 31–35, 39–41
Leghorn, Italy, 136

Lehman, John, 184–185, 190, 210, 233, 250
Leifer, Neil, 152–153
Leverton, J. Wilson, Jr. (*New Jersey* CO, 1948), 68–69, 78–80, 225
Lewis, John S., 180
Lewis Hancock, USS (DD-675)
Lexington, USS (CV-16), 32, 35
Leyte Gulf, Battle of, 40–41, 47
Libby, Ruthven, 122
liberty for crew members of *New Jersey*, in Australia, 247, 249; in Bahrain, 264; in Bremerton and Seattle, Washington, 52–53, 65, 182, 233, 257; in California, 98, 157–158, 175, 218; in the Caribbean, 12–13, 100, 126, 137; in England, 75–77, 129, 139–140; in Egypt, 205; in Florida, 127–128; in France, 102, 123, 133, 215; in Greece, 134–135; in Hawaii, 36–37, 86, 97, 106, 158, 177, 197, 200–201, 223, 229, 251; in Hong Kong, 114–115, 229, 262; in Israel, 208, 215; in Italy, 136, 215; in Japan, 57–58, 91, 111, 128, 169, 231; in Korea, 245; in New England, 76; in New York, 78, 121, 128, 144–145; in Norfolk, Virginia, 17, 85, 105, 119, 127, 131, 135; in Norway, 74–75, 138–139, 141–142; in Panama, 21, 201–202; in Philadelphia, 9-10; in the Philippines, 164, 198, 265–266; in Portland, Maine, 18; in Portugal, 102; in Portland, Oregon, 270; in San Francisco, 194, 223, 227, 270; in Scotland, 73, 141; in Singapore, 166, 198; in Spain, 123, 129, 131–132, 136–137; Tacoma, Washington, 177; in Thailand, 199–200, 264; in Trinidad, 12–13, 21; in Turkey, 135–136, Ulithi Atoll, 39, 44
library in *New Jersey*, 94, 99–100, 234
Lillis, Mark, 50–51
Lisbon, Portugal, 102, 141
Lockley, E. E., 116
Lockwood, USS (FF-1064), 259
London, England, 73, 76, 123
Long Beach, California, 62–64, 67, 98, 106, 118, 157, 173–179, 177–180, 185, 189, 201, 203, 205, 211, 216–218, 220–221, 224, 226–228, 233–235, 241–242, 244, 251–252, 254–255, 259, 266–274
Long Beach Naval Shipyard, 62, 157–158, 175, 184–193, 194, 196, 218–220, 222, 236–240, 243, 266–267, 271–274
Long Beach, USS (CGN-9), 227–228, 231, 260
Los Angeles, USS (CA-135), 91
Loughan, J. P., 33–34, 39–40, 52
Lowery, Don, 240
Lucas, Mike, 172

Lundquist, Jon, 258–259, 264, 266, 268
Luzon Island, 42–44, 47, 62
Lynde McCormick, USS (DDG-8), 259–260

MacArthur, Douglas, 29–30, 40, 56, 58, 71, 235, 245
Macon, USS (CA-132), 122, 130, 138, 150, 154
Magana, Alvaro, 201
magazines, powder, in *New Jersey*, 6, 8, 11, 16, 26, 28, 63, 107, 155, 170–171, 177, 204, 213
Maidstone (British submarine tender), 129
Maikaze (Japanese destroyer), 26
mail, 32, 36, 47, 112–113, 131, 165, 174, 203, 211, 222
main engines, *see* Engineering Plant
Majuro Atoll, 25, 27–33, 35, 39
Mallorca Island, 137
Mamroth, Ellis, 6, 19, 42–43
Manchester, USS (CL-83), 87
Manila, Philippines, 56, 61, 197–199, 230
Manitowoc, USS (LST-1180), 206
Manus Island, 38
Marianas Islands, 28, 30, 32–36, 40–41
Marine Corps, U.S., *New Jersey*'s detachment, 7, 27–29, 36, 38–39, 41, 44, 46, 48–49, 52, 61–62, 72, 83, 86, 91–92, 99–100, 116–118, 120, 124, 131–136, 143, 151, 186, 191, 205, 233, 239, 244–245, 258; supported by *New Jersey* in Lebanon, 203–215, 225; supported by *New Jersey* in Vietnam, 162, 165, 168–173; terrorist explosion at Beirut barracks, 204–205, 211; visitors to the *New Jersey*, 162, 165, 207
Marshall Islands, 24–25, 28, 36, 39, 55, 63
Marshall, USS (DD-676), 38
Martin, Chris, 265–266
Martin, Edward H., 203
Martin, Harold M., 87, 91, 94–95, 97
Massa, Eric, 218
Massachusetts, USS (BB-59), 31
Mathias, Charles McC., 58, 68–69, 72–73
Mattole, USS (AO-17), 14
Mayport, Florida, 127
McAdams, Carl, 199–200
McCarthy, Joseph, 100
McCorkle, Francis D. (*New Jersey* CO, 1951-52), 96–104
McCormick, John W., 14, 16, 18, 48
McCormick, Lynde D., 119, 121
McCrea, John L., 24, 29
McDonald, David L., 147–148, 150
McDonough, Barry, 209–210, 214
McDonough, James, 164

McDowell, Percival E., 6–9, 13, 19–20
McDowell, Richard, 131, 133, 136, 139
McElwain, Harry, 139–142, 144–145
McGuigan, David, 277
McGinnis, Joseph, 125
McGowan, Joseph A., 24–25
McIntire, Nait, 113
McKenna, Richard, 187, 192, 211–214
McLean, Heber H., 69, 75, 78
McNamara, Robert S., 151
Meanor, Rich, 279
Mehling, Ben, 128, 131, 139–140, 145
Meilandt, Ralph, 145
Melson, Charles L. (*New Jersey* CO, 1952-53), 103–104, 106–109, 111, 113, 115, 117, 122, 130
Menocal, George L. (*New Jersey* CO, 1947-48), 67–69, 72–73, 75, 79
Meredith, USS (DD-890), 69
Merrill, USS (DD-976), 227–228
mess decks in the *New Jersey*, 9–10, 19, 43, 45, 70, 82, 96, 104, 136, 148, 151–152, 163, 189, 210–211, 214, 227, 231, 241, 251, 254, 256, 271, 279
Metcalf, Joseph III, 136, 201, 237–238
Meyer, Harolyn Cheryl, 32, 67
Meyer, Leo, 86, 88–89, 91
Midway, USS (CV-41), 198, 260
Migrala, Walter, 151, 155, 158, 160, 174
Mikasa (Japanese battleship), 169
Mili Atoll, 28, 54
Miller, Greg, 209, 211, 213–214
Miller, Paul David, 248–249
Milligan, Richard D. (*New Jersey* CO, 1983-85), 140, 201–202, 204–207, 209, 211–216, 221, 224–225, 256
Miner, John O., 144
mines, 9, 15, 30, 57–58, 87, 107, 237
Minneapolis, USS (CA-36), 26, 51
missiles, Exocet, 200, 263–264; Harpoon, 185, 193–194, 198, 214, 224, 228, 230, 241, 244; Silkworm, 263; Styx, 157, 200, 264; Tomahawk, 185, 193, 195–196, 201, 224, 226, 228, 241, 244, 270–271
Mission Bay, USS (CVE-59), 82
Mississinewa, USS (AO-144), 136
Missouri, USS (BB-63), 50, 53, 55–56, 81, 84–86, 103, 106, 119, 122, 139, 182–183, 228, 234, 260, 262, 267–269, 271–272
Mitchell, William, 122
Mitscher, Marc A., 25–26, 30–32, 34, 51
Mog Mog Island, 39, 44

Molinaro, Richard, 100
Monaco, 215
Monaghan, USS (DD-354), 46
Monterey, USS (CVL-26), 14, 25
Moore, Charles J., 26
Moore, Lewis, 151, 168, 170, 173, 182
Moore, Robert, 118, 151
Moore, Robert L., 6, 14, 45, 62, 73
Moorer, Thomas H., 150, 174
Morse, Carl S., 154
Mota, Arturo, 219
Mothball Fleet, 79-81, 183-184, 274
Mount Fuji, Japan, 58
movies, 26, 42, 48, 69, 77, 94, 104, 122, 155, 211, 251, 266
Mrozinski, Roman V., 9, 21, 27, 31
Muir, Gene, 113
Mumford, Charles, 144
Mumpower, Thomas, 152, 162-163, 169
Murphy, Michael, 226-227
Musashi (Japanese battleship), 30, 40
Myers, Charles E., Jr., 183

NROTC units/midshipmen, 66-68, 101-102, 119, 140, 175, 238
Nagasaki, Japan, 55
Nagato (Japanese battleship), 59-60
Nantahala, USS (AO-60), 122
Naples, Italy, 136, 215
National Geographic magazine, 68, 70, 72, 74, 77
Naval Academy, U.S., 11-12, 65-68, 71, 82, 106, 122, 129-130, 137-138, 140, 175, 178, 238, 264
Naval Military Personnel Command (NMPC), 186, 206
Naval Reservists, 5, 7, 67-68, 72, 81-82, 94, 96, 99, 103, 118, 120, 129, 185-186, 200, 206-207, 209, 257
Nelson, Horatio, 76
Nelson, Ray, 121
Newcastle (British cruiser), 108-109
New Guinea, 29-30
New Jersey, USS (BB-16), 122
New Jersey, USS (BB62), band, 18, 43, 86; boats, 19, 75, 81, 86, 91, 113, 124, 127, 177, 143, 205, 223, 259, 266; collisions, 42, 50-51; construction of, 2-6; commissioning of, 6-7; cruise books, 136, 140, 157, 172, 232; deaths on board, 15, 88, 229-230, 251; decommissioning of, 79-80, 144-145, 182, 185, 272-274; design of, 1; drinking on board, 25, 42-43, 89, 168, 250; dry-docking, 4, 16-17, 66, 79, 84-85, 100, 124, 143-144, 187-188, 236-239, 281-282; fired at by enemy, 88-89, 108, 161-162; fires on board, 88, 252; galley, 82, 189; gambling, 39-40, 94; grounding of, 15-16, 143; inactivations of, 65-66, 78-79, 84, 142-145, 181-182, 271-274; keel-laying, 2; launching of, 1, 3-4, 10, 19; midshipman training cruises, (1947), 66-78, 129 (1952), 101-103, (1954), 122-124, (1955), 128-130, (1956), 138-140, (1969), 175-177; museum/memorial, 276-282; naming of, 1-2 ; newspapers published on board, 18-19, 116, 123-124, 164, 250; overhauls, 51-53, 57, 124-125, 143, 219-220, 236-240; reactivations of, 81-84, 144, 147-151, 185-189, 218; recommissioning of, 83-84, 153-154, 191-193; refresher training, 54, 100-101, 119, 194, 220-221, 241-242; shakedown training, 12-15, 84-85, 125-127, 157; ship's silver service, 279; size of crew, 7, 43, 63, 66, 90, 100, 119, 157, 186, 272; speed of, 11, 18, 41, 85, 125, 153, 202-203, 210, 240; trials under way, 18, 54, 85, 100, 125, 152-155, 189-191, 220, 240
Newmar, Julie, 145
New Orleans, USS (CA-32), 26
Newport, Rhode Island, 121-122
Newport News, USS (CA-148), 131, 164, 173, 175
news media, 20, 32, 83, 94, 108-109, 152, 157, 161, 175-176, 185, 199-200, 211, 230-231, 248, 250, 264, 267, 274, 276-277
New York City, 52, 78, 121, 128, 144-145
New York Naval Shipyard, 78-79, 83-84, 142-144
Nicaragua, 200
Nickols, James P., 254, 264, 271-272
Nimitz, Chester W., 27, 41, 46-47, 55-56, 59, 235
Nimitz, USS (CVN-68), 260
Nishimura, Shoji, 40
Nishman, Robert, 123
Nixon, Richard M., 162, 174
Norfolk Virginia, 11-12, 15, 17, 20-21, 67, 84-85, 98-99, 100-101, 103-106, 118-122, 125-126-128, 130-131, 135, 137-138, 140, 142, 144, 156, 158, 206
Norfolk Naval Shipyard, 85, 99-100, 103, 105, 124-125, 137, 142
Norris, USS (DD-859), 54
North Atlantic Treaty Organization (NATO), 140-142, 158
North Carolina, USS (BB-55), 23, 31-32
Norway, 17, 74, 138-139, 141-142
Nowaki (Japanese destroyer), 26-27, 41
nuclear weapons, *see* atomic bombs/projectiles
Numbers, Robert, 50

OS2U Kingfisher, U.S. scout plane, 10, 15, 19, 35, 37, 49, 54
O'Brien, USS (DD-975), 222
O'Bryen, Dale, 36, 44, 46, 52
Ocean (British aircraft carrier), 108–109, 111
Odenthal, Joseph, 116
O'Donnell, (*New Jersey* CO, 1955-56), 126–128, 130–133, 136–140
Ofstie, Ralph, 137
Ogle, Gerald B., 8, 14, 38
O'Hare, USS (DD-889), 69
Okinawa, 48–51, 56–57
Oldendorf, Jesse B., 40
Oliver, Frank, 90–91
Olongapo, Philippines, 164, 198
Onslow Beach, North Carolina, 121
Operational Propulsion Plant Examination (OPPE), 221–222
Orell, Barry, 223
Oslo, Norway, 74, 138–139, 141–142
Osterwind, Robert, 88, 99
Owasco, USCGC (WHEC-39), 171, 177
Ozawa, Jisaburo, 33, 35, 40–41

Pacific Exercise 1989 (PacEx 89), 259–262
Palau Islands, 29–30, 39
Palestine Liberation Organization (PLO), 203
Palladino, Jim, 239–241, 251, 253, 265–266
Palma, Mallorca, 137
Panama Canal/Canal Zone, 21–22, 67, 85–86, 106, 118, 156–157, 201–202, 208, 215, 275
Panmunjom, Korea, 113–114
Paravanes, 9, 15, 237
Paria, Gulf of, 12, 14–15
Paricutin, USS (AE-18)
Paris, France, 102, 123
Parker, Edward N., 131–132, 134, 136–137, 201
Parmelee, Robert, 26, 30
Parrish, Pervy F., 104
Parsons, Joseph, 126
Partain, William, 168
Pasadena, USS (CL-65), 60–61, 181
Pattaya Beach, Thailand, 199–200, 230, 264
payment of New Jersey's crew, 82, 94, 126, 135, 159, 173, 209, 234, 254–255
Pearl Harbor, Hawaii, 27, 30, 32, 36, 51, 54, 86, 97–98, 106, 117, 158, 177, 197, 200, 223, 229, 250–251, 266
Peek, Richard, 72

Peet, Raymond E., 124–125, 128, 130
Peleliu Island
Peniston, Fran, 178
Peniston, Robert C (*New Jersey* CO, 1969), 11–12, 66–67, 149, 178–182
Pennsylvania, USS (BB-38), 150, 182
Percival, Gene E., 57
Persian Gulf, 262–264, 271
Petrovitz, George, 151, 157
Phelan, James, 7
Philadelphia, Pennsylvania, 6, 9, 84, 145, 153, 277–278, 280
Philadelphia Navy Yard/Naval Shipyard, 1–10, 15–17, 25, 124, 147–151, 153–156, 274–277, 282
Philippine Islands, 33, 39–42, 44, 47, 56, 61–62, 71, 158–159, 164–165, 169, 173, 197, 200, 229–230, 235, 246, 265
Philippine Sea, Battle of, 34
Philippine Sea, USS (CV-47), 87, 112
Philip, Prince (Britain), 76
Pinney, Frank, 29
Pioneer drone, 261–262
plotting rooms in *New Jersey*, 6, 11, 15, 41–42, 88, 92, 107, 160, 162–163, 171, 174, 188, 209–210, 213–214, 231, 242
Poe, Donald, 100, 102
Point Heyer, USCGC (WPB-82369)
Polo Grounds, 94, 121
Ponape Island, 31
Portland, Maine, 18
Portland, Oregon, 268–270
Portsmouth, England, 75–76, 139
Portugal, 102, 123, 141
post office in *New Jersey*, 89, 94, 112, 222
Pousson, Larry, 155–157, 172, 187, 194, 198–199, 203–204
powder bags/cans in *New Jersey*, 8, 11, 14, 16, 48, 8, 16, 28, 63, 90, 143, 155, 157, 162, 170–172, 204, 211, 213, 246, 257, 270
Pratt, Richard R., 125, 127, 129, 131
Pringle, James, 119, 124–127
prisoners of war, 38–39, 57, 206
profanity, 32-33, 54
Program for Afloat College Education (PACE), 233–234
projectiles, 20-mm, 63; 40-mm, 63, 88, 143; 5-inch, 14, 23, 46, 63, 143, 156, 160, 171–173, 185, 213; 16-inch, 11, 20–21, 26–28, 33, 63, 66–67, 77, 84, 89–90, 92, 97, 105, 107, 113, 124, 128, 143, 155–157, 159–162, 165, 169–170, 173, 177, 180, 194, 204, 207, 212–215, 246, 257, 267, 270, 280

propellers/propeller shafts, *see* engineering plant
Propulsion Examining Board (PEB), 220
prostitution, 36, 129, 131, 137
protesters, 153–154, 177, 230, 248–249, 258, 269
Puerto Rico, 77, 85, 202–203
Puget Sound Navy Yard/Naval Shipyard, 51–53, 57, 63–66, 69, 180–183, 274–275
Pusan, South Korea, 108, 115–116, 231, 245, 262
Pyonggang-Kimhwa-Cheorwon, North Korea, 96

Quang Ngai, South Vietnam, 165
Queen Mary (British liner), 102, 157

racial issues, 119 -120, 128, 246–247, 256
radars, fire control, 16, 27, 29–30, 77, 162–163, 210; SG surface search, 24–25, 27, 41; SK air search, 29; SK-2 air search, 78, 99; SP height finder, ; SPS-6 air search, 99, 168–169; SPS-8 height finder, 124; SPS-10 surface search, 101; SPS-67 surface search, 236, 247
Radford, Arthur W., 49–50, 90, 106
radio communications, 10, 13, 25, 36, 41–42, 46, 57, 84, 101, 106, 109, 113, 124, 141, 159, 162–165, 171, 174–177, 215, 225, 236, 264
Randall, Henry, 124
Randolph, USS (CV-15), 48, 69
Rangekeeper, Mark 8, in *New Jersey*, 162
Ranger, USS (CV-61), 200–201, 232
Raven, USS (MSF-55), 177
Reagan, Frank, 49
Reagan, Ronald, 184, 191–193, 212
Reason, J. Paul, 257, 259, 261–264, 266, 269–270
Reasoner, USS (FF-1063), 223
Reed, Christopher, 150–151, 153, 156–157, 160, 164–166, 168, 181
Reeves, John, Jr., 35
refueling at sea, 14, 42, 44–46, 48, 68, 70, 90–91, 122, 194–195, 227
religious services in *New Jersey*, 19, 32, 74, 93–94, 136, 157, 228, 241, 254, 264
replenishment at sea, 63, 90, 133, 160, 162, 209, 211, 226–227, 258, 260–261
Reynolds, Harry O., 3, 6, 29, 44–45
Rhee, Syngman, 108, 112, 115
Rice, Rob, 245–247, 266–267
Rice, Robert H., 48–49, 52, 54, 58
Roane, Donald P., 157, 170
Roanoke, USS (CL-145), 101
Roark, USS (FF-1053), 200–201

Robie, William, 34
Robison, USS (DDG-14), 200–201
Rodney (British battleship), 73
Roeder, Bernard F., Jr., 58
Romer, Bill, 252, 260, 264, 270
Roosevelt, Franklin D., 2, 17, 25, 235–236
Roper, John W., 61, 63
Rose, Rufus E., 20, 23
Rossie, John P., 8, 16, 21–22, 43
Rosyth, Scotland, 69, 72–74
Rota, Spain, 203
Royal Navy (British), 17, 72–73, 108–109, 111, 129, 246, 249
Rupp, David O., 82, 86, 93–94, 100
Russell, Baxter, 38
Russell, Richard, 147
Russo, James, 32
Ryan, Dennis, 236–237, 240, 244

S-2 Tracker, U.S. surveillance plane, 160
SC-1 Seahawk, U.S. scouting plane, 54, 57
SH-2 Sea Sprite, U.S. helicopter, 201, 203
Sadler, Stuart, 107, 113–115, 118
St. Paul, USS (CA-73), 111, 150
St. Thomas, Virgin Islands, 137
Saipan Island, 33–35
Salinas, Daniel III, 237
San Bernardino Strait, Philippines, 40–41
San Clemente Island, 57, 175, 190, 194, 221, 225, 242, 256
Sanctuary, USS (AH-17), 57
Sandia Laboratory, 256, 267
San Diego, California, 151, 157, 177, 190, 220, 222, 234, 243, 257
San Francisco, California, 61–62, 176, 194, 223, 227, 244, 270
San Pedro, California, 54
Santa Catalina Island, 179, 218–219
Sapyong-ni, South Korea, 93
Sardinia Island, 136
Sasebo, Japan, 86, 90, 92, 97, 107, 111–112, 114, 230–231
Scanlon, Daniel, 45
Scarselletta, Albert, 182
Scharnhorst (German battle cruiser), 17
Schwarzkopf, Norman, 278
Schweitzer, Robert, 164
Scotland, 69–74, 141
Scott, Art, 34

Seal Beach, California, 180, 187–188, 218, 220–221, 225, 240, 252, 270
Sea of Japan, 175
Sea of Okhotsk, 231-232
Seattle, Washington, 52, 257
Second Fleet, U.S., 136, 140, 201
Seigenthaler, Thomas, 276–277
Seventh Fleet, U.S., 41, 87, 90, 97, 106, 109, 111, 113–115, 122, 170, 178, 198, 229, 248–249, 263
Severn, USS (AO-61), 101
sewage system in *New Jersey*, 221
Shand, MacDonald, 159
Sheffield (British destroyer), 200
Shemya Island, 260–261
Shepherd, Lemuel C. III, 133–134, 136
Sherman, Frederick, 24–25, 48, 61
Shikoku, Japan, 56
Shipley, William, 241–243, 246–247, 249, 260–261, 268
Shonan Maru No. 5 (Japanese trawler), 26
shore bombardment, in World War II, 25, 28, 31, 33, 42, 48–50, 54, 159; postwar period, 67, 77; Korean War period, 81, 85–90, 92–96, 107–101, 108, 111–113; mid-1950s, 121, 126, 136; Vietnam War period, 148–149, 157, 159–163, 165–166, 168–173, 175; in the 1980s, 194, 207, 209, 212–215, 221, 225, 234, 256
shore patrol, 129, 131, 151, 177, 270
Short, Roy, 170
Siboney, USS (CVE-112), 122
Sibuyan Sea, 40
sick bay/medical department in *New Jersey*, 31, 169, 200
Sides, John H., 137
Siemer, Harold, 137
Singapore, 166, 198–199, 215, 262, 264
Sixth Fleet, U.S., 131–137, 203
Slonim, Gilven, 38–39
Smaldone, Ron, 172
Smith, Arthur, 142, 144–145
Smith, Donald, 189
Smith, William H., 253, 255, 265
Snyder, J. Edward, Jr. (*New Jersey* CO, 1968-69), 150–152, 154, 157–164, 167, 170, 172–175, 178–179, 200, 264
Snyder, Edwin K., 175
Snyder, Philip W., 17
Sosnowski, William, 154, 161, 174, 177, 182
Soucek, Archie, 49, 53, 58, 60, 62, 65
Souda Bay, Crete, 133
Sousa, Ron, 168
South Dakota, USS (BB-57), 17, 23, 31, 119

South Korea, 93, 108, 112, 115–116, 229, 231, 245
Soviet Navy, 226, 232
Soviet Union, 134, 141, 200, 231–232, 263, 277
Spahr, J. L., 112
Spain, 123, 129, 131, 136, 203
Spence, USS (DD-512), 45–46
spotting guns' fall of shot, 92, 96, 107, 112, 136, 159–163, 165, 173, 261
Sproston, USS (DD-577), 12
Spruance, Raymond A., 25–30, 34, 37, 40, 48, 51, 55–59, 61
star shells, 14, 37–38, 77
Stark, USS (FFG-31), 263
State Society of the Battleship *New Jersey*, 20, 152
Stein, USS (FF-1065), 227, 259
Stephan, David R., 50–51
Stevens, P. H., 99
Stilwell, Joseph W., 56
store in *New Jersey*, 98, 151, 244, 267
Storm, Robert J., 82, 85, 88–90
Stribling, USS (DD-867), 69
Strock, Herman, 94
Strub, Henry, 163, 169, 175, 178–179, 181
Stuber, D. E., 113
Subic Bay, Philippines, 158, 164–165, 169, 173, 198, 200, 229–230, 246, 262, 265–266
Sullivan, James, 121
Sullivan, John W., 9, 31, 33, 41, 48, 50, 58
Swayze, Frank, 164
Sydney, Australia, 248–250
Sydney (Australian aircraft carrier), 97
Sykes, Harold, 170
Syrian Forces in Lebanon, 203, 206–207, 210–212, 214–215
Szimanski, Ryan, 243, 279

TA-4 Skyhawk, U.S. spotter plane, 159
Tacoma, Washington, 177
Taiwan, *see* Formosa
Tanchon-Songjin, North Korea, 96
Task Force 22 (1943), 17
Task Force 34 (1944), 40–41
Task Force 38 (1944-45), 38–40, 42, 44, 47, 87
Task Force 58 (1944-45), 25–26, 29–31, 34–35, 38, 48–51, 87
Task Force 60 (1983-84), 206, 214
Task Force 77 (1951-53), 87, 90, 96–97, 107, 114
Task Force 81 (1947), 69–78

Tattnall, USS (DDG-19), 210
Taylor, Raynor A. K., 228, 230–231
Taylor, Roger C., 103
television, 152, 158–159, 162, 164, 172, 187, 204, 215, 223, 225, 234–236, 241, 250, 258, 261–262, 264–265, 270, 279
Teller, George, 30–31
terrorism, 204–205, 211, 277
Terry, James, 4–5
Thach, USS (FFG-43), 227
Thailand, 199–200, 230, 264–265
Thai Navy, Royal, 230
Third Fleet, U.S., 36–44, 47–48, 55–56, 195, 244
Thomas, Charles, 130
Thompson, Edward M. (*New Jersey* CO, 1945-46), 57, 59–60, 63–64
Thompson, William, 148
Thomson, Robert B., 94
Thornton, Thomas, 176
Thurber, H. Raymond, 99–100, 102–104
Ticonderoga, USS (CVA-14), 128
Tiernan, William, 78
Tiger cruises, 250–251, 266
Tinian Island, 33
Tirpitz (German battleship), 17
Tobias, Andy, 169
Togo, Heihachiro, 169
Tokyo/Tokyo Bay, Japan, 48, 56–57
Toledo, USS (CA-133), 97, 150
Tony, Japanese fighter plane, 34
torpedoes, 14, 26–27, 33, 37, 58, 91, 117
Toricelli, Robert, 276–277
Touzin, K. T., 264–265
Towers, John H., 59, 61, 140
Towers, USS (DDG-9), 158–160, 165
Trail, John, 194, 197, 199, 202, 204–205
Trecartin, Allen, 46–47, 57
Trieste, Italy, 136
Trinidad, 12–14
Triola, Salvatore, 124, 133–135
Trost, Carlisle A. H., 241
Trujillo, Hector B., 126
Trujillo, Rafael Leonidas, 126
Truk Atoll, 26, 28–31, 41
Truman, Harry S., 56, 120
Tucker, Leon, 240–241, 247, 256–257, 259, 263, 267, 271–272
Tucker, Ronald, 253–255, 257–259, 262–269, 272–273

Tuffanelli, George, 95
tugboats, 4, 9–10, 15, 59, 79, 84, 121, 123, 127, 143, 152, 156, 181, 184–185, 239, 245, 274–276, 278, 282
Turkey, 135
Turner, Richmond Kelly, 34, 41
turrets in *New Jersey*, 16-inch, 4–9, 11–12, 15–16, 19, 27–29, 34, 42–44, 55, 66, 81–82, 85, 88–90, 107, 117–118, 151, 155, 159–160, 162–163, 168, 170, 172, 186–188, 191, 194–195, 201, 204, 210, 213, 219, 222–223, 241–242, 251, 256–257, 259, 271, 279
typhoons, 38, 45–46, 158, 198
Tyre, Lebanon, 205
Tyree, David M. (*New Jersey* CO, 1950-51), 82–84, 86–87, 90, 92–93, 96–97

Ulithi Atoll, 39, 43–44, 46–49, 51
United Nations, 92, 111, 113
United States (U.S. liner), 101

Valencia, Spain, 129, 131–132
Valenta, Joe, 257–258
Vance, USS (DER-387), 150, 158
Van Vleck, George, 46
Vasey, Lloyd, 175–177
Vaught, Roy Lee, 63
venereal disease, 129
Victory (British sailing ship), 76
Vietnam War, reactivation of *New Jersey*, 147–151; bombardment of North Vietnam, 153, 159–160; peace talks, 162, 179; support of friendly troops in South Vietnam, 162–163, 165–166, 168–173
Vigo, Spain, 123
Villefranche, France, 215
Vincennes, USS (CG-49), 231, 263
Vinh, North Vietnam, 149, 161
Vining, Pierre, 131, 140, 144, 146
Virgin Islands, 137
Virginia Capes Operating Area, 103–104, 138, 155
Vitt, John, 10

Wabash, USS (AOR-5), 227
Wakayama, Japan, 57
Wake Island, 54, 116
Walker, Edward K., Jr., 126–127, 129, 133, 135
Walsh, John, 133, 135
wardroom, officers' in *New Jersey*, 45–46, 69, 88, 133, 141, 195, 211, 214, 239, 241, 249, 251, 254, 265
Warner, John W., 178–179

INDEX

Washington, USS (BB-56), 23, 32
Watts, Charles R., Jr., 92–93, 101, 114, 117
Weather-Heavy, 21, 38–39, 43–46, 102–104, 116, 125, 130, 138, 158, 170, 198, 259–261, 266–267
Webb, James R., 239
Weinberger, Caspar, 201
Wellborn, Charles, Jr., 61, 140–142
Westcott, Robert, 10–13, 18
WETSU, 258, 272–273
Weymouth, England, 129, 139
White, Danny, 113
Whitman, Christine Todd, 275
Whitman, Larry, 174
Wichita, USS (AOR-1), 194
Wichita, USS (CA-45), 25
Wilhite, D. Raymond, 103, 108, 112–113, 116–117, 121
Wilkes, E. L., 37
Willenbrock, Eric, 199
Williams, Clarence, 122
Williams, Marvin, 255–256, 266, 271–273
Williamson, W. H., 112
Wilson, Gill Robb, 20
Winkelman, Val, 34

Winslow, Edward, 119, 124–125
Wisconsin, USS (BB-64), 50, 53, 69–70, 72–74, 78, 97, 116, 122, 126–127, 137–138, 142, 144, 147, 156, 262, 272
Wolpin, Richard, 186, 189, 191, 199, 208, 214–215
Wonsan, North Korea, 88–92, 95–96, 108, 113
Wooldridge, E. Tyler (*New Jersey* CO, 1945), 47–49, 51–52, 54–56, 59–60, 62
Wouk, Herman, 100, 235, 272
wrestling, 129, 262
Wright, George, 86
Wright, Jerauld, 121
Wright, William, 121

Yamato (Japanese battleship), 40, 51
Yangyang, North Korea, 90
Yeager, John, 58
Yokosuka, Japan, 57–59, 61–62, 87, 91–93, 97, 106, 111, 116–117, 169, 173–174, 231
Yorktown, USS (CV-10), 50
Yugoslavia

Zero/Zeke, Japanese fighter plane, 26, 34, 44, 49

ABOUT THE AUTHOR

PAUL STILLWELL is an independent historian. He retired in 1992 after thirty years of duty in the U.S. Naval Reserve. From 1966 to 1969 he served in the crew of the tank landing ship *Washoe County* during Vietnam War action. From May to October 1969 he was assistant combat information center officer on board the battleship *New Jersey*. Stillwell then worked on the staff of the U.S. Naval Institute from 1974 to 2004 as an oral historian, *Proceedings* managing editor, *Naval Review* editor, and founding editor-in-chief of *Naval History* magazine.

Battleship New Jersey is Stillwell's fourteenth book. Among his other publications is *The Golden Thirteen: Recollections of the First Black Naval Officers*, listed by the *New York Times* as one of the notable books of 1993 in the field of history. Stillwell's most recent book, *Battleship Commander: The Life of Vice Admiral Willis A. Lee Jr.*, received multiple awards, including the 2022 Samuel Eliot Award for Naval Literature, presented by the New York Commandery of the Naval Order of the United States.

THE NAVAL INSTITUTE PRESS is the book-publishing arm of the U.S. Naval Institute, a private, nonprofit, membership society for sea service professionals and others who share an interest in naval and maritime affairs. Established in 1873 at the U.S. Naval Academy in Annapolis, Maryland, where its offices remain today, the Naval Institute has members worldwide.

Members of the Naval Institute support the education programs of the society and receive the influential monthly magazine *Proceedings* or the colorful bimonthly magazine *Naval History* and discounts on fine nautical prints and on ship and aircraft photos. They also have access to the transcripts of the Institute's Oral History Program and get discounted admission to any of the Institute-sponsored seminars offered around the country.

The Naval Institute's book-publishing program, begun in 1898 with basic guides to naval practices, has broadened its scope to include books of more general interest. Now the Naval Institute Press publishes about seventy titles each year, ranging from how-to books on boating and navigation to battle histories, biographies, ship and aircraft guides, and novels. Institute members receive significant discounts on the Press' more than eight hundred books in print.

Full-time students are eligible for special half-price membership rates. Life memberships are also available.

For more information about Naval Institute Press books that are currently available, visit www.usni.org/press/books. To learn about joining the U.S. Naval Institute, please write to:

Member Services
U.S. NAVAL INSTITUTE
291 Wood Road
Annapolis, MD 21402-5034

Telephone: (800) 233-8764
Fax: (410) 571-1703
Web address: www.usni.org